SERIES VIII   CYCLE B

LECTIONARY PREACHING WORKBOOK

For All Users
Of The Revised Common,
The Roman Catholic, And
The Episcopal Lectionaries

Carlos Wilton

CSS Publishing Company, Inc.
Lima, Ohio

This book is dedicated to
Claire, Benjamin, and Anna,
with love

and to the people of the Point Pleasant Presbyterian Church
of Point Pleasant Beach, New Jersey,
who generously gave me time away on sabbatical
to finish this project.

Second Printing, 2005

Copyright © 2005 by
CSS Publishing Company, Inc.
Lima, Ohio

Some scripture quotations are from the *New Revised Standard Version of the Bible*, copyright 1989 by the Division of Christian Education of the National Council of the Churches of Christ in the USA. Used by permission.

Library of Congress Cataloging-in-Publication Data

Wilton, Carlos, 1956-
  Lectionary preaching workbook : Series VIII, Cycle B : for all users of the Revised Common, the Roman Catholic, and the Episcopal lectionaries / Carlos Wilton.
      p. cm.
   ISBN 0-7880-2362-4 (three-ring binder : alk. paper) — ISBN 0-7880-2371-3 (perfect bound : alk. paper)
   1. Lectionary preaching. Common lectionary (1992) 3. Bible—Homiletical use. I. Title.

BV4235.L43W55 2005
251'.6—dc22

                                                                              2005011719

For more information about CSS Publishing Company resources, visit our website at www.csspub.com or e-mail us at custserv@csspub.com or call (800) 241-4056.

Cover design by Chris Patton
ISBN 0-7880-2362-4 Binder
ISBN 0-7880-2371-3 Paperback   PRINTED IN U.S.A.

Table Of Contents

Sermon Planner / Builder

Date: _____   Cycle / Season: _____   Sunday: _____

Cycle/Season / Sunday theological clue _____

_____

Psalm / central thought: _____

_____

Collect / prayer concern/focus: _____

_____

Sermon text(s): _____

_____

Summary of sermon text(s): _____

_____

_____

_____

_____

_____

_____

_____

Pastoral perspective: _____

_____

_____

_____

_____

Stories / illustrations: _____

_____

_____

_____

_____

Type of sermon: _____

Sermon plan / sketch: _____

_____

_____

_____

_____

_____

The Church Year Calendar

The Christmas Cycle

Advent	**Color**
First Sunday Of Advent	purple or blue
Second Sunday Of Advent	purple or blue
Third Sunday Of Advent	purple or blue
Fourth Sunday Of Advent	purple or blue

Christmas	
Christmas Eve	white
The Nativity Of Our Lord	white
First Sunday After Christmas	white
Second Sunday After Christmas	white

Epiphany	
The Epiphany Of Our Lord	white
The Baptism Of Our Lord (First Sunday After The Epiphany)	white
Second Sunday After The Epiphany	green
Third Sunday After The Epiphany	green
Fourth Sunday After The Epiphany	green
Fifth Sunday After The Epiphany	green
Sixth Sunday After The Epiphany	green
Seventh Sunday After The Epiphany	green
The Transfiguration Of Our Lord (Last Sunday After The Epiphany)	white

The Easter Cycle

Lent	
Ash Wednesday	black or purple
First Sunday In Lent	purple
Second Sunday In Lent	purple
Third Sunday In Lent	purple
Fourth Sunday In Lent	purple
Fifth Sunday In Lent	purple
Sunday Of The Passion / Palm Sunday	scarlet or purple
Maundy Thursday	scarlet or white
Good Friday	black or no paraments
Holy Saturday	white

Easter	
Vigil Of Easter	white or gold
The Resurrection Of Our Lord / Easter Day	white or gold
Second Sunday Of Easter	white
Third Sunday Of Easter	white
Fourth Sunday Of Easter	white
Fifth Sunday Of Easter	white

Sixth Sunday Of Easter			white
The Ascension Of Our Lord			white
Seventh Sunday Of Easter			white
The Day Of Pentecost			red

The Pentecost Cycle

The Season After Pentecost

Revised Common / Episcopal	Lutheran (Other than ELCA)	Roman Catholic	Color
The Holy Trinity	The Holy Trinity	The Holy Trinity	white
		Corpus Christi	green
Proper 4	Pentecost 2	Ordinary Time 9	green
Proper 5	Pentecost 3	Ordinary Time 10	green
Proper 6	Pentecost 4	Ordinary Time 11	green
Proper 7	Pentecost 5	Ordinary Time 12	green
Proper 8	Pentecost 6	Ordinary Time 13	green
Proper 9	Pentecost 7	Ordinary Time 14	green
Proper 10	Pentecost 8	Ordinary Time 15	green
Proper 11	Pentecost 9	Ordinary Time 16	green
Proper 12	Pentecost 10	Ordinary Time 17	green
Proper 13	Pentecost 11	Ordinary Time 18	green
Proper 14	Pentecost 12	Ordinary Time 19	green
Proper 15	Pentecost 13	Ordinary Time 20	green
Proper 16	Pentecost 14	Ordinary Time 21	green
Proper 17	Pentecost 15	Ordinary Time 22	green
Proper 18	Pentecost 16	Ordinary Time 23	green
Proper 19	Pentecost 17	Ordinary Time 24	green
Proper 20	Pentecost 18	Ordinary Time 25	green
Proper 21	Pentecost 19	Ordinary Time 26	green
Proper 22	Pentecost 20	Ordinary Time 27	green
Proper 23	Pentecost 21	Ordinary Time 28	green
Proper 24	Pentecost 22	Ordinary Time 29	green
Proper 25	Pentecost 23	Ordinary Time 30	green
Proper 26	Pentecost 24	Ordinary Time 31	green
Proper 27	Pentecost 25	Ordinary Time 32	green
Proper 28	Pentecost 26	Ordinary Time 33	green
	Pentecost 27		green
	Reformation Sunday		red
All Saints	All Saints	All Saints	white
Thanksgiving Day, USA			white
Christ The King	Christ The King	Christ The King	white

The Advent Season

Advent presents preachers with a dilemma, a built-in conflict between the sacred and the secular. On the one hand is the church's historic teaching that Advent is a season of hope and expectation, linking Old Testament messianic prophecy with New Testament eschatology. On the other hand is the secular society's growing anticipation of the Christmas holiday.

Of the debate between those who favor messianic eschatology and those who favor "getting ready for Christmas" there will be no end. Most preachers come down on one side of the debate or the other. Some choose to swim upstream from the secular culture, stubbornly preaching eschatology to people with shopping lists and Santa on their minds. Others choose to soft-pedal church tradition, believing that the evangelical importance of contextual preaching trumps any externally-imposed theological regimen.

In practice, few preachers on either side of this interminable debate are purists — nor would it be good for the church if they were. Most pastors, feeling pulled in both directions, will include a mix of messianic prophecy and pre-Christmas preparation in their Advent sermons.

If either of these emphases is lost, the church of Jesus Christ is ultimately the poorer. On the one hand, if church members never hear the difficult eschatological texts during Advent, they will probably never hear them addressed at all. They will never grasp that, in the words of Thomas Merton, "eschatology is not *finis* and punishment, the winding up of accounts and the closing of books: it is the final beginning, the definitive birth into a new creation."[1] On the other hand, if worshipers — many of them seasonal attenders who return to the pews only in late Advent and Lent — sit through sermons that never address their personal, holiday-focused yearning for faith-renewal, they will go away with the impression that the church is out of touch with its people, caring little for their spiritual needs. There is the added disadvantage that the only time seasonal attenders will ever hear a sermon on the vitally important theme of the incarnation will be Christmas Eve / Christmas Day itself — the lectionary offers marvelous incarnational texts on the Sundays following Christmas Day, but this is only after attendance has dipped to its post-holiday lows.

The material presented in this Advent section self-consciously attempts to meet the needs of preachers who are following both approaches. We will take the Advent texts seriously, not ducking eschatology's challenging wake-up call; yet we will also remain aware of the great feast soon to come, that looms so large in the hearts and minds of God's people. The eschatological themes will naturally receive greater emphasis in the earlier Advent Sundays than in the latter, when Christmas expectation becomes all but inescapable: but they will be present throughout.

---

1. Thomas Merton, "The Time of No Room," from *Watch for the Light; Readings for Advent and Christmas* (Farmington, Pennsylvania: Plough Publishing House, 2001).

First Sunday Of Advent
November 27, 2005

Revised Common	Isaiah 64:1-9	1 Corinthians 1:3-9	Mark 13:24-37
Roman Catholic	Isaiah 63:16b-17; 64:1, 3b-8	1 Corinthians 1:3-9	Mark 13:33-37
Episcopal	Isaiah 64:1-9a	1 Corinthians 1:1-9	Mark 13:(24-32) 33-37

Theme For The Day   Jesus calls his people, awaiting his coming, to be watchful.

Old Testament Lesson   Isaiah 64:1-9   *The Heavens Torn*

"O that you would tear open the heavens and come down...." Many American worshipers will still be savoring pleasant memories of Thanksgiving turkey when they hear these prophetic words burst into their consciousness: a perhaps unwelcome interruption. The coming of Advent, the beginning of a new liturgical year, is meant to be intrusive. For the several prophets trading under the name of Isaiah, preaching to a despairing people in exile, the abrupt intrusion of God into human affairs is a sign of hope. Such is the case for oppressed people in every place and time, who have historically welcomed apocalyptic imagery far more readily than those who are complacent and satisfied. "Our God Is An Awesome God," we sing, with radiant smiles on our faces: yet can we, who are for the most part comfortable and secure, even begin to understand what God's "awesome deeds" (v. 3) are really like?

New Testament Lesson   1 Corinthians 1:3-9   *The Unveiling*

"Grace and peace," Paul begins his letter. These two words represent the two worlds from which he comes: the Greek world and the Jewish world. Grace (*xaris*) was a standard greeting in ancient Greek letters. The Hebrew *shalom*, or peace — translated here as the Greek *eirene* — was the standard greeting in Hebrew. In bringing the two salutations together, Paul is alluding both to his own dual background, and to the competing Greek and Jewish factions within the Corinthian church. More important, he sounds these themes just before launching into some intensely disturbing subject matter: the end of the world. The grace and peace Paul wishes for the Corinthians flow from his supreme confidence in Christ: that, at his coming, "you are not lacking in any spiritual gift as you wait for the revealing of our Lord Jesus Christ." The word for "revealing," here, is *apokalupsis*. We know it from the English words, "apocalypse" and "apocalyptic," which have taken on rather sinister meanings in our day. Apocalyptic, to the popular imagination, is wreathed in shadows and seasoned with doom. For Paul, however, it simply means "revealing" or "unveiling." That which is unveiled — while it may be a threat to evildoers — is ultimately good and life-giving. "Faith is not knowing what the future holds," a wise and anonymous writer reassures us, "but knowing who holds the future."

The Gospel   Mark 13:24-37   *Faith For The Wee Hours*

"Keep awake," warns Jesus — "for you do not know when the master of the house will come...." This is a faith for the wee hours, for those bleak watches of the night. Except for those whose employment is nocturnal, those who wait and watch sleeplessly at such hours generally have deep worries. A loved one is dying, an intractable problem blocks sleep, some dark fear looms large enough to call forth a bleary-eyed vigilance. The sudden return of a long-absent and powerful master would incite fear in most servants' minds: but for these true believers who are keeping vigil, the heavy footfall on the doorstep is a sign of hope.

Preaching Possibilities

Few biblical passages are more difficult to preach, in the dominant culture in North America, than apocalyptic. Many of our people seem inclined to receive such passages in one of two ways: either with fear and loathing, or with a perverse glee at the vanquishing of their enemies. There's something of the truth in both these viewpoints, but each one — taken on its own — is dangerously one-sided. Apocalyptic is meant to be a wake-up call: like the buzzer on an alarm clock, it's designed to be jarring. Yet hurling the clock out the window is not the answer. Apocalyptic is also meant to bear witness to the ultimate triumph of God's justice: but claiming to know anything of when that judgment is going to take place, or who will bear the weight of it, is the height of spiritual arrogance (Jesus himself warns, "about that day or hour no one knows, neither the angels in heaven, nor the Son, but only the Father" — Mark 13:32).

A sermon on any one of these passages could begin by exploring the experience of being startled. "Boo!" cries some practical joker, leaping out from the shadows — inciting a surge of adrenalin, a suddenly elevated heart rate, and the equivalent of a jangling alarm throughout the entire nervous system. For all but young children (whose supple nerves can take the strain), it's not a pleasant experience.

Yet this, in one way or another, is what all three of our scriptural authors are saying the human race's ultimate encounter with God will be like. The rending of the heavens, the sudden unveiling, the swift and sudden return of the absentee master — these brush strokes, added to one another, create a painting none of us would eagerly hang on our living room walls.

In making this kind of prediction, Jesus is a man of his times. For the past couple of centuries before Jesus' birth, Judaism had been developing an apocalyptic tradition far more detailed than the sketchy hopes of Isaiah. That emerging tradition was centered around the idea of a "Day of the Lord" that is to come, a day of darkness and tribulation. On that day, the prophets proclaim, God will scatter Israel's enemies and blast them with earthquake, wind, and fire — while carefully preserving the lives of the faithful.

Something rather like this did in fact happen, about seventy years after Jesus' birth — about the time the gospels were being edited into their final form. The Roman general Titus brutally put down a Jewish revolt, and in doing so destroyed the temple and much of the city of Jerusalem. Those dire events — while not precisely identical to Jesus' prophecy — would have been seen by the early church as fulfilling it, at least in part. Maybe 70 A.D. didn't bring global conflagration, but it did bring the destruction of the world as the Jewish people had known it. Apocalyptic texts of the Bible speak most loudly and clearly to those on this earth who have little to lose, because their lives are already in shambles.

Apocalyptic is strong medicine. Like a narcotic, it's best reserved for times of intense suffering. Use it in times of spiritual good health, as it were, and it becomes something like an addictive drug: first it seduces, then it kills. Let us neither hide these apocalyptic remedies away, nor use them indiscriminately.

Prayer For The Day

Lord of all ages, as season succeeds season and year supplants year, we come to you: trusting that your call — to wait, to watch, to trust — still has the same note of urgency about it as our forbears of old believed. Give us the courage to do as they have done, and stake our lives on your eternal promise in Jesus Christ. Amen.

11

To Illustrate

The anonymous African-American spiritual, "My Lord! What A Morning," goes like this:

> My Lord! what a morning,
> My Lord! what a morning,
> Oh, my Lord! what a morning,
> When the stars begin to fall.

There's something discordant here: a lovely melody, the comforting thought of welcoming the morning ... *and the stars beginning to fall?*

But remember who it was who first sang this song, and who cherished it over many generations. The view from the slave quarters was not a hopeful one — at least not concerning things of this earth. Unless those African-American slaves could find a way to escape to the North — a risky and possibly deadly proposition — their lives on this earth would be marked only by backbreaking labor, abuse, and the forced breakup of families. The only white people they knew — their oppressors — regarded them as subhuman (which the slaves themselves instinctively knew to be false).

Those slaves did find some measure of hope in singing, "My Lord! what a morning, when the stars begin to fall." For they believed that only when the stars did fall — or when they themselves died, whichever came first — would they and their people be at last free from suffering. When worshipers who are not from that tradition sing hymns like this today, they do well to try to see those words and hear that music through the eyes and ears of another people, the oppressed believers who wrote them.

***

Poet and spiritual writer Kathleen Norris says of "eschatology" (literally, "the doctrine of the last things"):

> *I have come to regard the word as life-affirming in ways far more subtle than any dictionary definition could convey. What I mean is this: an acquaintance of mine, a brilliant young scholar, was stricken with cancer, and over the course of several years came close to dying three times, but after extensive treatment, both radiation and chemotherapy, came a welcome remission. Her prognosis was uncertain at best, but she was again able to teach, and write. "I'd never want to go back," she told her department head, an older woman, "because now I know what each morning means, and I am so grateful just to be alive." When the other woman said to her, "We've been through so much together in the last few years," the younger woman nodded, and smiled. "Yes," she said, emphatically. "Yes! And hasn't it been a blessing!"*

"That," concludes Norris, "is eschatology."
— Kathleen Norris, *Amazing Grace* (New York: Riverhead, 1998), pp. 12-13

***

Fear has been much forgotten — both by the world and by Christians in general. We rush toward angels unafraid. We approach the blazing furnaces of the seraphim with no more apprehension than children who reach laughingly for fire.

This fearlessness is not a sign of the character of God, as if God has changed through the centuries that divide us from Moses and Isaiah, from Zechariah and Mary and the shepherds. Rather, it is a sign of the character of this present age, of arrogance or of ignorance, whether or not one admits to a living God.

Mindlessly do the bells of secular celebrations jingle for Christmas. Meaninglessly do carols repeat their tinny joys in all the malls in America. No richer than soda pop is every sentimentalized Christmas special on television. Fearless is the world at play with godly things, because godless is its heart.

If God is a laughing Santy, why should we be afraid?

— Walter Wangerin, *Preparing For Jesus*
(Grand Rapids, Michigan: Zondervan, 1999), pp. 59-60

***

He told me that once when he was a little boy, he spent all day Sunday watching at the window, waiting for Jesus to come to Bern. I asked him, "And in the evening, you were disappointed?"

He said, "No, the waiting was wonderful!" I think that attitude remained throughout his life.

— Eberhard Busch, speaking of his friend and teacher, Karl Barth

***

Sometimes you can observe a lot by watching.

— Yogi Berra

Second Sunday Of Advent
December 4, 2005

Revised Common	Isaiah 40:1-11	2 Peter 3:8-15a	Mark 1:1-8
Roman Catholic	Isaiah 40:1-5, 9-11	2 Peter 3:8-14	Mark 1:1-8
Episcopal	Isaiah 40:1-11	2 Peter 3:8-15a, 18	Mark 1:1-8

Theme For The Day   Prepare!

Old Testament Lesson   Isaiah 40:1-11   *From Condemnation To Comfort*

These lines begin the portion of the larger Isaiah collection known as Second Isaiah. As such, they mark one of the most significant transitions in the Judeo-Christian tradition — and indeed, in all of human religious thought. With the ringing proclamation that begins this passage, "Comfort, O comfort my people ... Speak tenderly to Jerusalem," the prophet's message changes from condemnation to comfort. Isaiah pushes back the very boundaries of human religious imagination: daring to envision a God who is larger than a single nation or culture, whose zeal for justice is tempered by tender love. Prepare the way for this just and loving Lord, Isaiah proclaims, who will lead dispirited exiles home again!

New Testament Lesson   2 Peter 3:8-15a   *Like A Thief In The Night*

"But the day of the Lord will come like a thief...." To modern ears, that sounds like bad news — not to mention a mixed metaphor that depicts God in morally questionable terms. To the ears of the recipients of this letter, however, it would come as good news (this also happens to be a metaphor Jesus himself uses, in Matthew 24:43). The church of 2 Peter is struggling to maintain the integrity of its teaching against the competing messages of certain contemporary Greek philosophers, who fault Christians for continuing to wait for their Lord's appearing. Not to worry, the author says: the Lord will come when the Lord will come. The reason for his delay is to allow time for repentance (v. 9); but when that time is up, his coming will be swift and unannounced. All is still unfolding according to plan: so be patient, and continue to live faithfully.

The Gospel   Mark 1:1-8   *John The Baptist Prepares The Way*

In his typically sparse narrative style, Mark launches right into telling "the good news of Jesus Christ, the Son of God." Unlike his synoptic colleagues — who begin their gospels with nativity stories — Mark locates his first scene on the banks of the Jordan, with the fiery John proclaiming a gospel of repentance, sealed by the sign of baptism. Mark's narrative imagery is vivid: to the admiring throng of penitents who have removed their sandals in order to wade into the river, John proclaims that he is not worthy even to perform the slave's gesture of untying the sandal of the holy one who is to come. An obvious problem (corrected by some later scribes, in textual variants) is that the first part of John's Old Testament citation (v. 2b) — which Mark attributes to Isaiah — is actually from Malachi 3:1. The rest of the citation (v. 3) is a rough translation of Isaiah 40:3 (the lectionary's Old Testament selection for today — see above). This loose attribution is perhaps faithful to the spirit of the fiery John: he is not the sort of person to be troubled by scholarly documentation!

Preaching Possibilities

A common theme linking today's passages — although one that means something a little different in each instance — is that of preparation. Isaiah hears a voice that thunders, "prepare the way of Yahweh!" — meaning: blast out a highway in the desert, more grand than the processional avenues of Babylon, down which your captors used to parade their puny idols on wheeled carts! The author of 2 Peter advises his long-suffering church, "prepare yourself," for you never know when the Lord is coming. Mark adapts Isaiah's words (which originally meant something quite different) to name John the Baptist as the one who prepares the way of the Lord. Rather clumsily, he links the Isaiah passage with similar, unattributed words from Malachi 3:1, which in their context actually refer to the Messiah himself — rather than his forerunner — as the one who prepares the way.

In any event, the concept of preparation is prominent, both in the texts and in the hearts and minds of our people — who have by now been inundated with secular admonitions to prepare ("*How* many more shopping days till Christmas?"). Due to the diverse meanings of "preparation" in each of the lectionary passages, however, it is wise to preach on just one text, thereby avoiding considerable confusion.

So what does it mean to be prepared? When I was growing up as a Boy Scout, it meant to always carry a dime in your pocket in case you needed to summon help for an accident victim (ten cents for a phone call certainly dates the story!). An entire industry — the insurance industry — exists to help people prepare for adverse financial circumstances. Several burgeoning educational businesses ("test preparation" companies, they call themselves) help college applicants prepare to take standardized examinations.

Advent preparation, of course, is different. A time-honored goal of Advent preaching, in a consumer culture, is to help worshipers shift their idea of preparation from commercial to spiritual activity. In Advent, we do not so much prepare *for* something, as we prepare *ourselves*. The focus is not so much on doing, as on being — always a tough task, in a season of multiple, conflicting demands on our time. Isaac Watts — in a hymn never intended as a Christmas carol, incidentally, but which has subsequently become one — puts it memorably: "let every heart prepare him room...."

It's like an expectant couple preparing to welcome a new baby. There are certain things couples do to prepare for a birth: scheduling prenatal doctor's appointments, attending Lamaze classes, purchasing nursery furniture. A well-known psychological phenomenon is the "nesting instinct," in which a woman in late pregnancy launches into frenetic activity to prepare a room of the house, after which — or even during which — labor begins. As *chronos*-time rolls over into *xairos*-time, however, a transformation takes place. Preparation, for the expectant parents, becomes not so much a matter of doing as of being: of preparing their hearts for the life-changing experience that awaits them both. Advent preparation, at its best, is a transition from *chronos* to *xairos*: from doing to being.

The figure of John the Baptist can help us focus on this transformative task. His is a call to radical repentance, to transformation. John appears from an unexpected quarter: a stranger, an outsider, an alien. He is a man of the wilderness, calling us out of the well-worn grooves of our workaday lives into a simple place of stark spiritual choices.

The wilderness, by the way, should never be portrayed as barren desert; what's meant by "wilderness," in biblical passages such as this, is merely uninhabited land. It's possible to "live off the land," in such a place — on locusts and wild honey, in John's case, or on quail and manna as the Israelites of old — fully dependent on God's provision.

15

And that, ultimately, is the spiritual goal of Advent: repentance, simplicity, total dependence on God. Our listeners, for the most part, already know they need to make such a transformation; nearly all of them are aware of the seductive spiritual pitfalls of yuletide commercialism, and don't need a preacher to enlighten them on this point. A sermon that communicates John's call to repentance — in a way that gently confirms this truth our people already know, but need to hear once again — will surely advance the gospel.

Prayer For The Day
Our lives, O God, are often filled with distractions. Time and again, we put our heart's desire on hold, forsaking the truly important to chase after the merely urgent. Give us, in these Advent days, the grace to discover moments of peaceful contemplation: that we may prepare ourselves aright to welcome the Savior. Amen.

To Illustrate
Stephen Vincent Benet once wrote a Christmas play in which the wife of the innkeeper, who intuitively realizes something momentous has happened back there in the stable, remarks: "Something has been loosed to change the world, and with it we must change."
Such is the message of John the Baptist. We must change.

***

We have become so accustomed to the idea of divine love and of God's coming at Christmas that we no longer feel the shiver of fear that God's coming should arouse in us. We are indifferent to the message, taking only the pleasant and agreeable out of it and forgetting the serious aspect, that the God of the world draws near to the people of our little earth and lays claim to us. The coming of God is truly not only glad tidings, but first of all frightening news for everyone who has a conscience.
Only when we have felt the terror of the matter, can we recognize the incomparable kindness. God comes into the very midst of evil and of death, and judges the evil in us and in the world. And by judging us, God cleanses and sanctifies us, comes to us with grace and love. God makes us happy as only children can be happy.
— Dietrich Bonhoeffer, from *Watch for the Light: Readings for Advent and Christmas* (Farmington, Pennsylvania: Plough Publishing House, 2001)

***

There's a recent book by Brian Czech on environmental and economic issues with the intriguing title *Shoveling Fuel for a Runaway Train* (Berkeley, California: University of California Press, 2002). It's a good metaphor. The damage we've done to the natural environment and society by our insistence on unlimited "growth" is the runaway train, and we keep doing things to make the damage worse....
The message of John the Baptist, the message of Advent, is "You're going the wrong way. Stop shoveling, slow down, and turn around. Repent." It's not surprising that we have trouble hearing that simple message because it calls for radical change. Turn 180 degrees and go in the other direction. The Greek word for "repent" in the New Testament, is equally radical. *Metanoeo* means "I change my mind" — not in the trivial sense of deciding to order soup instead of a

salad, but making a fundamental change in the way I think. The wrong way is to put myself first. The right way is to "love the Lord your God with all your heart, and with all your soul, and with all your strength, and with all your mind — and your neighbor as yourself."
— George Murphy, writing for The Immediate Word internet sermon resource,
December 14, 2003 <www.csspub.com/tiw.lasso>

***

A young rabbinical student once asked his teacher, "When is the best time to repent?"

The rabbi thought for a moment, then answered, "The best time to repent is at the last possible moment."

After he said that, the student replied, "But you never know when the last possible moment will be."

And the rabbi answered, "Exactly!"

Third Sunday Of Advent
December 11, 2005

Revised Common	Isaiah 61:1-4, 8-11	1 Thessalonians 5:16-24	John 1:6-8, 19-28
Roman Catholic	Isaiah 61:1-2, 10-11	1 Thessalonians 5:16-24	John 1:6-8, 19-28
Episcopal	Isaiah 65:1-25	1 Thessalonians 5:(12-15) 16-28	John 1:6-8, 19-28
			or John 3:23-30

Theme For The Day   In Advent we welcome Jesus, a stranger among us.

Old Testament Lesson   Isaiah 61:1-4, 8-11   *Good News ... And Justice*

"The spirit of the Lord God is upon me," announces Isaiah. The Lord is sending him "to bring good news to the oppressed, to bind up the brokenhearted, to proclaim liberty to the captives, and release to the prisoners; to proclaim the year of the Lord's favor ..." (Isaiah 61:1-2a). These words are doubly familiar to us, because they are the same words Jesus will quote, centuries later, as he begins his ministry in the Nazareth synagogue. In the second portion of this reading, the prophet speaks for God: "I, the Lord, love justice ..." (v. 8). Good news and justice are intertwined, inseparable — in Advent, or at any other time.

New Testament Lesson   1 Thessalonians 5:16-24   *Rejoice Always ...*
Be Sanctified Entirely

Paul concludes many of his letters with a "mixed bag" of closing advice and admonitions, and this passage is an example of that sort of collection. It's difficult to deal with this assortment of disparate sayings as a unified whole; each piece of advice is more or less distinct. Two excerpts, however, lend themselves to consideration during Advent: either one may explain why the lectionary editors chose this passage for this week. Verse 16 (one of the shortest verses in the Bible) says, "Rejoice always" — always an appropriate thought for Advent. Verse 23 says, "May the God of peace himself sanctify you entirely; and may your spirit and soul and body be kept sound and blameless at the coming of our Lord Jesus Christ." Note that God — and not the believer — is the principal actor here. Sanctification is never a human accomplishment, but is wholly the result of God's gracious intervention.

The Gospel   John 1:6-8, 19-28   *Among You Stands One*
Whom You Do Not Know

The lectionary returns us once again to John the Baptist's testimony (see last week's resource for reflections on the parallel passage in Mark). Two differences in this Johannine version are verse 8's assessment of John: "He himself was not the light, but he came to testify to the light" (providing an opportunity to address the theme of light); and John's words in verse 26, "Among you stands one whom you do not know." When John first spoke these words, he was alluding to the fact that Jesus had not, as yet, stepped forward as a public figure. Yet there is another, ironic sense in which these words may speak to us today: for is it not true that, even for us who profess to be his disciples, Jesus remains in some respect "one whom we do not know"? Every time we allow ourselves to be distracted from the true meaning of Christmas, we demonstrate that, to one degree or another, we still do not fully know him.

Alternate Gospel Lesson   Luke 1:47-55   *The World Turned Upside Down*

Preachers who have already spoken about John the Baptist the previous week may want to go with the alternate psalm for this Sunday, the Magnificat of Mary, instead. This stunning poem bears witness to the world-changing nature of the Messiah's coming. In entering the world in human form, God has brought down the powerful from the thrones and lifted up the lowly; God has filled the hungry with good things and sent the rich away empty. It's a divine reversal of the usual order of things — as revolutionary today as it was in biblical times.

Preaching Possibilities

All the passages, this week, touch in one way or another on the strangeness of the incarnation. It may sound odd to describe such a central doctrine of Christianity in this way, but in fact it is an event so utterly unique in human history that it continues to defy description. The fact that God became one of us changed everything, and continues to do so.

This is a counter-cultural message: because this time of year, whether in the church or outside it, just about everyone wants to claim the Christ-child in one way or another. Meditating on the sweet image of "the little Lord Jesus, asleep on the hay," it's hard to do anything but imagine embracing the child; yet all of today's passages remind us that Jesus is both one of us and not one of us. The doctrine of the incarnation teaches that he is fully human, yes, but also fully God — and that in that divine aspect of his being, he is always strangely remote from us in his holiness. Try as we may to confine him in our Christmas creches, he will not remain there, smiling beatifically. This child will grow to become the "one whom we do not know" (John 1:26), the one who will cast down the powerful from their thrones and raise up the lowly (Luke 1:52). He is the one to whom we will sooner or later look, to do for us what we could never do for ourselves: to "sanctify us entirely, spirit, soul and body" (1 Thessalonians 5:23). He will lead us in doing what we, left to our own devices, are so seldom capable of: bringing good news to the oppressed, binding up the brokenhearted, proclaiming liberty to the captives (Isaiah 61:1). At the last day, he will complete this work of justice through the last judgment.

There is reason to be suspicious of a domesticated Jesus, especially at Christmas time. The purpose of God becoming human is not to confirm us in our fallen humanity, but rather to transform us by grace. The herald angels who sing "Glory to the newborn king" are not rosy-faced choristers spreading Christmas cheer, but rather the vanguard of God's heavenly host (literally, God's army). Their songs are not carols, but military marching songs. The stable in Bethlehem is not so much the rustic, lantern-lit domestic tableau of many a Christmas card, as it is the beachhead of God's invasion forces, breaking into the world to do battle with sin. Yes, there is everything to celebrate about this birth: but not for the reasons the world typically expects. In celebrating the coming of the God-man, Jesus Christ, we acknowledge that our own lives — and indeed the future of the entire world — will never be the same again.

Prayer For The Day

We praise you and thank you, O God, that you care so deeply about this world as to be present in it: through the birth of your Son, Jesus, the incarnate word. May we never take this, your greatest gift, for granted. Amen.

To Illustrate

He comes to us as one unknown, without a name, as of old, by the lakeside. He came to those who knew him not. He speaks to us. He speaks the same word: Follow me! and sets us to the tasks which he has to fulfill for our time.

He commands, and to those who obey him, whether they be wise or simple, He will reveal himself, in the toils, the conflicts, the sufferings which they shall pass through in his fellowship, and, as an ineffable mystery, they shall learn in their own experience who he is.

— Albert Schweitzer, from *The Quest for the Historical Jesus*
(New York, New York: Macmillan, 1968)

***

In a famous and still-controversial poem, "Holy Sonnet XIV: Batter My Heart, Three-Person'd God," the Elizabethan poet John Donne employs a highly unusual image to speak of God. He describes God as an assailant, who breaks into his heart by force — but who, precisely because of the desperate nature of that assault, brings new life:

Batter my heart, three person'd God; for, you
As yet but knocke, breathe, shine, and seeke to mend;
That I may rise, and stand, o'erthrow mee, and bend
Your force, to breake, blow, burn and make me new.

Donne ends his poem by exclaiming,

Divorce mee, untie, or breake that knot againe,
Take mee to you, imprison mee, for I
Except you enthrall mee, never shall be free,
Nor ever chast, except you ravish mee.

***

Mary did you know that your baby boy would someday walk on water?
Mary did you know that your baby boy would save our sons and daughters?
Did you know that your baby boy has come to make you new?
This child that you delivered, will soon deliver you.

Mary, did you know that your baby boy will give sight to a blind man?
Mary, did you know that your baby boy will calm a storm with his hand?
Did you know that your baby boy has walked where angels trod?
When you kissed your little baby, then you kissed the face of God.

— Mark Lowry, "Mary, Did You Know?"; words by Mark Lowry,
music by Buddy Green, (Nashville: Word Music, 2000)

***

Since the evangelical century of the 1800s, America's Protestant majority has gravitated toward a Mister Rogers Jesus, a neighborly fellow they could know and love and imitate. The country's megachurches got that way in part because they stopped preaching fire and brimstone and the blood of the Lamb. Their parishioners are sinners in the hands of an amiable God. Their Jesus is a loving friend....

— Stephen Prothero, "The Personal Jesus," *New York Times* magazine, February 29, 2004

***

If the world is sane, then Jesus is mad as a hatter and the Last Supper is the Mad Tea Party. The world says, "Mind your own business," and Jesus says, "There is no such thing as your own business." The world says, "Follow the wisest course and be a success," and Jesus says, "Follow me and be crucified." The world says, "Drive carefully — the life you save may be your own" and Jesus says, "Whoever would save his life will lose it, and whoever loses his life for my sake will find it." The world says, "Law and order," and Jesus says, "Love." The world says, "Get" and Jesus says, "Give." In terms of the world's sanity, Jesus is crazy as a coot, and anybody who thinks he can follow him without being a little crazy too is laboring less under a cross than under a delusion.
— Frederick Buechner, from *Listening To Your Life* (New York: HarperCollins, 1992)

***

According to a story from the 1930s, when anti-Jewish pogroms were ravaging the villages of Eastern Europe, there was a Jewish grave-digger who saved many lives by hiding refugees in his freshly dug graves. One night, as a young woman and her family were hiding in just such a grave, the woman gave birth. "This," the grave digger cried, "is surely the Messiah — for who else would be born in a grave?"

Fourth Sunday Of Advent
December 18, 2005

Revised Common	2 Samuel 7:1-11, 16	Romans 16:25-27	Luke 1:26-38
Roman Catholic	2 Samuel 7:1-5, 8-12, 14, 16	Romans 16:25-27	Luke 1:26-38
Episcopal	2 Samuel 7:4, 8-16	Romans 16:25-27	Luke 1:26-38

Theme For The Day We can never fully prepare for miracles of God's grace, but can only resolve to be open to them when they come.

Old Testament Lesson 2 Samuel 7:1-11, 16 *God Promises To Build David A House*

Flush with victory and filled with pride in his accomplishments, King David grandiloquently declares that he will build the Lord a magnificent house: a temple. Yet God declines the king's offer. "I have not lived in a house since the day I brought up the people of Israel from Egypt to this day," says the Lord, "but I have been moving about in a tent and a tabernacle" (v. 6). Instead, God promises to build David a house (v. 11). What the Lord has in mind is not a physical structure, but rather a spiritual dynasty: "Your house and your kingdom shall be made sure forever before me; your throne shall be established forever" (v. 16). (For a fuller description of this passage, see Proper 11, on page 183.)

New Testament Lesson Romans 16:25-27 *Mysteries Revealed*

Paul ends the Letter to the Romans with a blessing, a closing doxology. What has undoubtedly attracted the attention of the lectionary editors (leading them to choose these two verses for this week's Epistle Lesson) is the line about "the proclamation of Jesus Christ, according to the revelation of the mystery that was kept secret for long ages but is now disclosed." This passage looks back upon the prophecies of the Messiah's coming and acknowledges that they have been but partially understood — until now, when Christ is revealed as their fulfillment.

The Gospel Luke 1:26-38 *Here Am I, Servant*

It's one of the most familiar of all biblical stories, one that has been celebrated in countless well-loved works of art: the angel Gabriel's announcement to Mary that she is to bear a child who will be Savior of the world. Luke's account also sets up the story that immediately follows: as the angel informs Mary that her aged kinswoman Elizabeth is likewise expecting a child. Mary responds in obedient humility, using words reminiscent of the great prophets' response to their divine calling: "Here am I, the servant of the Lord; let it be with me according to your word" (v. 38).

Alternate Gospel Lesson Luke 1:47-55 *The Magnificat*

Again, the Magnificat is an alternate psalm for today, and could be used as an alternate Gospel Lesson (see last week's resource).

Preaching Possibilities

As the candles on the Advent wreath burn lower and the days grow ever shorter, the pews fill with worshipers both familiar and unfamiliar to the preacher. Some of them understand that this is still Advent, and that Christmas (although near) has not arrived yet. Others who have not been present for the previous three weeks, have been listening incessantly to Christmas carols on the car radio and in the shopping mall, and would like nothing better than to sing carols and hear a nativity story. Still others will soon be traveling, to celebrate the holiday with family or friends in distant places, and would love to have something of a Christmas experience here in their regular place of worship.

With so many conflicting expectations, what's a preacher to do?

A sermon focusing on the Gospel Lesson is an appropriate solution. The *annunciation* is, technically, still an Advent story — although years of lessons-and-carols services have convinced many people it's the first part of the Christmas story. It is also an opportunity, particularly for Protestants, to celebrate the contribution of Mary: a giant of faith who has been neglected by our tradition for far too long.

For Mary, it begins as an ordinary day in an ordinary life. She rises early to do her household chores. Nothing about the day seems unusual. The sun is shining at its predictable angle, neighbors are following their customary routine. Outside, the street is dusty, the distant market noises raucous. Yet before this day is out, the teenager, Mary, will be visited by an angel. The angel will tell her she will soon be with child, and that the infant who will grow inside her is no ordinary baby, but God's own son. It is, for her, a day of wonder.

The church calls this event the *annunciation* — a word which simply means, "announcement." Over the centuries, artists have tried to picture the scene. Take a tour of Renaissance sites in Italy, and you will see churches and museums filled with dozens upon dozens of annunciation paintings. After a while, you no longer need to read the placards below the heavy gilt frames. The scene is always the same: there's Mary, kneeling devoutly, and beside her is a rather feminine-looking man in a golden robe, with flowing locks and his arm upraised in blessing.

The late-Medieval and Renaissance artists always seem to know what goes into the scene — although the real annunciation was private. Mary was the only witness. What really happened? Did she see an angel with her own eyes, or with the secret eye of her inmost heart? Did Mary hear a beautiful voice and suddenly turn around? Or did she hear someone speaking quietly, deep within her soul?

Mary's response to all this is, "How can this be, since I am a virgin?" It's a little like Mary asking Gabriel — after he has uttered that intricate, awe-inspiring prophecy about "Son of the Most High," and "throne of David," and "house of Jacob forever" — "Would you repeat some of that for me?"

"Certainly, which part?"

"The part after, 'You will conceive in your womb and bear a son....' "

There's something homely, and very human, about this story. Mary's certainly not ready to receive this wondrous news — but eventually it does sink in. The angel has just informed Mary that, after hundreds of years of waiting, after untold millions of prayers chanted in the temple, the Messiah is about to come to her people. This child whom she will bear will reclaim the throne of David — from which no legitimate Jewish king has ruled for centuries. More than that, all nations will pay him homage, and his kingdom will never end.

"But ... how can this be, since I am still a virgin?" Mary wonders at the angel's prophecy, all right — but hers, at least for the moment, is still a small wonder. Mary's not ready for Christmas. Are we?

Prayer For The Day
Have your own way, Lord, have your own way;
You are the potter, I am the clay.
Mold me and make me, after your will,
While I am waiting, yielded and still.
(Hymn text, "Have Thine Own Way," adapted)

To Illustrate
The world will never starve for wonders, but only for want of wonder.

— G. K. Chesterton

***

We die on the day when our lives cease to be illumined by the steady radiance, renewed daily, of a wonder, the force of which is beyond reason.

— Dag Hammarskjold

***

Mary, mother of our Lord, I wish I could be as pure a disciple as you were even from the beginning!

For you were invited to join a sisterhood — with Tamar and Bathsheba — of sorrow and human suffering, since the child of your womb would draw the hatreds and the outrages of a scoundrel world.

And you said, "Yes" ...

For it was an angel that spoke to you, a sky-strider, an inhabitant of holy heaven whose face caught fire from standing near to God, whose glory darkened all the common world in which you lived.

Yet you did not hesitate in fear or horror. You said, "Yes."

For history was pouring into your womb, the whole history of the Israel backward through David even unto Abraham; yet you were but a single person, one lone woman. How could a vessel of simple human limitation hold twenty centuries of national endeavor — triumph, failure, sin, atonement, trouble, prayer, and promise — and not burst open? But you would burst, Mary. You would spew the son of David into Judah again, and he would keep every past promise of God.

And you said, "Yes."

For heaven itself was swelling within you, and you were the door. Not in terrible glory would he come, this Son of the Most High God. Not in the primal blinding light, nor as the shout by which God uttered the universe, nor yet with the trumpet that shall conclude it, but through your human womb, as an infant bawling and hungry. By your labor, Mary, by the fierce contractions of your uterus, eternity would enter time. The angel said, Will you be the door of the Lord into this place?...

You, the first of all the disciples of Jesus, said, "Yes."

— Walter Wangerin, *Preparing For Jesus*
(Grand Rapids, Michigan: Zondervan, 1999), pp. 68-69

***

24

A woman went to the doctor's office. She was seen by one of the new doctors, but after about four minutes in the examination room, she burst out, screaming as she ran down the hall. An older doctor stopped and asked her what the problem was, and she explained. He had her sit down and relax in another room.

The older doctor marched back to the first and demanded, "What's the matter with you? Mrs. Terry is 63 years old, she has four grown children and seven grandchildren, and you told her she was pregnant?"

The new doctor smiled smugly as he continued to write on his clipboard. "Cured her hiccups though, didn't it?"

— Ralph Milton

***

Jesus observed, "Without me you can do nothing." Yet we act, for the most part, as though without us God can do nothing. We think we have to make Christmas come, which is to say we think we have to bring about the redemption of the universe on our own. When all God needs is a willing womb, a place of safety, nourishment, and love. "Oh, but nothing will get done," you say. "If I don't do it, Christmas won't happen." And we crowd out Christ with our fretful fears.

God asks us to give away everything of ourselves. The gift of greatest efficacy and power that we can offer God and creation is not our skills, gifts, abilities, and possessions. Mary offered only space, love, belief.

Try it. Leave behind your briefcase and notes. Leave behind your honed skills and knowledge. Leave the Christmas decorations up in the attic. Go to someone in need and say, "Here, all I have is Christ." And find out that that is enough....

The intensity and strain that many of us bring to Christmas must suggest to some onlookers that, on the whole, Christians do not seem to have gotten the point of it. Probably few of us have the faith or the nerve to tamper with hallowed Christmas traditions on a large scale or with our other holiday celebrations. But a small experiment might prove interesting. What if, instead of doing something, we were to be something special? Be a womb. Be a dwelling for God. Be surprised.

— Loretta Ross-Gotta, "Ready For Christmas?" in *Watch for the Light: Readings for Advent and Christmas* (Farmington, Pennsylvania: Plough Publishing House, 2001)

The Christmas Season

Each year, sacred and secular observances of "the holidays" run side-by-side: on a course that's roughly parallel, but at times intersects. The holiday season of 2005-2006 is one in which there are more intersections than usual.

Christmas Eve, 2005, occurs on a Saturday, and Christmas Day on a Sunday. A week later, New Year's Day coincides with the First Sunday After Christmas. Some churches will not hold Sunday morning services on December 25 at all, following the ancient tradition of the church that a new liturgical day begins at sundown (and that therefore the 2005 Christmas Eve services are technically Lord's Day services as well). Other churches, recognizing that daily and hourly habits of worship are deeply ingrained, will hold Lord's Day services on both Christmas Eve and on the morning of Christmas Day — although in most cases, their Sunday morning services will be simplified in one way or another, reflecting the practical awareness that attendance that day will be exceptionally low.

This year the lectionary provides but a single set of readings for Christmas Eve and Christmas Day (although the additional Propers provide more than enough variety for those needing to plan two distinct services). Then, the following week, the First Sunday After Christmas readings must also suffice for whatever observance the local church is planning for New Year's Day (not a liturgical holiday, of course — although the transition to a new year offers a pastoral opportunity to support worshipers as they reflect on the past year and look with hope to the future).

For most churches, Christmas Eve is one of the two best-attended services in the year. In some places, Christmas attendance is bigger even than on Easter (despite the fact that Easter is of greater importance theologically). Christmas Eve offers unique challenges to the preacher, in that the view from the pulpit is radically different on that date than on any other occasion.

"Who *are* these people?" the newly installed pastor may be led to ask, regarding the assemblage of faces in the pews. "Where have they come from?" (In some congregations, the cast of characters may be that different.) Longer-tenured pastors reach the point where even some of the "C & E" worshipers look familiar. They're part of the outer circle of the company of the saints: a few of them less-than-active members, but many of them non-members who feel some vague affinity with the congregation. For most of the year, this is the congregation they don't attend — but it's still *their* congregation.

These are the sort of people who — like the parishioner in the old anecdote — could very well call the pastor up to complain about too much repetition in hymn choices. "I don't think there's too much repetition," the pastor objects, defensively. "I try to choose a variety of hymns. Could you tell me which ones you think we sing too often?"

"Every time I come to church, it's the same old stuff," continues the critic: " 'Joy To The World,' 'Silent Night' and 'Jesus Christ Is Risen Today'!"

All pastoral gripes about C & E people aside, Christmas Eve provides preachers with an evangelistic opportunity like none other. For a few brief moments, in the very center of the North American shop-and-spend maelstrom, we've got them. Maybe they're exhausted, maybe they're disillusioned, maybe their eyes are glazed-over from a little too much eggnog of the spiked kind, but we've got their attention. Now, what to say?

There's one thing, for sure, we *shouldn't* say, for it's bound to be counter-productive: we shouldn't scold. The C & E types know perfectly well who they are. "Their sin is ever before them," to paraphrase the psalmist. They know the pretenses under which they've come. Some of them they may even expect a scolding. It's only fair, they think to themselves; a pastoral scolding's not a bad price to pay for the many Sundays they've risen late, to bagels and the funny papers. And besides, isn't the church just full of haughty, hypocritical people, who get their jollies from looking down their noses at others? If these occasional visitors get *that* impression on Christmas Eve, well that's reason enough for them to stay home for the next six months.

No, the best way to handle C & E worshipers is to extend to them, in every way we know how, the Christian virtue of hospitality. Treat them like they belong here. Maybe someday they will.

Christmas Eve / Christmas Day
December 24 & 25, 2005

Revised Common	**Isaiah 9:2-7**	**Titus 2:11-14**	**Luke 2:1-20**
Roman Catholic	**Isaiah 9:1-7**	**Titus 2:11-14**	**Luke 2:1-14**
Episcopal	**Isaiah 9:2-4, 6-7**	**Titus 2:11-14**	**Luke 2:1-14 (15-20)**

Note: The comments below are on the Proper I texts. Proper II and III texts (alternates for this day) are as follows:

Proper II

Revised Common	**Isaiah 62:6-12**	**Titus 3:4-7**	**Luke 2:(1-7) 8-20**

Proper III

Revised Common	**Isaiah 52:7-10**	**Hebrews 1:1-4 (5-12)**	**John 1:1-14**

Theme For The Day   The good news of Christmas is for everyone — no exceptions.

Old Testament Lesson   Isaiah 9:2-7   *To Us A Child Is Born*
"The people who walked in darkness have seen a great light" — and that great light, the prophet says, is the birth of a child. And who is this child? In Isaiah's historical context it can only be Hezekiah, son of King Ahaz of Judah. In young Prince Hezekiah the people can see God's future incarnate, living in flesh and blood in their midst. By the end of Hezekiah's reign, the dire threat from Assyria will be no more, and the nation will have regained a measure of stability. Isaiah says this new king will be called "wonderful counselor" and "prince of peace." The titles fit — but not the other ones Isaiah uses. Mighty God? Everlasting Father? No, these titles must await the birth of another....

New Testament Lesson   Titus 2:11-14   *Grace Has Appeared*
"The grace of God has appeared, bringing salvation to all ..." (v. 11). The word for "appeared" is a form of *epiphaino* — source of the word "epiphany." Epiphany has connotations both of sudden appearing and of illumination — fitting thoughts for a midwinter candlelight service, when days are short, but flickering flames symbolize the hope and confidence of light's return.

The Gospel   Luke 2:1-14 (15-20)   *Good News For All People*
For many people, these verses from Luke are *the* Christmas story. Significant in this passage is the care Luke takes to tell us that Jesus' coming is, in the angel's words, "good news of great joy for *all* the people" (v. 10). The Greek *laos* means people in general; adding the adjective "all" intensifies the gospel's universality. The Savior of the world comes not to princes, but to disreputable shepherds. He is born not in a palace, but in a stable. Over against the universal tendency of human governments to form hierarchies and favor special-interest groups, God's new order is truly egalitarian.

Preaching Possibilities

A particular difficulty in interpretation is the tendency to harmonize the birth narratives of Matthew and Luke, deftly ignoring the numerous differences and contradictions between them. Here's a quick comparison of those differences:

	Matthew	*Luke*
Genealogy	From Abraham (1:1-17) — Judaic	From Adam (3:23-28) — Universal
Annunciation	To Joseph, in a dream (1:20)	To Mary, in person (1:28)
Joseph's role	Adoptive father (2:24)	Supposed father (3:23)
Parallel story of Elizabeth and Zechariah	No	Yes
Appearance of angels to shepherds	No	Yes
Description of birth	Minimal (2:1a)	Detailed (2:1-21)
Location of birth	Unclear; Magi find Jesus in a "place" (2:9)	A stable (2:7)
Visit of Magi	Yes	No
Massacre of Innocents / Flight into Egypt	Yes	No
Final destination	Joseph settles in Nazareth (2:22-23)	Joseph's already from Nazareth (1:26)

Harmonization is hard to resist, especially with the well-loved traditions of Christmas pageants and "services of lessons and carols." Rather than depicting each birth-narrative in its individuality and integrity, however, such observances uncritically lump the two together. Preachers long accustomed to displaying historical-critical insights in their sermons may blanch at doing so on Christmas Eve; it's hard enough to explain that kind of stuff to the every-Sunday crowd, let alone to a roomful of near strangers!

Yet it's simply wrong to continue to encourage our listeners in the naive belief that Matthew's and Luke's nativity stories are like two halves of a treasure map; or, to use another metaphor, that Matthew and Luke are like tag-team historians. Just try to combine the two stories, and the contradictions multiply.

The length to which interpreters have gone, over the years, attempting to meld these two stories into one, approaches the comical. Pastoral sensitivity considers it a poor idea to reveal all these exegetical intricacies to an unsuspecting Christmas Eve congregation — particularly the biblically semi-literate, who will be out in great numbers. "Pay no attention to the preacher behind the curtain," we're tempted to mutter, if our exegesis should happen to show — all the while continuing to pull the levers and rotate the wheels that crank the star up into the sky, and cause the angel song to rumble over the hills in surround-sound. (Ain't it a great show, Christmas Eve? One of the best!)

Yet there *is* an alternative to simply capitulating to the harmonizers. That solution is, simply, to preach on one passage — scrupulously resisting the temptation to haul in details that occur only in the other book. Each birth-narrative has its own narrative and theological integrity — and while perhaps it's unwise to trumpet that fact from the rooftops without a whole lot of good, educational preparation beforehand, it can inform the direction we choose to go.

Luke, for example, has several distinctive theological themes, all of which lend themselves to preaching:

1. Jesus' coming prefigures *the reversal of the existing social order* (as Mary sings in the Magnificat, God "fills the hungry with good things, and sends the rich away empty" — 1:53).

2. *The gospel comes first to the poor and the outcast* (as symbolized by the shepherds, and by Jesus' birth in a stable).
3. *The gospel is for all people*, not simply the Jews (as symbolized by Luke's taking Jesus' genealogy back to Adam and Eve, and by the universality of the angels' song).

Prayer For The Day

Christmas! Holy night of nights
that made the very richest poor —
you pierce the darkness with your light;
powers of night cannot endure.

Jesus is the light of stars.
Jesus is the strength of life!
And he does for the world's poor,
things beyond the world's belief.

Make us poor through your great love,
Jesus, poor like you, we plead.
Make us weak — weak in your strength.
Show us mercy in our need.

— Eberhard Arnold

To Illustrate

As a magnifying glass concentrates the rays of the sun into a little burning knot of heat that can set fire to a dry leaf or piece of paper, so the mystery of Christ in the gospel concentrates the rays of God's light and fire to a point that sets fire in the spirit of man....

God is everywhere. His truth and his love pervade all things as the light and the heat of the sun pervade our atmosphere. But just as the rays of the sun do not set fire to anything by themselves, so God does not touch our souls with the fire of supernatural knowledge and experience without Christ.

— Thomas Merton, *New Seeds of Contemplation*
(New York: New Directions Publishing, 1949)

***

In 2003, the Christians of Iraq were wondering how they were going to celebrate Christmas, amidst the political instability of a nation at war. An article in the *New York Times* told the story:

> *Fears of guerrilla fighters and armed bandits called Ali Babas have led churches to move up the traditional midnight Mass. People are now resigned to celebrating Christmas barricaded in their homes. Some Christians are worried that churches will be bombed and congregations attacked, a fear given credence by American military officials who cite intelligence reports saying guerrillas may stage a wave of assaults this week partly to avenge the capture of the deposed Iraqi dictator Saddam Hussein.*

The article included an interview with Father Yousif Thomas Mirkis of St. Joseph's Cathedral in Baghdad. "Christmas this year will not be as special a day as it has been," Father Mirkis told the *Times*. "But maybe families will still celebrate it with trees and cake, and maybe it will be closer in spirit to the first Christmas. The first one took place in poverty and under difficult circumstances for that small family. Maybe that's our one consolation this year. We're having a true Christmas."

A true Christmas: what is that? Holly and carols and eggnog? Brightly-wrapped packages bound up with ribbon? Strings of icicle lights hanging from the eaves of the house? Or is it the birth-cry of a naked, shivering baby, held tightly in the apprehensive arms of his peasant-girl mother, his body covered with bits of straw from the feeding-trough in which he was born?

— Edward Wong, "In Iraq, Christians Warily Prepare an Early Christmas,"
New York Times, December 23, 2003

***

Gerald Coffee was an American navy pilot who was shot down over North Vietnam, and spent seven years as a prisoner of war. In his book, *Beyond Survival*, he writes of one of his Christmases as a prisoner.

For some reason — maybe because it was Christmas — his captors had given him three chocolate bars. The chocolate itself was almost inedible, but each bar had come wrapped in foil, red on one side and shiny silver on the other.

Taking one wrapper, Coffee flattened it, and folded it into an origami swan. The second he fashioned into a flower. The third he began folding, not sure of what it would become.

It became a star — the star of Bethlehem, he thought to himself. Plucking three straws from the broom in his cell, he jammed them into a crack in the wall, and used the straws to hang his homemade ornaments above his bunk, where he could lie and gaze up at them.

Captain Coffee thought, then, of the simplicity of the first Christmas — and of the faith that was sustaining him through his long ordeal. In his own words,

> *Here there was nothing to distract me from the awesomeness of Christmas — no commercialism, no presents, little food. I was beginning to appreciate my own spirituality, because I had been stripped of everything by which I had measured my identity: rank, uniform, money, family. Yet I continued to find strength within. I realized that although I was hurting and lonely and scared, this might be the most significant Christmas of my life.*

***

Where are his courtiers, and who are his people
Why does he wear neither scepter nor crown.
Shepherds his courtiers, the poor for his people,
With peace for his scepter and love for his crown.

— From John Rutter's "Christmas Lullaby"

***

When we say "it is Christmas" we mean that God has spoken into the world his last, his deepest, his most beautiful word in the incarnate word, a word that can no longer be revoked because it is God's definitive deed, because it is God himself in the world. And this word means: I love you, you, the world and humankind. And God has spoken this word by being himself born as a creature.

— Karl Rahner

31

First Sunday After Christmas
January 1, 2006

Revised Common	Isaiah 61:10—62:3	Galatians 4:4-7	Luke 2:22-40
Roman Catholic	Sirach 3:2-6, 12-14	Galatians 3:12-21	Luke 2:22-40
Episcopal	Isaiah 61:10—62:3	Galatians 3:23-25; 4:4-7	John 1:1-18

Note: The comments below are on the First Sunday After Christmas texts. Alternate texts for New Year's Day are as follows:

Revised Common:	Ecclesiastes 3:1-13	Revelation 21:1-6a	Matthew 25:31-46

Theme For The Day   God, the architect of time, has decreed that with Jesus' coming, the time is fulfilled.

Old Testament Lesson   Isaiah 61:10—62:3   *Let The Good News Resound!*

"For Zion's sake I will not keep silent" (62:1). How could the prophet do so, in light of the good news he has heard and seen? The "vindication that shines out like the dawn," the "salvation like a burning torch" belongs to the nation Israel, whose exiles are at last coming home. Yet these rejoicings could just as well belong to the whole world, once the world has received Jesus Christ, the Son of God.

New Testament Lesson   Galatians 4:4-7   *Fullness Of Time*

"But when the fullness of time had come, God sent his Son ..." (v. 4). "Fullness of time" (*pleroma tou chronou*) utilizes the word *chronos*, or clock time (as contrasted to *xairos*, or the right time). It's as though grains of sand had been falling into the lower portion of an hourglass, and that flow has finally ceased. High above Times Square on New Year's Eve, an illuminated ball slowly descends, marking the fullness of time that is the end of a calendar year. The old year is gone, never to return. So, too, the old order that once pertained — before Jesus' coming — is ended. A new order has begun. We can no more go on living in the old order than we can pretend to keep living in the old year.

The Gospel   Luke 2:22-40   *Out With The Old, In With The New*

The aged Simeon takes the young Jesus into his arms and sings a hymn of praise: "Master, now you are dismissing your servant in peace, according to your word; for my eyes have seen your salvation ..." (v. 29). The imagery is rather like that of the stock New Year's cartoons: a wizened old man, symbolizing the old year, rejoices in the presence of a chubby youngster in a diaper. Luke knows Jesus' coming changes everything. He tells us this tale of Simeon's blessing (along with its parallel, Anna's blessing) so we don't miss the point.

Preaching Possibilities

This is one of those Sundays when secular events trump the lectionary — but fortunately, the assigned readings allow ample opportunity to address contemporary need and still maintain the rhythm of the Christian year.

It's New Year's Day, and both the Epistle and Gospel Lessons happen to emphasize transitions of time. What the New Testament authors have in mind is the transition between the old, pre-incarnation order, and the new order, now that God's Son has been born among us — but still, they can be made to serve the other need as well.

Whichever passage is used, the trick is to keep the theme of Christmas prominent, so New Year's doesn't supplant it. (New Year's is of course not a Christian holiday — although it does call to mind a host of pastoral concerns about the future, that Christianity can and should address.) Out in the department stores, the Christmas merchandise has been packed up since December 26. The New Year's goods have remained out a bit longer, though very soon they, too, will be on their way to the warehouse (or the bargain bins, as the case may be). Time marches on, and retail waits for no one.

Indeed. But there are some things in life that are immutable, that cannot be swept out with yesterday's holiday decorations. Galatians speaks of time that has become "full." Ever play a game like Boggle, in which each turn is timed with a tiny, hourglass-like egg timer? The players rush to complete their tasks, nervously glancing over to the timer every few seconds. Eventually someone notices that the grains of sand have stopped falling. With this news, everything changes. The pressure is off. The reign of *chronos* is ended. The players have entered a new dimension, in which time is no longer so critical. What a relief!

Every twelve months, New Year's Day brings its own set of pressures. There's year-end accounting. Bills to pay. Resolutions to make — or not to make. (And what of those resolutions of last year? They're history.) The good news of the birth of Jesus Christ is not like that. Christ was born in time, but is not bound by it. When Christ was born, the sands stopped falling inside the hourglass of the old order — and that archaic timepiece will never be turned over again. A new order has begun. The old rules of bondage to the law no longer apply. We live by grace.

The Gospel Lesson likewise provides an opportunity to address New Year's themes. The stories of the wise elders, Simeon and Anna, blessing Jesus communicate the bittersweet joy of one season succeeding another. Always there is loss as well as gain. It may be profitable to explore, in a New Year's message, how people view the new year in different seasons of their lives: in youth, in middle-age, in maturity.

There's an old Jewish fable about an elderly man who spent all his spare time at the edge of his village, planting fig trees. People would ask him, "Old man, why are you planting fig trees? You're going to die before you can eat any of the fruit!"

But the wise old man replied, "I have spent so many happy hours sitting under fig trees and eating their fruit. Those trees were planted by others. Why shouldn't I make sure that others will know the same enjoyment I have had?" Simeon and Anna are like that. They know they will never see the Messiah in his prime, but one look into his infant eyes is enough.

Prayer For The Day

Holy God, we pray for your brightness to shine upon our hearts this day.
As we move forward into a new year,
may we know your grace
as it appears for us in the birth, life, death, and resurrection of Jesus Christ.
Help us to renounce sad outlooks and sorrowful attitudes
that threaten to darken our hearts.
Lead us, rather, to live lives that are joyous and just,
Godly and righteous,
as we await, in blessed hope,
the coming of your Son to shine on our world forever. Amen.

To Illustrate

During the darkest days of the Second World War in Britain, Prime Minister Winston Churchill made a speech in which he told his dispirited people, "Now this is not the end. It is not even the beginning of the end. But it is, perhaps, the end of the beginning."

***

There's a story about Benjamin Franklin, from the days when he served as his young nation's ambassador to France. Ever the keen scientist, Franklin jumped at the invitation to view the launching of a new French invention: the hot-air balloon.

Franklin traveled, in the company of others, to a field where the balloon ascent was to take place. A great fire was lit on the ground, and a pump and bellows were set up beside it, to fill the bag with hot air. After a great deal of difficulty, the great bag puffed out, and the whole apparatus ascended high into the air: only to descend to earth again, just a few moments later.

Franklin was entranced by what he saw. But then he heard a cynical voice by his side: "That's all well and good," the voice growled, "but what's it good for?"

Franklin is said to have turned to the man and asked, "Tell me, my friend, what a baby is good for?"

***

Time has no divisions to mark its passage; there is never a thunderstorm or blare of trumpets to announce the beginning of a new month or year. Even when a new century begins, it is only we mortals who ring bells and fire off pistols.

— Thomas Mann, *The Magic Mountain* (New York: Vintage Books, 1989)

***

When the primal Celtic tribe of *Tuatha de Danaan* first established their people in Ireland, Bres, the leader of the former inhabitants of the island, offered them a continual harvest. They refused him, saying,

> *This has been our way:*
> *Spring for plowing and for sowing,*
> *Summer for strengthening the crop,*
> *Autumn for grain's ripeness and for reaping,*
> *Winter for consuming its goodness.*

If we respect the gifts of each season, we will also find the thresholds and doorways of the spirit.

— Michael Rodgers and Marcus Losack, *Glendalough, a Celtic Pilgrimage*
(Harrisburg: Morehouse, 1996), p. 39

***

34

We can summarize the paradoxes of time as follows:

The Paradox of the Future: The future does not exist and never has existed, yet it is our most precious possession because it is all we have left. The future is where we will spend the rest of our lives. Since the future does not exist, it cannot be examined or measured.... It can only be studied by means of ideas based on knowledge from the past.

The Paradox of the Past: The past is the source of all our knowledge, including our knowledge of the future. But, despite everything we know about it and even our personal experience with it, we are powerless to improve the past or change it in any way because, by definition, the past no longer exists.

The Paradox of the Present: The present is the only period of time that exists and in which we can think and act, yet it is merely the boundary between the past and the future without any duration or existence of its own. These paradoxes lie at the center of human existence and shape profound dilemmas in our psychic life. After we recognize that we have made a terrible mistake, we can never alter that the fact that we made it.

— Edward Cornish, *The Futurist*, July-August, 2001

***

Don't fear tomorrow, God is there already.

— Anonymous

The Epiphany Season

There is division among lectionary users over what to call this season. The older title is "The Season Of Epiphany" or "Sundays After The Epiphany." More recently, there has been a growing trend to describe these Sundays between Epiphany and Lent as "Ordinary Time." The "Ordinary Time" designation is meant to reflect more accurately the character of these Sundays: for the season called Epiphany — unlike more thematically focused seasons like Advent and Lent — is not really a season at all. It has no unifying theme, and most of its texts have no relation to Epiphany at all. Counting Sundays "after the Epiphany" is a convenient device, that is all. A second period of Ordinary Time (with the numbering picking up where it left off just before Lent) begins after Pentecost, in the season some still designate — mostly for similar reasons of numeric convenience — "Sundays After Pentecost."

Whether or not we formally designate these Sundays as "ordinary," that is what they are. There is no need to apologize for that, or to scramble to find reasons to make them special. The very fact that God's Son has been born into ordinary human life — thus rendering it holy — is reason enough. The great celebration of the Advent / Christmas cycle is ended, and that of the Lent / Easter cycle has yet to begin. Now is the time for telling the story of Jesus' life and ministry.

The Baptism Of Our Lord
First Sunday After The Epiphany
First Sunday In Ordinary Time
January 8, 2006

Revised Common	Genesis 1:1-5	Acts 19:1-7	Mark 1:4-11
Roman Catholic	Isaiah 42:1-4, 6-7	Acts 10:34-38	Mark 1:7-11
Episcopal	Isaiah 42:1-9	Acts 10:34-38	Mark 1:7-11

Theme For The Day Jesus' baptism reminds us that our own baptism can be a powerful sign of God's presence in our lives.

Old Testament Lesson Genesis 1:1-5 *And God Created Light*

These are the beginning verses of the first of two creation stories in Genesis (the second begins at Genesis 2:4b). Out of the void — out of nothing — God creates the heavens and the earth. More a theological than a scientific commentary, this deeply loved poetic account portrays a Creator who pushes back the dark void — the sum of all human fears — displacing it with a good creation. Displaying mastery over the darkness, God names it *night.*

New Testament Lesson Acts 19:1-7 *Paul Baptizes Some Disciples Of John The Baptist*

In Ephesus, Paul encounters some believers who claim to be Christians — although upon closer examination it becomes clear that their baptism is in the tradition of John the Baptist, rather than one of the apostles. With a true missionary's flexibility and pastoral sensitivity, Paul affirms the essential goodness of the baptism these earnest seekers have received, then rebaptizes them in the name of Christ. The visible manifestation of gifts of the Holy Spirit that follows is a sign to all of the legitimacy of Paul's apostolic mission.

The Gospel Mark 1:4-11 *The Baptism Of Jesus*

We considered the first part of this passage not long ago, on the Second Sunday Of Advent, when Mark 1:1-8 was the Gospel Lesson. The overlapping portion, common to these two Sundays, vividly describes John the Baptist's activity in baptizing the repentant in the Jordan River. It also makes clear John's subordination to Jesus: he is awaiting one greater than himself, whose sandal he is not worthy to untie. The second part of today's selection describes the baptism of Jesus himself, with the heavens "torn open," the Holy Spirit descending "like a dove" and a heavenly voice declaring "You are my Son, the Beloved; with you I am well pleased." Mark's use of *schizomai*, "torn apart," in verse 10 is significant, because the only other time he uses this word is in 15:38, when the temple veil is torn from top to bottom at Jesus' death. The beginning and the end of Jesus' ministry are thus bracketed by God's direct intervention: cracking open the boundary between the heavens and the earth, the sacred and the profane.

Preaching Possibilities

The Baptism Of Our Lord — which for most churches today is one of the lesser celebrations of the Christian year — was of prime importance for the early church. One of the few events recounted in all four gospels, the details of each account are substantially similar. The details of this incident — particularly the clear subordination of John the Baptist to Jesus — served for the early church as an opportunity for teaching Christology, in opposition to various false teachers who portrayed Jesus as either pure spirit or less than divine. In submerging his body in the river in this very physical rite, Jesus takes his place with ordinary men and women. At the same time, in receiving the spectacular supernatural blessing from God, Jesus is shown to be spiritually unique.

Later generations have struggled with the question of whether Jesus' allowing himself to be baptized is consistent with his sinless nature, particularly since John's baptism is described as "a baptism of repentance for the forgiveness of sins" (v. 4). This does not appear to be a question that troubled the early church; they would have been far more interested in the theophany and divine benediction aspects of the story, and in John's comment about one greater than himself coming after him. There is, in fact, no mention of Jesus confessing sins in the context of his baptism. We can view it as an act of solidarity with fellow-believers, in much the same way as Jesus seems to have undergone every other religious rite an observant Jew of his day would have participated in. Does Jesus himself need to be baptized? No. Do *we* need him to have been baptized? Yes.

The Baptism Of Our Lord is a prime opportunity to teach the significance of the sacrament of Baptism. For centuries — at least in churches where infant baptism is the norm — the sacrament has been relegated to a peripheral role, becoming at times little more than a celebration of childhood and family life. In church architecture, the baptismal font itself has too often been located in an inconspicuous place — or worse yet, it has taken the form of a small bowl that's hidden away entirely, and brought out only when needed. The liturgical renewal movement has urged Christian believers to rediscover the centrality of our baptism — not just at the beginning of life, but through all our days. This is consistent with today's text: if Jesus thought it important enough a rite to receive it himself, and if all four gospel writers give it a central role, then who are we to let it degenerate into a celebration of babyhood?

This Sunday is an excellent opportunity to lead the people in one of the excellent modern liturgical rites for the reaffirmation of baptismal vows. Some congregations have started doing a formal vow-renewal celebration each year at this time.

George MacLeod, founder of Scotland's Iona Community, is well known for his concept of "thin places," geographical locations where God seems to be especially present. Baptism is a sort of thin place, although in a non-geographical sense. We no longer espouse the sort of cosmology evident in the narratives of Jesus' baptism — in which heaven is "up there" and we are "down here" — but still we can see the sacrament as an occasion in which God does create (if only for a moment) a gap in the boundary separating earth from heaven. As Martin Luther used to take comfort in recalling his own baptism, so we, too — at any stage in life — can discern the gracious intervention of the Spirit in our baptisms, and consider it as a sign of God's gracious accommodation to our needs.

Prayer For The Day

We acknowledge, O God, that we all have a watermark. It's not a mark that we or anyone else can see. But marked we are: marked with your love. Help us to remember that, in our baptism, we are set apart — set apart for service. Amen.

To Illustrate

"You are my Son, the Beloved; with you I am well pleased." What a wondrous thing it is to feel the pleasure of God. It's what we feel when we respond to God's call in our life — quite independently of any success we may experience.

It's what the character Eric Liddell feels in the movie, *Chariots of Fire*. Eric Liddell was a real person, a track star who just may have been the fastest man in the world in 1924. Yet, Eric is also the son of a missionary, and in the film his sister is trying to talk him into returning to China, rather than going for the gold in the Paris Olympics.

"God made me fast," Eric tells his sister, "and when I run, I feel his pleasure." Eric goes on to win the 400-meter race: a much longer race than the 100-meter for which he had trained, but from which he had dropped out because the qualifying heat was on a Sunday.

***

There is another Olympic story that has to do with feeling the pleasure of another — and it's one of the most remarkable stories in sporting history. In the 1992 Olympics in Barcelona, Derek Redmond of Great Britain had dreamed all his life of winning a gold medal in the men's 400-meter — the same race, incidentally, in which Eric Liddell won his gold. Redmond's dream seemed to be in sight, as the starter's gun sounded at the semifinals.

As he rounded the turn into the backstretch, Derek Redmond felt a piercing pain in the back of his right leg. The next thing he knew, he was lying face down on the track, having experienced the runner's worst nightmare: a torn hamstring.

What happened next has become the stuff of sporting legend. As the first-aiders approached, Redmond somehow struggled to his feet. "It was animal instinct," he would say later. He began hopping, in a crazed attempt to finish the race.

The crowds looked on, in silent amazement. When Redmond reached the home stretch, a large man in a T-shirt leaped down from the stands, hurled aside a security guard, and ran over to the runner, embracing him. It was Derek's father.

"You don't have to do this," he told his son.

"Yes, I do," insisted the son, through bitter tears. "Well, then," said his father, "we're going to finish this together." And there, before the eyes of the entire world, the son's head sometimes buried in his father's shoulder, the two men hobbled along in his lane all the way to the end, finishing the race.

The crowd went wild. Derek Redmond did not leave Barcelona with his dreamed of gold medal. But he did return home with a precious memory of a father who looked down on his beloved son, with whom he was well pleased.

***

It can be a powerful thing to know we are in God's favor. There's a story that illustrates this, told by the preacher Fred Craddock. It seems he and his wife were vacationing in the Smoky Mountains, when a distinguished older gentleman came to their table in the hotel dining room. He was, as it turned out, a celebrity: a former governor of Tennessee. When he discovered Craddock was a professor of preaching, the man said he had a story to tell him, about a preacher.

It seems that, when the governor was born, his mother wasn't married. He never knew his father. In the Southland of that era, that led to a difficult childhood. The other children used to

39

taunt him and call him names. They used to ask him when his father was coming back. Whenever he was out with his mother in public, he was painfully aware that he had but one parent.

One day, when he was about ten, this boy was in church. Usually, when the service was over, he found his way discreetly out the back door — which meant that he never talked to the minister, never had to share his name. On this particular occasion, though, the boy got swept up in the crowd — and before he knew it, there was the pastor, at the front door, his hand extended.

"Well, son," the preacher's voice boomed out, "whose boy are you?" He could hardly have asked a more embarrassing question. The boy flushed and started to stammer — but before he could say anything more, the preacher (still gripping his hand) said: "I know! ... You're God's son!" He slapped him on the shoulder and said, "Boy, go claim your inheritance."

The boy never forgot that incident. He never forgot the preacher's kindness in not drawing attention to his single-parent family. He never forgot the way he sent him out, either: "Go claim your inheritance!" Long after he became one of the most popular governors in Tennessee history, this man still delighted in telling the story of the day the preacher told him he was a child of God.

Second Sunday After The Epiphany
Second Sunday In Ordinary Time
January 15, 2006

Revised Common	1 Samuel 3:1-10 (11-20)	1 Corinthians 6:12-20	John 1:43-51
Roman Catholic	1 Samuel 3:3-10, 19	1 Corinthians 6:13-15, 17-20	John 1:35-42
Episcopal	1 Samuel 3:1-10 (11-20)	1 Corinthians 6:11b-20	John 1:43-51

Theme For The Day   God's call requires a receptive listener.

Old Testament Lesson   1 Samuel 3:1-10 (11-20)   *The Call Of Samuel*

It's a classic biblical call story: the young Samuel's growing awareness that the call he has heard in the stillness of the night is real. While the call in the story is auditory, its very quietness and subtlety would have spoken to its ancient readers of a private, inner experience. Also worth noting is the fact that God is calling Samuel to a difficult, perhaps even dangerous mission: to bring a word of judgment to Eli, exposing him for the unfaithful priest he is. Samuel will of course grow to become one of the greatest transitional figures in Israelite history, leading the people across the divide between the era of the judges and the era of the kings. Possible preaching points are that God's call is often subtle, is typically sustained over time, and sometimes leads us to go to places we would not otherwise be inclined to travel.

New Testament Lesson   1 Corinthians 6:12-20   *Yes, But Is It Beneficial?*

"All things are lawful for me," a popular saying of the day Paul is holding up for derision, sounds on the surface like it can be easily dismissed as a bit of narcissistic anarchism — but in fact it is a commonly repeated statement, in this or as any other age. (It may, in fact, be a corruption of something Paul once said himself, perhaps amidst the controversy over Jewish dietary laws, which his opponents are now hurling back at him.) The ideals of freedom at the basis of our present-day society are among our greatest strengths. Yet they can also be a terrible weakness, especially when they degenerate into bumper-sticker slogans that include the words "The right to _____" (fill in the blank). Certain members of the Corinthian church, intoxicated by a sense of individual entitlement, have been brashly proclaiming that they can flout longstanding and time-honored ethical principles, particularly regarding sexual behavior. To them Paul issues a wake-up call, introducing a higher standard: "Yes, but is it beneficial?" What, in other words, does it do to advance God's purposes? Paul also refutes the notion of a "victimless crime," when it comes to what is today euphemistically referred to as "the sex trade." Yes, there are victims of this trade — and the victims are not only those "sex workers" who are forced into selling, but also those customers who are buying.

The Gospel   John 1:43-51   *Come And See*

Unlike stories in the synoptic gospels of Jesus calling his disciples, in this case it is not so much Jesus discovering them, as them discovering him. Jesus has a distinctly laid-back approach to the task corporate America calls "head-hunting." Some of the evangelistic work is done by others, as Philip brings Nathanael to him (and Andrew brings his brother Simon in v. 41). Jesus' question "What do you seek?" (v. 48), displays his genius. Far from telling these men what they must do, Jesus opens a dialogue with them. When he finally pops the question, his offer, "Come and see," is more invitation than command. This is evangelism at its best.

(Nathanael, by the way — who is never mentioned in the other gospels — may or may not be one of the twelve, in John's eyes. Some have suggested that he is the same as Bartholomew, but it's possible that John sees him simply as one of the outer circle of disciples.)

Preaching Possibilities

Today's Old Testament and Gospel Lesson deal with aspects of calling. In 1 Samuel we hear of the boy, Samuel's, personal encounter with God, that leads to his accepting his prophetic vocation. In John, we hear of Jesus' gentle, winsome call to several of his disciples (his call to Andrew, Simon, and another unnamed disciple was related in the previous pericope).

A sermon based primarily on the Old Testament Lesson will likely emphasize the personal experience of receiving — and discerning — God's call. The key here is to emphasize the ordinary nature of Samuel's experience. While hearing a disembodied voice in the middle of the night may meet most modern listeners' definition of an extraordinary spiritual experience, from the standpoint of Hebrew thought (which does not sharply differentiate between mind and body) it is a way of saying Samuel's experience was quiet and inner. Also, the experience was not so definite that Samuel could be certain about it at first; hence, his three visits to Eli to ask, "Did you call me?"

The very notion of "hearing God's Word" is one that has lost its edge for many of us. We have become comfortable with the Word of God. We have printed it on elegant, India-paper pages with gilded edges, bound those pages between covers of the finest, hand-tooled leather, and given the end product an honored place in home and church.

The name of God rises to our lips many times each day: in table grace and bedtime prayer; in thoughtless expressions of "God bless you," or "God willing" — even in those meaningless (and slightly blasphemous) punctuations of speech, like "Oh, God," when the traffic light turns yellow, or "God, but it's cold today" (as though the Lord really needs to be so informed).

What a contrast this is to the Orthodox Jews, who write the name of God, "Yahweh," without vowels, so they cannot pronounce it, even accidentally — thereby bringing down calamity upon their heads!

"The word of God may not be chained," writes the preacher Barbara Brown Taylor, "but you would be hard pressed to believe it on most Sunday mornings. We read scripture out loud as though we were reading income tax instructions to each other. Children draw on offering envelopes during the sermon; adults balance their checkbooks. If someone breaks the rules and gets excited by the word, there are plenty of other people — including the preacher — who can be counted on to calm that person down. We are old friends with the word by now. There is nothing to get excited about. You can buy dish towels with the Beatitudes printed on them. You can give Bibles to your children without worrying that what they read will upset their lives. What has happened? Have we hobbled the word because we fear the harm it can do?"

A thoughtful sermon on 1 Samuel 3 can encourage the people to take God's Word more seriously, as well as giving some who have already heard God speaking the permission to name that experience for what it is: a divine call.

A sermon based on the Gospel Lesson could accomplish some teaching about true evangelism: what it is, and what it is not. In the late 1990s, the Lutheran church conducted a poll, in which researchers asked lots of Lutherans how it was that they had happened to come to their particular church in the first place. Here are the replies:

2-3% joined because of denominational identity (longtime Lutherans, obviously);
5-6% joined because of a particular program or church event;

42

3-4% joined because of the preaching / worship life;

A whopping 80% said they joined the church because a friend or family member invited them, and the new attender could see the importance of faith in the friend or family member's life.

Jesus' gracious, gentle invitation is "Come and see." It's extended to every one of us, all the time. Always we are invited into closer relationship with him — but the invitation is often extended through another person, taking the form not only of words but also example.

Prayer For The Day

Above the doorway of a church in London, a prayer has been carved into the stone:

O God, make the door of this house wide enough to receive all who need human love and fellowship; narrow enough to shut out all envy, pride, and strife. Make its threshold smooth enough to be no stumbling block to children, nor to straying feet, but rugged and strong enough to turn back the tempter's power. God make the door of this house the gateway to thine eternal kingdom.

To Illustrate

"Not a very promising crowd," the preacher thought to himself, looking out over the pulpit. Only a handful had turned out to hear him speak — even though he had traveled all the way to Scotland from South Africa.

The preacher's name was Robert Moffat. He was a missionary. That night, Moffat's "mission" was very particular: to find men, and bring them back to Africa, to the mission field.

Women, he wasn't especially interested in (this was the early 1800s, after all). The preacher would thank the women for their prayers and good wishes, but most everyone agreed that the hardships of Africa were not for members of "the fairer sex."

Yet, the fairer sex was all Robert Moffat had that night: and only a handful of them at that. To make matters worse, his pre-arranged text was Proverbs 8:4, "Unto you, O men, I call."

Moffat raced through his sermon, finishing early: trusting God to make something of it, somehow. When it was over, he departed: to the usual round of polite handshakes and smiling thank yous — but not a single recruit to show for his efforts.

Or so he thought. Moffat had no way of knowing it, but his words that night would make an enormous difference in the history of Christian mission.

Unbeknownst to him, there was a man in the sanctuary that night — well not a man, exactly, but a boy. High up in the choir loft he sat, waiting for the sermon to end, so he could do his job: pumping the bellows of the pipe organ with his feet.

As he waited, young David Livingstone could not help but listen to the preacher's words. It seemed as though they were directed to him alone.

Years later, by then a young man, David Livingstone would train as a doctor, and pack himself off to the most uncharted regions of Africa as a medical missionary and explorer. It was he whom Charles Stanley of the *New York Herald* would seek for months, and finally discover on the shores of Lake Tanganyika — greeting him with the immortal words, "Dr. Livingstone, I presume?"

All this took place because, one blustery Scottish night years before, a boy had listened — had really listened — in church.

***

43

A man was watching his two small children, ages six and four, on Wednesday, September 12, 2001, the day after the 9/11 atttacks. The television announcer said that the president was going to address the nation. The father said, "Now you have got to be quiet because the most important man in the world is getting ready to speak!"

The six-year-old then turned to the four-year-old and said, "You've got to be quiet now. God is about to speak to us."

**

In my class, as in any class, at any school, there were students who had a real flair, a real talent, for something. Maybe it was for writing or acting or sports. Maybe it was an interest and a joy in working with people toward some common goal, a sense of responsibility for people who in some way had less than they had or were less. Sometimes, it was just their capacity for being so alive that made you more alive to be with them. Yet now, a good many years later, I have the feeling that more than just a few of them are spending their lives at work in which none of these gifts is being used. This is the sadness of the game, and the danger of it is that maybe we find that in some measure we are among them or that we are too blind to see that we are.

When you are young, I think your hearing is in some ways better than it is ever going to be again. You hear better than most people the voices that call to you out of your own life to give yourself to this work or that work.

— Frederick Buechner, *The Hungering Dark* (New York: Seabury, 1968), p. 28

**

Frank McCourt, author of the best-selling autobiography, *Angela's Ashes*, also wrote a sequel to that book, the story of his young manhood as a newly arrived immigrant in New York City, just after the Second World War. That book is called, *'Tis*.

It is Christmas day. The young Frank McCourt is living alone in a rented room. It so happens that he's suffering from a chronic eye infection he's brought with him from Ireland, that makes his eye red and swollen all the time, and leads strangers to avoid looking at him. Because of the eye infection, he has trouble keeping a steady job, and so he's barely able buy enough food to eat. On Christmas day, McCourt — overcome by nostalgia and longing for something better in his life — decides to go someplace he hasn't been in years. He's going to go to church. The church he chooses is a fancy one on Park Avenue. Here is his account of the experience, in his own irrepressible style:

> *The People who go to St. Vincent's are like the ones who go to the Sixty-eighth Street Playhouse for Hamlet and they know the Latin responses the way they know the play. They share prayer books and sing hymns together and smile at each other because they know Brigid the maid is back there in the Park Avenue kitchen keeping an eye on the turkey. Their sons and daughters have the look of coming home from school and college and they smile at other people in the pews also home from school and college. They can afford to smile because they all have teeth so dazzling if they dropped them in snow they'd be lost forever. The church is so crowded there are people standing in the back, but I'm so weak with the hunger and the long Christmas Eve of whiskey, glug and throwing up I want to find a seat. There's an empty spot at the end of a pew far up the center aisle but as soon as I slip into it a man comes running at me. He's all dressed up*

44

in striped trousers, a coat with tails, and a frown over his face and he whispers to me,
You must leave this pew at once. This is for regular pew holders, come on, come on. I
feel my face turning red and that means my eyes are worse and when I go down the aisle
I know the whole world is looking at me, the one who sneaked into the pew of a happy
family with children home from school and college. There's no use even standing at the
back of the church. They all know and they'll be giving me looks, so I might as well
leave and add another sin to the hundreds already on my soul, the mortal sin of not
going to Mass on Christmas Day. At least God will know I tried and it's not my fault if
I wandered into a happy family from Park Avenue pew.

***

Long ago, there used to be a popular show on television: a police show called *Dragnet*. It still shows up on reruns from time to time. The original *Dragnet* — not to be confused with Dan Ackroyd's two recent movie versions — starred a rather odd actor named Jack Webb, who played detective sergeant Joe Friday.

Dragnet was originally a radio show, and it had two different television incarnations: in the 1950s and then again in the late '60s. It gave our culture a wealth of catch phrases — the most famous being "The story you have just seen is true; the names have been changed to protect the innocent." Jack Webb, in his role as Joe Friday, is single-handedly responsible for the other Dragnet catch phrase everybody knows. When faced, as he often was, with a somewhat hysterical woman who'd witnessed some dreadful crime, Sergeant Friday would pull out his notepad, stare coolly back at her, and say in his trademark monotone, "Just the facts, ma'am."

Joe Friday's just the sort of person you'd want to have as a witness in court: on *your* side. He's cold, analytical, and utterly unfazed by extremes of emotion. He's dead-on task-oriented: a law enforcement bulldog who stays on the job till it's done. Sergeant Joe Friday would make the ideal witness — or would he?

Joe Friday would be the ideal witness if the goal were simply to unearth the facts. But he'd be less than ideal for another sort of witnessing: the witnessing that leads others to faith.

Third Sunday After The Epiphany
Third Sunday In Ordinary Time
January 22, 2006

Revised Common	Jonah 3:1-5, 10	1 Corinthians 7:29-31	Mark 1:14-20
Roman Catholic	Jonah 3:1-5, 10	1 Corinthians 7:29-31	Mark 1:14-20
Episcopal	Jeremiah 3:21—4:2	1 Corinthians 7:17-23	Mark 1:14-20

Theme For The Day   Proclaiming the good news is the task of all God's people.

Old Testament Lesson   Jonah 3:1-5, 10   *The Ninevites Heed The Reluctant Jonah's Halfhearted Preaching*

Someone has pointed out that this sermon of Jonah's, "Forty days more, and Nineveh shall be overthrown," is the single worst sermon in all of scripture (at least as written). It's totally devoid of introduction and conclusion. Nowhere in it can you find so much as an illustration, or even a funny story. It's only got one point — and that single point is about the most offensive thing Jonah could possibly say to the people of Nineveh. He's just going through the motions, fulfilling the minimum requirement. Anything to keep the Lord off his back — and himself out of the digestive track of marine organisms. As Jonah turns on his heel after mouthing those unconvincing words, he notices something very strange indeed. The Ninevites are weeping. The Ninevites are wailing. The Ninevites are falling down on their knees and shouting "Amen!" It's amazing what God can do with the most halfhearted effort at sharing the good news.

New Testament Lesson   1 Corinthians 7:29-31   *The Present Form Of This World Is Passing Away*

Today's Epistle Lesson is an example of clumsy editing on the part of the lectionary committee. It begins in the middle of a pericope, omitting Paul's difficult-to-interpret words about marriage being a poor idea in light of the imminent end of the world, but marginally acceptable for those who cannot avoid it. As we join the argument midstream, hearing that "the appointed time has grown short; from now on, let even those who have wives be as though they had none," it's hard for a worshiping congregation, lacking context, to understand what the apostle is talking about. The only readily intelligible message in this unnaturally brief passage is the closing line, "For the present form of this world is passing away" (v. 31b). A sermon on this passage could emphasize the urgency of the gospel, but it will have to 1) back up and provide some of the context the lectionary omits and 2) deal with the problem of the delay of the *parousia*, of which Paul was just beginning to be aware at the time of writing, but which to our people — two millennia later — will be glaringly obvious.

The Gospel   Mark 1:14-20   *Jesus Begins His Preaching Ministry And Calls His First Disciples*

Immediately after telling of Jesus' temptation in the wilderness, Mark provides a condensed version of his essential preaching: "The time is fulfilled, and the kingdom of God has come near; repent, and believe in the good news." Jesus' sermon is every bit as brief as Jonah's — although a bit more positive in tone. Jesus then calls Simon and Andrew to be his disciples, in equally laconic fashion: "Follow me and I will make you fish for people." To which Mark matter-of-factly adds, "And immediately they left their nets and followed him." These are beloved and well-known words — even if they make us wish for more narrative detail, so we may understand what, psychologically, is going on in the minds of Simon and Andrew that makes them want to leave everything to follow this itinerant preacher. Even though Mark uses the word "immediately," his entire narrative is so stripped down and basic that we shouldn't necessarily assume that he means they dropped everything that second, happily trotting off down the beach after a man they scarcely knew. There was probably a bit more to it than that (although imagination is required to fill in the details).

Preaching Possibilities

An offbeat, though perhaps somewhat risky, approach would be to preach a sermon titled, "The Sermon You've Always Wanted To Hear." Begin by introducing the Jonah and Mark passages, holding up the one-sentence sermons within them as examples of messages that seem crashingly ordinary, but which have world-changing results. Then, ask the question, "What makes a good sermon, anyway?" (always a risky question to ask, as part of a sermon!) Then, turn the tables on the congregation: explaining that both Jonah's and Jesus' sermons are so simple, they could have been delivered by anyone (Jonah, in fact, seems singularly unqualified to enter a pulpit, his only credential being that God has ordered him to do so). What makes a sermon efficacious is the Holy Spirit. Since anyone could deliver such a sermon, then maybe it's something any member of the church could — or should — do. Maybe, we can say to our people, the sermon you've always wanted to hear is the sermon you ought to be preaching!

The Hebrew verb Jonah uses when he predicts, "Nineveh shall be overthrown" is one that's used in other places to describe something being flipped over: a bowl, a chariot on a battlefield, a piece of flatbread cooking in a pan. It bears with it the sense of reversal, of inversion, of things made topsy-turvy.

Our God is a God of reversals, of change. We know from the New Testament that the Lord works through both death and resurrection. In walking us through the on-again, off-again repentance of a reluctant prophet, the book of Jonah is a challenge: it is at once more demanding and more forgiving than we are naturally inclined to be.

Some of us want to proclaim the gospel only in its welcoming and inclusiveness — forgetting that the gospel includes also the baptism of death, and that there is no Easter without the cross. Others of us are all too eager to preach death and destruction, to imagine the Lord blasting malicious evildoers, and rewarding the righteous — forgetting that sin is a universal human trait, and that all have fallen short of the glory of God (even us!).

The whole point of the spiritual life is the discovery of new life, the bright dawning of love in the midst of darkness — and that discovery is a lifelong process. The more mature we all become in the life of faith, the more we come to realize that all is not simple, black-and-white, good-guys-vs.-bad-guys conflict. All of us have within us the seeds of both good and evil.

Jonah is saying to the Ninevites, "You people are going to be flipped, reversed, turned over by the power of the sovereign God. Your whole city, your whole world, will be turned over — what is up will be down, and what is down will be up."

Would that the preacher could have heeded his own message! It took a sojourn in the belly of a fish for Jonah to learn the error of his ways, to start paying attention to God's call. But still he falls short of the mark. Jonah, by the time the third chapter rolls around, has learned it's best to pay attention to God's leading: before he himself is overturned again.

This realization, this profoundly disorienting experience of reversal, is what qualifies Jonah to be a prophet. When Jonah is spewed up on that beach by the fish, he is no longer the naive, self-centered man he was just a few days before. God has turned him. God has reversed his natural inclination to run away from his problems. God has given him, at last, the perseverance to see his mission through.

A final note on dealing with Jonah: much ink has been spilled over the centuries in fruitless scholarly speculation over what sort of creature it was who swallowed Jonah, and how he could survive a three-day sojourn in the belly of the beast. Most congregations today can handle a frank description of this book as a fable or folktale. The Bible is not one book, but an entire library — and just as some libraries include books of fiction as well as history and other subjects, so, too, with the collection we cherish as scripture. The Hebrew people told and re-told the story of Jonah in much the same way as the ancient Greeks told and re-told the fables of Aesop. What makes it a true story is not its historicity, but its ability to speak to the human condition. It is only more recent readers who have sought to impose on this tale a burden of historicity it was never meant to bear.

Prayer For The Day
> Lord, speak to me, that I may speak
> In living echoes of your tone.
> As you have sought, so let me seek
> Your erring children, lost and lone.
> (Hymn, "Lord, Speak To Me That I May Speak," adapted)

To Illustrate
William Willimon, Dean of the Chapel at Duke University, tells of getting a telephone call from an irate parent:

"I hold you personally responsible for this," the father told him.

"Me?" the campus minister asked.

"Yes, you. I send my daughter off to college to get a good education. Now she tells me she wants to throw it all away, and go off to Haiti as a Presbyterian mission volunteer! Isn't that absurd? A B.S. in mechanical engineering from Duke, and she's going off to dig ditches in Haiti."

"Well," said Willimon, in a feeble attempt at humor, "I doubt the engineering department taught her much about that line of work, but she's a fast learner; she'll probably get the hang of ditch-digging in a few months."

"Look," interrupted the father, "this is no laughing matter. I hold you completely responsible for her decision. She likes you. You've filled her head with all those pie-in-the-sky ideas!"

"Now look," said Willimon, trying to keep his ministerial composure. "Weren't you the one who had her baptized?"

"Why, yes," the father replied.

"And didn't you read her Bible stories, take her to Sunday school, send her off on ski trips with the Presbyterian Youth Fellowship?"

"Well, yes, but ..."

"Don't 'but' me. It's your fault she believed all that stuff, that she's gone and thrown it all away on Jesus — not mine. You're the one who introduced her to Jesus, not me."

"But all we ever wanted was for her to be a Presbyterian," said the father, meekly.

"Sorry. You messed up. You made a disciple."

***

48

Repentance involves, first, a turning. In the story of Jonah we see that repentance also involves a tuning — a linking of our wills to God's, so they function in partnership.

It's rather like what goes on when a musical instrument is tuned. The musician sounds a tone on another instrument: a pitch-pipe or a tuning fork. That first tone is steady, unvarying; it will not slip up or down the scale, thrown off by changes in humidity or frequent use. Change in tone will happen, in time, to the strings of a piano or a violin, but it will not happen with a tuning fork. That primary tone remains the same.

So it is with God's way, the way of Christian discipleship. It is not enough to make cosmetic changes in our lives — to go around talking Christian talk, for a change — unless you and I earnestly desire also to bring our lives into harmony with God's will.

***

We are not saints, we are not heroes. Our lives are lived in the quiet corners of the ordinary. We build tiny hearth fires, sometimes barely strong enough to give off warmth. But to the person lost in the darkness, our tiny flame may be the road to safety, the path to salvation.

It is not given us to know who is lost in the darkness that surrounds us or even if our light is seen. We can only know that against even the smallest of lights, darkness cannot stand.

A sailor lost at sea can be guided home by a single candle. A person lost in a wood can be led to safety by a flickering flame. It is not an issue of quality or intensity or purity. It is simply an issue of the presence of light.

> — Kent Nerburn, *Make Me an Instrument of Your Peace: Living in the Spirit of the Prayer of Saint Francis* (San Francisco: HarperSanFrancisco, 1999)

***

My soul is a mirror in which the glory of God is reflected, but sin, however insignificant, covers the mirror with smoke.

> — Teresa of Avila

***

In her book, *Out of Africa*, Isak Dinesen tells the story of a young man from the Kikuyu tribe who worked for three months as a laborer on her farm. He surprised her one day by announcing that he was leaving her to work for a Muslim man nearby.

Surprised, Dinesen asked him if he had been unhappy working for her. He assured her that all was well, but that he had resolved to engage in a little experiment. He intended to work for a Christian for three months to study the ways of Christians, and then for a Muslim for the same period, to study the ways of Muslims. After observing the ways of both employers, he was going to decide whether to be a Christian or a Muslim.

What would a visitor like that learn about Christianity after a season of living in *our* homes?

Fourth Sunday After The Epiphany
Fourth Sunday In Ordinary Time
January 29, 2006

Revised Common	Deuteronomy 18:15-20	1 Corinthians 8:1-13	Mark 1:21-28
Roman Catholic	Deuteronomy 18:15-20	1 Corinthians 7:32-35	Mark 1:21-28
Episcopal	Deuteronomy 18:15-20	1 Corinthians 8:1b-13	Mark 1:21-28

Theme For The Day   What builds up the church is love, which is demonstrated concretely by mutual forbearance.

Old Testament Lesson   Deuteronomy 18:15-20   *Moses Promises That Prophecy Will Continue*

"The Lord your God will raise up for you a prophet like me from among your own people," says Moses (v. 15). He then goes on to suggest how the people may discern whether or not the words of a person claiming to be a prophet are true. At the time Deuteronomy was being compiled, prophecy was an important institution, a source of spiritual authority. Verses 9-22 describe some scenarios in which the question of a prophet's authority could prove problematic. Here the editors make certain to trace the authority of the prophetic office back to Moses, who provides some guidelines for discernment.

New Testament Lesson   1 Corinthians 8:1-13   *The Problem Of Food Offered To Idols*

What sounds, at first hearing, like obscure advice for solving a purely first-century church problem is in fact the great test case in the New Testament for mutual forbearance and tolerance of diversity. Two factions in the Corinthian church disagree over whether it is proper for Christians to eat food that has first been to the altar of a pagan temple as part of a sacrificial ritual. It was common practice in the Roman world for most meat to be brought to a pagan altar, where one portion would be incinerated as an offering to the gods, another portion would be roasted and either given or sold to people nearby and the remaining portion would be taken to the market for sale. Some commentators have suggested that, through the sacrificial system, the pagan priests in fact owned a *de facto* monopoly on the sale of meat. This is a sensitive subject for the Corinthian Christians, many of whom are rather close to their own pagan origins. Some still fear that pagan gods exercise power of some sort through the sacrificial meat, or that eating the meat renders the person who eats it unclean. Paul's answer is a masterpiece of theological precision and pastoral sensitivity. He declares that, since the pagan gods are as nothing, the question of whether to eat or not to eat their sacrificial meat is matter of indifference for Christians. Yet, since this is a question that causes anguish in the hearts of some Christians, it is a better course for all to abstain from eating pagan-sacrificed meat, out of sensitivity to the faith of one's brothers and sisters.

The Gospel   Mark 1:21-28   *Jesus Heals A Demon-Possessed Man*

At the synagogue in Capernaum, a mentally ill man accosts Jesus. According to the first-century understanding, he is demon-possessed, so Luke portrays him speaking in the first-person plural, as though a whole group of demons are speaking through him. The demons recognize Jesus as a threat, not only calling him by name, but addressing him as "the Holy One of God" (v. 24). Jesus rebukes the demons, and they leave the man, returning him to his right mind. "What is this?" Jesus' disciples marvel. "A new teaching — with authority! He commands even the unclean spirits, and they obey him" (v. 27). Authority is a key theme here: it is revealed not only by erudite words (as in the authority of the scribes), but more importantly by deeds of power. Also, Mark's use of the demon's speech to identify Jesus as "the Holy One of God" is a way of discreetly cluing the reader in to Jesus' true nature, even before his disciples are able to understand and articulate it.

Preaching Possibilities

A sermon on 1 Corinthians 8 could focus on what builds up the church. Paul gives the answer in verse 1: "Knowledge puffs up, but love builds up."

On the subject of food offered to idols, he advises the liberal faction in First Church, Corinth, to rein in their freedom and abstain from meat, for the sake of their more conservative brothers and sisters (see above). This advice flies in the face of the way most of us are accustomed to thinking in our culture. Along with the rest of American society, we are inordinately fond of our individual rights. We pride ourselves on having freedom to choose. We aren't used to hearing somebody tell us that maybe we ought to relinquish some of our cherished rights for the benefit of others.

Paul's actually saying there are higher priorities than individual choice. (Just try walking into the nearest supermarket and start talking about that — as you're standing in front of shelf upon shelf of cereal choices, soup choices, bread choices. They'll look at you like you've got three heads!) No one in our society seems to question the premise that freedom is all about having lots of choices.

Paul has a better idea. He's teaching the Corinthians that true freedom comes not from having lots of choices, but from the privilege of living together in community. God has called us Christians not only into responsibility for ourselves and our immediate families, but also for the neighbor down the street. "No man is an island, entire of itself," writes the Elizabethan poet, John Donne. "Each man is a piece of the continent, a part of the main...." We are, all of us, caretakers of each other — bound to one another in a complex web of relationships. When one weeps, all weep. When one rejoices, all rejoice.

So what is it that builds up the church? Lots of books you can buy today will tell you it's one thing or another. Some declare that the recipe for success calls for the teaching of true doctrine, others clever marketing, still others astute administration and planning. There are those who claim that a truly successful church has got to offer certain programs to keep up with the needs of today's families — or that there's got to be a certain ratio of parking places to worshipers.

Paul proclaims none of these things as the mark of success in the church. The most important feature of a successful church, he says, is love. A few chapters later, he tackles the subject with gusto. Many people think 1 Corinthians 13 is about marriage, because it's often read at weddings; but Paul's continuing on, in that chapter, with this very same subject: love-that-builds-up-the-church. Faced with a difference of opinion on food offered to idols, Paul affirms that love "is not envious or boastful or arrogant or rude. It does not insist on its own way; it is not irritable or resentful; it does not rejoice in wrongdoing, but rejoices in the truth." Before the overwhelming reality of Christlike love, the dog-eat-dog rules of debate are suddenly suspended. The negative campaign ads are no more. The mudslinging is over. The good of the community has become the highest value.

51

Prayer For The Day

When we are certain, Lord ... when we are convinced we are right ... when we feel our hackles rising as we consider that other person who has spoken to us in anger ... have mercy upon us. Open our minds, so the fresh air of your grace and forgiveness may blow through. Teach us that your church is bigger than anything we could imagine. Amen.

To Illustrate

When Ernest Gordon, formerly chaplain of Princeton University, was a young British officer in the Second World War, he was captured by the Japanese and held as a POW in a brutal prison camp in Southeast Asia. It's the same slave-labor camp that was dramatized in the classic Alec Guinness film, *Bridge Over the River Kwai*. In his wartime memoir, *Through the Valley of the Kwai* (New York: Harper, 1962), Gordon tells a remarkable story about the triumph of love.

Conditions in the POW camp have degenerated into a barbarous brutality. The guards beat the prisoners, and the prisoners try to beat each other out of food, water, a pair of shoes — any necessity that's in short supply.

It happens one day that a shovel goes missing. The Japanese officer in charge becomes enraged. He demands that the missing shovel be produced, or else. When nobody in the unit budges, the officer pulls out his gun and threatens to kill them all on the spot. It is obvious that the officer means what he's said.

Finally, one man steps forward. The officer puts away his gun, picks up a shovel, and beats the man to death. When it is over, the survivors pick up his bloody corpse and carry it with them to the second tool check. This time, no shovel turns up missing. It seems there was a miscount at the first checkpoint.

The word spreads like wildfire throughout the camp. An innocent man was willing to die to save the others! The incident has a profound effect. From that day forward, the men began to treat each other like brothers.

When the victorious Allies finally sweep in, the survivors, human skeletons, line up in front of their former captors. Yet instead of attacking them, they insist: "No more hatred. No more killing. Now what we need is forgiveness."

***

What, according to Fred Craddock, is "the most extraordinary piece of Christian furniture?" Why, it's "the pew, which invites former strangers to sit together as family."
— Fred Craddock, *First and Second Peter and Jude*, Westminster Bible
Companion series (Louisville: Westminster John Knox Press, 1995), p. 33

***

Queen Victoria was once at a diplomatic reception in London. The guest of honor was an African chieftain. All went well during the meal until, at the end, finger bowls were brought out. The guest of honor had never seen a British finger bowl, and no one had thought to brief him beforehand about its purpose. He took the finger bowl in his two hands, lifted it to his mouth, and drank its contents.

For an instant there was breathless silence among the British upper crust, who then began to whisper to one another. All that stopped in the next instant as the Queen silently took her own finger bowl in her two hands, lifted it, and drank its contents. A moment later, 500 surprised British ladies and gentlemen simultaneously drank the contents of *their* fingerbowls.

It was "against the rules" to drink from a fingerbowl, but on that particular evening Victoria changed the rules — because she was, after all, the Queen.

— Adapted from a story told by Brett Blair <www.esermons.com>, August 2003

***

We must love them both — those whose opinions we share and those whose opinions we reject. For both have labored in the search for truth, and both have helped us in the finding of it.

— Thomas Aquinas

***

Did you ever stop to think that the place that most exudes doing it decently and in order is the local cemetery? The people who manage it have their procedures down pat. New members are received in solemn ceremonies. An organizational chart on the office wall explains in detail where all the members stand (okay, lie) in relation to all the other members. There are no conflicts. Nobody ever encroaches on (or under) anyone else's turf. People don't quit and join another cemetery. They are all in their proper places every Sunday. Everyone knows his or her place and stays in it. It is the most decent and orderly place in town. There just isn't a whole lot of life there.

— John Galloway, Jr., *Ministry Loves Company: a Survival Guide for Pastors*
(Louisville: Westminster John Knox Press, 2003)

***

At its best, the local church functions as an arena in which conflict and hurts among participants who choose to stay can open up possibilities for spiritual progress. Where else will people still accept me after I stand up in a church meeting and harshly criticize something? "Ah, that's just Dave," they say. They know me. I learn about the Christian virtues of acceptance and graciousness even as I am not accepting and gracious. By not taking my toys and playing elsewhere — that is, finding a church that connects with my spiritual journey — I move forward in my spiritual journey. I give up control. I forfeit my options, in an environment of choices.

— David Goetz, "Suburban Spirituality," *Christianity Today*, July 2003, pp. 34-35

Fifth Sunday After The Epiphany
Fifth Sunday In Ordinary Time
February 5, 2006

Revised Common	Isaiah 40:21-31	1 Corinthians 9:16-23	Mark 1:29-39
Roman Catholic	Job 7:1-4, 6-7	1 Corinthians 9:16-19, 22-23	Mark 1:29-39
Episcopal	2 Kings 4:(8-17) 18-21 (22-31) 32-37	1 Corinthians 9:16-23	Mark 1:29-39

Theme For The Day   Jesus' example of personal prayer is one we all need to follow.

Old Testament Lesson   Isaiah 40:21-31   *With Wings Of Eagles*

This majestic prophetic passage moves from the austere majesty of an omnipotent and omniscient God to that same God's tender concern for the weakest members of the human race. In verse 22 the prophet celebrates the God "who sits above the circle of the earth, and its inhabitants are like grasshoppers." The passage ends with words of kindness for exiles who have suffered long enough: "those who wait for the Lord shall renew their strength, they shall mount up with wings like eagles, they shall run and not be weary, they shall walk and not faint" (v. 31). A pastoral sermon on God's comfort for the afflicted is always in season.

New Testament Lesson   1 Corinthians 9:16-23   *Gotta Preach*

The lectionary carves this piece off from a lengthy, complicated argument. To fully understand the issues, it's necessary to go back as far as last week's reading, in which Paul was advocating mutual forbearance in the case of whether Christians can legitimately eat food offered to idols. At the beginning of chapter 9, a new issue emerges: some antagonists have apparently been attacking Paul over the issue of his financial compensation. Again, Paul talks of rights: not the right to choose one's diet, but the right to "food and drink" in general and the right "to be accompanied by a believing wife" (vv. 4-5). Paul argues that, just as shepherds are entitled to the milk their flock produces, so too, as apostle, he is entitled to some of the "milk" from his Corinthian flock (v. 7). Yet, just as he did in the case of food offered to idols, Paul forgoes his rights for the sake of the weak. Twice he declares (vv. 12b, 15) that he has not made use of this right. No, Paul has determined that the only way to advance the gospel is for him to preach without compensation. After demanding his paycheck in the earlier part of this chapter, here in the latter part he hands it back uncashed. Paul insists that he proclaims the gospel "free of charge" (v. 18). He has made himself "a slave to all, so that [he] might win more of them" (v. 19). Everywhere he goes, he adapts himself to local circumstances. He has become "all things to all people" (v. 22). (This phrase, which has made its way into popular jargon, usually has derogatory connotations; here, in the original context, Paul cites it as a point of pride.) This is a difficult passage on which to preach, for it requires extensive background information about the situation in Corinth. The most relevant point for contemporary congregations is that Paul always puts the needs of the gospel first. As in Jeremiah 20:9, Paul has a fire in his bones: "Woe to me if I do not proclaim the gospel!" (v. 16b).

The Gospel   Mark 1:29-39   *Man Of Healing, Man Of Prayer*

Other biblical accounts of Jesus' healings offer more satisfying detail; here, describing the healing of Simon's mother-in-law, Mark provides the bare facts and little else. His closing comment, "and she began to serve them," is troubling to modern ears — most of us would assume that an elderly woman, healed of a serious illness, is entitled to a little bed rest! Mark is making the point, however, that Peter's mother-in-law is 100 percent healed, so much so that she returns immediately to her usual activities. News of this wonder gets around, and soon "the whole city was gathered around the door" (v. 33). Jesus casts out many demons, not permitting those demons to speak — "because they knew him" (v. 34). This echoes the story of the healing of the demon-possessed man in the previous passage (see last week's commentary). Not even Jesus' disciples fully understand who he is, but the denizens of the spirit-world certainly do. In the second part of today's reading, Jesus disappears briefly, and when his followers go looking for him, they find him praying. This may raise, for some, the question of why Jesus needs to pray. After all, if he is divine (as even the demons seem to realize), then in praying would he not be talking to himself? It's a similar question to that of why Jesus needs to receive baptism (see Mark 1:4-11, on Baptism Of Our Lord Sunday, p. 37) — although here the answer is different. Baptism, for a sinless person like Jesus, is an act of solidarity with the community. When it comes to prayer, however, we cannot assume that the earthly Jesus shares a common mind with God (otherwise, he could not be considered truly human). In John's Gospel, we may see Jesus described as having a certain amount of supernatural foreknowledge, but here in Mark there is little trace of that understanding.

Preaching Possibilities

Today's Gospel Lesson affords an opportunity to address the subject of prayer, and how to make room for it in our lives. Jesus evidently did: this is just one of a number of biblical passages that portray him as a man of prayer. Some other examples are Jesus praying alone on a mountain in Matthew 14:23; in "deserted places" in Luke 5:16; with his disciples in Luke 9:18; on a mountain in Luke 6:12; "in a certain place" in Luke 11:1; on the Mount of Transfiguration in Luke 9:18; in Gethsemane in Matthew 26:36ff; and on the cross in Matthew 27:46ff. Examples of prayers spoken by Jesus are legion, including: Matthew 11:25-26; Matthew 15:36; Matthew 19:13; Matthew 26:26-27; 1 Corinthians 11:24; Matthew 27:46; Luke 3:21; John 11:41ff.; John 12:27-28; John 17:1-26; Hebrews 5:7.

This incident happens after an incredibly busy sabbath day for Jesus. That day begins with him teaching in the synagogue at Capernaum. There, he's interrupted by a demon-possessed man, whom he subsequently heals. Next, he moves, along with his entourage, to the house of Simon and Andrew, where they discover Simon's mother-in-law sick in bed. Jesus heals her, too. Word of these wonders travels fast, and when the crowds appear at his doorstep, Jesus treats all comers. He's at it until well past sunset. By the time this incredible day is over, he's surely exhausted. He settles down to a well-earned night's sleep.

Morning dawns, and Jesus has disappeared — or so his disciples think. Unbeknownst to them, he has journeyed "to a deserted place," a place of prayer. The Greek word *eremos* that Mark uses here means "lonely" or "deserted." It's the same word that our word "hermit" comes from. It is in this sort of place that the disciples find their Lord and master: on his knees. We can almost hear the annoyance in Simon's voice, as he informs Jesus, "everyone is searching for you."

Well, that much is still true, even today. Everyone in the world, in one way or another (whether or not they would articulate it in those terms) is searching for Jesus. Where they don't expect to find him is in that desert place, the place of prayer. Most of the world is looking for Jesus in the place of action, the place of striving, the place of doing. They don't expect to find him in the place of being.

This picture of Jesus spending quiet time in prayer doesn't square with the image many of us have of him. We're busy people, most of us. Consequently, we look for a Lord who's even busier than we are: one who can burn brightly in workaholic excess without being consumed. This passage, however, shows us otherwise.

Prayer For The Day

Following is the full text of "The Serenity Prayer," adapted from a prayer of Reinhold Niebuhr. Its less-well-known second paragraph displays the true source of the serenity celebrated in the first:

> God, grant me the serenity
> to accept the things I cannot change,
> the courage to change the things I can,
> and the wisdom to know the difference.
>
> Living one day at a time,
> enjoying one moment at a time,
> accepting hardship as a pathway to peace;
> taking, as Jesus did,
> this sinful world as it is,
> not as I would have it;
> trusting that you will make all things right
> if I surrender to your will;
> so that I may be reasonably happy in this life
> and supremely happy with you forever in the next.
> Amen.

To Illustrate

There's a wonderful comic novel by a woman named Celia Gittelson. It's called *Saving Grace*, and it was also made into a movie (one that ought not to be confused with a more recent film of the same title). *Saving Grace* is about a newly elected pope, Leo XIV, who until a short time before had been very happy being a cardinal. Through a quirk of Vatican politics, he's proposed as a dark-horse candidate for pope, and to the world's surprise, he gets elected. This pope is somewhat reminiscent of John Paul I, who reigned only a few weeks before dying suddenly.

In the novel, this reluctant pope doesn't die; he runs away. Feeling like a fish out of water amidst the byzantine politics of the Vatican, he wishes he were someplace else. The opportunity arises one day for him to slip away: and, on the spur of the moment, he takes that opportunity. Dressed as a common priest, he eludes his entourage and bodyguards. This man is still so new as pope that his face is not recognizable to most.

Through a series of unpredictable events, Pope Leo ends up in a tiny Italian mountain village. There he discovers a church in ruins, whose congregation has no priest. The villagers naturally assume he's been sent to be their priest, and he doesn't contradict their assumption. He sets to work rebuilding the parish and the church building, reconnecting with God and his sense of calling in the process. Meanwhile, back in the Vatican, his handlers comically struggle to cover up the fact that they've somehow lost the pope. They issue vague press releases about him being sick in bed, hoping against hope that the *Pontifex Maximus* will show up on his own, before they're called upon to produce him.

There's a lot more that happens in this book, but this part of the story is enough to make the point: even a pope needs to find that "lonely place" from time to time, the place where striving ceases and true communion with God is to be found.

***

There's an old story that goes back to the days of the Industrial Revolution. In one of those early factories — a woolen mill where cloth was woven — there was posted over every piece of machinery a prominent sign: "If the threads become tangled, call the foreman."

It so happened that, on her first day at work at the mill, a new employee found the threads on her machine badly tangled. Immediately she set to work untangling them, which unfortunately only made matters worse. Finally the foreman walked by, scoped out the situation, and asked, "Why didn't you call for me?"

"I didn't want to bother you, Sir," she replied. "I was simply trying to do my best."

The foreman looked the frightened woman in the eye and said kindly, "Doing your best includes calling the foreman."

That's the way God looks on us as well. If we imagine we're completely self-sufficient in this life, we're only fooling ourselves. No matter how gifted, intelligent, or self-disciplined we may be, always there comes a time when our resources simply run out. In such an hour, there's nowhere else for us to turn but to the Lord.

***

Phillip Yancey advocates the rediscovery of an ancient monastic tradition called *statio*. What this means, simply, is ...

> *... stopping one thing before beginning another. Rather than rushing from one task to the next, pause for a moment and recognize the time between times. Before dialing the phone, pause and think about the conversation and the person on the other end. After reading from a book, pause and think back through what you learned and how you were moved. After watching a television show, pause and ask what it contributed to your life. Before reading the Bible, pause and ask for a spirit of attention. Do this often enough and even mechanical acts become conscious, mindful.... The visible world forces itself on me without invitation; I must consciously cultivate the invisible. I wish the process were spontaneous and natural, but I have never found it to be so. Indeed, I have found that such a process, like anything of worth, requires discipline.*

Yancey goes on to quote something the great concert pianist Arthur Rubenstein once said, about a different sort of discipline, that of musical practice: "If I omit practice one day, I notice it. If two days, the critics notice it; if three days, the public notices it." The same is true of prayer time, which is our devotional "practice."

— Philip Yancey, "Reaching for God," in *Plus* magazine, December, 2002, pp. 16-18

***

In the famous poetic words of T. S. Eliot, Christians in our work-driven culture have ...

> *... knowledge of motion, but not of stillness;*
> *Knowledge of speech, but not of silence;*
> *Knowledge of words, and ignorance of the Word.*
> *All our knowledge brings us nearer to our ignorance.*
> *All our ignorance brings us nearer to death,*
> *But nearness to death no nearer to God.*
> *Where is the Life we have lost in living?*
> *Where is the wisdom we have lost in knowledge?*
> *Where is the knowledge we have lost in information?*
> *The cycles of heavens in twenty centuries*
> *Bring us farther from God and nearer to the dust.*

— T. S. Eliot, Choruses from "The Rock"

Sixth Sunday After The Epiphany
Sixth Sunday In Ordinary Time
February 12, 2006

Revised Common	2 Kings 5:1-14	1 Corinthians 9:24-27	Mark 1:40-45
Roman Catholic	Leviticus 13:1-2, 44-46	1 Corinthians 10:31—11:1	Mark 1:40-45
Episcopal	2 Kings 5:1-15	1 Corinthians 9:24-27	Mark 1:40-45

Theme For The Day   God desires us to be partners in our own healing.

Old Testament Lesson   2 Kings 5:1-14   *Elisha Heals Naaman The Syrian*

This well-loved story is an example of how the Lord of Israel is powerfully at work behind the scenes, guiding the fortunes of everyone from slaves to kings — but working especially through prophets like Elisha. The story of the young Israelite girl, servant of Naaman's wife, is reminiscent of the stories of Joseph, Esther, and Daniel — all of them devout people who worked from a position of weakness to influence the mighty to fulfill the will of God. (It is unlikely that Naaman's affliction is Hansen's Disease, that which the New Testament typically calls leprosy; the Hebrew word used in verse 3 can refer to a variety of skin diseases. While society may have pitied Naaman, there is no indication that it shunned him.) When Naaman shows up at the king's palace seeking help (v. 7), the monarch's dismay is understandable: compared to Israel, Syria is a superpower, and the price of failure (which could incur the Syrian king's displeasure) is not something the king of Israel wants to think about. Protocol is central to this story: Naaman behaves in all the expected ways, showing the king due fealty, bringing costly gifts, and the like. Yet Dr. Elisha — as the agent of Yahweh — is indifferent to this sort of thing. When his VIP patient comes to see him, he declines to examine him. Elisha remains in his tent, sending out a prescription script that reads, "Go jump in the river. Repeat six times." Naaman is understandably miffed, but with the encouragement of his servants — again, the underdogs are the truly wise ones in this story — he gives it a try, and is healed.

New Testament Lesson   1 Corinthians 9:24-27   *Train Hard; Run Hard; Run To Win*

Beginning where we left off last Sunday (see p. 54), the lectionary has Paul concluding his argument by using one of his favorite metaphors: that of an athlete competing in a race. He encourages the Corinthian Christians to keep up their spiritual training, so that when the goal is at last in front of them, they may press on and win the wreath of victory. Paul continues to display himself as an example of self-discipline and spiritual zeal. The "perishable wreath" in verse 25 would have been well known to Paul's Greek readers, who were used to seeing such trophies distributed at the athletic games that were frequently part of their lives.

The Gospel   Mark 1:40-45   *The Leper Who Can't Keep Quiet*

This passage is a prime example of the "Messianic secret" theme that is so prominent in Mark's Gospel. Jesus heals a leper, sending him off to the priest to be judged ritually clean (this according to Leviticus 13 and 14). Jesus is healing far more than a disease, here; he is also healing the man from his rejection by society. In this case — unlike Naaman's, in today's Old Testament Lesson — the man does have a disease that, like Hansen's disease, leads to shunning by the community. Before sending the man off, Jesus sternly charges him — as he so often does in Markan healing stories — to tell no one. Overcome with joy, the former leper can't keep the secret, and tells everyone he sees. As a result, Jesus is mobbed by crowds of sick people seeking help. It's hard to know the reason for Jesus' reluctance to have the man identify him as the healer, but it may have something to do with Jesus' desire to have himself known as more than just a miracle worker. His mission is bigger than that. Healing, for him, is an act of compassion for the afflicted, not a means of accruing glory for himself.

Preaching Possibilities

A sermon based on either the Old Testament Lesson or the Gospel Lesson (or both) could focus on the need for us to be full participants in our healing. Elisha requires Naaman to go bathe in the Jordan seven times — something he's reluctant to do, and almost doesn't do at all (thereby coming very close to letting the thing he most desires slip through his hands). Jesus requires the leper to go off and be ritually cleansed by the temple priests.

The leper says to Jesus, "If you choose, you can make me clean." Notice that the man places the entire burden of success or failure on Jesus' shoulders. That's a common enough refrain: one which any doctor, therapist, or social worker has heard time and again. "Sure, I want to get better, Doc ... to lose weight ... to kick this addiction ... to stop hurting the ones I love. Make me better. Write me a prescription. Give me a pill. I'll write you a check, of course, that's only fair — but don't expect me to *do* anything. The last thing I want to do is to become a partner in my own healing."

Jesus doesn't allow the leper to get away with that kind of helpless, poor-me attitude — any more than Elisha permits the mighty Naaman to do so. Doctor Jesus whips out his prescription pad, and scribbles a few words. He tears the top sheet off, and hands it to his patient. "Here's what I've written," he tells him. "Go to the high priest, and perform the ritual cleansing prescribed by law. Then you will truly be well, inside and out."

There's wisdom in that prescription: both for the leper, and for the leper within ourselves. God's deepest desire is that we be strong and healthy, that we be free of addictions, that we avoid sin, that we live lives of faithful simplicity. Yet God will not bestow such treasures by magic; the Lord desires to walk beside us, as we pursue and achieve these goals ourselves. God will accompany us on our journey through life, and will even aid us at times: but at no time will the Lord allow us to be mere passive recipients of a magical healing process.

If a person with an alcoholism problem, for example, prays to the Lord for healing, then goes to Alcoholics Anonymous and works the twelve steps, and gets better, does the person then go right out and declare, "I guess I didn't need God after all; I really did it myself?" Of course not! God was part of the healing all along — both the healing action itself and the patient's response.

The two are, in fact, two sides of the same coin. We cry out for help; God touches us; then we do the thing that's necessary for healing. Maybe it's more like a couple on a dance floor: in claiming our healing, we are dancing with God. True, one partner may be leading — but it takes both partners to complete the dance.

Prayer For The Day

Come into our hearts, Lord Jesus. You know those parts of our deepest selves that are dark, hidden, shut off from the world. Yet we know there are no secrets with you. You know where we most need to be healed. Come into those places, we pray. Help us to throw open the shutters, so the healing light may enter. Come into our hearts, that we may be made whole. Amen.

To Illustrate

Theologian Ann Ulanov has written,

> *This task confronts all of us, to deal with what touches us and not avoid it, to collect our missing parts, the neglected and overlooked and banished parts of our inner and outer populations. We are never touched in the abstract, only in the flesh. The marks of our own frown lines, our overweight, our sleepless nights, our neighborhood crime, our neglected land or polluted air reveal this truth. God waits in those parts, waits for us to visit the part left in the prison of repression, waits for us to offer some life-giving water to outcast sexual parts, to give food to starving parts. All these bits must be gathered in and nourished. As Lady Julian of Norwich puts it, "All must be knit in, must be one with God."*

***

Phillips Brooks, the renowned nineteenth-century Congregationalist preacher, once said, "The true way to be humble is not to stoop until you are smaller than yourself, but to stand at your real height against some higher nature that will show you what the real smallness of your greatness is." The smallness of his greatness: the haughty General Naaman has to learn this lesson, before he can partake of the healing God has in store for him.

***

Celebrity is a mask that eats into the face. As soon as one is aware of being "somebody," to be watched and listened to with extra interest, input ceases, and the performer goes blind and deaf in his overanimation. One can either see or be seen.
— John Updike, *Self-Consciousness: Memoirs* (New York: Random House, 1989), ch. 6

***

Once there was a priest who traveled to see a renowned spiritual teacher, to spend a time on retreat with him. "Master," he said upon arriving, "I come to you seeking enlightenment."

"Well, then," the master said, "for the first exercise of your retreat, go into the courtyard, tilt back your head, stretch out your arms and wait until I come for you."

Just as the priest arranged himself in that position, the rains came. And it rained. It rained the rest of the afternoon. Finally, the old master came back. "Well, priest," he asked, "have you been enlightened today?"

"Are you serious?" the priest asked, in disgust. "I've been standing here with my head up in the rain for an hour. I'm soaking wet. I feel like a fool!"

The master said, "Well, priest, for the first day of a retreat that sounds like great enlightenment to me."
— Joan Chittister, *Light in the Darkness: New Reflections on the Psalms for Every Day of the Year* (New York: Crossroad Publishing Company, 1998)

Seventh Sunday After The Epiphany
Seventh Sunday In Ordinary Time
February 19, 2006

Revised Common	Isaiah 43:18-25	2 Corinthians 1:18-22	Mark 2:1-12
Roman Catholic	Isaiah 43:18-19, 21-22, 24b-25	2 Corinthians 1:18-22	Mark 2:1-12
Episcopal	Isaiah 43:18-25	2 Corinthians 1:18-22	Mark 2:1-12

Theme For The Day   Christ calls our churches to radical openness, especially to those who may be inclined to feel unwelcome.

Old Testament Lesson   Isaiah 43:18-25   *A New Thing*
"I am about to do a new thing," says the Lord, "now it springs forth, do you not perceive it?" (v. 18b). Isaiah's message to the exiles is truly "a new thing." The people have been used to hearing prophetic messages of condemnation; now Isaiah brings them a positive message of redemption and hope. Once they limited their thinking to the boundaries of their own nation, seeing Yahweh as primarily a God of one people; now they catch the vision of a universal God, who is able to work through Cyrus of Persia just as much as through one of their own rulers. The prophecy of Second Isaiah marks one of those great moments in human religious history when "a new thing" — spiritually speaking — becomes a real possibility.

New Testament Lesson   2 Corinthians 1:18-22   *God's Promise Is Always A "Yes"*
Paul has apparently been accused of fickleness because, for whatever reason, his travel plans changed. Here he defends himself, admitting that, while he did change his mind, he did so because he was acting under the guidance of the Holy Spirit. He is not one of those people who say "Yes" one day and "No" the next; he follows God's way. Unlike human beings, God is not changeable: "... every one of God's promises is a 'Yes' " (v. 20b).

The Gospel   Mark 2:1-12   *A Hole In The Roof*
In a story whose colorful details have always delighted children, the friends of a paralyzed man cut a hole in the roof of the house where Jesus is staying, and lower him down so he may be healed. (The roof they "dug through" was likely made of rushes, which explains how relatively easy it was to accomplish this feat.) Jesus forgives the man's sins — a theologically audacious act that raises the hackles of some Pharisees who are present. When they object, Jesus asks which is easier: to forgive sins, or to say, "Stand up and take your mat and walk?" Whereupon he tells the man to do just that, and he does — to the amazement of all. While this is a healing story, on a deeper level it is about legalism. It is a classic example of the style of Jesus' ministry, that so alienated him from the religious authorities and so endeared him to the common folk. Everything he proclaims in words is also manifested in deeds: and for words bereft of deeds he has little patience.

Preaching Possibilities
A sermon on the Gospel Lesson could begin by declaring that what every church needs is a hole in the roof. Once upon a time, there was a church that had one. This church is said to have been constructed in a far-off part of Central Asia during a time of great privation. A deadly epidemic was stalking the land. So familiar were the Christians of that place with the victims'

sufferings, that they built their church with great wide doors and gently sloping ramps, so the sick could easily be carried in.

As the people built their church, they also remembered the story in Mark, about the healing of the paralyzed man. And so, for many years, this particular church left the dome of its sanctuary unfinished, open to the elements — covered only by a large tarp. For those Christians, the hole in the roof became a sign, a powerful symbol of their calling to be open to the world, and to minister unto it. For whatever reason, outsiders may have needed to get in, this congregation was committed to finding a way.

The older a congregation is, the less likely it will be to keep a hole in the roof. New church developments, for example, aren't particular about such things. There are few traditions in such churches: no matriarchs or patriarchs to let the new pastor know "how we do things here, thank you," no one to stand around and chant the "seven last words" of a dying church — "We haven't done it that way before."

That openness and flexibility is sometimes difficult for members of established churches to understand. New church developments can sometimes seem like a threat to more established congregations' sense of what the church is all about: "What? No building yet? Without a building, you can't have pews. Without pews, you can't have hymnbook racks. And without hymnbook racks — why, you've got no way to keep your hymnbooks in order. A church without orderly hymnbooks, I always say, is a terrible thing. What's that you say? You don't even *use* hymnbooks? You say you use a digital projector? I'm beginning to worry whether you people are even Christian!"

What appears, to members of established churches, to be disregard of tradition — or even a dangerous flirting with chaos — is actually a newer church's greatest strength. It is the very absence of tradition, the lack of all those people bodily blocking the doors and windows, that enables new members to get in — that makes it possible for new churches to post a rate of growth that would be the envy of most established churches.

Churches sometimes have a way — quite unintentionally — of excluding certain people. They have a way of looking askance at those who are a little different, or who maybe don't have their lives all together and on display for all the world to see. Churches develop this unfortunate tendency very early in their history — and unless they work hard to overcome it, they quickly become an exclusive club, serving the needs of their members first, reaching out to the world for which Christ died only as an afterthought.

Once churches become even a little bit "established," they have to fight this tendency to block the doors and windows, to admit only those who are "our kind of people." It's always sad when this happens, because it means the church has lost something of its spiritual vision, and has become bogged down in earthly, institutional realities.

Prayer For The Day

O God who embraces the outcast, who welcomes the prodigal home: we pray for those people who are seated around us in worship. Their heads are bowed, as are ours; their minds are in repose, as are ours; their hearts are attuned, as are ours, to worship you. It is easy to pray for people such as these: our family members, our friends, our neighbors in Christ. Help us to pray for those who are not present with us, whose existence is symbolized by the empty seats. Some of them may feel unwelcome. Some may feel uncared for. Some may feel wounded at the thought that we might fear them. May we who are your body, O Christ, open wide our arms to embrace all your children. Amen.

To Illustrate

(I can tell this one because I am a Presbyterian. Those from other denominations who feel that "the shoe fits" may be able to adapt the denominational affiliation to their own. — Author)

Once there was a Catholic church, a synagogue, and a Presbyterian church, that occupied three of the four corners of an intersection. A terrible lightning storm came along one day. It happened that all three places of worship were struck, and set afire. The three spiritual leaders happened to be nearby, and arrived at their respective burning buildings at roughly the same time.

The Catholic priest rushed into his sanctuary, and emerged a few moments later with the most precious thing he could think of: the Blessed Sacrament.

The rabbi ran into his synagogue, and came out a moment later, carrying the Torah scroll.

The Presbyterian minister ran into her church, but didn't come out. The minutes ticked by. The fire got worse. Her two colleagues were beginning to wonder if she was all right. They ran around to the back of the building, and there they came upon their friend, the Presbyterian minister, sitting exhausted on the curb — covered with soot, her head in her hands.

"Are you all right?" they asked.

"Don't worry, I'm fine," she replied. "You simply have no conception of how heavy a photocopy machine is!"

***

The ruined cathedral on the Rock of Cashel, one of Ireland's holiest and most historic sites, contains a narrow window called "the Leper's Squint," that opens up into a tiny chamber that could in years past be reached by a concealed flight of stairs. The room was designed for lepers, who were permitted to climb the stairs into this little chamber, there to look on from a distance at the worship in the great cathedral.

Are there any today who feel they have to stand apart and squint at what is going on inside our churches?

***

In their book, *Where Resident Aliens Live*, Stanley Hauerwas and William Willimon tell of the old Baptist country preacher who was called to a church in rural Georgia. The church had tried to call a series of other pastors — better preachers, by reputation — and had failed.

So they turned to this lay preacher. After they hired him and heard one of his sermons they informed him that the church did not want any newfangled ideas and definitely did not want any "colored" members.

The next Sunday that preacher preached a sermon against this racial attitude, telling them, "If you love Jesus, you've got to love everybody Jesus loves."

A number of the congregation told him they did not like such attitudes. Still, the preacher persisted, saying, "If you love Jesus, you've got to love everybody Jesus loves."

Many people left the congregation in protest. A number of African-American people joined. More people left.

"I preached that congregation down to almost nothing before it started to grow again," said the preacher. "And then it grew and grew into a strong, inclusive congregation."

"Like I said," the preacher explained, "if you love Jesus, you've got to love everybody Jesus loves."

***

There are many reasons for the failure to comprehend Christ's teaching ... but the chief cause which has engendered all these misconceptions is this: that Christ's teaching is considered to be such as can be accepted, or not accepted, without changing one's life.

— Leo Tolstoy

Eighth Sunday After The Epiphany
Eighth Sunday In Ordinary Time
February 26, 2006

Revised Common	Hosea 2:14-20	2 Corinthians 3:1-6	Mark 2:13-22
Roman Catholic	Hosea 2:16-17, 21-22	2 Corinthians 3:1-6	Mark 2:18-22
Episcopal	Hosea 2:14-23	2 Corinthians 3:(4-11) 17—4:2	Mark 2:18-22

Theme For The Day   Jesus calls for an end to the prejudicial assumption that there are some people who cannot change.

Old Testament Lesson   Hosea 2:14-20   *God's Fidelity*

"I will take you for my wife forever," says the Lord to Israel — in the tender words of the prophet Hosea, who pictures the relationship between God and the people as that between an eternally faithful husband and an errant wife. "I shall take you for my wife in faithfulness, and you shall know the Lord" (v. 20).

New Testament Lesson   2 Corinthians 3:1-6   *Living Letters Of Recommendation*

Credentials. We all need them — especially in this security-conscious world. Who could even imagine trying to get on a commercial airplane these days without a photo ID? Credentials — "letters of recommendation" — were part of Paul's world as well. And what are the letters of recommendation Paul values most intensely? Why, they are the people of his churches themselves. In traveling from congregation to congregation, he needs nothing more than their good will: "You yourselves are our letter, written on our hearts, to be known and read by all ..." (v. 2). Paul's competence to carry on his apostolic mission comes not from any diploma or degree: his competence is "from God" (v. 5).

The Gospel   Mark 2:13-22   *New Wineskins*

Today's Gospel Lesson is two distinct pericopes. The first one describes Jesus' calling of Levi, the tax collector. As Mark tells it, Levi gets up and follows just as unhesitatingly as do the other disciples (see Mark 1:14-20, Third Sunday After The Epiphany, p. 46); yet there is a certain fallout to his joining "Team Jesus." "Why does he eat with tax collectors and sinners?" ask some of the Pharisees. Jesus replies, saying, "Those who are well have no need of a physician, but those who are sick; I have come to call not the righteous but sinners" (v. 17). In the second pericope, some people come up to Jesus and ask why he and his disciples do not fast, as do the Pharisees and the followers of John the Baptist. Jesus responds with three mini-parables: "The wedding guests cannot fast while the bridegroom is with them" (v. 20); "No one sews a piece of unshrunk cloth on an old cloak" (v. 21); "And no one puts new wine into old wineskins" (v. 22).

Preaching Possibilities

We have examined, in recent weeks, several stories from the Gospel of Mark about healings Jesus performed. In today's lesson, however, we see him heal an ailment that has no physical manifestations, no medical symptoms. The malady he addresses is the social isolation of one category of people by the judgment of another: in short, prejudice.

Jesus calls Levi, a tax collector, as one of his disciples. Levi is nothing like any tax collector any of us have ever experienced. He's more like a corrupt customs agent. The system works like this. Levi sits in his booth, observing the trade that goes back and forth along the road. Each item, Levi must examine. The government is owed a certain percentage on all imports, but it's up to Levi to assess the value of each item. The higher the assessment, the easier it is for him to cook the books — which he frequently does, for that's where his profit comes from. Many's the merchant who has walked away from Levi's booth feeling certain he's been cheated. Even more than that, Levi deals with the coins and the merchandise of many nations and peoples. Roman coins pass through his hands, bearing the idolatrous image of the emperor. So do pigs, which Levi has to hold up, to estimate their weight. It's no wonder a faithful and observant Jew would take offense at one such as him.

We have no idea what goes through Levi's mind when Jesus issues his call. In his typical terse fashion, Mark simply tells us that Levi leaves his customs booth, walks away, and never looks back.

The scene shifts to that same evening. Jesus is reclining at dinner in the house of Levi. Lots of others are there, too — for Levi is a man of considerable means, one who can afford to throw an opulent banquet in the Greek style, with a wise teacher as guest of honor and lots of others listening in. Part of the crowd present that night are Pharisees — people who, due to religious scruples, would not ordinarily be found in Levi's house. They're probably there because Jesus is the guest.

At the heart of the Pharisaical lifestyle is the community of shared meals. Many of the regulations Pharisees hold dear have to do with eating: how you cleanse your cup a certain way, how you reach into a bowl, how the food itself is prepared. A meal with a Pharisee is a beautiful and spiritual occasion, a time-honored ritual in which every action has its meaning. It's a far cry from the dinner Jesus and the disciples enjoy that night. Sure, there are Pharisees in attendance — but this is the house of Levi, after all. The tax collector's in charge. The wine pours freely, the laughter is raucous, the jokes are — as usual — just a bit off-color. Many of the other guests have, shall we say, "interesting" pasts. They're hard-living misfits like Levi himself. If Jesus is a holy man, he's sure stepped off holy ground that night (or so the Pharisees think, and eventually tell him so).

"Those who are well have no need of a physician, but those who are sick," Jesus responds. "I have come to call not the righteous but sinners." In point of fact, though, Levi does need a physician. Very likely he's strong in body and mind — he'd have to have a certain toughness, to make his assessments stick. Yet maybe there's a part of Levi — a secret part, locked up deep within him — that weeps bitterly as he remembers the love he's lost, that sadly mourns the respect of others he's been obliged to cast aside. God's forgiveness is a gift, Jesus is saying: an utterly free gift, with no strings attached. To receive it, all you need to do is open your hands. If that love flows into your life truly and completely, runs over your soiled heart like a cleansing waterfall, you'll never be the same again. You don't need to prove yourself first; you just need to hunger for it.

You can't sew a patch of new, unshrunk cloth onto an old garment, as everybody knows; the seam will pull right out, as the new cloth shrinks. Nor can you pour new wine into an old wineskin; the chemical reaction of the fermenting wine will burst it apart. "Behold," says the Lord (in Isaiah's words), "I am doing a new thing!" "Behold," says Jesus to the Pharisees, "I am doing a new thing as well, bringing God's love to tax collectors and sinners!"

Prayer For The Day

We give you thanks and praise, O God, that you did not give up on us. Give us the honesty, the courage and the grace not to give up on others. Amen.

To Illustrate

Some years ago, there was a television movie, *Separate But Equal*. It told the story of the U.S. Supreme Court's decision to desegregate the public schools. Anyone who lived through those days in American history knows the court's decision did not come easily. Centuries of racism exerted their accumulated weight, in opposition to change. A majority of Supreme Court justices clearly and honestly believed segregation was wrong. Yet they feared what would happen if they overturned the legal principle of "separate but equal," on which segregation was based. Among other things, the movie tells the story of Chief Justice Earl Warren: how he made up his mind how he was going to vote.

For months, the court has been struggling with the issue. The chief justice is exhausted. He decides to get out of Washington for a weekend. He takes along his African-American aide, Mr. Patterson, to drive his car and provide some company.

The two of them set off on a tour of Civil War battlefields. They stop for the evening at a beautiful country inn. The camera shows Chief Justice Warren eating a fine meal in the restaurant, while reading Carl Sandburg's biography of Abraham Lincoln. The next morning, he emerges from the inn, only to find Mr. Patterson sleeping in the backseat of the car. "Mr. Patterson," he asks him, "why are you sleeping in there?"

His assistant replies, "I couldn't find a place. Sir, there's no place within twenty miles of here where I ..." There's no need for Mr. Patterson to even finish his sentence. The chief justice silences him with a gesture. He climbs back into the car, Mr. Patterson straightens his tie, and the two of them drive off, returning to Washington.

The next scene shows Chief Justice Warren sitting with one of the other justices. He's saying, "The court must vote to desegregate. It is a moral issue, one that goes deep into the soul of our nation." Sometimes it takes a very specific experience to run a great, looming, abstract idea to ground — to make it truly real. Sometimes it takes the sight of a good man waking rumpled and unshaven from a night spent sleeping in a car. Sometimes it takes a dinner with a repentant tax collector.

***

There's an old rabbinic legend about the prophet Elijah. (Elijah, of course, did not die as other people did, but ascended to heaven in a whirlwind — see 2 Kings 2:11 — and the rabbis tell how he still walks the earth from time to time, always turning up in unexpected places.) One day, Elijah's walking through a town, when he hears the sounds of a party coming from a large and beautiful house. The prophet twirls himself around, and instantly he's clothed in the rags of a beggar. He knocks on the door.

The host, in his elegant garments, takes one look at the so-called beggar on his doorstep, clad in his miserable rags, and slams the door in his face.

Elijah twirls around a second time. Instantly, he's clothed in the fine garments of a gentleman. He knocks on the door again, and this time the host takes one look at his splendid attire, and says, "Come right in!"

Elijah makes a beeline for the buffet table. He begins to stuff food into his pockets. The other guests all step back, amazed at this rare sight. Then Elijah pushes even more food into his tunic, and pours wine over his shoulders and down the front of his fine suit of clothes. It's not long at all before the host runs over to him, and demands to know what he's up to.

"I came to your door dressed in rags," explains Elijah, "and you did not invite me in. Then I came to your door dressed in fine garments — the very same person — and you welcomed me to your feast. I can only conclude that it was not me you invited, but my clothing. That is why I feed my clothing with your food and drink."

The story concludes with the party guests feeling ashamed and looking down at the ground. When they look up again, Elijah is gone.

***

Killing wolves has to do with murder. Historically, the most visible motive, and the one that best explains the excess of killing, is a type of fear: theriophobia. Fear of the beast. Fear of the beast as an irrational, violent, insatiable creature. Fear of the projected beast in oneself.... At the heart of theriophobia is the fear of one's own nature. In its headiest manifestations, theriophobia is projected onto a single animal, the animal becomes a scapegoat, and it is annihilated.
— Barry Lopez, *Of Wolves and Men* (New York: Scribners, 1978), p. 24

***

All of us are somewhere on a journey to God ... the gap between least and most advanced is infinitely smaller than the gap between the most advanced and God himself.
— John Ortberg

The Transfiguration Of Our Lord
Last Sunday After The Epiphany
February 26, 2006

Revised Common	2 Kings 2:1-12	2 Corinthians 4:3-6	Mark 9:2-9
Roman Catholic	Daniel 7:9-10, 13-14	2 Peter 1:16-19	Mark 9:2-9
Episcopal	1 Kings 19:9-18	2 Peter 1:16-19 (20-21)	Mark 9:2-9

Theme For The Day   Let us be alert for the rare, visionary experiences when God allows us to glimpse something of glory — experiences which can sustain us through darker days.

Old Testament Lesson   2 Kings 2:1-12   *Elijah Is Conveyed Into Heaven*

Using his rolled-up mantle, Elijah strikes the waters of the Jordan, parting them. He and Elisha cross over, and shortly afterward Elisha asks for a double share of his mentor's spirit. Elijah says it will soon become clear whether or not his successor will be blessed with such a gift. Then, a chariot of fire with flaming horses appears and Elijah is taken directly up to heaven in a whirlwind.

New Testament Lesson   2 Corinthians 4:3-6   *To See Christ Glorified Is A Divine Gift*

"... if our gospel is veiled, it is veiled to those who are perishing. In their case the god of this world has blinded the minds of the unbelievers, to keep them from seeing the light of the gospel of the glory of Christ ..." (vv. 3-4a). God, says Paul, is the giver of light, and it is only by inward illumination that we are able to perceive "the glory of God in the face of Jesus Christ" (v. 6).

The Gospel   Mark 9:2-9   *The Transfiguration*

Peter, James, and John, on a mountaintop with Jesus, see him "transfigured before them, and his clothes became dazzling white, such as no one on earth could bleach them" (vv. 2b-3). Moses and Elijah appear also, and the awestruck Peter suggests that he and his fellow disciples construct temporary dwellings for all three of these mystical figures. A cloud "overshadows" them, and they hear a heavenly voice speaking a blessing similar to the one conferred upon Jesus at his baptism: "This is my Son, the Beloved; listen to him!" (v. 7). With that, the vision ends, and Jesus is restored to his normal state.

Preaching Possibilities

Today we end the season some call Epiphany, and others call Ordinary Time. This Wednesday, Lent begins. This season opened with the baptism of Jesus, with a voice from the clouds saying, "This is my beloved son, with whom I am well pleased." Now, it ends with that same voice, spoken from the mysterious cloud on the Mount of Transfiguration: "This is my beloved son; listen to him."

Both events, baptism and transfiguration, are epiphanies. The word "epiphany" means "appearance" — a sign of power emerging out of darkness, unexpectedly. Yet even with its glorious imagery, the Transfiguration Of Our Lord is one of the most difficult Sundays of the Christian year for preachers. First, its subject matter is baffling — a mystical experience, difficult to describe in words. Because the group of witnesses (Peter, James, and John) is so small, the story of the Transfiguration is very close to a personal spiritual experience, that has been made public only through the telling of it. Second, the Gospel Lesson is more or less identical each year — meaning that no matter what cycle of the lectionary the preacher may be working with, he or she is presented with essentially the same text. (There is a parallel, less-detailed recollection of the Transfiguration in 2 Peter 1:16-18, but it's not much help.)

Even so, there is something universal about the Transfiguration imagery. A figure glowing with light, as Jesus is here portrayed, has an iconic resonance in the hearts of worshipers. Hollywood has long known this: numerous science-fiction and fantasy films — from *Close Encounters of the Third Kind* to *Ghost* to *Lord of the Rings* — have portrayed characters who are visually transfigured in one way or another. When the good wizard Gandalf the Grey reveals himself to his companions as Gandalf the White in *The Lord of the Rings: The Two Towers*, his computer-generated special-effects aura is a more-than-obvious allusion to the biblical imagery. It is precisely the light-and-darkness interplay that makes the Transfiguration imagery resonate in believers' hearts.

Peter, James, and John have just heard Jesus tell them of things to come: "The Son of Man must undergo great suffering, and be rejected by the elders, the chief priests, and the scribes, and be killed, and after three days rise again" (8:31). The disciples have never heard Jesus talk this way — so intense, so passionate, and at the same time, so weighed down with care. He sounds like a herald of doom. Even more ominous are the words he goes on to utter: "If any want to become my followers, let them deny themselves and take up their cross and follow me" (8:34).

For the past eight days, Peter and his friends have felt surrounded by gloom. Their holy quest, begun so cheerfully in the bright Galilean sun, has become overshadowed by ominous clouds. Each night, as the disciples lie down to rest, sleep eludes them. They stare into the night, until exhaustion overwhelms them.

This night on the mountain is different. As Peter and his companions look over to their master, still engaged in prayer, they see him change before their very eyes. Praise to God for sustaining visions of goodness and light, that sustain us through dark times!

Prayer For The Day

Lord, you created the light. Into the dark, swirling chaos you spoke the word of creation: and darkness retreated. There are times in life when we fear that darkness will have its victory. May we never forget that, in the gift of your Son Jesus, you have given us light not only by which to see, but through which we may triumph. Amen.

To Illustrate

I can remember, as a boy, hiking the Appalachian Trail with my scout troop. One of the things we used to do, from time to time, was hike at night. Our leaders would take us out, away from the reassuring glow of the campfire, to a place where the only illumination was the moon and stars. Then they would tell us to turn off our flashlights.

Instantly, the group was plunged into darkness. It was a little unsettling, to say the least — to be suddenly stripped of our hand-held electric power, our ability to push back the darkness with the click of a button. Without flashlights, the night surrounded us, as the sea surrounds a swimmer. For a time, we would stand in silence, startled by each snapped twig and every wind-rustled leaf, until finally we achieved the promised state called "night vision." When the pupils of our eyes had become fully dilated, we would find to our amazement that if we were fully attentive, the light of moon and stars were sufficient to pick out the white-painted blazes on the trees. We could navigate the trail, even by night.

The irony is that, with night vision, you can see much better than with a flashlight. The flashlight brilliantly illuminates a single point, but it dazzles the eyes. If you turn away from that projected circle of light, your eyes have lost all power to pierce the darkness. Night vision is dim vision, to be sure, but it extends 360 degrees around. With just a little help from moon or stars, it is enough.

In the "dark nights of the soul" we all experience, the way of discipleship is to stop trying to pierce the darkness by artificial means. It is to put aside our lanterns and flashlights, and to trust the night. It is to feel the darkness surrounding us like a cloak, and to allow it to do so — knowing that God, who is Lord of darkness as well as light, will provide us with the light we need to see.

***

Oceanographer tell us that deep-sea divers pass through several worlds of darkness, as they descend into the ocean depths. The first is "the world of fishes," that bright, sun-dappled world near the water's surface, where harlequin fish dance in reflected sunlight.

The deeper the divers descend, the more murky the waters become. The fish become fewer. Light becomes dimmer. The divers pass through a somber, gray-black curtain into "the world of the abyss" — an undersea void, containing nothing but deep darkness and bone-chilling cold. Only the strongest and most persistent venture into this world, and then only with special equipment. League upon league they descend, penetrating further into the gloom, until they reach another world altogether.

This is a world rarely seen by land-dwellers. It is "the world of luminous darkness." In this world, the sea is just as dark, and colder even than the worlds above, but everywhere there are lights — phosphorescent fish, glowing, luminous, casting their weird, colored lights into the void. An anonymous diver who has often penetrated this world has written of the experience:

> *... the diver discovers that the fear has lost its significance. It is possible to see in the darkness, if you are still. At the level of the luminous darkness, you begin to understand what God meant when God first spoke. You hear the sound of the genuine in yourself and in the world.*

***

The poet, William Butler Yeats, tells of a visionary experience he had — and in a very ordinary place indeed, a coffee shop:

> *My fiftieth year had come and gone.*
> *I sat, a solitary man,*
> *In a crowded London shop,*
> *An open book and empty cup*
> *On the marble table top.*

While on the shop and street I gazed
My body for a moment blazed,
And twenty minutes, more or less,
It seemed, so great my happiness,
That I was blessed, and could bless.

— "Vacillation, IV"

Another poet, Elizabeth Barrett Browning, recalls a similar transfiguration — that of Moses'
burning bush — in these famous lines:

Earth's crammed with heaven,
And every common bush aflame with God;
But only he who sees, takes off his shoes;
The rest sit round it and pluck blackberries.

— *Aurora Leigh*, Book vii

And again, the mystical English poet, William Blake, captures the true visionary's talent for
wonder:

To see a World in a Grain of Sand
And a Heaven in a Wild Flower
Hold Infinity in the palm of your hand
And Eternity in an hour.

— *Auguries of Innocence*

The Lenten Season

Unlike some other liturgical seasons, Sundays belonging to the season of Lent are described as seasons "in" Lent. There are Sundays "of" Advent, or expectation; and there are Sundays "of" Easter, or new life. But in Lent, Sundays are islands in the midst of a forty-day sea of penitence. In churches with a strong tradition of sacrificial Lenten disciplines, Lenten Sundays are a small break, a celebration (albeit a low-key one) that provides some relief. Lenten Sundays are sometimes considered "days off" from these disciplines. The word "Lent" is derived from an old form of the verb "to lengthen," referring to the lengthening days that characterize these late-winter and early-springtime weeks. Thus, even as the church is engaged in Lenten penitence, there is a growing intuitive awareness that the power of light is incrementally increasing — until the great celebration of Easter, when light bursts forth once and for all, invincible.

But even so, the overall theme of Lent is penitential, and the scripture texts (particularly the Gospel Lessons) have been chosen to assist Christians in the spiritual journey of accompanying Jesus on his way to the cross. In our pleasure seeking, "I want it now" culture, Lent can be a hard sell for preachers. Many worshipers are suspicious of any sustained emphasis on human sin, or on darker subjects like suffering and death. They're not sure there's anything to be gained in waiting forty days for Easter to come. Some will frankly admit that they much prefer worship they consider "inspiring" or "uplifting" — meaning by those words, worship that is set in a major (as opposed to a minor) key.

Yet there are considerable rewards to keeping Lent in the traditional way. In the larger context of the Christian year, it is hard to imagine a meaningful Easter celebration for people who have not first been to the cross. Lent is an important time of preparation. Also, for those who are experiencing the darker side of life — due to illness, bereavement, depression, or any of life's periodic reversals — a frank acknowledgment of these difficult times can be an important step on the road to healing.

Ash Wednesday
March 1, 2006

Revised Common	Joel 2:1-2, 12-17	2 Corinthians 5:20b—6:10	Matthew 6:1-6, 16-21
Roman Catholic	Joel 2:12-18	2 Corinthians 5:20—6:2	Matthew 6:1-6, 16-18
Episcopal	Joel 2:1-2, 12-17	2 Corinthians 5:20b—6:10	Matthew 6:1-6, 16-21

Theme For The Day   Return to the Lord!

Old Testament Lesson   Joel 2:1-2, 12-17   *Return To The Lord With All Your Heart*

This passage begins with a shout, "blow the trumpet in Zion" — the same signal typically used to warn of an enemy attack. Here, however, the invader is not so easily defended against: it is an invading army of locusts (1:4). Joel calls the people to repentance: "... return to me with all your heart," says the Lord, "with fasting, with weeping, and with mourning; rend your hearts and not your clothing" (v. 12). Who can fend off an army of locusts? Who, for that matter, can fend off sin? The Lord is the only refuge.

Alternate Old Testament Lesson   Isaiah 58:1-12   *A Fast Truly Pleasing To God*

Isaiah criticizes those in Israel who go through the motions of fasting, but who have not truly changed their behavior. "Is such the fast that I choose.... Is it to bow down the head like a bulrush, and to lie in sackcloth and ashes?" (v. 5). No, God is looking for a different sort of fasting: "Is not this the fast that I choose: to loose the bonds of injustice...?" (v. 6a). What God cares about most is not the outward veneer of religious practice, but rather the transformation of the heart. God welcomes not so much words of penitence, as deeds of justice.

New Testament Lesson   2 Corinthians 5:20b—6:10   *Now Is The Acceptable Time*

Advising against judging others "from a human point of view," Paul has just observed that "anyone who is in Christ is a new creation" (5:17). We who have received this good news have been given "the ministry of reconciliation" (v. 18), by which we are "ambassadors for Christ, since God is making his appeal through us ... " (v. 20). Quoting Isaiah 49:8, about the "acceptable time" and "the day of salvation" in which the Lord heard the people's pleas, Paul says, "See, now is the acceptable time; see, now is the day of salvation!" (6:2). The lectionary editors have undoubtedly included this passage because "now is the acceptable time" can serve as a call to renewal of spiritual discipline. Also, in the latter part of this passage, Paul speaks of his triumphs over adversity.

The Gospel   Matthew 6:1-6, 16-21   *Spiritual Practices That Are Not Ostentatious*

Here is pastoral advice from Jesus that is particularly timely for those who will soon undertake intentional spiritual disciplines: "Beware of practicing your piety before others in order to be seen by them; for then you have no reward from your Father in heaven" (v. 1). Do not pray in an ostentatious public way, Jesus advises, but go into a room and pray in private. Then, as an example of how to pray, Jesus teaches his disciples the text we have come to know as the Lord's Prayer. Finally, there is his advice for those who are fasting: try not to look "dismal, like the hypocrites" (v. 16).

Preaching Possibilities

Joel calls the people to repentance "with fasting, with weeping, and with mourning." What's all that about, Joel? You oughta lighten up! (That's one reaction many of us may have to what seems to be a blanket indictment of the human race.)

But Joel's right. It is said that there was once a wise old rabbi, who carried in his pocket two stones. One stone had written on it, "For me the world was created." The other said, "I am dust and ashes." The rabbi carried those two stones as a constant reminder that he lived his life within a certain tension. His life contained two contradictory aspects: an aspect of celebration, and an aspect of penitence.

Most of us in twentieth-century America much prefer celebration. It's no mystery why. To reach into our pocket and pull out the stone that says "for me the world was created" is to revel in God's love, in the simple, joyous exuberance of living. It's optimistic, upbeat, "can-do," affirming. The stone that says "I am dust and ashes" is a very different matter. It appears gloomy, morose, life negating.

"Dust and ashes" is the dominant theme of Lent. Whether we follow the worship tradition of literally placing ashes on our foreheads or whether we don't, the theme of Ash Wednesday worship is still the same. In the old days, back when every house contained a fire for cooking and warmth, ashes were a part of everyday life. (Those of especially long memory among us may recall what it was like to carry the ashes from the coal or wood stove outside each morning, and deposit them in the "ash can.") In biblical times, whenever tragedy intruded — in the form of death or some horrible deed that called for extreme repentance — those in the household knew what to do. They reached into the leftover ashes and smeared their faces with them, a sign to all the world of inconsolable grief.

The church picked this custom up from ancient Israel, and from a very early date used ashes as a symbol of penitence, especially during Lent. Yet, this whole idea doesn't sit so well with us modern folk. This is, after all, the era of self-help, of self-improvement, of shedding our negative emotions and realizing our fullest potential. The whole concept of sin seems, to many, a curious anachronism. All we have to do to achieve true happiness (our culture insists) is to eat healthy, think positive thoughts, avoid hurting anyone else, and follow our dream.

Yet — as the two stones of the old rabbi insistently remind us — that's only the half of it. If we go around proclaiming all the time, "For me the world was created," our lives will quickly degenerate into shallow self-centeredness. When we hurt those around us — and it's inevitable that we will, despite our best intentions — we will then have no way to deal with that experience, no framework in which to place it. In short, we will end up living a lie, spinning for ourselves sugary self-affirming fantasies that have no more capacity to nourish the soul than cotton candy. It is better, by far, to carry two stones than one — even if one of them bears the "dust and ashes" message.

Prayer For The Day

O God of our salvation,
we come before you
on this beginning of the season of repentance and reflection,
of turning and returning.
May we always trust in your mercy,
seek the reign of Christ in our lives
and rely upon the Spirit's power.

Through Jesus Christ,
who is the path homeward to you.
Amen.

To Illustrate

T. S. Eliot once said that repentance is getting on the right track, not just slowing down on the wrong track.

***

There is a choice before us during Lent, and the theologian Karl Barth put it very bluntly, with respect to our attitude toward our own sin: each of us can choose, he said, to be either a sick person taking medicine, or a well person taking poison.

***

This story was told by Rabbi Shelton Donnell of the Wilshire Boulevard Temple, in Los Angeles:

It is Yom Kippur, the Day of Atonement, and the rabbi is waxing eloquent before his congregation about the importance of true penitence. At the climax of his sermon, he raises his arms before the Ark of the Covenant, cries out, "O Lord, I am nothing, I am nothing!" and throws himself face down onto the floor.

The cantor's looking on, rather surprised. He figures he'd better follow the rabbi's example, so he too cries out, "O Lord, I am nothing, I am nothing!" and throws himself down beside the rabbi.

Now this creates an awkward moment for the president of the congregation. He doesn't know what he should do, but then he decides, "Oh, why not?" and so he laments, "O Lord, I am nothing, I am nothing!" and joins the others on the floor.

At this point, a little man who hardly ever goes to temple, sitting way up in the balcony, is so caught up in the spirit of the occasion that he also stands up, and cries out, "O Lord, I am nothing, I am nothing!" and throws himself onto the floor.

The president of the congregation recognizes the man's voice. He leans over to the cantor and whispers, "Just look who thinks he's nothing!"

***

Community requires the confession of brokenness. But how remarkable it is that in our culture brokenness must be "confessed." We think of confession as an act that should be carried out in secret, in the darkness of the confessional, with the guarantee of professional, priestly, or psychiatric confidentiality. Yet, the reality is that every human being is broken and vulnerable. How strange that we should ordinarily feel compelled to hide our wounds when we are all wounded! Community requires the ability to expose our wounds and weaknesses to our fellow creatures. It also requires the ability to be affected by the wounds of others. But even more important is the *love* that arises among us when we share, both ways, our woundedness.

— M. Scott Peck, *The Different Drum* (New York: Simon & Schuster, 1997)

***

77

I would rather be ashes than dust; I would rather that my spark should burn out in a brilliant blaze than it should be stifled by dry-rot; I would rather be in a superb meteor, every atom of me in magnificent glow than in a sleepy and permanent planet; the proper function of man is to live, not to exist; I shall not waste my days in trying to prolong them; I shall *use* my time.

— Jack London

***

Repentance is not a fruit problem; it is a root problem. It is the root of who we are that is a problem in God's eyes. So repentance cannot be composed of "I can" statements. "I have sinned God. I am sorry God. I can do better." Repentance, rather, must be composed of "I can't" statements. "I have sinned, God. I am sorry, God. I've tried and tried and tried but I just don't produce good fruit. I can't seem to do better. I need your vinedresser to work on the roots of my life. Give me a new life, God. Give me your life. I can't. You can."

— Richard Jensen, *Preaching Luke's Gospel* (Lima, Ohio: CSS Publishing, 1997), p. 147

***

We must first peer into the darkness, feel strangled and entombed in the hopelessness of living without God, before we are ready to feel the presence of his living light. The essence of Jewish religious thinking does not lie in entertaining a concept of God but in the ability to articulate a memory of moments of illumination by his presence.

Our quest for God is a return to God; our thinking of him is a recall, an attempt to draw out the depth of our suppressed attachment. The Hebrew word for repentance, *teshuvah*, means return. Yet it also means answer. Return to God is an answer to him, for God is not silent. The stirring in man to return to God is actually a "reminder by God to man." It is a call that man's physical sense does not capture, yet the "spiritual soul" in him perceives the call. God's grace resounds in our lives like a staccato. Only by retaining the seemingly disconnected notes do we acquire the ability to grasp the theme.

It is within man's power to seek him; it is not within his power to find him. God concludes what we commence.

— Abraham Joseph Heschel, *Between God and Man* (New York: Harper & Row, 1959)

First Sunday In Lent
March 5, 2006

Revised Common	**Genesis 9:8-17**	**1 Peter 3:18-22**	**Mark 1:9-15**
Roman Catholic	**Genesis 9:8-15**	**1 Peter 3:18-22**	**Mark 1:12-15**
Episcopal	**Genesis 9:8-17**	**1 Peter 3:18-22**	**Mark 1:9-13**

Theme For The Day   Let us rejoice in the covenant God makes with us, by sheer grace, beyond our deserving!

Old Testament Lesson   Genesis 9:8-17   *The Bow In The Clouds*

"I establish my covenant with you," says the Lord to Noah, "that never again shall all flesh be cut off by the waters of a flood ..." (v. 11). Then the Lord gives Noah the rainbow sign: an emblem of a new covenant of peace. Because of the quaint image of animals walking two by two, we often relegate this story to the world of children's tales, but in fact it is an example of what biblical scholar Phyllis Trible calls a "text of terror." The Almighty, here, is fierce and dangerous. The gently curving rainbow is quite literally, God's bow, God's weapon (v. 16). To the ancient Hebrew people, it is only God's covenant that saves them from destruction, that prevents the Lord from taking down the celestial bow, stringing it once again and wreaking havoc with creation.

New Testament Lesson   1 Peter 3:18-22   *Preaching To The Dead*

Many people are baffled by the phrase in the Apostles' Creed, "he descended into hell." This passage is the biblical basis for it: "He was put to death in the flesh, but made alive in the spirit, in which also he went and made a proclamation to the spirits in prison ..." (vv. 18b-19). There is further elaboration in 4:6: "For this is the reason the gospel was proclaimed even to the dead, so that, though they had been judged in the flesh as everyone is judged, they might live in the spirit as God does." Matthew 27:52-53 describes how, at the moment of Jesus' death, many of the righteous are raised from their graves. Ephesians 4:8-9 may also refer to this early Christian belief. Medieval Christian art frequently portrays this theme in the form of "the harrowing of hell," an iconic image in which the risen Christ triumphantly tramples down the gates of hell, allowing the righteous whose lives predated Jesus' earthly life to walk right past their demonic jailers to freedom. The modern pastoral message in this text is akin to that of Romans 8:38: "... neither death, nor life, nor angels, nor rulers, nor things present, nor things to come, nor powers, nor height, nor depth, nor anything else in all creation, will be able to separate us from the love of God in Christ Jesus our Lord."

The Gospel   Mark 1:9-15   *Baptism, Temptation, Proclamation*

For a third time, the lectionary returns us to Mark's account of the baptism of Jesus (see Advent 2, p. 14, and The Baptism Of Our Lord, p. 37). Today's selection continues further, however, to include Mark's sparse account of Jesus' temptation in the wilderness — a traditional way to open the season of Lent — and on from there to describe, in equally laconic terms, the beginning of his preaching ministry (we've also seen this passage previously, on the Third Sunday After The Epiphany, p. 46). These three brief pericopes present preaching challenges precisely because they are so brief. Mark provides very little narrative detail on which to hang a sermon. It may be worthwhile to reflect on all three at once, examining what Jesus has to go through before he is prepared to share the gospel. First, he must be baptized — publicly acknowledging who his Lord is. Then, through his wilderness temptation experience, he must learn to rely utterly on God for survival — realizing who his Savior is. The basic Christian confession of faith is that Christ is both Lord and Savior. Having these three brief passages displayed in sequence reminds us that Jesus' spiritual journey here on earth was similar to our own.

Preaching Possibilities

"I have set my bow in the clouds," declares the Lord to Noah, "and it shall be a sign of the covenant between me and the earth." The bow God places in the clouds is not so much a colorful decoration, as a weapon. The Hebrew word for "bow," used here and in other, more martial settings, is exactly the same.

Most of us find this image of God with a bow and arrows difficult to accept. It's far more comforting to imagine the Lord as a talented celestial artist, paintbrush in hand, festooning the heavens with all the colors of the rainbow. It's jarring, to say the least, to picture God as a sweaty, musclebound warrior, weary from battle, unslinging the bow from across his shoulders and hanging it high.

Yet that's precisely the image of God enshrined in this Hebrew text. We've simply forgotten what it means — so familiar have we become with all those sweet nursery school paintings of Noah in his ark, rejoicing that the storm clouds have passed. How easily we forget that it's God who sent the storm clouds in the first place — who savagely unleashed the flood waters, obliterating nearly all of creation.

The first thing the bow in the sky tells us is that God is dangerous. "Our God is an awesome God," church youth group members proclaim — but this doesn't mean "awesome" as in "really cool," the way most people use the word today. It means "inspiring fear." It's not popular, these days, to think of God as dangerous. God has become, for many, a friend, a buddy, a congenial traveling companion. *God is My Co-Pilot* was the title of a book, written by a WWII Army pilot. He found it comforting, as he flew into mortal peril over China, to imagine the Lord of heaven and earth sitting in the seat beside him. Soldiers in wartime are entitled to take comfort wherever they can find it — but from the standpoint of Noah, that book title seems just a trifle presumptuous. The God who places the bow in the clouds is not anybody's co-anything!

The second thing we can observe about the God who hangs the bow in the clouds is that this all-powerful God wants to be in relationship with the human race. The particular relationship God establishes with Noah is the covenant. There are many types of covenants in the Bible. The covenant with Moses, for example, takes the form of what the scholars call a suzerainty agreement; it's laid out according to the same format as the treaty a conquering emperor would impose upon a newly defeated king. There's an element of negotiation to it: "I'll do something for you, and you do something for me in return."

This covenant with Noah is different. It's what biblical scholars refer to as a "royal grant." In a royal grant covenant, a king rewards a loyal subject by granting an office, or land, or an exemption from taxes. In a royal grant covenant, it's only the superior party who is bound by its terms. There are no conditions imposed upon the inferior party. The covenants God makes with Noah, Abraham, and David all fit this pattern. In each of these cases, it is God alone who chooses to make covenant, to be bound by a solemn oath.

Why does the Lord do it? Out of love. There's no other explanation. There's no one on earth who could disarm this fearsome and mighty warrior; yet the warrior voluntarily chooses to hang up the bow, resolving to practice war no more.

There's another example of this kind of covenant in the Bible — a covenant leading to a deeper relationship. It happens in the New Testament, at the Last Supper. "This cup is the new covenant in my blood," Jesus proclaims. "Do this, as often as you drink it, in remembrance of me." Here, God's covenant with Noah enters a new, and even surprising, phase. The Son of God, Jesus Christ, goes far beyond merely laying aside his weapons: he delivers himself up to be crucified, for the sins of the world. He buys a new relationship with humanity at the price of his own blood.

Prayer For The Day

When we are sad and despairing, O God ... show us the rainbow.

When we are racked with doubt ... show us the rainbow.

When we fear we are all alone ... show us the rainbow.

When we find ourselves believing sin has won its final victory over us ... show us the rainbow.

In the name of Christ, who by his cross brings us redemption. Amen.

To Illustrate

In C. S. Lewis' much loved children's fantasy novels, *The Chronicles of Narnia*, the figure who's symbolic of Jesus Christ is the fierce lion, Aslan. The two girls, Susan and Lucy, are getting ready to meet Aslan for the first time. They admit to Mrs. Beaver, who's preparing them for the encounter, that they're feeling a bit anxious. "Is he quite safe?" asks Susan. "I shall feel rather nervous about meeting a lion."

"That you will, dearie," replies Mrs. Beaver. "And make no mistake, if there's anyone who can appear before Aslan without his knees knocking, he's either braver than most or else just silly."

"Then isn't he safe?" asks Lucy.

"Safe," said Mr. Beaver, "don't you hear what Mrs. Beaver tells you? Who said anything about safe? Of course, he isn't safe, but he's good. He's the king, I tell you!"

***

A rainbow itself is made of tiny droplets of water, suspended in the air. The sun shines through these drops of water, and its light is refracted, as through a prism. It is this refraction, this splitting up, of white light that creates the rainbow's bands of color.

In a certain sense, therefore, the rainbow is made up of the storm itself. The water that once cascaded down upon the earth, sweeping everything before it, has now become a sign of grace. The dread reality that once called forth only terror is transformed into something beautiful.

We can see a similar thing in certain churches and shrines that are renowned as places of healing. Displayed on the walls of such places are items like canes and crutches: cast aside by confident people who believed God had healed them. A cane or a crutch is not often a symbol of hope; rather, it is a mark of sadness, a reminder of human limitations and the frailty of the flesh. Yet, when hung upon the wall of a church where people come for healing, that very thing is transformed into a symbol of hope: and all by the power of God.

The same is true of relics of the Berlin Wall. Before the collapse of Communism, the Wall had been the very icon of political oppression, a symbol of despair before the stifling power of the totalitarian state. Yet, after that giddy night in 1990, when demonstrators, realizing the guards had departed, hoisted themselves upon it, smashing it with sledgehammers — the wall was transformed into a symbol of freedom. The Germans broke it into tiny pieces, and sent the pieces all over the world, so freedom-loving people everywhere could rejoice in their new, hopeful reality.

The same may be said of another symbol, even better known to us than the rainbow, or any other image. It's the symbol that occupies the central place in our sanctuary: the cross.

***

The journalist, Bill Moyers, produced a television series for PBS several years ago, called *Genesis: A Living Conversation.* On one of the shows he asked the guests on his panel what kind of headline each one would write to describe the Noah story. A newspaper editor responded with something predictable, like "God Destroys World." One of the other panel members was the Reverend Dr. Samuel Proctor, for many years pastor of the great old Abyssinian Baptist Church, the leading African-American church in Harlem. Proctor suggested an alternative headline: "God Gives Humans Second Chance."

Proctor then went on to share something of how he had learned the Noah story: from his father, a Sunday school teacher. "Sometimes we laughed at the ridiculous aspects of it," he said, with a smile, "[but] we didn't try to rewrite it. We drew from it what it said right then to the people and went on. Every Wednesday, though, my daddy would press his trousers and go down to the Philharmonic Glee Club rehearsal. These sixty black guys — table waiters, coal trimmers, truck drivers — would give one big concert a year to the white population. [We] couldn't sit where we wanted to, even though our daddy was singing — we had to sit in the back. But in the midst of all that rejection, hate, and spite, they went. And do you know the song they sang at the close of the concert? They sang, 'Yesterday the skies were gray / but look this morning they are blue / The smiling sun tells everyone come / Let's all sing, hallelujah / for a new day is born / The world is singing the song of the dawn.' Noah! Sixty black guys in tuxedos in the 1920s, with lynching everywhere and hatred — 'n____' this and 'n____' that. But they had something we need to recover right now. I can't turn loose this story of Noah and the flood because after all of the devastation ... there's a rainbow ... I'm not going to live without that kind of hope."

Second Sunday In Lent
March 12, 2006

Revised Common	Genesis 17:1-7, 15-16	Romans 4:13-25	Mark 8:31-38
Roman Catholic	Genesis 22:1-2, 9-13, 15-18	Romans 8:31-34	Mark 8:31-34
Episcopal	Genesis 22:1-14	Romans 8:31-39	Mark 8:31-38

Theme For The Day   Jesus' call to cross bearing is a call to redemptive suffering.

Old Testament Lesson   Genesis 17:1-7, 15-16   *A Laughing Matter*

At the age of 99, Abram receives from the Lord an impossible-sounding promise: that he will become "the ancestor of a multitude of nations" (v. 4). As a mark of this new covenant, the Lord directs Abram to change his name to Abraham (v. 5). More than that, the Lord will give Abram a son by his aged wife, Sarai (v. 16). The lectionary editors end their selection before Genesis gets around to describing Abram's reaction. He "fell on his face and laughed" — probably in disbelief (v. 17). But God gets the last laugh. Later we will learn that Abraham's laughter provides the etymology for his son, Isaac's, name ("Isaac" means "son of laughter" — see 21:6). For more on types of divine covenant, see "Preaching Possibilities" for the First Sunday In Lent, page 80.

New Testament Lesson   Romans 4:13-25   *It All Depends On Faith*

One of the theological problems the early church struggled with was how the Old Testament patriarchs fit into salvation history. Paul provides an answer: "For the promise that he would inherit the world did not come to Abraham or to his descendants through the law but through the righteousness of faith" (v. 13). "It depends on faith" (v. 16). Now some may think Paul's saying here that God has established a special, second-class procedure reserved for certain virtuous patriarchs and matriarchs — a sort of general equivalency diploma (G.E.D.) for those unable to graduate in the proper way — but in fact, he's saying that their way of salvation is no different than that relied upon by every Christian: "... the words, 'it was reckoned to him,' were written not for his sake alone, but for ours, also. It will be reckoned to us who believe in him who raised Jesus our Lord from the dead, who was handed over to death for our trespasses and was raised for our justification" (vv. 23-25).

The Gospel   Mark 8:31-38   *A Growing Resolve*

We have already referred to this passage as an antecedent to the Gospel Lesson for The Transfiguration Of Our Lord (see p. 70). Just after Peter makes his famous confession of faith, identifying Jesus as the Messiah (v. 29), Jesus gets serious about what, realistically speaking, lies ahead for him and his disciples. The Son of Man, he tells them, must be rejected, killed, and after three days raised. Peter "rebukes" Jesus for saying this, to which Jesus responds, "Get behind me, Satan!" (in other words, he tells his friend, "Get out of my sight!" because what Peter is saying is a fearsome temptation to him — v. 33). It is then that Jesus says, to all present: "If any want to become my followers, let them deny themselves and take up their cross and follow me" (v. 34). Those who follow him in this way may in fact lose their lives, but they will gain life eternal (v. 35). Although it is by no means certain that the phrase "Son of Man" always refers to Jesus in Mark's Gospel, it is clear that Peter takes the expression here to refer to his master.

Alternate Gospel Lesson   Mark 9:2-9   *The Transfiguration*

Primarily for those who have not observed The Transfiguration Of Our Lord two Sundays earlier, the lectionary provides that story here as an alternate. (See notes on this passage for The Transfiguration Of Our Lord, p. 70.)

Preaching Possibilities

Jesus' words seem challenging, even confrontational: "If any want to become my followers, let them deny themselves and take up their cross and follow me" (Mark 8:34b). Many of us feel inclined to respond to those words just as Peter has responded to Jesus' prediction about the Son of Man's suffering and death: to "rebuke" Jesus for them. They seem so harsh.

Yet, there are some in the human community — even some in our congregations — for whom they do not seem harsh at all. These are the people who know suffering. This message is especially for them.

We all wish life could be free of suffering — but the truth is, it's a rare life indeed that knows nothing of heartache. "Human beings are born to trouble, just as the sparks fly upward," says Job 5:7.

What is there that human wisdom can offer, as an explanation for suffering? That it builds character? Perhaps — but then, there are some who seem to be allotted far more "character-building" experiences than others. That suffering is God's judgment upon evildoers? Perhaps — but then, none of us have to look far to see that, as Jesus puts it in Matthew 5:45, God "sends rain on the righteous and on the unrighteous."

As with many difficult sayings of the Bible, with this one it helps to look at the context. Not long before Jesus utters these words, he has asked his disciples, "Who do people say that I am?" and Peter has replied, "You are the Messiah." Then Jesus goes on to unfold to these, his closest friends, what he foresees happening to "the Son of Man" in Jerusalem: suffering, rejection, death — and, after three days, a glorious rising. All this is simply too much for Peter to handle in one day. He has taken the supreme risk of identifying Jesus as Messiah: yet how can it be that the Messiah will suffer such things? How can it be that the Messiah will enter Jerusalem in triumph, only to die?

"Get behind me, Satan!" is Jesus' tight-lipped response. He will not be deterred from doing what he must do. If Peter, his closest friend, will not accompany him, he will go alone. It is only after these curt exchanges that Jesus gathers the whole body of his disciples together, as well as the perpetual crowd of hangers-on, and puts to them his hard teaching about cross bearing. He wants his disciples to have no illusions about what lies ahead in Jerusalem, the fate that is in store for any who will follow him. The way of discipleship leads, inevitably, to a cross. In the words of Dietrich Bonhoeffer (who himself perished for the faith at the hands of the Nazis), "When Christ calls a person, he bids that one to come and die."

It is necessary to interject, here, that there are some forms of suffering, some crosses, that ought never to be borne by anyone. Domestic violence is an example. Some have tried to twist Jesus' words to justify a battered woman's remaining in an abusive relationship, even at the risk of her life. "It's just the cross you have to bear," clucks the well-meaning friend, applying ointment to the bruises.

Similar words have been spoken, over the years, to members of racial minorities who have been victimized by discrimination. There are true crosses and there are false crosses — crosses that lead to the center, to Christ, and crosses that lead only to loneliness and desolation. Christ's call to carry the cross never requires that we abandon our sense of justice.

The response of Christianity to the problem of human suffering is that even pain can have a place in God's plan. Not every incident of human suffering is an example of cross bearing, of course. Yet, there is some suffering that can — if it is embraced as an act of faith, and particularly if it witnesses to justice or serves neighbors — actually be redemptive. The process of living through suffering, of taking up "the cross we have to bear" can, amazingly, lead to new life.

This is a startling, even original, teaching. There are other religions that portray suffering as a path to spiritual development: as in the Hindu yogi on a bed of nails, for example, or the Buddhist sage aspiring, through meditation, to the state of no-mind — but these are, ultimately, paths *around* suffering. In the eastern religions, suffering is seen most often as a spiritual obstacle: something to be overcome on the way to true enlightenment. It has no real existence, in and of itself; in the great scheme of things, suffering is illusion.

That is not the view of Christianity. We are the faith that boldly hangs the image of an instrument of capital punishment in our worship places, and even around our necks — proclaiming to all the world that there is no experience in human life which God's love does not have the power to transform. Our spiritual tradition charts a course not around suffering, but *through* it.

Prayer For The Day
Lord Jesus, we do not wish to bear a cross. We pray that you would keep pain from us. Yet, if it is your will that suffering should come our way, we ask that — by the power of your Spirit — we may discover your powerful presence beside us. We know you do not promise to lift all our burdens; but you do promise to help us bear them. Amen.

To Illustrate
The world breaks all of us, and some of us become strong at the broken places.

— Ernest Hemingway

***

The medieval spiritual writer, Thomas à Kempis, once said a very profound thing about cross-bearing: "If you bear the cross gladly, it will bear you."

— *The Imitation of Christ*

***

A journey not around suffering, but through it, is described by Ernest Gordon, formerly chaplain of Princeton University. Gordon, who served as a young British officer in the Second World War, wrote of his experiences as a POW in a Japanese prison camp in his wartime memoir, *Through the Valley of the Kwai* (New York: Harper, 1962; this is the same slave-labor camp that was dramatized in the classic Alec Guinness film, *Bridge Over the River Kwai*). It was in the camp that Gordon met a soldier nicknamed "Dodger." Dodger suffered from serious stomach ulcers — a condition that caused him almost unbearable pain. More than that, he suffered from a despair so black that his fellow prisoners feared it would kill him before the ulcers would.

But then Dodger came to trust Jesus Christ in a special way. He became a Christian, there in the camp: and one of the first things he did was to look around for a way he could be of service.

"The filthiest job in camp," says Gordon, was collecting the rags the prisoners used as bandages, to cover the sores on their arms and legs. The rags had to be collected, scraped clean of infection, then boiled, before being returned so others could use them. "A smelly, unpleasant job it was, but Dodger volunteered for it. Regularly I would see him going from hut to hut, carrying his can of rags, and whistling as he walked."

Who but a Christian would whistle as he carried a cross?

***

Viktor Frankl, the well-known psychologist who wrote of survival in the Nazi death camps, also knew some people like that: "We who lived in the concentration camps can remember the men who walked through the huts comforting others, giving away their last piece of bread. They may have been few in number, but they offer sufficient proof that everything can be taken from human beings but one thing: The last of their freedoms — to choose one's attitude in any set of circumstances, to choose one's own way."

— Viktor Frankl, *Man's Search For Meaning* (Boston: Beacon Press, 1963)

***

Give up your self, and you will find your real self. Lose your life and you will save it. Submit to death, death of your ambitions and favorite wishes every day, and death of your whole body in the end: submit with every fibre of your being, and you will find eternal life. Keep back nothing. Nothing that you have not given away will ever really be yours. Nothing in you that has not died will ever be raised from the dead. Look for yourself, and you will find in the long run only hatred, loneliness, despair, rage, ruin, and decay. But look for Christ and you will find him, and with him everything else thrown in.

— C. S. Lewis, *Mere Christianity*

***

Walk in faith and love. If the cross comes, accept it. If it does not come, do not search for it.

— Martin Luther

Third Sunday In Lent
March 19, 2006

Revised Common	Exodus 20:1-17	1 Corinthians 1:18-25	John 2:13-22
Roman Catholic	Exodus 20:1-17	1 Corinthians 1:22-25	John 2:13-25
Episcopal	Exodus 20:1-17	Romans 7:13-25	John 2:13-22

Theme For The Day   As the commandments tell us, and as Jesus' cleansing of the temple shows us, we need to be ever-vigilant in keeping ourselves from idolatry and injustice.

Old Testament Lesson   Exodus 20:1-17   *The Ten Commandments*

God speaks the Ten Commandments to Moses. An alternate version is found in Deuteronomy 5:1-22.

New Testament Lesson   1 Corinthians 1:18-25   *The Foolishness Of The Cross*

The Corinthian church is divided into factions, each one declaring allegiance to a specific teacher. Each faction is claiming their own teacher to be wiser than the others. Paul observes that, far from seeming to be wisdom, the message of the cross is "foolishness to those who are perishing, but to us who are being saved it is the power of God" (v. 18). God, he promises (alluding to Isaiah 29:14), "will destroy the wisdom of the wise." "Why are you people fighting over wisdom?" Paul is asking, in effect. "There's nothing 'wise' about our proclamation of Jesus Christ, the son of God crucified. To the world, we are the people who preach utter foolishness!"

The Gospel   John 2:13-22   *Cleansing The Temple*

At Passover time, Jesus enters the temple precincts, where the officially sanctioned concessionaires are changing money from Roman into Jewish currency, and selling animals for the temple sacrifices. Making for himself a whip of cords, he drives these merchants from the temple area. When challenged to say by what authority he does this, Jesus responds with the cryptic comment, "Destroy this temple, and in three days I will raise it up" (v. 19). John explains that by this Jesus is referring not to the temple, but to his own body (although no one understood this at the time).

Preaching Possibilities

Jesus' cleansing of the temple is a difficult passage for many modern readers. Some have trouble with Jesus' evident anger; their image of the Savior is of a more even-tempered, placid personality. Others see his action as a sort of civil disobedience, a demonstration: a tactic they consider ethically questionable. To John, however, Jesus' rampage through the temple is no fit of pique. It is righteous anger. It's the sort of emotion true prophets are supposed to feel, when confronted with injustice. Some prior knowledge about the temple system is necessary to understand why.

The temple of Jesus' day is riddled with injustice. Pilgrims — diaspora Jews — come here from around the Roman world. Some of them have saved for years to make the journey. When these travelers arrive at the temple, they must pay a temple tax — and this is no minor admission charge. Biblical scholar, William Barclay, reckons the tax to have been about two days' wages for a laborer.

The problem is not so much the high amount, but that many of the pilgrims' money is no good. Most of them carry either Roman *denarii* or Greek *drachmas*: coins with emperors and gods engraved upon them — but the temple authorities will accept only the coins of Israel, that do not display potentially idolatrous images. That's where the moneychangers come in. With so many pilgrims arriving from so many places, there's quite a market in currency speculation. The moneychangers have a monopoly, so their commissions are impossibly high (Barclay estimates as high as fifty percent).

There's one other thing religious pilgrims to Jerusalem need, besides Judean currency to pay the temple tax. They need an animal to sacrifice. Well, those thoughtful temple merchants have remembered that, too. Located conveniently nearby, in the court of the Gentiles, are live-animal stalls. The prices are several times higher than the market stalls in town, but these are special animals. The merchants guarantee them to be clean and without blemish, just as the law requires.

If any pilgrims should happen to bring animals in from outside, they must first stop at the booth of one of the temple inspectors, who will look the beast over for defects. The inspectors are meticulous in their examination of any animal not purchased from one of the official dealers. It's a rare day indeed when one of those animals passes inspection.

But that's not the end of it: all this commercial activity is taking place in the court of the Gentiles. That's the name given to the outer courtyard of the temple, the only place where non-Jews are permitted to enter. The court of the Gentiles is the only place of worship for Gentile adherents of Judaism, seekers after Israel's God who were not born into the faith, and who have not yet converted into it through circumcision. The atmosphere in the court of the Gentiles, filled with the raucous shouts of the moneychangers and the lowing of the livestock, is hardly conducive to worship.

It is a monstrous, unfair system, designed for the benefit of a favored few who profit at the expense of the faithful. No wonder Jesus gets angry. Contrary to the claims of some commentators, he's not upset because of the close proximity of commercial activity to a place of worship, as though money itself were evil. It's a matter of injustice.

The Bible has a word for this sort of thing: idolatry. The first commandment (from today's Old Testament Lesson) is, "You shall have no other gods before me." That's what Jesus is really saying as he pushes over the moneychangers' tables: "No other gods!" The second commandment says, "You shall not make for yourself an idol." Jesus knows that, for the moneychangers, the only object of worship is the coins in their purses. Money is not evil or dirty in itself, in Jesus' eyes. It's part of God's creation, and like all creation it can be redeemed for God's purposes. Money is no more evil than the wood or stone used to construct an idol — but if money is the vehicle used to exploit those who have come to worship God, then it has indeed become an idol.

Prayer For The Day

Bring us, O Lord, from out of the cacophony of this striving world into that place of peace and stillness, that holy of holies, where you dwell in all purity and righteousness. Help us to seek out and cast down every idol that threatens to block our path to you. Bring us through this Lent to the simple beauty of the empty tomb, to the place where we are able to worship your son, Jesus, in spirit and in truth. Amen.

To Illustrate

Idolatry is worshiping anything that ought to be used, or using anything that ought to be worshiped.

— Anonymous

***

Echoing the World War II era, a company called Innovative Marketing Alliance is publishing the God's Armor New Testament, a bulletproof pocket-sized Bible for loved ones who are at risk. "While its fundamental function is to provide the spiritual assurance that comes from carrying God's Word next to the heart, its antiballistic qualities built into the cover provide a reminder of the world we live in." However, the armor is only capable of resisting a .38 caliber bullet.

— Brian Kelcher, "Not So Good News," *The Door*, November-December 1996, p. 41

***

Rising above all the other buildings at the center of the city of Groningen in the Netherlands is the great and the ancient Martini Church. The people began building it in the twelfth century. When we moved to Groningen in 1975, the Martini Church was undergoing a major renovation and had been closed to visitors for about ten years. Friends of ours knew the custodian who lived in a house embedded in one corner of the large church. On a Saturday morning, he gave us a private tour and lecture. Among other things, he explained how the Protestants assumed control of the church in the sixteenth century and whitewashed all the frescoes on the walls and ceiling.

Gazing at the veiled frescoes, I felt in a new way the tension of the Reformation and the intention of the Reformers. They believed that artwork was a dangerous flirtation with idolatry and a possible violation of the ten commandments. Images, graven or otherwise, stirred up strong emotions in the hearts of people and encouraged them to worship the thing created rather than the Creator. The Reformers wanted a white sanctuary so that nothing could distract the worshiper from concentrating on the preaching of the Word of God. They tried to recreate the experience that the people of Israel had had on Mount Horeb. As Moses recalled: "The Lord spoke to you out of the fire. You heard the sound of words but saw no form; there was only a voice" (Deuteronomy 4:12).

The custodian told us that unknown to the Protestants, the whitewash had a chemical in it that leeched into the frescoes and sealed them. Rather than destroying the artwork, the whitewash preserved it for future generations. After the renovators meticulously flaked off the white coating, the frescoes emerged four hundred years later in their original beauty. I remember the custodian telling this story with relish....

— Thomas A. Boogaart, "Preparing the House of God: A Theme in Four Movements," in *Perspectives: A Journal of the Reformed Faith*, November 1999, p. 16

***

The second commandment implies more than the prohibition of images; it implies rejection of all visible symbols for God; not only images fashioned by man but also of "any manner or likeness, of anything that is in heaven above, or that is in the earth beneath, or that is in the water under the earth." And yet there is something in the world that the Bible does regard as a symbol of God. It is not a temple or a tree; it is not a statue or a star. The symbol of God is man, every man. God created man in his image, in his likeness.

— Abraham Joseph Heschel

***

As long as we look for some kind of pay for what we do, as long as we want to get something from God in some kind of exchange, we are like the merchants. If you want to be rid of the commercial spirit, then by all means do all you can in the way of good works, but do so solely for the praise of God. Live as if you did not exist. Expect and ask nothing in return. Then the merchant inside you will be driven out of the temple God has made. Then God alone dwells there. See! This is how the temple is cleared: when a person thinks only of God and honors him alone. Only such a person is free and genuine.

— Meister Eckhart, from *Meister Eckhart: A Modern Translation* (New York: HarperCollins, 1972)

Fourth Sunday In Lent
March 26, 2006

Revised Common	**Numbers 21:4-9**	**Ephesians 2:1-10**	**John 3:14-21**
Roman Catholic	**2 Chronicles 36:14-17, 19-33**	**Ephesians 2:4-10**	**John 3:14-21**
Episcopal	**2 Chronicles 36:14-32**	**Ephesians 2:4-10**	**John 6:4-15**

Theme For The Day We look to the cross of Jesus for salvation.

Old Testament Lesson Numbers 21:4-9 *A Snake On A Pole*

Because the Israelites have been grumbling about Moses' leadership — and have gone even further, complaining about the Lord — the Lord sends poisonous snakes to afflict them. The word "poisonous" literally means "fiery," a vivid description both of God's anger and of the sensory experience of being bitten. When the people come to Moses repenting of their sin, the Lord instructs Moses to make a bronze image of a snake and place it on a high pole. When snakebite victims gaze upon this statue, the Lord says, they will live. Moses does so, and the snakebite problem is solved. 2 Kings 18:4 relates how, centuries later, Moses' bronze serpent (or perhaps a facsimile of it) has become an idolatrous object of worship, which Hezekiah pulls down as part of his reform.

New Testament Lesson Ephesians 2:1-10 *Saved By Grace Through Faith*

This passage, describing the mercy and grace of God in bringing true believers to salvation, includes one of the greatest of all scripture verses for Protestants: "For by grace you have been saved through faith, and this is not your own doing, it is the gift of God — not the result of works, so that no one may boast" (vv. 8-9). This verse became the source of the slogans, *sola gratia, sola fide* ("by grace alone," "by faith alone") that became the theological battle cry of Luther and others. This is God's doing, not the believer's — and it is a free gift. The verb "to boast" is one that occurs frequently in the Pauline tradition. Boasting does not have quite the pejorative connotation of prideful puffery that it has in English (indeed, in other letters, Paul uses it frequently to refer to himself); but it does mean taking credit for what one has achieved, and the author of Ephesians wants to make it absolutely clear that Christians can have nothing to do with earning their own salvation. It is the free gift of God. Verse 10 says that Christians are "created for good works." The good works, here, are a response to grace — not a prerequisite for it.

The Gospel John 3:14-21 *For God So Loved The World ...*

(See The Holy Trinity, p. 152, for a discussion of the larger story of which this passage is a part.) The lectionary abruptly breaks into the conversation between Jesus and the Pharisee Nicodemus at the point where Jesus is using Moses' bronze serpent as an example: "just as Moses lifted up the serpent in the wilderness, so must the Son of Man be lifted up, that whoever believes in him may have eternal life" (v. 14). The thought of the Son of Man (whom John identifies with Jesus) being "lifted up" occurs elsewhere in John (8:28; 12:32). John apparently sees the image of the serpent lifted up on the pole as an allegorical type of the cross and resurrection: just as the Israelites gazed on the bronze serpent and lived, so they gaze at the image of Christ — raised on the cross as well as raised from death — and live. The linkage of the Son of Man with the Numbers passage — and indeed, the very allegorical method of interpretation being applied here — is a bit obscure for modern ears. John 3:16, of course, is one of the most famous verses in the New Testament. It has been called "the gospel in miniature." It is overflowing with preaching possibilities. Like most verses, though, it is best interpreted in context — so it is important, here, to tell the full story of Jesus' encounter with Nicodemus, so worshipers may understand what led Jesus to say this. John may well be using Nicodemus as a composite example of all the learned, pious people of his own day who have investigated faith in Christ, but found it wanting. The fact that they have looked and looked but have never truly seen is a source of some considerable frustration for the evangelist, one he explores through passages such as this one. Verses 19-20 bring up, once again, the great Johannine theme of light versus darkness. Jesus' words here echo those of the Prologue (1:4-5, 9). Some people turn to the light, and others do not. "Those who do what is true come to the light" (v. 21).

Preaching Possibilities

The anthropologists would positively have a field day with Moses' bronze serpent on a stick in Numbers 21:4-9. They'd flip open their notebooks and write it up as a totem, a fetish, a talisman. "Such things are used in primitive cultures," they would surely pontificate, "to ward off plagues and evil spirits. Displaying an image of the thing one most fears unleashes a certain sympathetic magic, that causes its maker to feel protected. Primitive people the world over practice this sort of 'sympathetic magic.' "

It is, admittedly, a bit of a shocker to discover this sort of thing here in the Bible. With all the layers of redaction and editing that went into the composition of the Pentateuch, this little story has survived — and, in fact, its very strangeness suggests that it's an absolutely genuine historical artifact. Nobody could make this sort of thing up. Every once in a while, in the Bible, these wild images of very ancient religious ideas crop up (Jacob wrestling with the angel is one example, as is the account of the clay household gods that Jacob and his wives carry around with them).

This ancient tale would have remained buried deep within the Old Testament, squirreled away like some dusty family heirloom, were it not for the fact that Jesus refers to it. In the third chapter of John's Gospel, in the middle of his famous dialogue with the Pharisee Nicodemus, Jesus trots out the old story of Moses' snake-on-a-stick. From here, Jesus goes on the quote the sublime words of John 3:16, the memory verse beloved both of Sunday school kids and guys in football stadiums holding bedsheets.

So what does Jesus mean when he says, "the Son of Man be lifted up"? Some say he's talking about the cross, some the resurrection, some the ascension. Most likely, it is the cross — because the cross bears the closest physical similarity to what this ancient object must have looked like. When the poor, afflicted snakebite victims gazed upon that magical talisman, they were healed. When you and I look in wonder upon the cross of Jesus Christ, we, too, are touched to the heart.

Just after Jesus speaks of the Son of Man being lifted up like Moses' snake in the wilderness, he adds these words: "that whoever believes in him may have eternal life." The cross of Jesus is not altogether an image of abandonment and despair. For the human race, it is also an image of hope.

Moses raises the bronze serpent in the wilderness so the Israelites may look upon it and live. Maybe God raises Jesus on the cross for all to see, so the people of the world may look on him, and live. If the bronze serpent is a way for ancient people to deal with their fear of snakebites, then maybe the cross of Jesus Christ is the way in which people of every age may deal with their fear of death — and not just death as the cessation of biological life, but eternal death, cosmic oblivion, the black hole of existential despair. In the wilderness, Moses elevates an image of the thing ancient Israel most fears. On Calvary's hill, God raises up an image of the thing you and I most fear — and somehow, gazing upon God's crucified Son, we know that there is no human suffering that is utterly beyond the reach of our Lord's healing and sustaining love.

Yet what of Nicodemus? John leaves us hanging, at the end of chapter 3. Does Nicodemus ever get Jesus' point?

We're not entirely sure, but John does give us two hints. He mentions Nicodemus two other times. The first is when the chief priests and the scribes are plotting against Jesus. Nicodemus stands up in the council and argues for fairness; he insists that due process be followed. Not a ringing endorsement, exactly — but it may reveal a little sympathy.

The real evidence, though, comes near the end of John's Gospel. Jesus has been crucified, and his fearful disciples have scattered to the four winds. No one dares to come forward, at first, to claim the body. But then, two unlikely people show up. The first is a man named Joseph of Arimathea, who offers the loan of his own tomb. And the other? Why, it's Nicodemus, that cautious Pharisee. Nicodemus is the one who goes with Joseph to anoint Jesus' body for burial. He carries on his back 100 pounds of embalming spices — far more than what's needed. In a time when it's extremely risky to confess loyalty to Jesus, it is Nicodemus, that secret visitor in the night, who walks the streets of Jerusalem in broad daylight, carrying on his back a weighty bundle, 100 pounds of pure devotion. Nicodemus has come into the daylight.

Prayer For The Day

The cross has become for us, O God,
a piece of jewelry around the neck,
a logo for the top of the letterhead,
a symbol of pride to set us apart,
dividing us from your other children with whom we share this planet.
In these Lenten days, we ask for vision:
that we may come to see the cross not only as a symbol of who we are,
but also of how deep and abiding is your love for us and all people. Amen.

To Illustrate

An issue of *Newsweek* magazine from the year 2000 contained an insightful article about how other religions of the world view Jesus of Nazareth. While these other religions do not consider Jesus the Son of God, some do esteem and respect him highly — calling him prophet, or teacher, or enlightened one. Yet, as the article points out in its concluding paragraphs, the one thing about Jesus these other religions do not have room for is his cross:

> *Clearly, the cross is what separates the Christ of Christianity from every other Jesus. In Judaism there is no precedent for a Messiah who dies, much less as a criminal as Jesus did. In Islam, the story of Jesus' death is rejected as an affront to Allah himself. Hindus can accept only a Jesus who passes into peaceful* samadhi, *a yogi who escapes the degradation of death. The figure of the crucified Christ, says Buddhist Thich Nhat Hanh, "is a very painful image to me. It does not contain joy or peace, and this does not do justice to Jesus." There is, in short, no room in other religions for a Christ who experiences the full burden of mortal existence — and hence there is no reason to believe in him as the divine Son whom the Father resurrected from the dead.*

***

Homiletician, John R. Brokhoff, tells of seeing a film called *The Bridge*. It narrates the life of a beautiful young couple who have a son. The boy is trying to grow up to be just like his father. "Then the film shows the father going off to his work. He is the switchman for a railroad line that carries people on holiday from one place to another. Part of the line lies over a river, where it must be kept back most of the time for the boats to pass. It is his job to wait until the last moment and then pull the switch that will swing the bridge into place before the thundering approach of the train. We, the viewers of the film, see what the father does not see — his little son has followed him down to the river and is coming across the bridge. As the train whistle blows to signal the approach of the speeding train, the father sees the boy. If he closes the track, the boy will die. We watch the agony on his face. He loves the boy better than anything in his life. But finally he pulls the lever and the bridge locks into place. We see the people on the train laughing and having a good time as the train races across the bridge. They do not know how narrowly they have averted disaster — or what it has cost the switchman."

— *Homiletics* magazine, May 26, 1991

***

There's a wonderful passage in C. S. Lewis' *Chronicles of Narnia* when Aslan, the huge lion who symbolizes Jesus Christ, calls the young girl Lucy over to him. It's been a frightening time, and the young girl cries out ...

"Aslan, Aslan. Dear Aslan — At last." The great beast rolled over on his side so that Lucy fell, half sitting and half lying between his front paws. He bent forward and just touched her nose with his tongue.

His warm breath came all round her. She gazed up into the large wise face.

"Welcome, child," he said.

"Aslan," said Lucy, "you're bigger."

"That's because you are older, little one," answered he.

"Not because you are?"

"I am not. But every year as you grow older, you will find me bigger."

Fifth Sunday In Lent
April 2, 2006

Revised Common	**Jeremiah 31:31-34**	**Hebrews 5:5-10**	**John 12:20-33**
Roman Catholic	**Jeremiah 31:31-34**	**Hebrews 5:7-9**	**John 12:20-30**
Episcopal	**Jeremiah 31:31-34**	**Hebrews 5:(1-4) 5-10**	**John 12:20-30**

Theme For The Day   God promises a new covenant, to welcome the penitent back into relationship.

Old Testament Lesson   Jeremiah 31:31-34   *A New Covenant*

God is making a new covenant with Israel, of a radically new type: "this is the covenant that I will make with the house of Israel after those days, says the Lord: I will put my law within them, and I will write it on their hearts ..." (v. 33). This exalted view of the law has less to do with knowledge of detailed ordinances and more to do with Israel's fundamental attitude toward the law. The accent is on obedience: on the alignment of Israel's hearts with the heart of God, through the ministrations of God's Spirit. It is a relational view of the law: the Lord addresses the "house" of Israel (not the nation of Israel), and describes the former, shattered covenant in familial terms, as "a covenant that they broke, though I was their husband" (v. 32). The language used is not that of violation of specific legal points, but rather of personal betrayal.

New Testament Lesson   Hebrews 5:5-10   *Jesus, The Great High Priest*

Here the author begins to develop further the idea of Jesus as high priest, introduced earlier (2:17; 3:1). Jesus did not volunteer for the position, but was appointed by God. Quoting Psalm 2:7 and Psalm 110:4, the author links Jesus' high priesthood with the high priesthood of ancient Israel. Jesus is "a priest forever, according to the order of Melchizedek" (v. 6, quoting Psalm 110:4). Yet he is more than that, as the quotation from Psalm 2:7 indicates. Jesus is God's Son. The full implications of the priesthood "according to the order of Melchizedek" are developed in chapter 7. The image of the high priest is a rich one, christologically speaking, and is worthy of further sermonic development. It portrays Jesus as the great mediator between God and humanity. In the words of Thomas Long, "The task of a priest is to approach God on behalf of the people, to gather what the people bring — their offerings, their prayers, the symbols of their repentance, their cares, their deepest needs — and to take these offerings into the very presence of God. The priest, therefore, faces in two directions. On behalf of the people, he faces toward God and travels to the holy place with their offerings.... This high priest participates in human suffering; he "sympathizes with our weaknesses" (4:15). Therefore, Jesus does not place ordinary offerings — mere lambs or grains or money — on the heavenly altar; he carries, instead, the human condition to God.... But if the priest faces toward God on behalf of humanity, the priest also faces toward humanity on behalf of God. The priest represents God's holy presence among the people. What does the church see when it looks into the face of its great high priest? It sees in the face of Jesus "the reflection of God's glow" (1:3). It sees a God who stoops down from the holy heights to bear our griefs and carry our sorrows. It sees a God to whom it can pray freely, confident that we will "receive mercy and find grace to help in time of need" (4:16). (*Hebrews*, in the *Interpretation* series [Louisville: John Knox Press, 1997], p. 64)

Some Greeks come to Philip, saying, "Sir, we wish to see Jesus." When Andrew and Philip go to tell Jesus about these visitors, he speaks cryptically of a grain of wheat that must first fall to the ground and die before it is able to bear fruit (v. 24). "Those who love their life lose it, and those who hate their life in this world will keep it for eternal life" (v. 25). He then goes on to speak of his own death. Shall he beg God to save him, he asks? Jesus answers his own question by turning to the heavens and imploring, "Father, glorify your name." Then a voice from the heavens replies, "I have glorified it, and I will glorify it again" (v. 28) — words the bystanders cannot make out, but which sounds to them like thunder. Jesus interprets for them, telling them this thunderous voice is indicating that God's judgment and the defeat of "the ruler of this world" is near. "And I, when I am lifted up from the earth, will draw all people to myself" (v. 32). John's theological commentary is so melded with his narrative that it's hard to conceive of the events taking place exactly as he describes. Yet the message of self-sacrifice for the sake of the gospel — that the way of God is one that often leads to struggle and suffering in this life, contrary to the "gospel of success" message so prevalent in some circles today — is one that always bears repeated emphasis.

Preaching Possibilities

From that day forward, life would never be the same again. In the days after the attack, life seemed to lose some of its luster. Many residents of the city spoke of a loss of innocence that would never return. The smoky haze, rising up from fires still not extinguished, made the sunsets more brilliant; but it also served as an aching reminder of all the people had lost, in that one dreadful day.

It was the day the armies of Nebuchadnezzar, King of Babylon, burst through the gates of Jerusalem, and ended the royal line of David and Solomon. Jehoiachin, the boy king, was soon packed off — along with his mother, all the members of the royal court, and 10,000 captives — to Babylon. None of them would ever see Jerusalem again. The temple, that wonder of Solomon's reign, was burned, as were many of the houses in the city. Nebuchadnezzar set up his own puppet king as a sort of royal governor, and Babylonian administrators moved into every civil-service job of any importance.

For Israel, the covenant people of God — the people whom the Lord had led through the wilderness — this was an ignominious defeat. But more than that, it represented a spiritual crisis. For them it was true: life would never be the same again. Life would never be the same, because it seemed the Lord God had abandoned the chosen people. In time, they would mournfully sing the song of the exiles that eventually became Psalm 137: "How could we sing the Lord's song in a foreign land?"

Jeremiah would show them how. Jeremiah — that grim prophet of doom who had been about the only one sharp enough to warn of what was really happening — abruptly changed his tune, and began preaching comfort. The theological high point of Jeremiah's message of comfort, in the eyes of many, is his promise of the new covenant in chapter 31. It's the promise of a new allegiance to God's Law that will be written on the heart.

When the Hebrew people speak of the heart, they mean something very different than what we do. The heart, to us, is the seat of the emotions. To the Hebrews, it's more than that. The heart is the place where our very personhood is centered: all the things you and I mean by the heart, yes, but also many of the things we mean by the mind and the will. To say that God's Law will be written on the human heart is to predict that, one day, obedience to the law will become second nature to us. We human beings will follow the law, then, not because we fear God: but because we love God.

It's a promise that does not appear to have been fulfilled in the ensuing centuries. The people would continue to be just as disobedient as ever, breaking covenant again and again with the God who remains eternally faithful. But at least the promise was uttered.

It's a promise that would wait hundreds of years to be fulfilled, in the person of Jesus Christ. Jesus, too, speaks of a new covenant, as he pours a cup of wine in the upper room: "This cup that is poured out for you is the new covenant in my blood." The disciples don't understand, at first, what he means. Yet, after his death and resurrection, they will. They will know, then, that even as he carries his cross, he is demonstrating a new way of being human, a new way of being faithful.

God's end of the new covenant has been upheld, in Jesus Christ. The question is: how are we doing on upholding our end?

Prayer For The Day

We thank you, Lord, that you are a God who keeps your promises. From the days of patriarchs and matriarchs, through the times of judges, kings, and prophets, you always kept your word. Then, when it all seemed lost, you gave us your word in a new way: in the form of your Son Jesus, the living word. Keep us ever faithful, we pray, to the way of discipleship he lays out before us. Amen.

To Illustrate

Thornton Wilder, in his play, *The Skin of Our Teeth*, depicts a WWII soldier, George, who returns home to his wife, Maggie. He's been away for years, and the experience has broken him. George announces to Maggie that he's decided to leave her for another woman.

Faced with her husband's moral weakness, Maggie mounts a spirited defense: "I married you," she says, "because you gave me a promise.... That promise made up for your faults. And the promise I gave you made up for mine. Two imperfect people got married, and it was the promise that made our marriage."

To this, George objects that the war has changed him, but Maggie refuses to let it go: "Oh, George," she continues, "you have to get it back again. Think! What else kept us alive all those years? Even now, it's not comfort we want. We can suffer what's necessary; only give us back the promise."

In the play, George and Maggie do reconcile. It's a difficult road, but they find a way to get the promise back.

Jeremiah is also concerned with how to get the promise back: only he's talking not about marriage, but about the relationship between the people, Israel, and their God.

***

Nothing is more surprising than the rise of the new within ourselves. We do not foresee or observe its growth. We do not try to produce it by the strength of our will, by the power of our emotion, or by the clarity of our intellect.... The new being is born in us, just when we least believe in it. It appears in remote corners of our souls which we have neglected for a long time. It opens up deep levels of our personality which had been shut out by old decisions and old exclusions. It shows a way where there was no way before.

— Paul Tillich

***

Covenants have a way of lasting a long time, as seen in this wire-service news story:

NEW ROCHELLE, N.Y. (AP) — A bunch of out-of-towners who think New Rochelle owes them something forced the city to round up an innocent farm animal to honor a 311-year-old real estate deal. "Where's the beef?" William Rodman Pell, III, said Thursday before Mayor Timothy Idoni handed over a six-month-old Holstein named Jessie, this year's payment on a never-ending debt. Pell is a descendant of Sir John Pell, who sold 6,000 acres of his holdings in 1688 to French Huguenots who had escaped religious persecution. The parcel became New Rochelle, now a New York City suburb. Sir John received the equivalent of $11,625 and was promised "one fatt calfe on every fouer and twentieth day of June yearly and every year forever, if demanded."

— "Family collects cow from sale of land 311 years ago,"
Associated Press, June 25, 1999

***

The novelist Walter Wangerin tells of an incident from his own life, from his experience as a parent. The Wangerins were going through a difficult time with their son, Matthew, who was on the threshold of adolescence. He seemed to be rebelling against every value the family held dear. On more than one occasion, the boy had been caught stealing comic books from a local store. After the latest incident, Walter was in despair. Feeling he'd run out of every other alternative, he resorted to a technique he'd not used with his son for years: he gave him a spanking.

The father performed the act gravely, deliberately, almost ritualistically. When it was finished, he was so upset that he ran from the room and wept. After pulling himself back together, he went back in to his son, Matthew, and hugged him, long and hard. Nothing more was said, by father or son, about the incident — but Matthew never stole another comic book.

Years later, Matthew the grown man and his mother were doing some reminiscing, and the subject came round to the comic book incident. "Do you know why I finally stopped?" he asked his mother.

"Of course," she said. "It was because Dad finally spanked you."

"No," replied Matthew, "it wasn't the spanking at all. It was because Dad cried."

This is something like what Jeremiah means, when he predicts the law will be written on our hearts. No longer will it be the threat of punishment that makes the difference. It will be because "they will all know [the Lord], from the least of them to the greatest."

Sunday Of The Passion / Palm Sunday
April 9, 2006

Revised Common	Isaiah 50:4-9a	Philippians 2:5-11	Mark 11:1-11
			or Mark 14:1—15:47
			or Mark 15:1-39 (40-47)
Roman Catholic	Isaiah 50:4-7	Philippians 2:6-11	Mark 14:1—15:47
Episcopal	Isaiah 45:21-25	Philippians 2:5-11	Mark (14:32-72) 15:1-39
	or Isaiah 52:13—53:12		(40-47)

Theme For The Day   When Jesus enters our lives, he demands a response.

Old Testament Lesson   Isaiah 50:4-9a   *The Third Servant Song*

In this, the third of his famous servant songs, Isaiah portrays a mysterious figure who has been given "the tongue of a teacher, that [he] may know how to sustain the weary with a word" (v. 4) This suffering servant, however, appears to communicate more by deeds than by words: "I gave my back to those who struck me, and my cheeks to those who pulled out the beard; I did not hide my face from insult and spitting" (v. 6). This is a truly tough, resilient individual: "I have set my face like flint, and I know that I shall not be put to shame ..." (v. 7). The servant is able to persevere because he knows he is not alone: "he who vindicates me is near" (v. 8). In verse 8, Isaiah introduces a courtroom setting: the servant dares his adversaries to contend against him — for his defense attorney is none other than the Lord God (v. 9a). The scholarly debate over the identity of the suffering servant in these songs of Isaiah will probably never end. The church, of course, looks to these songs and sees Jesus (indeed, at times the resemblance between the details of the servant's torture and that of Jesus is uncanny) — yet the text also had to have a meaning apparent to the people of Isaiah's own day. Absent a fully developed messianic hope at this time in history, scholarly consensus seems to be that, for Isaiah, the servant is an idealized version of the people of Israel.

New Testament Lesson   Philippians 2:5-11   *Christ Emptied Himself, Taking*
                                                          The Form Of A Servant

Today's Epistle Lesson is one of the treasures of the first-century church: the famous *kenosis* passage from Paul's letter to the Philippians. This is undoubtedly an early Christian hymn, well known to Paul's readers, which the apostle embeds in the text of his letter. The word *kenosis*, or self-emptying, refers to verse 7, in which we read that Christ "emptied himself, taking the form of a slave, being born in human likeness." This early hymn displays a dramatic movement of descent, followed by ascent. Christ begins in the heavenly places, but sheds every heavenly prerogative in order to take on human life. He becomes not only human, but steps into the lowest position imaginable in human society: a slave and a criminal, suffering capital punishment imposed by the state. Then, from the low point, the ascent begins. God lifts him up, exalting him to the heights, so that heaven and earth will one day bow the knee before him. Christ is described as the actor in the first, "descent" portion of the poem — this is self-sacrifice, after all — but after that, it is God who is the actor, raising up this completely self-emptied individual and filling him once again.

Palms Or Passion?

Depending on the degree of flexibility present in their liturgical tradition, lectionary preachers have an important choice this Sunday: between using the assigned Gospel Lesson for Palm Sunday or one of the two longer, Passion Sunday readings. The difference, of course, is that the Palm Sunday lesson is limited to Jesus' triumphal entry into Jerusalem, and the Passion Sunday lesson is a longer narrative, telling of Jesus' trial before Pilate and death on the cross. Some pastors go even further, using this Sunday for an extended reading of the entire Passion narrative in lieu of a sermon. Passion Sunday sermons typically focus on a smaller portion of whichever Gospel Lesson is being read that day (since it is difficult to do justice to the extended reading in a single sermon).

The choice is complicated by the fact that, in many churches, attendance at Maundy Thursday and Good Friday services has declined in recent years, so the only opportunity many church members have to hear of Jesus' suffering and death is this Sunday before Easter. All too many modern Christians go directly from the "Hosannas" of Palm Sunday to the "Alleluias" of Easter — without ever stopping anywhere else in between. This makes Holy Week appear to be a rollicking good time: all sugar and no vinegar, all light and no darkness.

That is, of course, a distorted view: not only of the gospel, but of life in general. If the Sunday before Easter has a purely triumphal tone, emphasizing the spirited exuberance of the palm procession and little else, then an important part of the story will go unheard by many. On the other hand, many congregations have long-established traditions focusing on the palm procession, and the displacement of these traditions by a Passion Sunday observance would be acutely felt.

Pastoral sensitivity is required, either way. If the choice is Palm Sunday, then including some mention of Jesus' suffering and death is essential. If it is Passion Sunday, then flexibility that honors local Palm Sunday traditions is also of great value.

The Gospel — Palm Sunday   Mark 11:1-11   *Jesus' Triumphal Entry*

Ironically, John's version of the story of Jesus' triumphal entry (John 12:12-19) is the only one that mentions palm branches — and John's version never comes up in the lectionary. Here in Mark's version, Jesus sends some representatives ahead of him to secure a colt. Once they assure its owner that Jesus needs it (and will return it), he relents. (In Luke's version, by contrast, the phrase "The Lord has need of it" appears to be some kind of pre-arranged password; there is no mention of a promise to return the animal, for this would not have been necessary if the use of the beast had been agreed upon ahead of time.) Since Jesus never refers to himself as "Lord" elsewhere in Mark's Gospel, the appearance of that word in the statement, "The Lord needs it," is noteworthy. The people spread "leafy branches" out before him; there's no specific mention of palms (as in John's Gospel) — which would have had the specific connotation of Jewish nationalism — although it's possible that Mark's readers would have understood these leafy branches to be palms. Nor is there any mention of crowds from the city coming out to welcome Jesus — the procession could (and, in this version, probably is) comprised mostly of his entourage. The spreading of cloaks on the road probably refers to an ancient coronation custom described in 2 Kings 9:13. The cry of the people is "Hosanna!" — literally, "Save us!" The full quotation, "Hosanna! Blessed is he who comes in the name of the Lord" comes from Psalm 118:25-26, a royal psalm that was also traditionally sung by pilgrims as they entered the city. It would have had connotations of pilgrims coming into the city in any event, but the addition of the royal accoutrements means that Jesus' followers are also invoking the enthronement connotations.

The Gospel — Passion Sunday   Mark 14:1—15:47 or Mark 15:1-39 (40-47)

The longer Passion Sunday reading includes the following pericopes:

The Plot To Kill Jesus (14:1-2)
The Anointing At Bethany (14:3-9)
Judas Agrees To Betray Jesus (14:10-11)
The Passover With The Disciples (14:12-21)
The Institution Of The Lord's Supper (14:22-25)
Peter's Denial Foretold (14:26-31)
Jesus Prays In Gethsemane (14:32-42)
The Betrayal And Arrest of Jesus (14:43-51)
Jesus Before The Council (14:53-65)
Peter Denies Jesus (14:66-72)
Jesus Before Pilate (15:1-5)
Pilate Hands Jesus Over To Be Crucified (15:6-15)
The Soldiers Mock Jesus (15:16-20)
The Crucifixion Of Jesus (15:21-32)
The Death Of Jesus (15:33-41)
The Burial Of Jesus (15:42-47)

The shorter Passion Sunday reading includes just the trial and the crucifixion.

Preaching Possibilities

(**Note:** The following comments refer to a Palm Sunday sermon on Mark 11:1-11.)

A fundamental question for the preacher, when it comes to this well-documented public event in Jesus' life, is "What is it?" Is it a genuine outpouring of affection and respect on the part of the capital city's residents, who will turn on him as soon as the political winds change? Is it a well-orchestrated effort by Jesus' supporters to advance his cause, amidst a curious but not altogether supportive populace? Or is it what some have called an act of revolutionary street theater — a political demonstration satirizing those with pretensions to power, an act deliberately calculated to provoke a certain degree of hostility on the part of the ruling authorities?

Combined study of the four gospels' differing accounts of this incident, using a tool such as *Gospel Parallels*, is extremely fruitful. From such a study it becomes clear that each writer has a slightly different interpretation of the meaning of this very public event. There are numerous factual differences as well, some more significant than others. While it may be difficult (not to mention confusing, for the sermon's listeners) to introduce much of this parallel material, it is advisable that the sermon focus on one text or the other — rather than on a harmonization that does justice to none of them.

So what is this event, as Mark describes it? Some commentators have claimed that the people of Jerusalem were hailing Jesus as a conquering political/military hero, but that's extremely unlikely. The people of Jerusalem knew what military parades were all about — particularly Roman military parades. Typically, the victorious general would ride in, driving a chariot or sitting astride a magnificent warhorse. Around him would march legions upon legions of his troops — all looking forward to "a hot time in the old town tonight," in the tradition of soldiers from time immemorial. Also in the procession — barefoot, in chains, whipped along by overseers — would be the prisoners of war: miserable unfortunates who, after they'd been displayed to the cheering multitude, were not long for this world.

Jesus is no general, and his followers no professional army. The very way he rides into the city — on a donkey (as it says in the Gospel of John) or on a colt (as it says here in Mark, and also in Luke), or on both a donkey and a colt (as it says in Matthew) — was hardly the sort of conveyance favored by the rich and powerful.

So what is Jesus doing, with his triumphal entry, if he doesn't intend to lead an armed insurrection? Very likely, he is making fun of the powers-that-be. He is engaging in what some commentators today have called "street theater" — a satirical demonstration that lampoons the mighty and self-important. Jesus is a religious reformer, who wants to call the Jewish people back to the true worship of God. By revealing how insignificant and ridiculous the civil rulers appear in God's eyes, he is hoping to focus the people's devotion on what's truly important.

It's a very dangerous strategy. Jesus knows he could end up dead — and in fact, as we all know, that's exactly what did happen, in a matter of days. There was simply too much money, too much power, riding on the status quo for an upstart rabbi from the provinces to be permitted to call the whole system into question.

In Jerusalem, the palm branches — if, indeed, that's the type of branch the people are waving — have a particular meaning. Palms are the symbol of Judas Maccabeus and his followers: Jewish revolutionaries, who more than a century earlier briefly overthrew the Seleucid Greek rulers. Waving palm branches is a symbol, to Jewish Zealots, of their desire for a new Judas Maccabeus to come forward, and overthrow the Romans. Does Jesus intend the spectators to be waving palm branches? Do they make this gesture of their own accord? We have no way of knowing.

From the standpoint of today's worshipers, hearing the Palm Sunday story and wondering what difference it makes in their lives, perhaps the most important question is whether or not it will lead them to leave the sidewalk and join the procession. Will they remain mere spectators — or will they personally enter into the events of this week we call "Holy"?

Yet how easy it can be to slide into a comfortable, predictable, sidewalk Christianity — a faith that expects little and demands even less!

Prayer For The Day

Lord Jesus, we saw you coming. Someone pressed a palm branch into our hand. We cheered with the best of them. We shouted "Hosanna!" as our spirits rode high, on the crest of the applause. But now you've gone. You've ridden on. The palm-strewn street is before us, empty — except for the others who have stepped forward to follow. Give us the courage, Lord, to join them. Amen.

To Illustrate

Several years back, watching the television news, you would have seen palm branches waving. The year was 2003, and the scene was Baghdad. Rolling into that ancient near-Eastern city were the tanks and Humvees and Bradley Fighting Vehicles of the United States Army. The monumental statue of Saddam Hussein had been pulled down just hours before. Smiling Iraqi children approached fierce-looking Marines, offering flowers. And there, in the background of many of the television news shots, you could actually see them: jubilant crowds waving palm branches.

Truly it is an ancient gesture in the Middle East. A powerful army rolls into the streets of an ancient city, and the people do what they've always done to greet conquering heroes: they wave palms.

***

It's a well-loved institution in many of our communities: the small-town parade. Imagine that it's Memorial Day, or the Fourth of July, or maybe a high school homecoming. In the typical small-town parade, there's a marching band or two, some homemade floats, a few classic cars, and a convertible with local dignitaries sitting in the back, waving to the crowds. Following it up is a procession of fire engines, ambulances, and other emergency vehicles, driven by the proud volunteers who maintain them. At the very end, a police cruiser advances slowly, lights flashing, its driver nodding solemnly to friends in the crowd. It's all good fun.

Once that final police car passes, the people lining the sidewalks have a decision to make: they can either turn and go home, or they can join some of their fellow spectators in stepping out into the street. The parade has already passed them by — or at least the official parade has. Some of the spectators pour out into the street, turn in the direction the parade's heading, and begin marching. The parade's not over, after all: for they are continuing it.

Did something similar happen in Jerusalem, as Jesus and his disciples passed by? Mark seems to suggest it did: "... those who went ahead and those who followed were shouting, 'Hosanna! Blessed is the one who comes in the name of the Lord!' " (Mark 11:9).

***

Do you know who it is you're cheering, this day?

Maybe you believe you're cheering that auburn-haired young man, meek and mild, a ray of sunlight beaming over his shoulder, whom you remember from the Sunday school pictures. This same man is the one who will take a whip of cords and drive the moneychangers from the temple.

Maybe you believe you're applauding the one who gently said, "Let the children come to me." This same man is the one who proclaims, "I come to bring not peace, but a sword."

Maybe you believe you're welcoming the one who is always on your side to do your bidding — the one you signed on with years ago, and who, ever since, you've felt was with you. This same man is the one who will wake you from sleep one night and ask, "Could you not watch with me one hour?"

Maybe you believe you're cheering the one who "will come on the clouds of heaven, and all the angels with him," and will separate the sheep from the goats, blasting the evildoers who confound your life. This same man is the one who tells tales of a self-centered runaway whose father welcomes him home with open arms, and of field-workers who are paid the same wage at the end of the day, no matter how many hours they've been working.

He's a man of contradictions and complexity ... one who defies every attempt to place him into logical pigeonholes or psychological categories ... one whose spirit, living today, "blows where it will, and you know not where it comes from or whither it goes." Yet he is also the one whose teaching is so simple, it can be boiled down to a single sentence: "Love the Lord your God with all your heart, soul, mind, and strength, and love your neighbor as yourself."

They thought they knew who he was back in old Jerusalem, too. How wrong they were!

Maundy Thursday
April 13, 2006

Revised Common	Exodus 12:1-4 (5-10) 11-14	1 Corinthians 11:23-26	John 13:1-17, 31b-35
Roman Catholic	Exodus 12:1-8 (11-14)	1 Corinthians 11:23-26	John 13:1-15
Episcopal	Exodus 12:1-14a	1 Corinthians 11:23-26 (27-32)	John 13:1-15 *or* Luke 22:14-30

Theme For The Day   Jesus' call to his disciples to love one another is a call to radical servanthood.

Old Testament Lesson   Exodus 12:1-4 (5-10) 11-14   *The Institution Of The Passover*

Just prior to this passage, after Moses' pleadings to Pharaoh to let the people go, "the Lord hardened Pharaoh's heart, and he did not let the people of Israel go out of his land" (11:10b). As chapter 12 begins, the Lord instructs Moses and Aaron in how to prepare for the last, most dreadful demonstration of power: God's slaying of the Egyptian firstborn sons. These events will, of course, provide the inspiration for subsequent celebrations of Passover. The plentiful liturgical detail provided with these instructions marks this passage as belonging to the priestly tradition. Each household is to slay, prepare, cook, and eat a lamb in the prescribed fashion, smearing some of its blood on the doorposts of their home. "This is how you shall eat it: your loins girded, your sandals on your feet, and your staff in your hand; and you shall eat it hurriedly" (v. 11a). Blood is at the heart of this ritual: "when I see the blood," says the Lord, "I will pass over you, and no plague shall destroy you when I strike the land of Egypt" (v. 13b). Parallels with the sacrificial death of Jesus ("the Lamb of God") are legion, as are connections with Jesus' institution of the Lord's Supper.

New Testament Lesson   1 Corinthians 11:23-26   *The Institution Of The Lord's Supper*

Paul begins this passage, "For I received from the Lord what I also handed on to you," indicating that what he is about to pass on belongs to the most solemn and important traditions of the faith. The opening is noteworthy because Paul, alone among the apostles, was not present when Jesus established this tradition. He "received it from the Lord," therefore, not firsthand but through the witness of the community — which is how any of us receive and hand on this tradition. What follows, of course, are Jesus' words of institution of the Lord's Supper. The synoptic gospels' versions of these words can be found at Matthew 26:26-29; Mark 14:22-25; and Luke 22:14-23 (although, in date of composition, these words from 1 Corinthians are older). The occasion that leads Paul to recount Jesus' institution of the Lord's Supper is the problem of either factionalism or class distinctions within the Corinthian church. This problem has intruded even into the sacramental meal. This was more of a full meal than is the practice in our day, and — since there were no church buildings — it was celebrated in a private home. Some at the sacramental feast, who evidently consider themselves more privileged than others, eat their fill and become drunk — showing contempt for their fellow believers, who go hungry. Paul is extremely angry about this, as seen in the harsh scolding he gives: "What should I say to you? Should I commend you? In this matter I do not commend you!" (v. 22b).

The name "Maundy Thursday" is a corruption of the Latin *mandatum,* or commandment. This refers to Jesus' "great commandment" that Christians are to love one another — a passage that is found in the second part of today's selection from John (13:31b-35), along with the prior narration of Jesus' washing of the disciples' feet. The footwashing is both the setting for Jesus' commandment and its practical illustration. It is, in fact, a sort of visual parable. The great difficulty his disciples have in receiving this simple, loving gesture is demonstrated in Peter's sputtering objection. Jesus immediately suppresses his friend's complaint with the stern promise that, if Peter does not receive the footwashing, he will be expelled from the fellowship. Jesus' stern, even angry response is similar to that of Paul in 1 Corinthians 11 (see above) — the maintenance of class distinctions within the Christian community is not something Jesus will tolerate, any more than Paul. Peter repents completely of his error, impetuously begging Jesus for the privilege of having his hands and head washed, as well. Jesus commands his disciples to wash each others' feet on future occasions, an act performed only rarely in the modern church — which is curious, given the direct and unequivocal nature of the Lord's commandment to his followers to do as he has just done (vv. 14-15). Some have observed that Jesus' demonstration of footwashing, followed by his unequivocal commandment to do so, has the same level of authority as his commandment to baptize or to celebrate the Lord's Supper — although the modern church has, for the most part, neglected it.

Preaching Possibilities

A sermon on "The Two Basins" could compare the basin of Jesus' footwashing with the basin Pilate uses to wash his hands after condemning Jesus (John 13:1-17). Time and again, we all have to choose between them. Do we, most often, choose the basin of humble discipleship — or do we choose the basin of guilty denial of responsibility, our responsibility to love and care for one another?

The Last Supper is a banquet — and at a banquet in Jesus' day, it was the custom for guests to wear special robes, gleaming white. (We have no way of knowing if Jesus and his company, being of humble origin and being visitors to Jerusalem, would have had the means to celebrate in such a fashion; but this would have been their society's ideal.) Before leaving home, banquet guests carefully washed themselves, so as to be clean in body as well as spirit. There was a practical problem, though: in a land of dirt roads, it was impossible to keep their feet clean. So when guests arrived at a banquet, they would have their feet washed — usually by a servant.

But Jesus and his disciples have no servants. This means that, according to custom, the task of washing the others' feet should fall to the most junior of the disciples. But that presents a problem: for, as the gospel writers indicate, the disciples are always arguing among themselves. Luke relates how, even at the Last Supper, they are disputing as to "which one is greatest" (22:24). No one wants to take the servant role. So Jesus, their rabbi and leader, quietly takes up the basin and towel and becomes their servant.

So often in our lives, we choose not the basin of footwashing: of care and concern for neighbors. We choose the other basin: the basin of Pilate.

Pilate knows the charges against Jesus are nonsense. He has seen plenty of political revolutionaries in his day, and the man before him does not have the look of a revolutionary about him. Yet Pilate has little regard for Jesus' life. He has sacrificed others in the past on the altar of political expediency, and this pathetic prisoner is no different. Yet, Pilate has the larger political situation to think of. This activist rabbi does have his supporters. If he's to be a martyr, better to have the Jewish and Roman authorities together pass sentence on him, than to have the Roman governor do so alone. If Pilate can arrange things so the members of the Sanhedrin can also walk away from this trial with blood on their hands, so much the better.

Pilate knows of an obscure portion of the Jewish law that describes what to do if a dead man is found outside a village, murdered by thieves. In such an instance, the village elders are obliged to slay a heifer, and publicly wash their hands over the slain animal, declaring by their act that their village is innocent of the dead man's blood (Deuteronomy 21:1-9). So Pilate calls for a basin and washes his hands, saying to the mob outside his window, "I am innocent of this man's blood."

This is a slap in the face to the crowd. The hated Roman governor is using their own law to call them murderers. And the crowd shouts back, "We take responsibility for this man's blood — for he is guilty!" Jesus never has a chance. Caught between the Sanhedrin and Pilate in their endless struggle for power, he is crushed without a word.

Pilate's basin is a travesty of forgiveness and justice; compared to Jesus' basin of footwashing, it is a twisted, tragic imitation. But we must be honest with ourselves, and admit that it is that basin we choose again and again in our lives.

There is hope, though. The hope lies in doing what Peter finds it so difficult to do — allowing Jesus to wash our own feet. If we let down our guard enough to allow the Lord to do that, we just may be able to take up the basin of humility ourselves.

Prayer For The Day

Wash us thoroughly from our iniquity, O God, and cleanse us from our sin. Purge us with hyssop, and we shall be clean; wash us, and we shall be whiter than snow! Restore to us the joy of your salvation, and uphold us with your free Spirit. Amen.

— Adapted from Psalm 51

To Illustrate

We live in a society that's obsessively concerned with rights. Our nation is founded on a "Bill of Rights." Our Declaration of Independence talks of "inalienable rights ... to life, liberty, and the pursuit of happiness." We have a proud tradition of democracy in our country, but it's not without its dark side.

It's often said that we Americans are the most "litigious" people in the world. That means we love to litigate — to take one another to court, to claim our rights. Because of this love of litigation, two-thirds of all the lawyers in the world practice in the United States of America.

At the Last Supper, Jesus completely renounces his rights. He takes the lowliest role in the place, as he takes up the basin.

***

C. S. Lewis compares our self-love to a man who looks down the road at a line of telephone poles and concludes that the pole closest to him is the largest. Our happiness looms so much larger in our hearts than our neighbor's happiness, even though God created us as equal in our capacity for happiness, just as a row of telephone poles are equal in height.

***

There's a term in the art world known as *chiaroscuro*. It's an Italian word: the Italians invented the technique. Before *chiaroscuro*, paintings were uniformly bright, often enclosed in gilt frames and matting.

But with the advent of this technique, things changed in the world of painting. Artists discovered the dramatic power of shadow — of painting a person whose face was illuminated by a single candle, surrounded on every side by darkness. This technique somehow captured the ambiguity and uncertainty of life. Against the background of darkness, light seems all the more brilliant.

Easter is a glorious celebration, whether or not we have paid Lent, or Maundy Thursday, or Good Friday any mind. Yet the sunlight of Easter morn never seems so bright, unless we come to the empty tomb by way of the upper room, and unless we have stood for a time at the foot of the cross.

***

Some background on the setting for the Lord's Supper in the Corinthian church:

> *Archaeological study of Roman houses from this period has shown that the dining room (triclinium) of a typical villa could accommodate only nine persons, who would recline at table for the meal. Other guests would have to sit or stand in the atrium, which might have provided space for another thirty to forty people.... It is reasonable to assume, therefore, that the host's higher-status friends would be invited to dine in the* triclinium, *while lower-status members of the church (such as freedmen and slaves) would be placed in the larger space outside.*
>
> *Furthermore, under such conditions it was not at all unusual for the higher-status guests in the dining room to be served better food and wine than the other guests — just as first-class passengers on an airliner receive much better food and service than others on the same plane. A number of surviving texts from this period testify to this custom among the Romans.... For example, Pliny the Younger describes his experience of dining as guest of a man who boasted of the "elegant economy" of his hospitality: "The best dishes were set in front of himself and a select few, and cheap scraps of food before the rest of the company. He had even put the wine into tiny little flasks, divided into three categories, not with the idea of giving his guests the opportunity of choosing, but to make it impossible for them to refuse what they were given." (Letters 2.6)*

Paul regards such practices — however "normal" in respectable Roman culture — as an outrage. He does not deny the right of the more prosperous Corinthians to eat and drink however they like in their own homes (v. 22a), but he insists that the church's common meal should symbolize the unity of the community through equitable sharing of food at the meal.

— Hays, R. B., First Corinthians, in the Interpretation series
(Louisville: John Knox Press, 1997), p. 196

***

"Why doesn't anyone see God nowadays?" a wise rabbi was asked.
He answered: "People are not willing to look that low."

***

107

Meister Eckhart, who repeats this message dozens of times in his writings, points out that the word "humility" comes from the word *humus* or earth. In the creation tradition, then, to be humble means to be in touch with the earth, in touch with one's own earthiness, and to celebrate the blessing that our earthiness, our sensuality, and our passions are.

— Matthew Fox, *Original Blessing* (Santa Fe: Bear & Co., 1983), p. 59

***

"We can do no great things; only small things with great love."

— Mother Teresa of Calcutta

Good Friday
April 14, 2006

Revised Common	Isaiah 52:13—53:12	Hebrews 10:16-25	John 18:1—19:42
Roman Catholic	Isaiah 52:13—53:12	Hebrews 4:4-14; 5:7-9	John 18:1—19:42
Episcopal	Isaiah 52:13—53:13 *or* Genesis 22:1-18	Hebrews 10:1-25	John (18:1-40) 19:1-37

Theme For The Day   Do not look away from the cross: for there we see the fullest expression of God's love.

Old Testament Lesson   Isaiah 52:13—53:12   *The Fourth Servant Song*

In this, the fourth of his famous servant songs, Isaiah describes an unfortunate victim whose appearance is "marred ... beyond human semblance" (52:14). Perhaps more than any of the other servant songs, Christians are inclined to identify this dying figure with that of Christ on the cross, because of what this great poem says theologically about suffering that brings redemption to others: "Surely he has borne our infirmities and carried our diseases; yet we accounted him stricken, struck down by God, and afflicted. But he was wounded for our transgressions, crushed for our iniquities; upon him was the punishment that made us whole, and by his bruises we are healed" (53:4-5).

Yet the match, while close, is not perfect. Inevitably, Isaiah's words must have had meaning for the people of his own day, quite apart from what subsequent generations would come to see in them. The following lines in particular are an imperfect match with the figure of Christ, for what they say about the suffering servant "seeing his offspring": "When you make his life an offering for sin, he shall see his offspring, and shall prolong his days" (53:10).

In the context of the limited Jewish conception of individual afterlife prevalent at the time of Isaiah, it is hard to see this section as applying to any individual person. It is more likely that it refers to the nation Israel, personified as a human being; or, more specifically, to the cultural elite of Judah who went through a death-like experience in their Babylonian captivity, and who only at the time of return are collectively able to "see their offspring" or "prolong their days." A problem that was undoubtedly present at the time of the return from exile was the reintegration of the returnees with those who had remained behind. Speaking to this problem, Isaiah evidently sees the suffering of the exiles as vicariously redemptive for the residents of Babylonian-occupied Judah (whose lives, while far from easy, were still not characterized by outright captivity). Inasmuch as Isaiah sees Cyrus of Persia as God's instrument in releasing the exiles (44:28; 45:1; 45:13), it is possible that the first-person plural voice ("Surely he has borne *our* infirmities") is that of not only those who remained in Jerusalem but also the nations of the world — who in the prophet's imagination are coming to see Israel's suffering as redemptive for all humanity. Christian preachers need to be cautious in making too quick an identification of Isaiah's suffering servant with Jesus Christ; while we can affirm that his role was very much like this servant figure, it is important to preserve the original sense of these poems, however ambiguous the identity of their central figure may be.

New Testament Lesson   Hebrews 10:16-25   *Jesus, The High Priest, Reveals*
What Was Once Hidden

Alluding in verse 16 to Jeremiah's new covenant (Jeremiah 31:31), the author declares — accurately, in light of the then-recent Roman destruction of the temple — that the temple sacrifices once performed by the old high priest are no more (v. 18). Therefore, Christians are now — metaphorically speaking — able to enter the once-forbidden sanctuary "by the blood of Jesus, by the new and living way that he opened for us through the curtain ..." (v. 19b-20a). Christians may enter the holy of holies "in full assurance of faith, with our hearts sprinkled clean from an evil conscience and our bodies washed with pure water" — an allusion to the blood-sprinkling rites of the priestly ordination and Day of Atonement rituals described in Exodus 29:19-21 and Leviticus 16:14-19 (and now replaced by the once-for-all sacrifice of Jesus), and also to Christian baptism (v. 22). This passage ends with an appeal to community: "... not neglecting to meet together, as is the habit of some, but encouraging one another ..." (v. 25a).

Alternate New Testament Lesson   Hebrews 4:14-16; 5:7-9   *Jesus, The Great*
High Priest

An alternate option for this day is two earlier passages from Hebrews, about the role of Jesus as high priest (the second of the two, from chapter 5, has already come up in the lectionary on the Fifth Sunday In Lent, see p. 95). "For we do not have a high priest who is unable to sympathize with our weaknesses, but we have one who in every respect has been tested as we are, yet without sin" (4:15).

The Gospel   John 18:1—19:42   *John's Passion Account*

This lengthy section of John's passion narrative begins with Jesus' trial before Pilate and continues through his burial. This long lesson could be read in its entirety — in which case there may not be time for more than the most perfunctory sermon — or a smaller portion of it could be chosen for a more intense focus. The section describing the crucifixion (19:16b-30) is especially appropriate for a more focused treatment on this day, for obvious reasons. As with the Nativity stories — which have some similarities among them, but also some widely differing details — it is best to avoid harmonization, concentrating instead on what a single text says. This may be a challenge in certain liturgical settings — such as the ubiquitous "Seven Last Words" Good Friday services, in which individual verses are lifted out of context and combined with those from other biblical books — but it is still the most textually faithful way of approaching these materials. As for John's account, there is mention of Jesus carrying his cross (but not of Simon of Cyrene assisting — v. 17). There is crucifixion alongside two others (but no mention of them being thieves — v. 18). John has the fullest account of Pilate's posting of the sign inscribed "Jesus of Nazareth, the King of the Jews" — fullest both in terms of the length of the inscription and the account of how it came to be written. John alone includes the detail about the chief priests objecting to the wording, and of Pilate refusing to make changes, saying, "What I have written, I have written" (v. 22). The detail of the seamless tunic (v. 23) is unique to John, although all four gospel accounts include the soldiers' casting of lots for his clothing (alluding to Psalm 22:18). Only John has the three Marys standing directly at the foot of the cross (or possibly four women, depending on whether Jesus' aunt and "Mary the wife of Clopas" are one person or two). The detail of Jesus assigning "the disciple whom Jesus loved" to care for his mother is also unique to John (vv. 26-27). In common with Matthew and Mark, John includes the detail of the sponge full of sour wine — though only John has the soldiers place it on "a branch of hyssop" (an allusion to either Exodus 12:22 or Psalm 51:7). At the end,

Jesus says, "It is finished" and gives up his spirit (v. 30). There is a sense in which he is in control of the entire process right up to the end. Of the four gospel writers, John's Jesus is the most aloof, displaying not the least sign of pain or despair (except perhaps for his expression of thirst in v. 28, which John explains as necessary "to fulfill the scriptures").

Preaching Possibilities

Good Friday is among the most challenging of days for preachers, but also among the most rewarding. Those who come for Good Friday services are, for the most part, highly committed believers, who refuse to let themselves be cowed by the secular culture's tendency to avoid all that is painful or unpleasant in life. Most will have come because they understand the importance of reflecting on the enormity of Jesus' sacrifice. It is well to remind the people — in a restrained and not a maudlin way — of the Savior's pain: although this is a difficult task if John's Gospel provides the text, because he tends to downplay the human elements of the crucifixion — being more concerned (as he is throughout his gospel) with presenting abstract theological ideas.

John's passion account requires special care, also, because his collective statements about "the Jews" easily lend themselves to anti-Jewish assumptions on the part of listeners who may be inclined to think in prejudicial terms. It is, in fact, possible to substitute the words "the religious authorities" or "the religious leaders" for "the Jews" throughout John's passion narrative, and do no violence to his central meaning. It is absurd to blame the Jews, as a people, for Jesus' death, when Jesus was himself a faithful, observant Jew. John's use of this label reflects the highly charged atmosphere of persecution in which he lived, in which Christians — including many Christians of Jewish origin — were being abandoned by reactionary groups, and in some cases turned over by them to the Romans. John's church had begun to distance itself from Judaism as a matter of survival, and his frequent references to "the Jews" say more about his polemical attitude toward his contemporary opponents than about Jerusalem's population during the days just before the crucifixion.

Above all, it is best to avoid the saccharine proclamation, "It's Friday, but Sunday's coming!" To touch down briefly on Golgotha and immediately leap from there to the empty tomb does no justice to the gospel writers, who relate the details of the Savior's death for a reason. Soberly "surveying the wondrous cross" on Good Friday is as much a part of the Christian devotional life as singing "Jesus Christ Is Risen Today" on Easter morn. Sunday's coming, to be sure — but today's Friday, and we need to live through it.

In the words of a contemporary folk hymn of Scotland's Iona Community, the church's task on Good Friday is to:

Wonder and stare,
Fear and beware,
Heaven and Hell are close at hand.
God's living word,
Jesus the Lord,
Follows where faith and love demand.

Prayer For The Day

We remember your passion, Lord. It seems you're always on your cross, and your children cringing in some hole while bombs burst, or cheated in some supermarket, refused in some bank, or cursed in some crowd; dying one way or another. And you refuse to quit your suffering and your crawling down into the holes where we hide, and you call us to share your suffering, but to remember the third day, and to keep moving. We give thanks for that. Amen.

— John Vannorsdall

To Illustrate

One of the most famous crucifixion images in Christian art is a panel from what's called the Grunewald Altarpiece. It was painted in the village of Isenheim, Germany, in the early 1500s. What's so famous about this painting is the graphic detail with which the artist, Matthias Grunewald, portrays Jesus' sufferings.

This painter doesn't hold back — not one bit. Those viewing the painting for the first time are apt to react very much like several small figures the artist paints off to one side. John, the beloved disciple, has turned his face away in revulsion. Just at that moment, he's catching the fainting Mary, mother of Jesus, as she passes out. Just in front of them, Mary Magdalene has collapsed to her knees, hands clenched high above her head in anguished prayer.

They're reacting to the visible sufferings of Jesus. There he hangs, pulled down by a misery so great that it bends the very crossbeam to which he's nailed. His mouth is gaping, his breath gasping. His fingers have become like claws surrounding the cruel spikes driven through the palms, and he's so emaciated he looks like a concentration camp inmate. Jesus' entire body is covered with hundreds of welts and wounds.

This altarpiece might well have been displayed in any great cathedral in the Middle Ages — for graphic portrayals of the crucifixion were common in those days. But this painting was never designed to hang in a church. It was created, instead, for the chapel of a hospital. It was hung in such a way that patients could contemplate it from their beds.

Now the sight of such a gruesome painting may not sound very therapeutic, but, in fact, it is. The patients in that particular hospital, in the early 1500s, were suffering from a dreaded plague that had swept the continent of Europe. The wounds on the body of the crucified Jesus are identical to the symptoms of this plague. That meant the patients of the hospital could gaze up at the altarpiece and see there a Lord who, in the words of Isaiah, "has borne our griefs and carried our sorrows." They would realize, then, there was no suffering they could undergo that had not already been experienced in full by their Lord and Savior.

***

J. Barrie Shepherd, retired pastor of the First Presbyterian Church of New York City, tells the story of a time when he was flying back to the USA after a visit to his native Scotland. It so happened that, on that day, Shepherd was carrying back, for his church, a large Celtic cross from the Isle of Iona.

He had wrapped the cross carefully in layers of paper and padding. Not trusting the baggage handlers, he thought it best to carry it onto the plane himself. As he approached the airport X-ray machine, the guards eyed him up and down: his bundle looked suspiciously like an automatic weapon. When the image of a two-foot-tall Celtic cross appeared on the X-ray screen, the guards relaxed.

Early the next morning, Shepherd and his fellow passengers made their way into the customs area of New York's John F. Kennedy Airport. "Do you have anything to declare?" asked the customs agent.

"Only this cross," Shepherd replied, still sleepy from his long flight. The agent looked down and scribbled something on a form in front of him. It was only later that Shepherd got to see what he had written: "Item of a sentimental nature, of little or no value."

The customs agent's words were significant. The words he wrote down were perhaps correct from the standpoint of bureaucratic regulations, but in a theological sense they were all wrong. Yet isn't that description — "Item of a sentimental nature, of little or no value" — exactly what the world thinks of the cross of Jesus?

Unfortunately, it is. On Good Friday, the customs officer's question is put, disturbingly and directly, to every Christian: "Do you have anything to declare?"

What will we say, in reply?

**

I remember being at a retreat once where the leader asked us to think of someone who represented Christ in our lives. When it came time to share our answers, one woman stood up and said, "I had to think hard about that one. I kept thinking, 'Who is it who told me the truth about myself so clearly that I wanted to kill him for it?'" According to John, Jesus died because he told the truth to everyone he met. He was the truth, a perfect mirror in which people saw themselves in God's own light.

What happened then goes on happening now. In the presence of his integrity, our own pretense is exposed. In the presence of his constancy, our cowardice is brought to light. In the presence of his fierce love for God and for us, our own hardness of heart is revealed.... In his presence, people either fall down to worship him or do everything they can to extinguish his light.

A cross and nails are not always necessary. There are a thousand ways to kill him, some of them as obvious as choosing where you will stand when the showdown between the weak and the strong comes along, others of them as subtle as keeping your mouth shut when someone asks you if you know him.

Today, while he dies, do not turn away. Make yourself look in the mirror. Today no one gets away without being shamed by his beauty. Today, no one flees without being laid bare by his light.

— Barbara Brown Taylor, "Truth to Tell," from *The Perfect Mirror*
reprinted in *The Christian Century*, March 18-25, 1998

**

There's a story about a young French priest who came into his country church and found an old peasant man sitting in the front pew, staring at the crucifix. He didn't seem to be praying, or reciting the rosary, or doing anything except staring into space. The priest went about his business, and after a very long time he looked over at the man again. He had not moved. The priest went over, and asked the old farmhand what he was doing. The man turned to him and said simply, "I am looking at him, and he is looking at me."

That's the only thing you or I can do, really, on Good Friday: to observe with awe the spectacle of Jesus on the cross.

The Easter Season

The forty days from Easter to Pentecost counterbalance Lent's forty days of penitence. Having walked with Jesus to the cross, we now walk with him and his astonished disciples through forty days of revelation and wonder. First Lessons from the lectionary this season are from Acts, rather than the Old Testament — reminding us that, just as the angels instructed the disciples to follow the risen Lord into Galilee, our proper response to the resurrection is to follow where the Holy Spirit leads. The Lord is risen, but his spirit does not allow us to linger long by the empty tomb in wonder. The church is gathering to undertake its worship and work, and there is a place for each one of us in those efforts.

During Year B, the Easter season is heavily invested in Johannine theology. Both the Epistle and Gospel Lessons move in *lexico continuo* fashion through the First Letter of John and the Gospel of John, respectively. Because a certain amount of thematic repetition is inevitable in this approach, it is advisable for preachers to plan ahead: surveying the texts that are coming up, and deciding in advance which texts best lend themselves to particular topics. That way, a situation may be avoided in which the texts for a given day all point toward a theme that has just been covered in the previous week's sermon.

It is always good to remember, in dealing with John's Gospel (and, to some extent, with the Johannine letters that mirror it) that it is a fundamentally different type of literature than the synoptic gospels. Not only is John's Gospel decades later in composition, it is, in its design, more of a theological treatise hung on a narrative framework. John organizes his narrative not so much chronologically, as around certain themes. In the lengthy discourses and prayers of Jesus that are his trademark, he appears more interested in imaginatively constructing a compendium of Jesus' teaching — one that speaks to the church of his own day — than he is in absolute historical accuracy. To say this is in no way to demean the Gospel of John, or to question its authority; it is simply to observe that the book is a different type of literature, and ought not to be interpreted using the same hermeneutical approach that is used for the synoptics.

In the lectionary, the Old Testament Lesson is replaced during the season of Easter with another New Testament Lesson, typically from Acts. Given the heavy emphasis on New Testament texts in this season, it is advisable to include some Old Testament passage, liturgically — perhaps the Psalm for the day — in order to avoid any hint of a Marcionite preference for the Greek scriptures over the Hebrew.

The Resurrection Of Our Lord / Easter Day
April 16, 2006

Revised Common	Acts 10:34-43	1 Corinthians 15:1-11	John 20:1-18
			or Mark 16:1-8
Roman Catholic	Acts 10:34-43	Colossians 3:1-4	John 20:1-19
Episcopal	Acts 10:34-43	Colossians 3:1-4	Mark 16:1-8

Theme For The Day   The good news of resurrection beckons us to follow after the risen Lord.

Old Testament Lesson   Isaiah 25:6-9   *No More Tears*

A visionary poem about a great mountain, atop which the Lord will one day offer a great banquet of the richest foods and finest drink: "And he will destroy on this mountain the shroud that is cast over all peoples, the sheet that is spread over all nations; he will swallow up death forever. Then the Lord God will wipe away the tears from all faces ..." (vv. 7-8a).

The imagery is striking, and appropriate indeed for Easter. The passage is reminiscent of 2:1-4, in which the nations likewise are portrayed as streaming to Zion, the mountain of the Lord. In chapter 2, however, they are coming to the mountain to be judged. Here, in chapter 25, they are coming to be comforted. The veil that is spread over the nations should not be read as a lack of understanding, but rather as the universal experience of suffering.

Alternate First Lesson   Acts 10:34-43   *Peter's Easter Testimony*

Here in chapter 10, Peter has just been approached by the centurion Cornelius, a Gentile adherent of Judaism, who is interested in hearing the gospel. Cornelius' way has been prepared before him by the Holy Spirit, through which Peter has received a vision of a gospel belonging to all people (vv. 9-16). This passage contains Peter's address to Cornelius and to the gathered community of disciples, in which he shares his vision and proclaims his new conviction "that God shows no partiality" (v. 34). Peter delivers a mini-sermon in which he shares the essential proclamation about Jesus Christ — part of which is that, "We are witnesses to all that he did both in Judea and in Jerusalem. They put him to death by hanging him on a tree; but God raised him on the third day ..." (vv. 39-40a).

New Testament Lesson   1 Corinthians 15:1-11   *Paul's Easter Testimony*

Just as in chapter 11, when he shares the words of institution of the Lord's Supper, here Paul once again "hands on" important traditions. This is the Pauline equivalent of Peter's sermon in Acts 10: a digest of the essential Christian message, which contains, at its heart, the good news "that [Christ] was raised on the third day in accordance with the scriptures, and that he appeared to Cephas, then to the twelve. Then he appeared to more than five hundred brothers and sisters at one time ..." (vv. 4b-6a). It's possible that these verses are the text of an early creed. Paul carries the story forward to encompass his own experience, his own calling as an apostle: "Last of all, as to one untimely born, he appeared also to me" (v. 8) — the phrase, "one untimely born," translates an especially coarse and earthy Greek term that essentially means "miscarried fetus," and witnesses to Paul's profound ambivalence about the life he led before coming to Christian faith. "But by the grace of God," he affirms, "I am what I am" (v. 10a). Paul's very life story bears witness to the power of the resurrection.

Alternate New Testament Lesson   Acts 10:34-43   *Peter's Easter Testimony*

The Alternate First Lesson (see above) may also be used as an alternate New Testament Lesson.

The Gospel   John 20:1-18   *Mary Magdalene Meets Her Lord In The Garden*

The first of two possible Gospel Lessons is the most famous of the resurrection narratives: the encounter between Mary Magdalene and the risen Jesus outside the empty tomb. In pre-dawn darkness, Mary Magdalene comes to the tomb and finds it empty. She alerts Peter, who — along with another disciple, "the one whom Jesus loved" (possibly John himself) — runs to the tomb, observes the carefully rolled up graveclothes, and goes back home in awe and wonder with his companion in tow (vv. 6-10). The weeping Mary remains, however — she apparently believes the grave has been robbed, despite the rolled up head-cloth — and discovers within the tomb a pair of angels, who ask her why she is weeping. Their appearance is evidently ordinary enough that she does not recognize them as angels at first. Then, Mary is blessed with the first encounter with the risen Jesus. She does not recognize Jesus at first — whether it is because of her tears or because his post-resurrection appearance is somehow different is unclear. It is only when he speaks her name that she recognizes him. "Do not hold on to me," he warns, "because I have not yet ascended to the Father" (v. 12). A Latin Vulgate mistranslation (*noli me tangere*, "do not touch me") has led some to speculate that Jesus' post-resurrection body was qualitatively different from ordinary human flesh in some way, but more likely, this phrase means that he has urgent things to accomplish in the short time before his ascension, and therefore cannot linger. Mary Magdalene finds her fellow disciples and announces, "I have seen the Lord" — making her the first Christian preacher. There is no credible biblical evidence, by the way, for the early medieval church tradition that Mary Magdalene had been a woman of low morals before becoming a follower of Jesus. Too many Easter sermons have played on this lurid and false speculation, besmirching the reputation of this great Christian leader, the *apostola apostolorum* — "apostle to the apostles."

Alternate Gospel Lesson   Mark 16:1-8   *Into Galilee ...*

This is the "year of Mark" in the lectionary, so it is appropriate that one of the Gospel Lesson options is Mark's account of the resurrection. This account, which ends abruptly at verse 8 with the words, "and they said nothing to anyone, for they were afraid," caused considerable consternation in the early church. Other accounts of Jesus' resurrection had been circulating, and it seemed odd to Mark's readers that he would end his gospel without including any of these — and, furthermore, without presenting any evidence of the resurrection at all except for the empty tomb. There are two alternate endings to Mark, but strong linguistic and textual evidence suggests that they were added in some later manuscripts. They are a second part of verse 8 (the "shorter ending") and verses 9-19 (the "longer ending"). So why does Mark end his story so abruptly? Very possibly, it is for dramatic effect: he wants to leave the line, "and they said nothing to anyone, for they were afraid," resonating in his readers' minds, as an encouragement not to do the same thing. In the prior verse, an angel has just said, "But go, tell his disciples and Peter that he is going ahead of you to Galilee; there you will see him, just as he told you." The implication is that the good news of resurrection is an urgent call to action: those who hear it are to get themselves "to Galilee" — to witnessing in the world — without delay.

Preaching Possibilities

Among the various gospel accounts of Jesus' post-resurrection appearances, there is considerable confusion as to detail. The gospel writers are not at all consistent in their reporting. It's almost as though they are at a loss to explain it. In one place, we read of the risen Lord walking through walls; yet elsewhere — even in the same gospel, John — we hear that his flesh is substantial enough for Mary to cling to and for Thomas to touch. Luke makes it a point to tell us how he ate a piece of fish. Scripture clearly declares that the risen Lord is the same Jesus; yet even his closest friends have a hard time recognizing him. Most definitely he is Jesus, but he's different somehow: he is perfected, complete.

Then there are the accounts of Peter and Paul — not narrative accounts, as in the gospels, but rather testimony from witnesses. Acts records Peter's declaration: "We are witnesses to all that he did both in Judea and in Jerusalem. They put him to death by hanging him on a tree; but God raised him on the third day...." Even Paul, who never met Jesus before his resurrection, met him afterwards, on the Damascus Road: "Last of all, as to one untimely born, he appeared also to me." Sure, it wasn't the typical way to meet the risen Jesus — but is there ever a typical way to meet a man risen from the dead? "By the grace of God," Paul affirms, "I am what I am."

Of all the accounts of Jesus' resurrection, though, it is the simple story of Mark's that is the most innocent, the most direct — and, in its own way, the most beguiling. Mark provides no eyewitness accounts from those who have met the risen Lord. There's just an empty tomb, and an angel saying, "He's gone from here." For Mark, the central feature of the story seems to be the angel's command: *Go.* Go and tell the disciples and Peter. Go and follow the risen Lord to Galilee. Go and share with all who will hear it this glorious news that death has been vanquished forever, that Jesus who was crucified now reigns triumphant.

It is Mark's account that is closest to our own, modern-day experience. No one in the church today has embraced Jesus, as Mary Magdalene did, or put their finger in his side, as Thomas did. All that is left to us are the stories, the testimony. That, and the command of the angel: Go. Go to Galilee. There he awaits you.

The same will be true for our Easter congregations. Let us share the good news with them: yet as we do so, let us not fail to share the angel's command as well. Along with the glorious Easter proclamation "He is risen!" there is the instruction of the angel to go and leave the place where we presently are, in our spiritual lives: to venture out and see if the risen Lord does indeed meet us.

To set out on a journey is a risk, to be sure. It's the risk called faith. But it's a risk worth taking.

Prayer For The Day

Great are you, O God, and greatly to be praised! For you have raised your son, Jesus, from the dead, vanquishing every power of darkness. He has gone before us into Galilee: give us the courage, the conviction and the inquisitive faith to follow him there. Amen.

To Illustrate

One of the new and different amusements this computer age has brought to our culture is "interactive entertainment." On computer blogs and bulletin boards, people sometimes write murder mysteries together, as a community effort. One person writes the first chapter, another the second, and so on — with no one knowing exactly how it's all going to turn out, until it does.

A few years back, Hollywood produced a movie, *Clue*, based on the same principle. Based on the popular murder-mystery board game, the film had three or four separate endings. When the time for the final scene arrived, the audience — equipped (in at least some theaters) with computer keypads — got to vote on which ending they wanted. They got to decide which suspect had committed the murder.

Interactivity is the principle behind all computer and video games. Players impact the story by what they punch into the keyboard, or how they wiggle the joystick. Every game session is, by definition, different from the last.

There's an interactive story in the Bible. It's Mark's account of Jesus' resurrection. It ends abruptly because what happens next is up to the readers to decide.

***

The great composer of operas, Puccini, died suddenly before he had a chance to finish his final work, *Turandot*. One of his fellow-composers, Franco Alfano, wrote two final scenes that completed the story. When the opera premiered at Milan's La Scala opera house in 1926, the famous Arturo Toscanini was the conductor. Toscanini got to the place where Puccini had left off, and he stopped the performance. With tears in his eyes, he turned to the audience and announced, "This is where the master ends." Then he raised his baton again and said, "This is where his friends continue." And he concluded the performance.

***

Thomas Jefferson also came up with a short ending to the Easter story — though for very different reasons than Mark. Jefferson, the rationalist, could not accept scripture's miraculous events, so he edited his own version of the New Testament with all supernatural references removed. The emphasis in Jefferson's Bible is on moral teachings: Jesus is an eastern sage, teaching kindness and justice. Jefferson's gospel account closes with these words: "There laid they Jesus and rolled a great stone at the mouth of the sepulcher and departed."

Mark's short ending points us in a very different direction.

***

Canadian preacher and writer Ralph Milton has written:

> *One of the fundamental things about Christ's resurrection is that we can't argue anyone into believing it. We can offer a whole bunch of circumstantial evidence, but when push comes to shove, there is no proof. That's because we can't prove love.*

Ralph goes on to testify how certain he is of the love he shares with Bev, his wife of forty years:

> *If you were a psychiatrist, you might say we've got a co-dependent relationship. If you were a sociologist, you might say we're living out our gender roles. If you were an accountant, you might say there is a financial advantage in sticking together. And all would be true, to a degree. But proof of love? There is no such thing. At least, not*

scientific proof. But if you believe, then you know. If you believe, then it becomes the central fact of your life. If you believe, you can see no other fundamental reality.

***

Many years ago, a friend told me that his young son was a great fan of both Captain Kangaroo and Mister Rogers. The boy faithfully watched both of their television shows, and one day it was announced that Mister Rogers would be paying a visit to the Captain Kangaroo show. The boy was ecstatic. Both of his heroes, together on the same show! Every morning the boy would ask, "Is it today that Mister Rogers will be on Captain Kangaroo?" Finally the great day arrived, and the whole family gathered around the television. There they were, Mister Rogers and Captain Kangaroo together. The boy watched for a minute, but then, surprisingly, got up and wandered from the room.

Puzzled, his father followed him and asked, "What is it, son? Is anything wrong?"

"It's too good," the boy replied. "It's just too good."

Maybe that's it. Maybe the news of the empty tomb, the news of the resurrection, the news of Jesus' victory over death is just too good to believe, too good to assimilate all at once.

— Thomas G. Long, "Empty Tomb, Empty Talk,"
in *The Christian Century*, April 4, 2001, p. 11

***

On the third day, the friends of Christ coming at daybreak to the place found the grave empty and the stone rolled away. In varying ways they realised the new wonder; but even they hardly realised that the world had died in the night. What they were looking at was the first day of a new creation, with a new heaven and a new earth; and in a semblance of the gardener God walked again in the garden, in the cool not of the evening but the dawn.

— G. K. Chesterton

***

Let no one fear Death, for the Savior's death has set us free!
He that was taken by Death has annihilated it.
He descended into Hell, and took Hell captive!...

"O Death, where is your sting? O Hell, where is your victory?"

Christ is risen, and you are overthrown!
Christ is risen, and the demons are fallen!
Christ is risen, and the Angels rejoice!
Christ is risen, and Life reigns!
Christ is risen, and not one dead remains in the tombs!

For Christ being raised from the dead, has become the first-fruits of them that slept.
To him be glory and dominion through all the ages of ages!

— Easter acclamation of John Chrysostom (paraphrased)

Second Sunday Of Easter
April 23, 2006

Revised Common	Acts 4:32-35	1 John 1:1—2:2	John 20:19-31
Roman Catholic	Acts 4:32-35	1 John 5:1-6	John 20:19-31
Episcopal	Acts 3:12a, 13-15, 17-26	1 John 1:1-22	John 20:19-31

Theme For The Day   The events of the Easter story demand a response of faith.

First Lesson   Acts 4:32-35   *Everything In Common*

Such is the impact of the resurrection, and of the descent of the Holy Spirit at Pentecost, that the early church enters into a remarkable period of signs and wonders (2:43). Among the greatest of signs is the impressive unity of the people, including the holding of possessions in common: so the needs of all — and especially the needy — may be met. Some today may scoff at this account, doubting that such communal living is possible (and indeed, the church was not able to maintain it very long) — but ever since then there have been communities of Christians who have risked this sort of daring lifestyle, and some have been able to maintain it. Monastic communities are a notable example. The courageous, Christ-centered economic lifestyle of the early Christians is an example to us all.

New Testament Lesson   1 John 1:1—2:2   *What We Have Heard And Seen*
And Touched

The testimony of the First Letter of John — concerning not only "what was from the beginning," but "what we have heard, what we have seen with our eyes, what we have looked at and touched with our hands" (1:1) — is presented here as the account of a firsthand witness. Chapter 1 is strongly linked, in language and themes, with the prologue to the Gospel of John (John 1:1-18). The author introduces a central theme of this letter — *koinonia* or fellowship — from the very first verses (v. 3). That fellowship is not only with fellow-believers, but with Jesus Christ. "God is light and in him there is no darkness at all": the quality of the fellowship among believers is the barometer by which the world can tell if the Christian community is truly dwelling in God's light (v. 5). Verses 8-10 are familiar to worshipers in most churches, because one or more of them is often used as either a call to confession or an assurance of God's pardon. Another great Johannine theme is that of Christ as advocate (*parakletos*); this is introduced in 2:1. In the Hellenistic world this word has a legal sense: that of one who stands by another in court, as a sort of defense attorney. It has a more generic sense as well: of a helper or comforter.

The Gospel   John 20:19-31   *Jesus Appears To Thomas*

This passage occurs on the Second Sunday Of Easter in all three cycles of the lectionary. In this, the first post-resurrection appearance in John (after the resurrection story itself), Jesus miraculously appears to a roomful of disciples behind locked doors. The Lord's greeting to them is "Peace be with you" — in Hebrew, it is the perfectly ordinary, everyday greeting, *"Shalom"* (v. 19). There is a sort of understated humor to a man returning from the dead to deliver the first-century equivalent of "Hi, there" — although, of course, the wish for peace also has profound meaning for this confused and troubled band of believers. Jesus shows them his hands and side as a mark of authenticity (and also, from John's standpoint, to counter the

Docetists, who were claiming, in his own day, that the resurrection was a spiritual and not a bodily reality). Jesus then commissions the disciples, saying, "As the Father has sent me, so I send you," giving them through his own breath the gift of the Holy Spirit (vv. 21-22). Some have called this passage "John's Pentecost," for it is in fact an alternate version of the descent of the Holy Spirit upon the church (in contrast to Luke's more famous account in Acts 2). In verse 23, Jesus gives the disciples what has been called elsewhere "the power of the keys" or "the power to bind and loose" — the authority to forgive in his name. The second part of this passage is the story of Jesus' self-revelation to Thomas — who is sometimes (in a regrettable turn of phrase) called "Doubting Thomas." In fact, Thomas is only asking for what his fellow disciples have already been given in verse 20: a chance to see Jesus' hands and side, to assure himself of the truth of this amazing claim that the Lord has risen. Jesus graciously returns a week later, in similar circumstances, to allow Thomas to have the same experience as his fellows (vv. 26-28). John concludes with an epigram that is evidently meant as much for the larger church as for those gathered in that room: "Blessed are those who have not seen and yet have come to believe" (v. 29). Many scholars think the Gospel of John originally ended at this verse.

Preaching Possibilities

Poor Thomas! History has been hard on him. He's the only one of the twelve disciples with an adjective permanently attached to his name. We don't speak about "Unfaithful Peter," or "Uppity James and John." We don't even talk about "Treacherous Judas." It's only Thomas who's been unfortunate enough to come through the centuries with a label attached to his name.

It's not even a well-deserved label. Every other mention of Thomas, throughout the New Testament, is positive. The first time Thomas' name appears is in chapter 11 of John. Jesus has received an urgent request to go help his good friend Lazarus of Bethany, who is gravely ill. Jesus waits around longer than he should before departing, then informs the disciples they're all going to Bethany. Lazarus has died, he informs them, but they're going anyway. He's going to perform a mighty act, so they all may believe.

Most of the disciples object. It's a dangerous trip. The last time they were all in Judea, the locals just about ran them out of town. Only Thomas stands unequivocally behind his Lord and master: "Let us also go," he says, "that we may die with him." Based on that account, you could just as well call him, "Courageous Thomas."

A bit later, in John 14, Jesus is teaching his followers about the life to come: "In my Father's house are many dwelling places." He's going before them to prepare a place for them: "And you know the way to the place where I am going."

Thomas is intrigued. He responds, "Lord, we do not know where you are going. How can we know the way?"

Jesus replies, "I am the way, and the truth, and the life. No one comes to the Father except through me."

Instead of sitting there like a bump on a log, Thomas actively engages his teacher, seeking to understand. We might just as well call him, "Thoughtful Thomas."

But no, Doubting Thomas he is, in all of our minds: and Doubting Thomas he will remain (even though the nickname is not especially fair). The Greek word John uses is not actually a word that means "doubt." (There are other Greek words for "doubt," and John doesn't use them.) Jesus' statement is best rendered as some translations have it: "Do not be faithless, but believing." The Greek word for "faith" is *pistos*; the word translated either "doubt" or "faithlessness" here is *apistos* — which literally means "unfaith."

It's almost as though Thomas is practicing a kind of anti-faith. He's not at all indifferent to the amazing claims his friends have just made, about having seen the risen Lord. He's just as passionate and committed as they are, but in an opposite direction: "unless you show me otherwise, I will not believe."

What does Thomas ask for that day, anyway, that's so terrible? All he wants is exactly the same evidence his friends have seen! Thomas seems to have a pretty clear idea what it's going to take for him to believe: "Unless I see the mark of the nails in his hands, and put my finger in the mark of the nails and my hand in his side...." What preconditions do you and I place on our faith? What are our "unlesses"? What is it we want to see happen, before we risk offering our hearts to God in return?

Some of us are looking for miracles. Others are looking for evidence. Still others are looking for assurances that God will take care of them. Whatever it is we're looking for, many of us have found it: as the risen Lord has graciously come to us, providing what we need.

Prayer For The Day

God of power and love, who meets our every need,
we give you thanks for this story of Thomas:
passionate doubter, even more-passionate believer.
We give thanks also for the questions with which we all struggle,
the puzzling problems that flow from our human condition:
for in the very struggle, our faith deepens.
Help us to be numbered among those who "have not seen and yet have come to believe."
Whenever we find ourselves locked behind doors of fear,
come among us, Lord. Amen.

To Illustrate

We've all heard of "bulletin bloopers" — typographical errors in church bulletins. A bulletin blooper that's not so much funny as unintentionally wise happened in a larger church, in the pastor's sermon title for Easter.

This church staff used to plan out their worship services many months in advance. They wrote everything up in a fancy worship-planning chart that listed sermon titles, scripture passages, and hymns. The office staff would then use this chart to prepare the weekly bulletin. Not long after Christmas, the pastor was trying to figure out what his Easter sermon topic was going to be. It was awfully early in the year for him to be doing that, and — try as he might — he just couldn't get his mind in gear to think about Easter. Finally, he gave up. He wrote into the appropriate box on the chart, "I don't know yet."

You can probably see what's coming. On Easter Sunday, the ushers were handing out bulletins with this as a sermon title: "I Don't Know Yet."

On the other hand, maybe that's not such a bad theme for Easter. The good news of Jesus' resurrection breaks into our world with such suddenness, that the first reaction — even among Jesus' closest friends — is confusion. Those disciples simply don't know yet what it is they've just witnessed.

***

Garrison Keillor has some wonderful words to say on the subject of miracles and where to find them:

> *What else will do except faith in such a cynical, corrupt time? When the country goes temporarily to the dogs, cats must learn to be circumspect, walk on fences, sleep in trees, and have faith that all this woofing is not the last word.*
>
> *What is the last word, then?*
>
> *Gentleness is everywhere in daily life, a sign that faith rules through ordinary things: through cooking and small talk, through storytelling, making love, fishing, tending animals and sweet corn and flowers, through sports, music and books, raising kids — all the places where the gravy soaks in and grace shines through.*

— Garrison Keillor, "The Meaning of Life," in *We Are Still Married*
(New York: Viking, 1989)

***

If a dead man is raised to life, all people spring up in astonishment. Yet every day one that had no being is born, and no one wonders ... that it is a greater thing for that to be created which was without being than for that which had being to be restored. Because the dry rod of Aaron budded, all people were in astonishment; every day a tree is produced from the dry earth ... and no one wonders ... Five thousand people were filled with five loaves; every day the grains of seed that are sown are multiplied in a fullness of ears, and no one wonders. All wondered to see water once turned into wine. Every day the earth's moisture, being drawn into the root of the vine, is turned by the grape into wine, and no one wonders. Full of wonder then are all the things which people never think to wonder at, because they are by habit become dull to the consideration of them.

— Pope Gregory I (Saint Gregory the Great), *Moralia*

***

Perhaps the greatest threat to the gospel story, that the Jesus whom Jerusalem murdered, God raised from the dead, is the well-intentioned effort of preachers and theologians to make these scandalous, mysterious happenings comprehensible by suggesting that they mirror the familiar. In particular, illuminating analogies are frequently adduced from the phenomenon of the cyclic: the rhythms of sleep and waking, death and birth, which we experience night and morning and observe through all of nature's seasons, as well as in our own passages from infancy to parenthood to death. Above all, the Easter victory over death is domesticated as the supreme instance of a generic immortality — the inherent capacity of human beings, or more usually of the human soul or spirit, to survive the grave and achieve eternal unity with our transcendent source. All these attempts to treat the events of Good Friday and Easter Day as particularizing a familiar universal, either anthropological or cosmological, disregard the very narrative which presents them as history — as new, unique happenings, involving a particular, unsubstitutable person at an unrepeatable point in time and space.

— Alan E. Lewis, *Between Cross and Resurrection: A Theology of Holy Saturday*
(Grand Rapids: Eerdmans, 2001), pp. 59-60
Lewis completed this book shortly before dying of cancer.

***

Don't be so consumed by seeing the empty tomb that you miss seeing the gardener.

— Barbara Brown Taylor

***

It's not his absence from an empty grave that convinces us. It's his presence in our empty lives.

— Frederick Buechner

Third Sunday Of Easter
April 30, 2006

Revised Common	Acts 3:12-19	1 John 3:1-7	Luke 24:36b-48
Roman Catholic	Acts 3:13-15, 17-19	1 John 2:1-5	Luke 24:35-48
Episcopal	Acts 4:5-12	1 John 1:1—2:2	Luke 24:36b-48

Theme For The Day   The risen Christ calls us to be witnesses.

First Lesson   Acts 3:12-19   *Peter Calls The People To Repentance*

After healing the lame man at the beautiful gate, Peter is surrounded by a curious crowd. At Solomon's Portico he addresses them in his second major speech, crediting God with the healing. He berates the people for rejecting Jesus and choosing a murderer in his place, then bears witness to how he has himself seen the risen Christ. Of the man who has just been healed, Peter says: "... by faith in [Jesus'] name, his name itself has made this man strong ..." (v. 16a). Acknowledging that the people acted in ignorance, Peter calls them to repentance (vv. 18-19).

New Testament Lesson   1 John 3:1-7   *Children Of God*

John celebrates that those who follow Christ and "do right" are considered children of God. Once again, there is an allusion to the prologue of the Gospel of John: "The reason the world does not know us is that it did not know him" (v. 1). The author takes confidence in the future promise of seeing Christ as he is: "Beloved, we are God's children now; what we will be has not yet been revealed. What we do know is this: when he is revealed, we will be like him, for we will see him as he is" (v. 2). He confirms that sin is incompatible with Christian discipleship, and that Christian disciples necessarily display a righteous way of life (vv. 4-7).

The Gospel   Luke 24:36b-48   *Proof Of The Resurrection And*
                                                A Call To Bear Witness

In this, the concluding story of Luke's Gospel before Jesus' ascension, Jesus suddenly stands among the disciples, says "Peace be with you," and shows them his hands and his side. This is to reassure their fears, assuring them that it is him they are looking at, and not a ghost (vv. 36-40). Luke observes that "in their joy they were disbelieving and still wondering" — a psychologically realistic portrait of human faith (v. 41). Jesus eats a piece of boiled fish — further evidence of his corporeal existence (vv. 42-43). Jesus confirms that the prophecies of old are fulfilled, and "opens their minds to understand the scriptures" (v. 45) — an action similar to what he has just done for the disciples he met on the road to Emmaus (vv. 27, 32). The gospel is to be preached "to all nations, beginning from Jerusalem" — explicitly including the Gentiles (v. 47). "You are witnesses of these things," he says to them (v. 48). Luke then sets his readers up for the account of Pentecost that will follow in the second volume of his work, relating how Jesus charges the disciples to "stay here in the city until you have been clothed with power from on high" (v. 49).

Preaching Possibilities

"The Third Sunday Of Easter." It seems the epitome of anti-climax — like being elected second vice-president, or winning the bronze medal, or sitting in the bleachers way up high at a baseball game. Two weeks ago, our churches were filled, and the spirit among the people was electrifying. Now, it's back to business as usual.

And what *is* our business? It's a fair question. Luke gives us the answer: "You are witnesses of these things" (24:48). Witnesses. *Martyres*, in the Greek. "You are martyrs of these things."

"Martyrs," as we've come to understand that word, are true believers who sacrifice their lives for the faith — but our English word "martyr" is really no more than a direct transliteration of this Greek word for "witness." The early church believed that the martyrs — those who were killed in the arena, or thrown to the lions, or turned into human torches for the diabolical Emperor Nero's amusement — were witnesses to Christ. Their courage in going to their deaths told the world that what they had heard and seen was quite unlike the proclamation of any other religion.

In a law court, a witness is someone who has seen something important, something the court needs to know. Often we speak of "eyewitnesses" — those who were right there at the scene of the crime, who can tell the jury firsthand what really happened. Yet Christians are not called to be eyewitnesses when it comes to the good news of resurrection — how could we? We weren't there! What Christian believers do proclaim about the resurrection of Christ, we proclaim on faith.

The kind of witness Christ needs of us is a witness of another sort. Christ needs us to be "character witnesses." If defense attorneys are angling to undermine the prosecutor's argument, they are likely to call one or more character witnesses — people who know the defendant, who are willing to vouch for that person, to observe how unlikely it is that their esteemed friend or colleague would ever commit a crime.

That's the kind of witnesses you and I are called to be for Christ: character witnesses. We can't tell firsthand stories about the resurrection — other than the timeworn, smooth-as-a-piece-of-beach-glass stories that have been passed on across the generations. But we can witness to a personal Christ, a living Lord whom we know, one who has touched our lives and made a difference.

There are times when witnessing will be difficult. The world will try, from time to time, to assail our Christian faith. It will seek to declare that God is not on our side at all: that life is "nasty, brutish, and short," in the words of the grim, seventeenth-century philosopher Thomas Hobbes, and that there is no life beyond this one. The world will endeavor to convince us, from time to time, that Jesus did not rise from the dead, that there is no power in this world beyond the orderly forces of nature — gravity and muscle, magnetism and electricity, and the orderly decay of atoms that fuels the nuclear power plants. The world will try its hardest to win us over to the view that the rush of joy that "strangely warms" our hearts — in Wesley's famous phrase — is not the work of the Holy Spirit, but a mere projection of our inner, most cherished fantasies.

Our Lord calls us to be his character witnesses — "martyrs" in the most ancient sense — to speak not so much of proofs, or evidence, but rather of the Lord we personally know, and the difference he has made to us. It is not the mind that Christian witness touches, so much as it is the heart.

Prayer For The Day
Lord Jesus, long ago you came among your disciples: you spoke to them, touched them, reassured them. We praise you and thank you that you still come among us today, amidst the gathered fellowship of your worshiping people. As we depart this place, may we fulfill for others the role you filled for those first disciples. May we be for our neighbors the voices of

good news they hear, the helping hands they touch, the embrace of love they feel — for your sake, always for your sake. Make us your witnesses, we pray. Amen.

To Illustrate

When I was a student at Princeton Theological Seminary in the early 1980s, several of us were planning for a special event called the Easter Vigil — a many hours long extravaganza of worship and the arts, that took place literally all over campus. We were planning an outdoor sequence in which a hidden student, playing the role of God, was to speak out in a booming voice to various other students, who were playing Old Testament prophets. We were short on microphones, and so it made perfect sense for somebody to ask, of the male student reading the part of the Almighty, "What about God? Does he need amplification?"

The question is a good one. Does God need amplification?

***

The greatest proof of Christianity for others is not how far a man can logically analyze his reasons for believing, but how far in practice he will stake his life on his belief.

— T. S. Eliot

***

The personal character of Christian witness is captured in a little parable told by the English philosopher Basil Mitchell.... One night in wartime, in an occupied country, a member of the resistance meets a stranger, who deeply impresses him. The two men talk into the wee hours of the morning — of life and death, of the struggle for justice, of the things that need to happen to make their country great again. Finally, the stranger admits to the partisan that he himself is on the side of the resistance — and not only that, that he is its commander. He urges the underground fighter to have faith in him no matter what happens. The partisan is utterly convinced at that meeting of the stranger's sincerity and constancy, and decides that he will trust him.

The two men never have a conversation again. But from time to time, the partisan glimpses the stranger from afar. Sometimes he sees him helping members of the resistance — then he is grateful, saying to his friends, "He is on our side."

Sometimes the partisan sees the stranger in the uniform of the police, handing over patriots to the occupying power. On such occasions, his friends complain that he is no good: but the partisan still affirms, "He is on our side." The partisan still believes that, in spite of all appearances, the stranger did not deceive him.

Sometimes he sends word to the stranger for help, and receives it. Then he is thankful. Sometimes he asks for aid, and does not receive it. Then he observes, "The stranger knows best." Sometimes his friends demand in exasperation, "Well, what would he have to do for you to admit that you're wrong, that he's not on our side after all?"

Always the partisan refuses to answer. He will not put the stranger to the test. And sometimes his friends complain, "Well, if that's what you mean by his being on our side, the sooner he goes over to the other side the better."

But still the partisan is a faithful witness.

***

There is an old story of a Civil War chaplain, who one day happens upon a wounded soldier on the battlefield. The chaplain asks him if he'd like to hear a few verses from the Bible. "No," says the wounded man, "but I am thirsty. I'd rather have some water." The chaplain gives him a drink, then repeats his question.

"No, Sir," says the wounded man, "not now — but could you put something under my head?" The chaplain does so, and again repeats his question.

"No, thank you," says the soldier. "I'm cold. Could you cover me up?" The chaplain takes off his greatcoat and wraps the soldier in it. Afraid now to ask, he does not repeat his question. He makes to go away, but the soldier calls him back. "Look, Chaplain, if there's anything in that book of yours that makes a person do for another what you've done for me, then I want to hear it."

Fourth Sunday Of Easter
May 7, 2006

Revised Common	Acts 4:5-12	1 John 3:16-24	John 10:11-18
Roman Catholic	Acts 4:8-12	1 John 3:1-2	John 10:11-18
Episcopal	Acts 4:(23-31) 32-37	1 John 3:1-8	John 10:11-16

Theme For The Day   Christ's call to discipleship is a call to sacrificial love.

Note: Those inclined to preach on either the Epistle or the Gospel Lesson would do well to look ahead in the lectionary. We are currently proceeding step-by-step through both the First Letter of John and the Gospel of John, and the texts chosen from both these books for the next several weeks are rather heavily focused on a single subject: love. Advance planning — taking the form of either a sermon series or a balance among First Lesson, Epistle, and Gospel texts — is advisable, to avoid repetition. Next Sunday — which, in 2006, is Mother's Day in the United States — is a day when a sermon on love may be especially appropriate. That may affect homiletical strategies for today.

First Lesson   Acts 4:5-12   *Jesus, The Cornerstone*
     After attracting a great deal of attention through healings they have performed, Peter and John are brought before the council — including Caiaphas, Annas, and others who condemned Jesus. They ask them by what name they have performed these wondrous works, and Peter resolutely replies that it is "by the name of Jesus Christ of Nazareth, whom you crucified, whom God raised from the dead" (v. 10). He goes on to cite Psalm 118:22: "the stone that was rejected by you, the builders; it has become the cornerstone." This stone, he declares, is Jesus Christ, and says of him that, "There is salvation in no one else, for there is no other name under heaven given among mortals by which we must be saved" (v. 12).

New Testament Lesson   1 John 3:16-24   *Love In Deed*
     The author has been speaking of "the message you have heard from the beginning, that we should love one another" (v. 11). We know what true love is because Jesus laid down his life for us, and that example ought to lead us to do the same for others. Love that does not manifest itself in loving action is no love at all (v. 17). From the perspective of this letter, the gospel may be summed up in these words: "And this is his commandment, that we should believe in the name of his Son, Jesus Christ, and love one another, just as he has commanded us" (v. 23). John's is a down-to-earth, practical conception of love: don't talk the talk if you can't walk the walk.

The Gospel   John 10:11-18   *The Good Shepherd*
     "I am the good shepherd," says Jesus. "The good shepherd lays down his life for the sheep (v. 11). Earlier, in verse 7, Jesus has said he is "the gate for the sheep" — alluding to a common sort of semi-circular stone sheepfold enclosure, that had an opening across which the shepherd would lie at night, to protect the animals from predators. This is a homey, practical analogy that would have been familiar to many of Jesus' listeners. The shepherd who owns the flock naturally cares more for the individual sheep than does the hired hand, who is only earning a salary. When danger comes, the hired hand will typically run, while the shepherd will stay with the

flock — for "I know my own and my own know me ... And I lay down my life for the sheep" (v. 14). Verse 16 is somewhat cryptic, and has led to much scholarly discussion, particularly with regard to the relationship between Christianity and other world religions: "I have other sheep that do not belong to this fold. I must bring them also, and they will listen to my voice. So there will be one flock, one shepherd." It's possible that John shares these words of Jesus because he wants to make the point that there are other people who have not yet heard the gospel, but who will hear it in the future. The important point is that it is an all-inclusive message of welcome, which always ought to be the church's stance.

Preaching Possibilities

In the time of Jesus, sheep wandered all over the hillsides of what we now know as Palestine. Their shepherds, for the most part, journeyed with them. Each night, it was the shepherd's task to round the sheep up, herding them into a circular enclosure called a sheepfold. Now a sheepfold wasn't much to look at — a low wall, and not much more. From within the sheepfold, the shepherd could look out, searching for enemies roundabout. From within the sheepfold, the sheep could feel secure.

Most sheepfolds didn't have doors. Doors would have been hard to maintain and would have interfered with the process of getting sheep in and out. The shepherd solved the problem with his own body, stretching himself across the opening as he lay down to sleep at night: "I am the gate. Whoever enters by me will be saved...." It is a self-sacrificing role, this role of the shepherd.

There is a nagging voice within us that distrusts the idea of sacrifice. Sacrifice seems to run against the grain of our very culture. After all, doesn't the Declaration of Independence promise "life, liberty, and the pursuit of happiness?" (Where does sacrifice fit into that equation?) Didn't all those Depression-era children Tom Brokaw talks about in *The Greatest Generation* pretty much corner the market on sacrifice? And isn't this the era of self-actualization, of discovering our deepest potential, of nurturing the inner child? Self-sacrifice sounds awfully like that old psychological bogeyman called "co-dependence" — which, we all know, is the bane of the human-potential movement.

Sacrifice does not mean trampling individuality under foot, nor does it mean subordinating our every desire to the dreams of another. It most certainly doesn't mean being a doormat. There's such a thing as true, selfless sacrifice, and co-dependence is certainly not an example of it.

There is a healthy kind of self-sacrifice that represents the human spirit at its very best. It's the sort of inner motivation that fuels the most exemplary human lives. "I am the good shepherd. The good shepherd lays down his life for his sheep." It could just as well be, "I am the good teacher ... or the good nurse ... or the good parent ... or the good spouse ... or the good neighbor. I am the one who has taken it upon myself to look out for others: to nurture them, guide them, sustain them with love."

This gift of self is offered up not as the result of compulsion, but freely, willingly: "I lay down my life in order to take it up again. No one takes it from me, but I lay it down of my own accord. I have power to lay it down, and I have power to take it up again."

Now there's a model of self-sacrifice that's anything but neurotic. It's the self-sacrifice of a healthy individual, who's counted the cost and who's prepared to pay it. May that person's tribe increase!

Prayer For The Day

We know, O God, that sometimes faith is a risk: and never does it feel more risky than in those moments when we feel called to give of ourselves, so others may live more fully. When such situations present themselves, help us to discover within ourselves a reservoir of courage, courage that comes from Christ himself: so we may follow in his way, bearing witness to what he has already done for us. Amen.

To Illustrate

For a certain boy named Bradley, age eight, an awareness of the meaning of sacrifice arrived one morning just before breakfast. Somehow, he had managed to slip under his mother's plate a folded piece of paper. It was a bill. Scrawled in crayon were these words: "Mother owes Bradley: for running errands, 25 cents, for being good, 10 cents, for taking piano lessons, 15 cents; for extras, 5 cents. Total, 55 cents."

Bradley's mother smiled when she saw the note, but said not a word. As he returned for lunch, Bradley discovered to his delight that at his place was a little pile of coins: 55 cents. He discovered something else, as well: another folded piece of paper. Opening it, he read, in his mother's handwriting, these words: "Bradley owes mother, for nursing him through the chicken pox, nothing; for being good to him, nothing; for clothes, shoes, and playthings, nothing; for his playroom, nothing; for his meals, nothing. Total, nothing."

Bradley got the point. He learned a valuable lesson that day, a lesson about love: that it has no price.

***

Everybody can be great, because anybody can serve. You don't have to have a college degree to serve. You don't have to make your subject and verb agree to serve. You only need a heart full of grace, a soul generated by love.

— Martin Luther King, Jr.

***

A farmer named Bert — from the "Northern Kingdom" of New England, from rural Maine — traveled to the faraway metropolis of Boston. There he heard a lecture on socialism. To Bert, socialism sounded like a pretty good thing: everyone sharing with each other and helping each other out. He went back home and announced to his friend and neighbor, Harry, that he had become a socialist.

"So tell me what this socialism thing is, Bert," said Harry. Bert explained that it was all about sharing with each other and helping each other out.

"Let me see if I understand this. Are you saying that, if you had two farms, you'd give me one?"

"Sure," said Bert.

"If you had two pickup trucks, would you give me one?"

"Sure."

"If you had two hogs, would you give me one?"

Bert suddenly got red in the face and began looking at his shoes. "Now Harry," he said, "you know I've got two hogs!"

— From a story told by Jack Stotts

***

Once an elderly general practitioner consulted me because of his severe depression. He could not overcome the loss of his wife who had died two years before and whom he had loved above all else. Now, how could I help him? What should I tell him? Well, I refrained from telling him anything but instead confronted him with the question, "What would have happened, Doctor, if you had died first, and your wife would have had to survive you?" "Oh," he said, "for her this would have been terrible; how she would have suffered!" Whereupon I replied, "You see, Doctor, such a suffering has been spared her, and it was you who have spared her this suffering — to be sure, at the price that now you have to survive and mourn her." He said no word but shook my hand and calmly left my office. In some way, suffering ceases to be suffering at the moment it finds a meaning, such as the meaning of sacrifice.

    — Viktor Frankl, *Man's Search for Meaning* (Boston: Beacon Press, 1963), p. 135

***

Love in action is a harsh and dreadful thing compared with love in dreams. Love in dreams is greedy for immediate action, rapidly performed and in sight of all. Men will give their lives if only the ordeal does not last long but is soon over, with all looking on and applauding as if on the stage. But active love is labor and fortitude.

    — Fyodor Dostoevsky, *The Brothers Karamazov*

***

What people don't realize is how much religion costs. They think faith is a big electric blanket when, of course, it is the cross.

    — Flannery O'Connor

Fifth Sunday Of Easter
May 14, 2006 (Mother's Day)

Revised Common	Acts 8:26-40	1 John 4:7-21	John 15:1-8
Roman Catholic	Acts 9:26-31	1 John 3:18-24	John 15:1-8
Episcopal	Acts 8:26-40	1 John 3:(14-17) 18-24	John 14:15-21

Theme For The Day   Jesus encourages us to set fear aside and risk loving others.

First Lesson   Acts 8:26-40   *Philip Baptizes An Ethiopian Eunuch*

This passage is remarkable for the ways in which the Holy Spirit is active. Philip is the principal character, but in a certain sense it is not Philip, but the Spirit, that determines everything that happens. The story opens with the account of an angel directing Philip to travel along a certain road. There he encounters an exotic foreign visitor: an Ethiopian eunuch, who is the royal treasurer of that nation. The eunuch, apparently a Jewish proselyte (according to Deuteronomy 23:1, his sexual condition bars him from full participation in the faith), is returning home from a pilgrimage to Jerusalem. "Seated in his chariot" — apparently resting from his journey by the roadside — he is reading the Prophet Isaiah (v. 28). The Spirit directs Philip to run up and join the chariot, and he does so. Engaging the Ethiopian in conversation, he ascertains that this foreigner would appreciate a little help in scriptural interpretation, and he provides it — interpreting Isaiah 53:7-8 to refer to Jesus. At some point, the eunuch recommences his journey, this time with Philip riding beside him. When they reach "some water" the eunuch asks, "What is to prevent me from being baptized?" (v. 36b). Nothing, evidently, because Philip baptizes him on the spot. Then, in the tradition of great prophetic figures like Elijah, "the Spirit of the Lord [snatches] Philip away," depositing him in a location far away. A key point in the story is the Ethiopian's question, "What is to prevent me from being baptized?" Whenever the inclusion of a person in the church is in question, it is always instructive to pose the question in such a way (as opposed to asking "Why should this person be admitted?"). Sometimes there are unseen barriers to full inclusion, and it is always useful to try to determine what they may be, or if they really exist.

New Testament Lesson   1 John 4:7-21   *God Is Love*

In this section, the author celebrates the glories of Christian love, and so fully identifies God with love that he is able to make it an absolute equivalence: "God is love" (v. 8b). This love proceeds in a one-way direction at first: "... not that we loved God but that he loved us and sent his Son to be the atoning sacrifice for our sins" (v. 10). We are called to respond to this unconditional love by loving neighbors in return (v. 11). It is through love that we come to know the otherwise unknowable God (v. 12), and even to "abide" in God (v. 16) — a favorite Johannine word. Verse 18 is a favorite sermon text: "There is no fear in love, but perfect love casts out fear." As Martin Luther King, Jr., and others have noted, it is really fear — rather than hatred — that is the chief obstacle to love. In verse 19, the author reiterates love's divine origin: "We love because he first loved us." In verses 20-21 he returns to a theme he has considered before: that genuine faith must necessarily be accompanied by loving deeds. Reflecting on the Johannine perception that love originates with God, it may be worthwhile to raise the homiletical question of whether our culture does not in fact believe the opposite: not that God is love, but that love is God.

The Gospel   John 15:1-8   *Jesus, The True Vine*

Some acquaintance with horticulture (and its specialty field, viniculture) is necessary to understand the intricate extended metaphor at the heart of this passage. Jesus is "the true vine." God is "the vinegrower." Like any good vinegrower, God must prune unproductive branches from time to time, removing the ones that are not producing (and thereby detracting from the health of the whole plant, by consuming resources without contributing any produce in return). The Greek verb for "prune," *kathairo*, has a principal meaning of "cleanse"; evidently farmers in the ancient world spoke of "cleansing" their vines when they were pruning them. Those who follow Jesus have already been pruned / cleansed by the word he has spoken (v. 3). "Abide in me as I abide in you. Just as the branch cannot bear fruit by itself unless it abides in the vine, neither can you unless you abide in me" (v. 4) — the verb "abide" (*meno*) bespeaks a very intimate, side-by-side living relationship. Those branches that do not continue to abide in the vine are cast into the fire to be destroyed (v. 6). While that may sound harsh, it is in fact the common agricultural practice of the day; its opposite — continuing to abide in the vine — brings a positive reward: "If you abide in me, and my words abide in you, ask for whatever you wish, and it will be done for you" (v. 7).

Preaching Possibilities

Besides being the Fifth Sunday Of Easter, today is Mother's Day in the United States — a day which, while not a formal liturgical occasion, is often observed in churches. The debate about whether the secular Mother's Day holiday deserves liturgical emphasis is a never-ending one — although, for pastoral reasons, most American churches will want to observe the day in one way or another. Fortunately, the confluence of texts this Sunday affords ample biblical basis for preaching on love, which is always appropriate on Mother's Day.

It is important, of course, when mentioning Mother's Day in worship, not to assume that all congregants have either known their mother or have had a positive relationship with her. The dark side of Mother's Day observances in church is that the subject sometimes evokes secret pain. Sensitive pastors will be aware of that possibility, and will choose their words carefully — avoiding all-inclusive sorts of statements that may unintentionally create discomfort for those who were adopted as children, are estranged from their mothers, or have recently been bereaved.

Having said that, let us point out that 1 John 4:18, "there is no fear in love, but perfect love casts out fear," is highly suitable for a sermon text. It's remarkable how often the words "love" and "fear" occur together — and not just in the case of the love-struck teenage boy trying to pick up the phone to ask the object of his crush to the school dance. Throughout life, the decision to love is a choice — one that's often affected by the amount of fear that's lurking in the background. To love is to make ourselves vulnerable.

The modifier "perfect" in this verse may cause some consternation. The minute you slam down the adjective "perfect" in front of "love," it raises the stakes just a bit. Who on earth could ever imagine loving perfectly? Isn't there such a thing as "good enough love," without it having to be perfect all the time?

That word "perfect" bears closer examination. The Greek word is *teleios*. Literally, it means "finished" or "complete." When an artist working on a statue takes her last chisel stroke and lays down her tools, the statue is said to be perfect. It's finished. In a parliamentary meeting, when delegates work to "perfect" a motion, it means they've made all the changes they want to make to it. In English class, when the teacher asks a student to say something in a "perfect" tense, it means he wants the pupil to describe an action that's been completed.

When most of us use the word "perfect," we mean "without flaw or blemish" — but that's not the literal meaning of the word, here in First John. The Greek *teleios* means "ended." When this wise Christian teacher speaks of perfect love that casts out fear, he's referring to loving actions that have been completed. It's not just a matter of feeling love, of getting warm and goose bumpy all over ... it's actually getting up and doing something. It's going out and making a difference.

It's like follow-through in sports. Athletes have to swing that tennis racket or golf club, and they can't stop after they make contact with the ball. Their swing has to continue, until it has reached its natural conclusion — until, in other words, the swing has been perfected. Sometimes what athletes do, to improve their tennis or golf swing, is to actually focus on the follow-through. Now it may seem to make no logical sense to think about where the arm is placed *after* making contact with the ball — but wise coaches have learned over the years that working on the follow-through is the key to success.

The same is true in life. In any situation in which love seems risky, the only thing to do is take the swing — to complete the action, and trust God to bless it. Love is always a risk worth taking.

So what kind of love is it, that casts out fear? It's *perfect* love: love that began as a feeling ... then went on to become an inclination to do something ... and, finally, has taken on flesh and blood, in the form of loving action.

Prayer For The Day

Lord, we confess that we are people of fear. We wish we were people of love. You have the power to make us so. Take our fears, we pray, for they are a burden. Where fear once reigned, sow seeds of love. Free us to risk reaching out to neighbors, for the sake of Christ. Amen.

To Illustrate

When we operate out of fear, we will never feel secure. There is not enough money, property, or things to possess to compensate for fear. The dark side of money is rooted in fear ... growing out of fear is guilt, greed, vengeance, violence and ultimately war.

— Walter Brueggemann

***

Stalin, absolute dictator of the Soviet Union, was one of the most powerful men on earth — yet he was afraid to go to bed at night. Stalin had seven different bedrooms. In order to foil would-be assassins, he slept in a different one each night. Stalin also had five chauffeur-driven limousines. Every time he went out, all five cars left the garage, each one with curtains drawn, so no one on the streets would know which one contained the mighty Stalin.

If possessions could conquer fear, then the late billionaire Howard Hughes would have been fearless. But we've all heard his story. Hughes lived his last days a pathetic hermit, closed up in his Las Vegas penthouse suite. He had all the money anyone could ever dream of, but he was so afraid of germs that he breathed through pieces of Kleenex and refused to cut his beard or his nails.

There's always popularity. If popularity — or fame — could cast out fear, then the rock musician John Lennon would have been utterly fearless. Yet, the more fame accrued to this former Beatle, the more of a recluse he became. Lennon's biographers report that, in the months before his tragic assassination, he refused to sleep with the lights off and was afraid to touch anything because of possible germs.

"All you need is love," John Lennon sang, back in his Beatles days. It's a pity he didn't understand what love means — at least, not love in the Christian sense, the sort of love that perfects itself in giving oneself away to others.

***

The longest, most arduous trip in the world is the journey from the head to the heart. Until that round trip is completed, we remain at war with ourselves. And, of course, those at war with themselves are apt to make casualties of others, including friends and loved ones.
— William Sloane Coffin, *Credo* (Louisville: Westminster John Knox, 2004), p. 126

***

Now I want to tell you a lie. Hate is an emotion we can't help. Hate is a feeling we cannot overcome. If we hate someone, it is because we just can't help ourselves. We're human. We have no choice but to hate. That is a lie.

Unfortunately, it is a lie many people believe. They believe this lie in order to excuse their hatred. After all, if we can't help but hate, if hate is a feeling we simply cannot help, then hatred is never our fault, is it?

But we can help it. Hatred is a choice. We choose to hate, just as we choose to love. Oh, I know, there are people out there who believe love isn't a choice, that love is primarily an emotion, a feeling, a stirring in the loins. These are the same people who stay married for six months, then divorce. These are the people who love the idea of love but seem unable to stay in it. Love is a matter of the will — something we decide to do. Love is a choice.
— Philip Gulley, *For Everything a Season* (Sisters, Oregon: Multnomah, 1999), p. 204

***

Do not hesitate to love and to love deeply. You might be afraid of the pain that deep love can cause. When those you love deeply reject you, leave you, or die, your heart will be broken. But that should not hold you back from loving deeply. The pain that comes from deep love makes your love ever more fruitful. It is like a plow that breaks the ground to allow the seed to take root and grow into a strong plant. Every time you experience the pain of rejection, absence, or death, you are faced with a choice. You can become bitter and decide not to love again, or you can stand straight in your pain and let the soil on which you stand become richer and more able to give life to new seeds.
— Henri J. M. Nouwen, *The Inner Voice of Love* (New York: Doubleday, 1996)

136

Sixth Sunday Of Easter
May 21, 2006

Revised Common	Acts 10:44-48	1 John 5:1-6	John 15:9-17
Roman Catholic	Acts 10:25-26, 34-35, 44-48	1 John 3:18-24	John 15:1-8
Episcopal	Acts 8:26-40	1 John 3:(14-17) 18-24	John 14:15-21

Theme For The Day   Friendship with Jesus is a liberating experience.

First Lesson   Acts 10:44-48   *The Gentiles' Pentecost*

While Peter is preaching about his vision of a gospel that's inclusive of all people, the Holy Spirit falls on all those present, including particularly the Gentile household of Cornelius. There is a mini-Pentecost, with even the Gentiles receiving gifts of the Spirit and prophesying ecstatically. Peter then asks the same question that Philip and the Ethiopian eunuch considered together in last week's selection from Acts: "Can anyone withhold the water for baptizing these people who have received the Holy Spirit just as we have?" (v. 47). And they are baptized.

New Testament Lesson   1 John 5:1-6   *Love And Obedience*

First John continues with the same themes that have been expressed so far. There is an absolute unity between the Son and the Father; to love one means necessarily to love the other, also. The true sign of loving God is obedience to God's commandments: this love is no mere emotion, but is hard work. It issues in deeds of love. The commandments of God, however, "are not burdensome, for whatever is born of God conquers the world" (v. 3). The question could be asked, in a sermon, whether it is possible to love God solely, without loving one's fellow human beings; and, conversely, whether it is possible to love other people alone, without also having faith in God? A satisfactory answer to this question could help unite those perpetual factions in the church, those who emphasize evangelism and spirituality on the one hand and those who emphasize social justice on the other.

The Gospel   John 15:9-17   *I Chose You*

Continuing the "True Vine" discourse, John once again emphasizes several of his distinctive themes: abiding in Christ's love (v. 9), and the necessity of keeping Christ's commandments as a demonstration of genuine love (v. 10). Verse 12 brings a classic expression of the importance of loving sacrificially, as Christ has loved: "This is my commandment, that you love one another as I have loved you. No one has greater love than this, to lay down one's life for one's friends" (vv. 12-13). Those who abide in him are no longer slaves, but "friends" (v. 15). The initiative in the call to discipleship lies with Christ, not the believer: "You did not choose me but I chose you" (v. 16a).

Preaching Possibilities

After several weeks of *lexico continuo* selections from both the First Letter of John and the Gospel of John, preaching from either the Epistle or Gospel Lesson becomes a challenge. The style of both writers is so repetitive that the same themes occur again and again. They are great themes, to be sure: but preachers will inevitably find themselves scanning the latest selection of texts and asking themselves, "So what's new?"

One possible answer, in this week's selection, is the concept of friendship with Jesus, found in John 15:15: "I do not call you servants any longer, because the servant does not know what the master is doing; but I have called you friends...." He is the rabbi and master; they are his followers and servants. Yet Jesus Christ, son of God, raises his servants up. He raises them to friendship.

By the standards of first-century Judaism, this is extraordinary. Relationships between rabbis and pupils are formal and highly structured. Rabbis hold an exalted position in Jewish society. They are to be kind and caring to their disciples, but they generally do not befriend them. What is more, it is extraordinary that Jesus would raise his disciples above the level of servant — for if Jesus is God's Son, then the disciples, as his servants, already hold an exalted position. In the Bible, only the greats like Moses or Abraham are called "servants of God." In raising the disciples above the level of servant, Jesus is giving them a higher station even than the patriarchs.

By the standards of other world religions, Jesus' friendship with his disciples is even more amazing. The founders of other great religions — Mohammed, Confucius, Gautama the Buddha, even Moses — are austere and lofty figures, dwelling (as it were) with one foot in the heavenly places and one on earth. They do not have time for such niceties as friendship. Yet, Jesus' words to his disciples are, "I have called you friends." It's one of the most radically original insights in the annals of religion.

Concretely, being friends with Jesus means three things. First, we are no longer servants. Second, when Jesus is our friend, something changes in our human relationships — we approach others as friends in a new way. Third, this divine friendship has transforming potential for our lives — for when we are friends with Jesus, the world itself becomes a friendly place.

Jesus' friendship with us transforms us, and all our relationships as well. Just look at how it is with those people Jesus approaches in the gospels — he approaches them as friends, and their lives are never the same again. Remember how Jesus walks up to the hated tax collector Zacchaeus, perched up in his sycamore tree? He doesn't shout harshly up to the little man, asking, "Zacchaeus, are you saved?" No, Jesus says instead, "Let's have dinner."

Then there is the woman at the well. In New Testament times, a Jewish man would not approach even an unknown Jewish woman in public — and the woman at the well wasn't even Jewish. She was a Samaritan, a member of the race Jews despised more than any other. More than that, she was a Samaritan woman of doubtful reputation. Yet this Samaritan woman from the wrong side of the tracks is the one Jesus approaches at the well, to ask for a drink. He treats her as a friend.

Our text from John, "I do not call you servants any longer ... but ... friends," is one of the most alluring, compelling messages in all of scripture. People want to hear that. They need to hear it. Even more than hearing it, our neighbors need to see it lived out, by Christians who know they are Jesus' friends, and who extend that gift of friendship to others.

Prayer For The Day
You have not called us servants, O Christ. You have called us friends: allowing our spirits to soar over every barrier that separates us from true faith. How glorious it is to realize your love for us — yet how easy it is for our frail hearts to forget it! Keep our hearts ever close to yours, we pray. Amen.

To Illustrate

In the movie, *Driving Miss Daisy*, the title character is an elegant Southern aristocrat, played by Jessica Tandy. She is getting on in years, and her son has decided she is now a traffic hazard behind the wheel of her car: so he has hired her a chauffeur. The chauffeur, played by Morgan Freeman, is an African-American — in the South, at the time in history this movie is set, a member of the servant class.

Miss Daisy doesn't like the idea of a chauffeur one bit, and the early part of the movie tells of her stubborn efforts to resist change. In time, though, Miss Daisy discovers that she and her chauffeur, Hoke, have more in common than either one ever imagined.

The two come from different economic classes, it is true. Yet, Miss Daisy is Jewish, and has lived her whole life in the American South — so both she and Hoke know what discrimination feels like. Both are getting up in years, and know physical limitations. Both have rich memories, extending back over many years.

By the end of the film, Hoke and Miss Daisy are truly each other's best friend. They keep up the pretense of the master-servant relationship, but that's for the world to see. By mutual consent, they have crossed the boundaries of race and class, to discover a friendship that is priceless. In the movie's final scene, Miss Daisy is living in a nursing home, and her son has brought Hoke with him to visit her. It becomes perfectly clear that the person Miss Daisy most wants to see is not her own son, but her chauffeur and friend of many years.

***

It's one of the odd quirks of American history that, in many parts of the South, slavery persisted after the Civil War was over. Lincoln had signed the Emancipation Proclamation. Union troops occupied state capitals across the South. The infamous carpetbaggers were running the state houses. Yet still, in the smaller towns and villages of the rural South, life continued very much as it had before.

The slaves were free, but they couldn't claim their freedom. Acts of Congress had been passed, presidential proclamations had been signed — and, in many cases, news of those actions had reached the plantations. The changes were too sudden, too far-reaching, to take in all at once. Life on the plantation, for all its hardship and misery, seemed less threatening. So most of the former slaves stayed where they were, and it wasn't long before the oppressive system of sharecropping rose up, a new kind of slavery.

It can be the same way for us, even after we hear Christ calling us "friend." If we've grown up fearing God as a horrible taskmaster, dreading him as the dispenser of harsh punishments, it can be positively threatening to hear God's Son calling us friend. It upsets the applecart. It changes our whole perspective.

We may end up acting much like those former slaves of the American South. Acknowledging that a proclamation has been passed somewhere on high, confessing with our lips that we are free people, we yet live as though we were still in bondage. The shackles are removed; the locked gate is now open — more fearful yet the open road appears to us, stretching on to who knows where.

***

The love of our neighbor is the only door out of the dungeon of self, where we mope and mow, striking sparks, and rubbing phosphorescences out of the walls, and blowing our own breath in our own nostrils, instead of issuing to the fair sunlight of God, the sweet winds of the universe.

— George MacDonald

***

You cannot take Jesus to India. You cannot take Jesus to Africa. The call to take Jesus to the heathen is ridiculous. We cannot take Jesus anywhere. He is already in Africa. He is already beside the mother in the hut in India. He is already there loving and healing and ministering. He takes us to join him in his loving service to his children. He has already been there. Before we were born, he was there. Before we could think of going, he was already there. He takes us, we never take him.

— D. T. Niles

***

He is the Way. Follow him though the Land of Unlikeness;
you will see rare beasts
and have unique adventures.

He is the Truth. Seek him in the Kingdom of Anxiety:
you will come to a great city
that has expected your return for years.

He is the Life. Love him in the World of the Flesh:
and at your marriage
all its occasions shall dance for joy.

— W. H. Auden, from the "Christmas Oratorio"

***

E. Stanley Jones tells of a missionary who got lost in the African jungle. When he happened upon a native hut, he asked if the man who lived there could guide him out. The native agreed to do so. "All right," said the missionary, "show me the way."

The native said just one word: "Walk." Together they walked for more than an hour, hacking their way through the thick undergrowth with machetes.

When they finally stopped for a rest, the missionary had grown worried. "Are you quite sure this is the way? Where is the path?"

"Bwana," replied his companion, "in this place there is no path. I am the path."

***

There is a God-shaped vacuum in the heart of every man which cannot be filled by any created thing, but only by God, the Creator, made known through Jesus Christ.

— Blaise Pascal

Seventh Sunday Of Easter
May 28, 2006

Revised Common	Acts 1:15-17, 21-26	1 John 5:9-13	John 17:6-19
Roman Catholic	Acts 1:15-17, 20-26	1 John 4:11-16	John 17:11-19
Episcopal	Acts 1:15-26	1 John 5:9-15	John 17:11b-19

Theme For The Day   Christ's prayer for the church is that it would have gifts of unity, protection, and truth.

First Lesson   Acts 1:15-17, 21-26   *The Selection Of Matthias To Fill Judas' Place*

Peter reminds the company of the faithful of the vacancy among the twelve apostles that was created by Judas' death. (Luke interjects some parenthetical detail here, omitted by the lectionary, about Judas' death — not by suicide but by some dreadful abdominal illness.) Peter announces that a man must be chosen from among the outer circle of disciples to become "a witness with us to his resurrection" (v. 22b). The crowd proposes two names, and Matthias — about whom we know almost nothing — is chosen by prayer and the casting of lots (v. 26). Peter's prayer preceding the casting of lots indicates that the choice is made not by chance, but by God. This passage is important because it includes Luke's definition of an apostle as an authoritative eyewitness to the resurrection. Apostolic ministry, by extension, is any ministry that communicates this apostolic testimony. The church's leadership is not without its human weaknesses — Luke's graphic description of Judas' death and the community's recent memory of Peter's betrayal are evidence of that — but God accommodates human weakness in order to allow the church's witness to continue.

New Testament Lesson   1 John 5:9-13   *Whoever Has The Son Has Life*

The lectionary concludes its march through 1 John with this passage, which begins with an affirmation that the greatest testimony is not any human proclamation, but the work God has done in giving Jesus to the world. There is a choice set before every human being: to believe in Jesus Christ, or not to believe in him. Our decision reveals the degree to which we trust God. Eternal life is found in Jesus alone: "Whoever has the Son has life; whoever does not have the Son of God does not have life" (v. 12). This selection concludes with the first verse of the epilogue to this letter, in which the author declares his purpose for writing: "that you who believe in the name of the Son of God ... may know that you have eternal life" (v. 13).

The Gospel   John 17:6-19   *Christ's Prayer For The Church*

Jesus' lengthy prayer, of which this passage is a part, is sometimes called his High Priestly Prayer, and sometimes his Great Prayer for the Church. It is highly unlikely that this is an exact transcription of a public prayer offered by the historical Jesus. Rather, it reflects John's theological understanding of the person and work of Christ, and of Christ's desire for unity among his followers — particularly those late first-century disciples to whom John is writing. The concerns addressed in the prayer are very much those facing the Johannine church toward the end of the first century. Speaking of his followers, Jesus asks God "that they may be one, as we are one" (v. 11). He asks for God to protect them from the evil one, and from the world's hatred (vv. 14-15). Like him, he declares, these believers now belong not to the world, but to heaven

(v. 16). Jesus prays that God will "sanctify them in the truth," in conformity to God's Word, which "is truth" (v. 17). These concerns — unity, protection, and orthodoxy — all reflect the situation of the Johannine church, which was beginning to undergo persecution and to experience problems of disunity resulting from false teaching.

Preaching Possibilities

What would Jesus say to the contemporary church, if he reappeared among us?

A similar question was undoubtedly in John's mind, as he composed the lengthy discourses and prayers which are, for him, a compendium of Jesus' teaching. John is concerned about a church increasingly troubled by internal conflicts, vulnerable to persecution and tempted by teachings that are, to his mind, unorthodox. The lengthy prayer of Jesus that John reconstructs in chapter 17 — far too long a prayer to have been recorded verbatim — is in fact John's imaginative answer to the question of what Jesus would say to the church of his own day.

The three concerns — unity, protection from evil, and the maintenance of true teaching — are remarkably relevant to the needs of today's church. They could provide the outline for a sermon.

First, unity. It is especially apparent in North America how splintered the church of Jesus Christ has become. The "melting pot" nature of our culture, uniting immigrants from around the world into a single society, has created a situation that is historically unique. The historic national divisions among European churches have become, in our setting, denominational divisions within a single nation. The inertia present in all human bureaucracies — of which ecclesiastical bureaucracies are, sadly, no exception — has resisted most efforts at denominational union. The twentieth century, which began hopefully in the United States with unity movements like the Federal Council of Churches (later the National Council of Churches), and continued with the post-Second World War Consultation on Church Union, has ended in an ecumenical stalemate. In Canada, a bold move to create a united Protestant church has resulted in a situation in which some are in, but many others still out. There have been small gains, to be sure, but the overall witness of our varied denominations is still one of scandalous disunity. Jesus' prayer for the twenty-first century church would undoubtedly still include a plea that, "that they may be one, as we are one."

Second, Jesus' prayer for the first-century church includes a wish for protection from "the evil one" (or, in some variant texts, simply from "evil"). Persecution was an obvious threat in the days of John, so a prayer for protection from evil would have been clearly understood to mean protection from the imperial authorities — who had already wreaked havoc within Judaism, through the sack of Jerusalem and destruction of the temple. The church in North America is not, of course, under persecution (despite the rhetoric from certain extremist factions in our midst, who see the separation of church and state — affecting issues such as the wording of the Pledge of Allegiance and the posting of the Ten Commandments in courthouses — as a form of persecution). Far from outright persecution, we are more in danger of being consigned to irrelevance by a culture that increasingly turns a deaf ear to Christianity's witness. The contemporary threat from the evil one — from which we do need to be protected — takes the form more of studied indifference than deliberate persecution.

Third, Jesus prays that God will sanctify the church in the truth. So many of our neighbors, in this diverse society, have trivialized truth. Some have come to disbelieve that there is such a thing as ultimate truth at all. For such individuals, there is only utility: the things that work and the things that don't. If Christianity works for you, many seem to be saying, then believe it; if it doesn't, then find something else that works better. As long as you end up feeling happy, it doesn't matter. This is no basis on which to select a religious allegiance. Jesus is not asking God to sanctify his followers in the truth so they can flit here and flit there, sampling every dish on the spiritual smorgasbord. No, he is giving them the Spirit of truth so they may discern the one true path, and follow it.

Prayer For The Day
> Come, my Way, my Truth, my Life:
> Such a way as gives us breath,
> Such a truth as ends all strife,
> Such a life as killeth death.
> Come, my Joy, my Love, my Heart:
> Such a joy as all can move,
> Such a love as none can part,
> Such a heart as joy in love.

— George Herbert (adapted)

To Illustrate

Many years ago, the United States Army issued a guidebook for its noncommissioned officers.

One of the topics in this guidebook was how a sergeant could deal with two soldiers who had been quarreling: how they could rediscover unity and become friends again.

The guide suggests that the two men should be assigned to wash the same window: one outside, one inside. As they stand looking at each other, rags and cleaning fluid in hand, absorbed in a common task, it is all but impossible for them to continue being angry.

***

An old, but still serviceable comic story about ecumenical disunity ...

A shipwreck victim was marooned alone on a desert island for many years. Like Robinson Crusoe, the castaway cleverly constructed everything he needed out of materials he found on the island: bamboo, gourds, coconut shells. He was proud of his handiwork — so proud that, when a rescue ship finally arrived, he refused to leave, until the captain had accompanied him on a walking tour.

Proudly, the castaway showed the captain everything he'd made: his dugout canoe, the treehouse where he lived, his storehouse bulging with food, the little shed where he kept his fishing gear. Finally they came to the largest structure of all: a magnificent, thatch-roofed building, made of bamboo poles lashed together, with what appeared to be a steeple rising from its roof. Inside, there were rows of handmade benches. Up in front was a pulpit carved from the trunk of a tree, and high in the steeple hung a hollowed-out gourd in the shape of a bell.

It seemed to the captain that this church was the cleverest creation of all. But then he looked out the window ... and saw another building, very much like the one he was standing in.

"If this is your church," he asked the man, "then what do you call that?"

"Oh, pay no attention to that building," answered the castaway. "That's the church I used to go to."

***

A group of pastors from India was once talking with an American relief worker. "You Americans," they told him, "are utterly unequipped for life in the real world."

"You think that life is supposed to be pleasant: life, liberty, the pursuit of happiness, and all that stuff. When it's not, you think something is wrong that you need to fix. Once fixed, you can get back to a normal state: pleasant."

"On the contrary," he continued. "We think life is hard. We know we will suffer. Our challenge is to learn how to trust God in the midst of suffering, find his purposes through it, and still have the courage and hope to change it."

***

One of the items that circulated anonymously by e-mail following the terrorist attacks of September 11, 2001 was this set of comparisons — between Monday, September 10th, and Tuesday, September 11th. What follows is edited from a longer list....

On Monday we e-mailed jokes
On Tuesday we did not
On Monday we thought that we were secure
On Tuesday we learned better
On Monday we were talking about heroes as being athletes
On Tuesday we relearned who our heroes are
On Monday we were irritated that our rebate checks had not arrived
On Tuesday we gave money away to people we had never met
On Monday there were people fighting against prayer in schools
On Tuesday you would have been hard pressed to find a school where someone was not praying
On Monday people argued with their kids about cleaning up their room
On Tuesday the same people could not get home fast enough to hug their kids
On Monday people were upset that they had to wait six minutes in a supermarket line
On Tuesday people didn't care about waiting up to six hours to give blood for the dying
...
On Monday there were people trying to separate each other by race, sex, color, and creed
On Tuesday they were all holding hands ...
Remember, the front of all U.S. coins say ... In God We Trust

***

It's well known that the official seal of Harvard University includes an open book, and the motto, *Veritas* — Latin for "Truth." What is not so well known is that this is not the seal Harvard has always had. The original university crest showed three open books — one of them face-down, to show the limitations of human knowledge. The motto underneath was not simply *Veritas*, or "Truth," but *Veritas Christo et Ecclesiae* — "Truth for Christ and the Church." It is interesting to note how one of the greatest universities in our land, founded originally for the purpose of training young men for the ministry, has strayed so far from its roots. Is there such a thing as independent truth, unmoored from the divine truth in which truth is meant to be grounded? The Gospel of John would say, "No."

***

144

What is worst of all is to advocate Christianity, not because it is true but because it might prove useful.... To justify Christianity because it provides a foundation of morality, instead of showing the necessity of Christian morality from the truth of Christianity, is a very dangerous inversion.... It is not enthusiasm, but dogma, that differentiates a Christian from a pagan society.

— T. S. Eliot

***

The inspirational writer Robert Fulghum tells the story of how he once traveled to Greece, to attend a seminar. On the last day of the conference, the teacher walked over to the bright light of an open window and looked out. Then, he asked if there were any questions. Fulghum, as anyone who's read any of his books knows, is something of a jokester. He laughingly asked the seminar leader what was the meaning of life. Everyone laughed and got ready to leave. But then the leader held up his hand, to ask for silence. He responded, "I will answer your question."

Then, he took his wallet out of his pocket, and removed from it a small round mirror about the size of a quarter. "When I was a small child during World War II," he explained, "we were very poor and we lived in a remote village. One day on the road, I found the broken pieces of a mirror. A German motorcycle had been wrecked in that place. I tried to find all the pieces and put them together, but it was not possible, so I kept the largest piece. This one. And by scratching it on a stone, I made it round. I began to play with it as a toy and became fascinated by the fact that I could reflect light into dark places where the sun could never shine. It became a game for me to get light into the most inaccessible places that I could find. I kept the little mirror, and as I grew up, I would take it out at idle moments and continue the challenge of the game.

"As I became a man, I grew to understand that this was not just a child's game, but a metaphor of what I could do with my life. I came to understand that I am not the light or the source of the light. But light — be it truth or understanding or knowledge — is there, and it will only shine in many dark places if I reflect it. I am a fragment of a mirror whose whole design and shape I do not know. Nevertheless, with what I have, I can reflect light into the dark places of this world — into the dark places of human hearts — and change some things in some people. Perhaps others seeing it happen will do likewise.

"This is what I am about. This is the meaning of my life."

The Pentecost Season
Sundays In Ordinary Time

Depending on one's ecclesiastical tradition, the season in which we now find ourselves is known either as the Season of Pentecost or as the second part of Ordinary Time. Whatever name we give the season, the first two Sundays of this season are special days: The Day Of Pentecost and The Holy Trinity, respectively. Once these two special days are past, the following Sunday is either the third Sunday after Pentecost (Pentecost 4) or the eleventh Sunday in Ordinary Time (the numbering of days in Ordinary Time picks up where the last Sunday in Ordinary Time left off, prior to Lent).

There is more theological continuity to the Season of Pentecost than to the Season of Epiphany. While scripture texts for Sundays following Epiphany have little to do with Epiphany themes of revelation and light, many of the selections for Sundays following Pentecost can, broadly speaking, be said to belong to the era of the church — the time in which the Holy Spirit is uniquely active. Proponents of the Ordinary Time designation would assert that this is not universally true of all the lections for this season and that, besides, by the time the autumn months are upon us, Pentecost is but a distant memory.

Whether or not we use the "Ordinary Time" designation, this season represents, by far, the largest portion of the Christian year — approximately half. These Sundays are, therefore, ordinary in a certain sense: they are the gathering of God's people to celebrate the Lord's Day, pure and simple. God is just as present among the people in this season as in any other.

The Year B version of Pentecost / Ordinary Time contains a seven-week series of Second Lesson Readings from the Letter to the Hebrews, beginning in early September. While it is common for Second Lesson Readings to come from the same book for several weeks in succession, this series is particularly long and contains much repetition in content. Planning ahead is always advisable in lectionary preaching, but is particularly wise when it comes to this material.

The Day Of Pentecost
June 4, 2006

Revised Common	Acts 2:1-21	Romans 8:22-27	John 15:26-27;
	or Ezekiel 37:1-14	*or* Acts 2:1-21	16:4b-15
Roman Catholic	Acts 2:1-11	1 Corinthians 12:3-7, 12-13	John 20:19-23
Episcopal	Acts 2:1-11	1 Corinthians 12:4-13	John 20:19-23
	or Isaiah 44:1-8	*or* Acts 2:1-11	*or* John 14:8-17

Theme For The Day   The gift of the Holy Spirit at Pentecost is a gift of mutual understanding.

First Lesson   Acts 2:1-21   *The Day Of Pentecost*

The details of this story are well known: the disciples gathered fearfully in one place, the sound of a rushing wind, "divided tongues as of fire" appearing over each one's head and the newfound ability to speak — and, more remarkably, to be understood — in other languages. The Holy Spirit, of course, gets the credit for these ecstatic gifts. In verses 5-11, Luke tells of the astonishment of the polyglot Jerusalem crowd, who hear individual disciples speaking in their own languages. It should be pointed out that, in this passage, the only tongues being spoken are intelligible human languages, not the *glossolalia* of 1 Corinthians 14. Luke's list of the various nations represented in the crowd is a catalogue of all the places to which the apostles will soon travel, spreading the good news — first to the people of the Jewish diaspora in those lands, and then (after the events of Acts 10) to the Gentiles. Not everyone "gets it," though: there are some bystanders who only sneer, "They are filled with new wine" (v. 13). This story sets the stage for all that will follow in the rest of the book: the drama of the growth of the church of Jesus Christ, in which the Holy Spirit is the principal actor.

Alternate First Lesson   Ezekiel 37:1-14   *The Valley Of Dry Bones*

This is Ezekiel's mystical vision of the valley of the dry bones. Essential to understanding this passage is the fact that the "vast multitude" in verse 10 is in fact the slaughtered army of Israel. In vivid imagery, the prophet describes how the bleached bones on this ancient battlefield come together, become enfleshed, and live. The people say, "Our bones are dried up, and our hope is lost; we are cut off completely" (v. 11b); but nothing is impossible with God. There are some standard prophetic devices here: the Spirit of the Lord miraculously transporting Ezekiel to the place (v. 1), the dialogue between the Lord and the prophet (v. 3 and elsewhere), the Lord telling the prophet what to say (v. 4), and the predicted result that humans "shall know that I am the Lord" (v. 5). A powerful story, and appropriate indeed for Pentecost.

New Testament Lesson   Romans 8:22-27   *The Spirit Helps Us In Our Weakness*

It is unfortunate that the lectionary breaks into the middle of this great Pauline argument as it does — although if the text is used only as a subsidiary reading to support the story of Pentecost from Acts 2, that is perhaps not so great a matter. Romans 8 is certainly deserving of a sermon in its own right, though, and those who undertake such an effort would do well to back up and begin the scriptural teaching at an earlier point in this letter, perhaps with verse 18 (and possibly earlier). Much of this chapter has been devoted to a detailed exposition of the difference between flesh and spirit. Beginning with verse 18, Paul speaks of human suffering.

Although suffering is very much a part of human life, help is on the way: all creation will soon be set free (v. 21). The suffering of this present time, is in fact, not futile. It is a productive kind of suffering, like labor pains (v. 22). There is much groaning, to be sure, but a new birth of hope is coming soon. Hope, by its very nature, is in things unseen (v. 24). In these between-times, "the Spirit helps us in our weakness; for we do not know how to pray as we ought, but that very Spirit intercedes with sighs too deep for words" (v. 26). The Spirit is our intercessor, our helper.

Alternate New Testament Lesson   Acts 2:1-21   *The Day Of Pentecost*
   If the Pentecost story from Acts has not been used as a First Lesson, it may be used as an alternate Second Lesson (see above).

The Gospel   John 15:26-27; 16:4b-15   *The Coming Of The Advocate*
   For the larger context of this passage, see the Fifth Sunday Of Easter (p. 129). Jesus has been speaking of himself as the *true vine* and, beginning at verse 18, has been speaking to the disciples about persecutions and sufferings that will inevitably come upon them. Here in this passage, he comforts them with the teaching that the Holy Spirit will be with them through those times of trial, as their "advocate" (*parakletos* — v. 26). This is courtroom imagery: a *parakletos* is like an attorney for the defense. The lectionary selection then jumps to chapter 16, v. 4b: Jesus must depart from the disciples, he tells them, for the Spirit will not be able to come and advocate for them until after he is gone (v. 7). The advocate "will prove the world wrong" — more courtroom terminology: the Spirit will literally "convict the world of its error" (v. 8). Throughout the Gospel of John, the Spirit is powerfully associated with truth ("he will guide you into all truth" — v. 13). As with the Romans 8 passage, a sermon on this passage should go beyond the fragmented lectionary selection and treat the larger block of material.

Preaching Possibilities
   The story of the coming of the Holy Spirit at Pentecost is precious to every denominational and theological tradition within the Christian church, yet no biblical account has inspired such widely varying interpretations. One major branch of Christianity — the Pentecostal tradition — views this incident as the source of its most cherished and distinctive beliefs; yet in truth, the Pentecost story belongs to no single tradition. Were any single tradition to try to claim this unique and miraculous event for its own, it would be contradicting the wild, unbridled diversity that is at the heart of this story. As William Willimon points out, one has the impression, in reading the second chapter of Acts, that Luke's account — strange as it seems — barely scratches the surface of the strangeness that was in the Jerusalem air that day:

> *More than one interpretation can be offered for what happened in the upper room at Pentecost. No single formulation can do it justice. We are listening to the account of something strange, beyond the bounds of imagination, miraculous, inscrutable, an origin which, as far as Luke is concerned, was the only way one could "explain" the existence of the church. No flat, prosaic explanation can do justice to the truth of how the church came into being and how the once timid disciples found their tongues to proclaim the truth of Christ.*
> — William H. Willimon, *Acts*, in the *Interpretation* series
> (Atlanta: John Knox Press, 1988), p. 29

It couldn't have been very organized, or very genteel. It isn't high tea, with all the disciples sitting around and conversing with the delicacy of diplomats. No, Pentecost is a little bit of heaven breaking in. There is the rush of a mighty wind, and tongues of fire dancing around; there's screaming and sweating and running and embracing. No one — not even the eloquent Luke — could ever convey the experience in words. It is a joyous, chaotic, frightening moment. Confusion and bewilderment, and more than a little wonder — that's Pentecost.

At the heart of it all is this remarkable experience of mutual understanding. According to the Pentecost story, understanding is a gift of the Spirit. And so it is — for we human beings are so prone to misunderstanding one another, that it sometimes seems a miracle we can communicate at all.

Language is only one thing that divides us. There are also differences of experience, of economic status, of gender, of age. Sometimes it feels like each of us is ultimately alone — sealed up in our private world, never able to see into the heart of another. The lesson of Pentecost, however, is that, by the power of the Holy Spirit, communication — and communion — can and does take place.

There are certain writers in the field of church growth who insist that the fastest way for a church to grow is to gather a group of people who are similar to each other as possible. If the church is a voluntary association of like-minded people, then the more things your people have in common, the more likely they will be to invite all their friends.

Pretty simple, isn't it? — if it weren't for one small problem. This kind of thinking flies in the face of Pentecost. A Pentecost church does not form itself out of "like-minded people"; it will be a motley assortment of all types and conditions of humanity. There will be rich and poor, young and old, the accepted and the rejected. There will be those who proclaim, "I've made it!" and those who lay in their beds after the alarm clock rings and pray, "Lord, just get me through another day." The mixed-ups, the up-and-comings, the down-and-outs and the down-to-earth all find a place in Christ's church.

There is unity in the church of Jesus Christ, but not a whole lot of uniformity. In the Roman world, everyone knew where unity came from — it came from power. The tramping boots of Roman legions had brought to the world a sort of superficial unity. You could travel from the British Isles to the Arabian desert, and if Latin were the only language you knew, it was enough to get by.

Yet, that is not the unity of Pentecost. Luke lists all those diverse nationalities, then points out that *in their own languages* they hear them speak. In the unity of God, no language is elevated higher than any other. No one is cast out, set aside or put down. God comes and speaks to us, on our own terms.

And, more than that, by that same Spirit we are empowered to understand. Would that the church of Jesus Christ could claim this spiritual gift more often, and with boldness!

Prayer For The Day
Teach us to love you as your angels love,
One holy passion filling all our frame
The baptism of the heaven-descended dove,
Our hearts an altar, and your love the flame.
— Adapted from George Croly, "Spirit of God, Descend Upon My Heart," 1854

To Illustrate

It was Winston Churchill who said that England and the United States are "two countries divided by a common language." Yet how often that can be true even within the most intimate of human institutions, the family. How easy it can be for husband and wife, parent and child, brother and sister, to talk with each other for hours on end, both parties speaking English — yet neither one truly understanding the other on the deepest level! Pentecost celebrates the Holy Spirit's gift of understanding on the deepest level.

***

Those who work in hospice ministry tell how frequently it happens that certain dying patients, who have functioned perfectly well using English as a second language, gradually revert to their first language on their deathbed. If their dying is prolonged, they may lose English altogether — creating certain practical difficulties for the hospice team, who may have to scramble to find a translator.

It's a beautiful thing, though, in its own way: how, when certain people prepare to cross over into the next life, they are focusing so clearly on seeing their parents and grandparents, those who have gone before them — and how they may journey, in memory, back to the time in distant childhood when they first met Jesus. It only makes sense that they would want to function, from that point onward, in the language of home — for home is where they are headed.

The miracle of Pentecost is that our God addresses us in the language of home: "In our own languages we hear them speaking about God's deeds of power." That's because our relationship with God is meant to be intimate. God means there to be no barriers to our understanding, no obstacles to block our awareness that God is near.

When Jesus himself is dying on the cross, he speaks not Greek, the language of commerce and learning, which is a second language for him. Nor does he speak Hebrew, the language of his religious faith. He speaks Aramaic: *Eloi, Eloi, lama sabachthani*: "My God, my God, why have you forsaken me?" In his dying agony, he reverts to the language he learned at his mother's knee.

There is another occasion when the gospel writers record Jesus speaking Aramaic. When he's teaching the disciples to pray, he instructs them to address God as "Abba" — the Aramaic diminutive for "Father." Literally, he's advising them to address God as "Daddy."

In death and in prayer ... in times of extreme solitude — when (as the gospel hymn puts it), "we've got to walk that lonesome valley, we've got to walk it by ourselves" we hear God speaking to us in our own language. And that's a wonder and a joy.

***

In the Christian vision, one Greek word has consistently characterized the Holy Spirit: *dynamis*, from which we get our word dynamite. The Spirit is Power, the Spirit is dynamite.
— Walter J. Burghardt

***

Power can be used in at least two ways: it can be unleashed, or it can be harnessed. The energy in ten gallons of gasoline, for instance, can be released explosively by dropping a lighted match into the can. Or it can be channeled through the engine of a Honda in a controlled burn and used to transport a person 350 miles. Explosions are spectacular, but controlled burns have lasting effect, staying power. The Holy Spirit works both ways.

At Pentecost, the Holy Spirit exploded on the scene; its presence was like "tongues of fire" (Acts 2:3). Thousands were affected by one burst of God's power. But the Spirit also works through the church — the institution God began to tap the Holy Spirit's power for the long haul. Through worship, fellowship, and service, Christians are provided with staying power.

— Anonymous

***

Dean Heather Murray Elkins of Drew Seminary speaks of the power of God's Holy Spirit as we con-spire with it in the work of co-creation. To con-spire means "to breathe with." The Hebrew word for God's breath is *ruah*; God *breathed* life into the first human beings. *Ruah* translated to Greek becomes Spirit. The Holy Spirit then is literally God's breath, breathing new life into our very bodies, breathing into the plant and animal life of the earth, as we respire in perfect balance in this delicate dance of life. We are called to be agents of the Holy Spirit's con-spiracy to transform humanity, to bring us back into right relationship with all that is and with God.

— Cynthia Crowner, "A Conspiracy of Healing Power," in *The Ridgeleaf*,
newsletter of the Kirkridge retreat center, March 1999

The Holy Trinity
June 11, 2006

Revised Common	Isaiah 6:1-8	Romans 8:12-17	John 3:1-17
Roman Catholic	Deuteronomy 4:32-34, 39-40	Romans 8:14-17	Matthew 28:16-20
Episcopal	Exodus 3:1-6	Romans 8:12-17	John 3:1-16

Theme For The Day   God's holiness awes, cleanses, inspires, and sends forth.

Old Testament Lesson   Isaiah 6:1-8   *The Call Of Isaiah*

The opening lines of this passage, "In the year that King Uzziah died ..." set the reader up for an event of great significance. Yet, what follows is a vision of cosmic, not merely national, importance. "I saw the Lord," Isaiah bluntly declares, "sitting on a throne, high and lofty; and the hem of his robe filled the temple." The statuary and decorations of the temple interior mingle with Isaiah's vision, as in some strange dream: the seraphs — huge, winged, angelic creatures that were carved on the sides of the throne in the temple — come to life, hovering over the smoke-enshrouded area where the Lord has appeared. Their words, "Holy, holy, holy is the Lord of hosts," have since come to be included in thousands of hymns and anthems. The smoke from the sacrifice that ordinarily fills the temple becomes, in Isaiah's vision, an element of the vision itself (v. 4). Holiness is the predominant theological idea in Isaiah's vision: the image of the Lord the young prophet is blessed to see is at once fearsome and powerful. The Hebrew word translated as "holy" is *qadosh*, which literally means that which is separated or removed from our ordinary lives. In verses 5-7 we learn that Isaiah's response to this awe-inspiring vision is to confess his sin — to acknowledge himself as nothing by comparison. That he confesses himself to be "a man of unclean lips" is significant, in light of the prophetic vocation he will soon take up. The Lord's response is to send one of the seraphs flying over to him with a burning coal in a pair of tongs; the heat from the glowing coal purifies the prophet's lips, so his speech, henceforth, will be in service to God. Then, in verse 8, comes the divine calling itself: "Whom shall I send, and who will go for us?" Isaiah's humble and faith-filled response is, "Here am I, send me!"

New Testament Lesson   Romans 8:12-17   *Adopted, Through The Spirit's Power, As God's Children*

Last Sunday's New Testament Lesson was Romans 8:22-27; now we move back a dozen or so verses in this same chapter. As this passage opens, Paul is in the midst of expounding a favorite theme of his, the dichotomy between flesh and spirit. Rather than living as those in debt (or bondage) to the flesh, he advises the Roman Christians: "If by the Spirit you put to death the deeds of the body, you will live" (v. 13). What we have received from God, he continues, is not a spirit of slavery but a spirit of adoption (v. 14). Adoption was a well-established institution in the Roman world; a young man who had been officially adopted by a noble patron became, in every respect, that noble person's son. It is an extraordinary claim Paul's making here: that, through the Spirit, Christians are offered a spirit of adoption that gives them, in God's eyes, the same status as God's Son, Jesus. We are privileged to employ the same form of address Jesus used in speaking to God: the familiar term, "Abba" (v. 15). We are "heirs of God and joint heirs with Christ." Yet, there is something expected of us in return: that "we suffer with him so that we may also be glorified with him" (v. 17). As a text for The Holy Trinity, this passage may be useful as an example of the close, familial relationship between the first and second persons of the Trinity, and of the role of the third person (the Holy Spirit) in gracefully leading believers into that same familial relationship.

The Gospel   John 3:1-17   *Jesus And Nicodemus*

We return now to the encounter between Jesus and Nicodemus. We have already considered a smaller section of this passage, verses 14-21, on the Fourth Sunday In Lent (see p. 91). This fuller version includes the narrative portion of the Nicodemus story in its entirety, omitting only the closing lines of Jesus' final discourse. (This omission is probably due to the fact that this closing section has recently appeared in the lectionary; logically, the entire block of material belongs together.) Readers could, perhaps, wish for a fuller exposition of the character of Nicodemus. John uses him in this passage primarily as a straw man against whom Jesus' argument is played out — and the learned Pharisee is about as uncomprehending as if he were literally made of straw.

This is another example of how, in John, narrative details are subservient to the overarching purpose of expounding theology. This is especially evident here, in the fact that, once Jesus' discourse is finished, John never finishes the Nicodemus story. The question of whether or not the Pharisee ultimately buys Jesus' argument is evidently unimportant to him. Nicodemus comes to Jesus by night — a fact that has led many commentators to suggest that he is fearful to be seen conversing with the Nazarene. At the very least, it means Nicodemus is seeking a private conversation. The Pharisee's opening words (v. 2) express his admiration for Jesus, and particularly for signs of power he has performed — demonstrating that he is intending this to be a goodwill visit, and not an adversarial confrontation. Rather abruptly, Jesus states, "No one can see the kingdom of God without being born from above" (v. 3). This is a notoriously difficult expression to translate. The verb *gennao*, here translated "born," can also mean "begotten" — referring, in other words, to either the male or female mode of parenting. The adverb *agothen* can mean both "from above" and "again." It is possible that John is aware of, and exploits, the double meaning: either one — or both — makes sense in the larger context. Seemingly oblivious to the possibility of metaphor, Nicodemus asks, "How can anyone be born after having grown old? Can one enter a second time into the mother's womb and be born?" (v. 4).

Jesus repeats his previous assertion about the necessity of rebirth, adding only the detail that this rebirth must be "of water and Spirit" (v. 5). It is unclear what Jesus means here by "water" — possibly the baptism of John, possibly Christian baptism, possibly Jewish purification rituals (with which Nicodemus would have been familiar), possibly amniotic fluid. There is no definite article before "spirit," so it is possible Jesus means the Holy Spirit, and possibly some more generic sense of the word — although the fact that he uses "Spirit" with the definite article in verses 6 and 8 suggests the former.

In any event, Jesus is drawing a distinction between flesh and Spirit (v. 6), and is indicating that a decision for the way of the Spirit is the better course. In verse 8, most translators choose to translate *pneuma* as "wind" the first time it occurs and as "spirit" the second time. Like the Hebrew *ruach*, the same word suffices for both — another Johannine double meaning. John is probably not operating under Greek mind-body dualism, in any event. For him and for most of his contemporaries, the moment of human death is when the breath, the wind, leaves the body. Flesh is the lower nature that is animated by breath, which is synonymous with the life-force. With its allusion to the unpredictable wind, this verse testifies to the utterly free and unbounded nature of the Holy Spirit. In verse 9, Nicodemus responds with a total lack of comprehension, and in verse 10, Jesus speaks to him in a rather condescending fashion.

153

From this point on, John drops his narrative framework and enters full discourse mode. See the Fourth Sunday In Lent (p. 91) for comments on the remainder of this passage.

Preaching Possibilities

There's a certain fascination that sends people out into storms, just to experience the power of the elements. My family and I sometimes venture out onto the beach, when a hurricane or nor'easter passes by our portion of the Atlantic coast. Tasting the grit of sand in our mouths, squinting our eyes between the wind-gusts to look at the storm's fury, we gaze out over what is usually a broad bathing-beach, but on this night is simply no longer there.

Not most of it, anyway. The waves break close to the line of sand dunes that are held in place by the wooden snow fencing and what's left of the dune grass. As for the waves themselves, they look different. No longer are they that sequential series of rollers, typical in calmer weather. No: in the midst of a storm, the sea seems as one, huge wave. Above the roiling mass of olive-green water there hangs a wreath of mist. The sound the sea makes is a continuous crashing.

Why do we do it? What makes otherwise sane, logical people so bold as to go down to the beach — the beach, of all places — on a cold night, in the middle of a storm? Fascination sends us down there: the same fascination that sends people careening over Oklahoma backroads in pickup trucks, chasing tornados ... the same attraction that fills theaters with moviegoers eager to witness the watery demise of a steamship named "Titanic." It's an encounter with what theologian Rudolf Otto calls, in his famous book, *The Idea of the Holy, mysterium tremendum et fascinans* — "tremendous and fascinating mystery." That's his definition of holiness.

It's much bigger than we are, this mystery. What's intrinsically fascinating about it is how little we, ourselves, can dream of controlling it — not to mention the whiff of danger that lurks around its edges! In the lee of the storm, you and I glimpse ourselves, outlined in a flash of lightning, as we really are: small and vulnerable, finite and limited.

In the year that King Uzziah died, Isaiah has his vision: Uzziah, the king who had begun his reign with such promise, but who died in disgrace. Who is it who has power to cast down kings from their thrones? It can only be the Lord! The God who cursed King Uzziah with leprosy, and who appears to Isaiah "sitting on a throne, high and lofty," in the temple, is a figure of dreadful power, who calls forth incredible fear. The very foundations of the temple seem shaken.

"Woe is me!" cries Isaiah. "I am lost, for I am a man of unclean lips, and I live among a people of unclean lips; yet my eyes have seen the king, the Lord of hosts!" It's the kind of thing you just might shout into the wind as a nor'easter is raging: but the wind whips your words away, off into space. What are words, anyway? How long do they last? Words are but fragile, transitory things: so much like us, our fleeting human lives. In the presence of the holy, ego-inflated pride shrinks away to nothingness.

This text from Isaiah is troubling to modern ears. Few of us come to church expecting to hear someone cry out, "Woe is me! I am lost, for I am a man of unclean lips...." The truth is, most of us would rather not hear about that sort of thing. Wouldn't we rather practice "the power of positive thinking"? Wouldn't we prefer to surround ourselves with self-affirmation ... to build up our self-esteem ... to reassure ourselves with the mantra of televangelist Robert Schuller: "Every day, in every way, I am getting better and better"?

The problem is, for Isaiah, that his vision doesn't allow him to do that. The light of God's glory has cast the prophet's shadow onto the wall behind him, in sharp relief — and he doesn't much like the silhouette he sees. Before Isaiah can do a thing more, the angel must hover over him: touching his lips, for the briefest instant, with a burning-hot coal from the fire on the altar. The heat from the sacrificial fire burns all his sin away.

Is Isaiah trying, in this passage, to bad-mouth the human race? Is it his goal to declare that people are just no good, that deep down within us we're all rotten to the core? No, his first intention is to elevate God, not to denigrate humanity. Isaiah is declaring that this God whom he has encountered in the temple is so huge, so awe-inspiring — so wholly other — that his life is as nothing by comparison.

What this great text is about, fundamentally, is awe. It's about the feeling the psalmist calls, "fear of the Lord." Isaiah's God is a God who cannot be trivialized — yet don't we try, so often, to do just that? Don't we endeavor to drag God down to our level? The one of whom the angels sing, "the whole earth is full of his glory" is not our buddy, our friend, our congenial traveling companion. This God can never be the great cosmic vending machine we sometimes wish we had — into which we plunk our prayers, like coins, expecting a sugary treat to fall out. This God is not the one who is responsible, in any way, for insuring that our lives on this earth are happy.

Once you and I are touched by holiness, our lives are never the same again. That empty place within is unveiled to the light: and the revealing of it can be (and often is) a fearful experience. Yet, thank the Lord, that "empty place" within each of us is a God-shaped place. Into that empty place comes Jesus Christ, the Lord.

Prayer For The Day

Holy, holy, holy are you, Lord God of hosts: the whole earth is filled with your glory! Give to us, we pray, in moments of your own choosing, some glimpse of your glory — and of our own unworthiness. May such a vision be, for us, like a burning coal placed to our lips. May we be sanctified by your presence, and sent out on the road of life to respond obediently to your call to serve. Amen.

To Illustrate

Our brains are no longer conditioned for reverence and awe. We cannot imagine a Second Coming that would not be cut down to size by the televised evening news, or a last judgment not subject to pages of holier-than-thou second-guessing in *The New York Review of Books.*

— John Updike

***

What I mean is that if we come to a church right, we come to it more fully and nakedly ourselves, come with more of our humanness showing, than we are apt to come to most places.... Like Moses [at the burning bush], we come here as we are, and like him we come as strangers and exiles in our way because wherever it is that we truly belong, whatever it is that is truly home for us, we know in our hearts that we have somehow lost it and gotten lost. Something is missing from our lives that we cannot even name — something we know best from the empty place inside us all where it belongs.

— Frederick Buechner

***

In an interesting homiletical move, John Donne emphasizes the infinite distance between us and holiness by a mathematical argument. It doesn't matter how many times one multiplies it, zero is still zero (among many apt analogies, he includes one about the span of life — prophetic, considering the fact that he couldn't have known how long modern medicine would be able to expand the duration of life):

> If I twist a cable of infinite fadomes in length, if there be no ship to ride by it, nor anchor to hold by it, what use is there of it? If Mannor thrust Mannor, and title flow into title, and bags powre out into chests, if I have no anchor, (faith in Christ) if I have not a ship to carry to a haven, (a soule to save) what's my long cable to me? If I adde number to number, a span, a mile long, if at the end of that long line of numbers, there be nothing that notes, pounds, or crownes, or shillings; what's that long number, but so many millions and millions of nothing? If my span of life become a mile of life, my penny a pound, my pint a gallon, my acre a sheere; yet if there be nothing of the next world at the end, so much pace of conscience, so much joy, so much glory, still all is but nothing multiplied, and that is still nothing at all. 'Tis the end that qualifies all; and what kinde of man I shall be at my end, upon my death-bed, what trembling hands, what lost legs, what deafe ears, what gummy eyes, I shall have then, I know; and the nearer I come to that disposition, in my life, (the more mortified I am) the better I am disposed to see this object, future glory. God made the Sun, and Moon, and Stars, glorious lights for man to see by; but mans infirmity requires spectacles; and affliction does that office.
>
> — John Donne, Sermon XXXI, in *Complete Poetry and Selected Prose*
> (London: Nonesuch, 1946), pp. 699-700

***

Eugene Peterson, in one of his books, says every church worthy of the name should be required by law to post a sign warning, "Beware the God."

***

There is no less holiness at this time — as you are reading this — than there was the day the Red Sea parted.... There is no whit less enlightenment under the tree by your street than there was under the Buddha's bo tree. There is no whit less might in heaven or on earth than there was the day Jesus said, "Maid, arise" to the centurion's daughter, or the day Peter walked on water, or the night Mohammed flew to heaven on a horse. In any instant, the sacred may wipe you with its finger. In any instant, the bush may flare, your feet may rise, or you may see a bunch of souls in a tree. In any instant, you may avail yourself of the power to love your enemies; to accept failure, slander, or the grief of loss; or to endure torture.

— Annie Dillard, *For the Time Being* (New York: Knopf, 1999)

Proper 6, Pentecost 4, Ordinary Time 11
June 18, 2006 (Father's Day)

Revised Common	1 Samuel 15:34—16:13	2 Corinthians 5:6-10 (11-13) 14-17	Mark 4:26-34
Roman Catholic	Ezekiel 17:22-24	2 Corinthians 5:6-10	Mark 4:26-34
Episcopal	Ezekiel 37:1-6, 10-14	2 Corinthians 5:1-10	Mark 4:26-34

Theme For The Day   A primary task of fatherhood is the symbolic anointing of children.

Old Testament Lesson   1 Samuel 15:34—16:13   *Samuel Anoints David As King, Replacing Saul*

Some background: in 15:26, Samuel rejects Saul's confession of sin, refusing to accompany the king any longer. In a poignant scene, the king reaches out to grasp the edge of the prophet's robe, tearing it. "The Lord has torn the kingdom of Israel from you this very day," Samuel responds at the time (v. 28). Now, in verse 35b, we learn that "the Lord was sorry that he had made Saul king over Israel." The Lord directs Samuel to stop moping, to fill his horn with anointing-oil, and seek out the sons of Jesse, from among whom God has chosen a successor to Saul (16:1). There is a clandestine nature to this undertaking — which is, in effect, a secret coronation. The Lord gives Samuel a cover story: he is to take a sacrificial cow with him, explaining his visit to Bethlehem as a religious, and not a political, mission. The fact that the village elders respond to Samuel's arrival with alarm suggests that he is indeed a powerful political figure in Israel; it's likely that news of the rift between the king and his chief prophet has reached their ears (v. 4). Samuel examines seven promising-looking sons of Jesse, one by one, but the Lord rejects them all. It is only then that he discovers there is an eighth son, David, who is out watching the sheep. Samuel orders that David be brought, and the Lord indicates that he is the one. Although the Lord has previously indicated that it is not outward appearance that matters, but a faithful heart, the author can't resist adding that David is "ruddy, and [has] beautiful eyes, and [is] handsome" (v. 12). Samuel anoints David, with his brothers for witnesses (v. 13). Verses 14-16 describe Saul's descent into madness, and set the scene for the entry of David into the royal court as a musician. The scriptures take pains to point out that, in the choice of David as king, the initiative belongs wholly to God.

Alternate Old Testament Lesson   Ezekiel 17:22-24   *The Lord Will Plant A New Tree On Mount Zion*

Speaking in metaphorical terms, the prophet declares that the Lord will plant a new tree on Mount Zion. Taking "a sprig from the lofty top of a cedar," the Lord will plant it, and in time it will mature into a tree that will provide many benefits. "I bring low the high tree, I make high the low tree" — God, in other words, will establish a new ruler for Israel, to offer the blessings of the Davidic kingship.

New Testament Lesson   2 Corinthians 5:6-10 (11-13) 14-17   *A New Creation*

On the subject of eternal life, Paul has just reassured the people that "if the earthly tent we live in is destroyed, we have a building from God, a house not made with hands, eternal in the heavens" (v. 1). Now we hear him speaking of supreme confidence in the Lord, because in this life "we walk by faith, not by sight" (v. 7). Knowing what he knows about life and death, the apostle admits that he naturally feels desire to be "away from the body and at home with the Lord" — although that is not what God wills for him at the present time (v. 8). Because Christ died for all, those who realize this truth must now live no longer for ourselves, but for him (v. 15). We must regard others no longer "from a human point of view" (literally, "according to the flesh"), but as God sees them (v. 16). That new vision, Paul says, is that "if anyone is in Christ, there is a new creation: everything old has passed away; see, everything has become new!" (v. 17). Conventional wisdom affirms, "You can't teach an old dog new tricks." In this great verse, Paul contradicts that pessimistic old saw by affirming that, in Christ, rebirth and renewal are always possible. Paul's assertion that Christ "died for all" (v. 15) is cryptic; there has been much debate over what the apostle means by it. Is it an offer of salvation to all, or is that salvation an accomplished fact (universalism)?

The Gospel   Mark 4:26-34   *Seed Parables*
We return now to the Gospel of Mark, after our long, Easter-season sojourn in Johannine literature. This passage contains three separate pericopes: the parable of the growing seed, the parable of the mustard seed, and a brief postscript in which Mark explains Jesus' use of parables. These are among the most elegantly simple of Jesus' parables: an allusion to the miracle of growing plants as symbolic of the coming reign of God, and another parable that focuses in on a particular type of seed, the mustard seed. That type of seed is the smallest and seemingly least significant of all, but it grows into an impressive plant. Jesus, here, reflects on a universal human experience: the feeling of wonder as we observe the growth of the natural world around us. Even today, with all that we know about biology, there is still something mysterious about that growth. Science has still not been able to define the life-force that is at the heart of the natural world. Farmers may manipulate nature in order to produce the most useful crops, but in the final analysis it is God who is responsible. Jesus is saying here, too, that the signs of God's reign in our midst may seem insignificant and nearly invisible: but just wait, they will result in remarkable growth.

Preaching Possibilities
Because this is Father's Day in the United States, the story from 1 Samuel of Jesse and his sons provides an excellent opportunity to consider the theme of fatherhood. "For the Lord does not see as mortals do; they look on the outward appearance, but the Lord looks on the heart" (1 Samuel 16:7b). A good father is one who aspires to "look on the heart" in just such a way.

Jesse has eight sons, and who knows how many daughters — but the name of only one of them has become a household word: David, the greatest of Israel's kings. Today's passage begins the story of how David came to be king over Israel.

God has decided it's time for a change: King Saul isn't working out so well, so God dispatches the Prophet Samuel on a secret mission: to go find the sons of Jesse, look them over, and see which one is to be the new king. Samuel doesn't ask how he'll recognize the new king; that's God's department.

The first one to step forward is Eliab — and a fine example of Israelite manhood he is, too. Samuel's all set to whip out his vial of anointing-oil and do the prophetic deed when God interrupts him, saying, "Do not look on his appearance or on the height of his stature, because I have rejected him; for the Lord does not see as mortals see; they look on the outward appearance, but the Lord looks on the heart."

One by one, Jesse parades his other sons before Samuel. Guided by the Lord, he rejects each one in turn. Finally, he ascertains that there is another son, and when David is at last brought before him, he is the one who passes the Lord's heart-test. Samuel reaches, mysteriously, into the folds of his robe, and pulls out a horn — in which is stored a carefully prepared supply of scented olive oil. He uncorks the horn, and pours the oil over young David's head. Then all the sons of Jesse know that David, the youngest among them, is destined to be king over Israel.

Yet what about those older brothers? As they paraded by that venerable, snowy-haired gentleman, the last living judge of Israel, they may not have known they were auditioning for kingship — but as they regard their youngest brother standing there, oil dripping down from his hair onto his tunic, and that giddy smile on his face, do they feel they have missed out? Why is it David, and not them, who has received the anointing?

This whole concept of anointing is symbolic of what children receive from their fathers (in the ideal world, anyway). Samuel wasn't David's father, of course, but in this story he steps into a fatherly role: blessing the boy who is on the verge of manhood, and performing for him a simple ritual he will remember all his life. Maybe, as David will shortly stand before the hulking champion Goliath, twirling his sling as it gradually picks up speed, he will remember the smell of that scented oil, and all that it symbolizes.

Fathers don't receive a lot of encouragement, in our society, for taking that role — for anointing their children. The shadow of John Wayne (or maybe, today, Clint Eastwood) looms large: the strong and silent figure riding off into the sunset, his work completed, the grateful women and children left behind. "Maw, who was that masked man?"... "I don't know — but he left a silver bullet!"

Some of the writers of today's Men's Movement have zeroed in on this particular deficit — especially as it relates to sons. It used to be that men worked in the fields, or in a cottage industry at home, and sons got to watch them, as day succeeded day, doing their work. Yet beginning with the Industrial Age, and continuing on into today's Information Age, many men leave home in the morning — sometimes even in the dark — and never see their children until evening.

According to one study of two-parent households, fewer than 25 percent of young children experience an hour or more per day of contact with their fathers. The average daily amount of one-to-one father / child contact reported in this country is less than thirty minutes. Almost twenty percent of junior-high and high-schoolers have not had a good conversation with either of their parents, lasting more than ten minutes, in more than a month. All this, according to the poet Robert Bly, can lead to a kind of hunger — especially as sons seek to relate to fathers. It used to be, Bly writes, that "standing next to the father, as they repair arrowheads, or repair plows, or wash pistons in gasoline, or care for birthing animals, the son's body has the chance to retune. Slowly, over months or years, the son's body-strings begin to resonate to the harsh, sometimes demanding, testily humorous, irreverent, impatient, opinionated, forward-driven, silence-loving older masculine body. Both male and female cells carry marvelous music, but the son needs to resonate to the masculine frequency as well as to the female frequency" (Robert Bly, *Iron John* [New York: Random House, 1999]).

The whole subject of Father's Day may not be a happy one for everyone. There are many who gladly honor their fathers, but there are others who find that difficult. They find it difficult because they are still mourning their fathers' passing — maybe a literal passing, because the grief-wound is recent; or maybe a figurative passing, for the wound has simply never healed.

Some adults — both male and female — have yearned to be anointed, as Samuel anointed David, but have never had that experience. They watched other young people receive it —

maybe at the time they learned to drive, or graduated, or came to church to get married — but they never did.

There's not any single occasion in life at which the anointing ought to take place; most often it's a process, extending over many years. Every time a parent says to a child, "You've done well" — or even, "You've made a mistake, but I still love you" — that child is anointed, set apart, for the task of responsible adulthood.

The anointing is part of the essential equipment for striking out on one's own, in life. You can't take it out and inspect it later (any more than David could call forth Samuel's horn of oil) — but you can cherish it, in heart and mind and memory. And no matter what may happen in life, the anointing is like an educational degree: no one, but no one can take it away from you.

But what of those haven't received it? How do they satisfy the hunger within? The answer is a very ancient ritual of the church — one that, in some traditions, is still associated with anointing-oil. It's baptism. Through remembering our baptism, we can experience a sense of having been anointed by God to a life not of kingship, but of discipleship — after the example of Jesus Christ.

Prayer For The Day

Today, Lord, we celebrate fatherhood — the real, as well as the ideal. We celebrate those men who courageously take that role on — though society these days gives them precious little encouragement and few positive examples. We celebrate the men who can be tender as well as tough; present as well as providing; who are faithful to their God, their wives and their children. May we always hold up such a way as an example — and let us encourage more men to live it! Amen.

To Illustrate

There's a story of a Roman Catholic nun who works as a prison chaplain. One day an inmate came to her, and asked if she could find him a Mother's Day card he could send. She had the bright idea of asking a greeting card manufacturer to donate some. They donated a whole case, as it turned out, and the sister handed them out to many a grateful inmate.

A few weeks later, Father's Day came around, and the nun approached the same greeting-card manufacturer. Sure enough, the case of cards arrived — only this time, things were different. Not a single inmate would accept a Father's Day card from her, not even a free one. Years later, the sister still had the entire case of cards sitting in her closet. Such is the impact of missing one's fatherly anointing.

***

The Irish-born actress Roma Downey was one of the stars of television's *Touched By An Angel*. When she was twenty years old, her father died. Before he died, however, he anointed his daughter. He did so very simply, and in a rather unusual place: in his hospital room, on his deathbed.

Of all the things he could have shared with his daughter, at that moment, he chose this (and to this day, she declares, she finds it empowering): "Remember," he told her, "if you can bury your dad, you can do anything." What a gift of courage that man gave, in naming his own death — so his daughter wouldn't have to name it alone!

***

160

These words were written by a man who evidently feels some regrets about the amount of time he spent with his children:

If I had my child to raise all over again,
I'd build self-esteem first and the house later.
I'd finger-paint more, and point the finger less.
I would do less correcting and more connecting.
I'd take my eyes off my watch and watch with my eyes.
I would care to know less and know to care more.
I'd take more hikes and fly more kites.
I'd stop playing serious and seriously play.
I would run through more fields and gaze at more stars.
I'd do more hugging and less tugging.
I'd see the oak tree in the acorn more often.
I would be firm less often and affirm much more.
I'd model less about the love of power and more about the power of love.

***

Our most painful suffering often comes from those who love us and those we love. The relationships between husband and wife, parents and children, brothers and sisters, teachers and students, pastors and parishioners — these are where our deepest wounds occur. Even late in life, yes, even after those who wounded us have long since died, we might still need help to sort out what happened in these relationships. The great temptation is to keep blaming those who were closest to us for our present condition, saying: "You made me who I am now, and I hate who I am." The great challenge is to acknowledge our hurts and claim our true selves as being more than the result of what other people do to us. Only when we can claim our God-made selves as the true source of our being will we be free to forgive those who have wounded us.

— Henri J. M. Nouwen, *Bread for the Journey* (New York: HarperCollins, 1997)

***

Any fool can have a trophy wife. It takes a real man to have a trophy marriage.

— Diane Sollee

***

Don't worry that children never listen to you; worry that they are always watching you.

— Robert Fulghum

Proper 7, Pentecost 5, Ordinary Time 12
June 25, 2006

Revised Common	1 Samuel 17:(1a, 4-11, 19-23) 32-49 *or* 1 Samuel 17:57—18:5, 10-16	2 Corinthians 6:1-13	Mark 4:35-41
Roman Catholic	Job 38:1, 8-11	2 Corinthians 5:14-17	Mark 4:35-41
Episcopal	Job 38:1-11, 16-18	2 Corinthians 5:14-21	Mark 4:34-41 (5:1-20)

Theme For The Day   The presence of Jesus is sufficient to conquer our fears.

Old Testament Lesson   1 Samuel 17:(1a, 4-11, 19-23) 32-49   *David Slays Goliath*

Despite its gory details, this story is a favorite of children — and no wonder. The image of young David standing up against the fearsome giant Goliath, then slaying him with a single, well-aimed stone flung from his sling, has become a byword for the victory of good over evil, no matter what the power differential may be. Because the story is so lengthy, the lectionary provides an edited version. The heart of the story, however, is in verses 32-49. Some of the most colorful description is found in the optional section, verses 4-11, as Goliath's stature and armor are described in detail, and as he issues his taunting challenge to the Israelites. Verses 17-18, omitted from both the shorter and longer lectionary versions, contain the important narrative detail that David is not apparently intended for the battle at all: his father Jesse has sent him on a mission to bring food supplies to his brothers. David has been ordered to carry cheese to the front, not to engage the enemy. The omitted section from verses 24-31 tells how David (a political natural) works the crowd. It then provides a psychologically true-to-life description of sibling rivalry between Eliab and his younger brother. In the section beginning with verse 32, we hear of David's offer to Saul to become Israel's champion and fight Goliath himself. The feisty David boasts of his prowess with the sling, and more than that, about how the Lord has made his stones effective, in the past, against many a wild beast. Saul, who flatly refuses David's request at first, is inexplicably convinced by this logic — particularly by what David says about the Lord's guidance and protection — and relents. Verses 38-39 provide the homey, almost comical detail of how the diminutive David cannot fit into the king's armor, and so decides to take the field without it. David is armored not in bronze, but in virtue and in the fear of the Lord. Against the taunts of the mighty Philistine, David speaks of the true armament he has at his disposal: "You come to me with sword and spear and javelin; but I come to you in the name of the Lord of hosts, the God of the armies of Israel, whom you have defied" (v. 45). After more tough talk — reminiscent of the pre-match "trash talk" of certain professional wrestlers — David quickly sends his stone flying toward the giant's forehead, felling him with one precise blow. David is the only character in this story who mentions the name of the Lord; the others are all depending on their own devices. David goes into battle equipped with little more than his total reliance on divine providence, and he prevails.

Alternate Old Testament Lesson   1 Samuel 17:57—18:5, 10-16   *David And Jonathan Conspire Against Saul*

An alternate lesson takes up the story just after the death of Goliath. Abner, Saul's general, brings David into the royal presence. Despite the story in 16:14-23 of David's having consoled Saul in his madness by playing the lyre, Saul does not know the young man; and even now, David somewhat coyly does not share his name, saying only that he is one of Jesse's sons. In 18:1 we learn of the close friendship that develops between David and Saul's son Jonathan. "Then Jonathan made a covenant with David, because he loved him as his own soul. Jonathan stripped himself of the robe that he was wearing, and gave it to David, and his armor, and even his sword and his bow and his belt" (vv. 3-4). This is the beginning of an implicit alliance between David and Jonathan against Saul. David ends up being so successful as a military leader that Saul promotes him to commander of his army (v. 5). Omitted from this lectionary selection is the taunting song of the Israelite women, "Saul has killed his thousands, and David his ten thousands" (v. 7), as well as the ominous observation that, as a result of his growing jealousy, "Saul eyed David from that day on" (v. 9). The second portion of this lectionary reading tells how Saul, in a fit of madness, tries to kill David with his spear (vv. 10-16). But even so, Saul is not able to remove him totally from military command, because of David's great popularity with the people.

New Testament Lesson   2 Corinthians 6:1-13   *Now Is The Acceptable Time*

See the description of 2 Corinthians 5:20b—6:10 for Ash Wednesday (p. 75).

The Gospel   Mark 4:35-41   *Jesus Stills The Storm*

In this passage, attested to also in the other synoptic gospels (Matthew 8:23-27; Luke 8:22-25), Jesus and his disciples set off across the Sea of Galilee by boat, accompanied by some other boats as well (although these other boats are never mentioned again). Jesus falls asleep on a cushion at the rear of the boat. A sudden storm arises, but Jesus continues sleeping soundly. The disciples awaken him, saying, "Teacher, do you not care that we are perishing?" (v. 38b). Jesus awakens, rebukes the wind and the waves, and suddenly all is calm. Jesus gently chides his followers, saying, "Why are you afraid? Have you still no faith?" Filled with awe they ask one another, "Who then is this, that even the wind and the sea obey him?" (vv. 39-40). "Faith" can mean many things, but in this passage it clearly means trust: Jesus is encouraging his followers not so much to believe in a doctrine, as to trust in a person. In the midst of life's storms, that sort of faith is a lifeline. The viewpoint from which one views this story is crucial to its meaning: looking on it theologically, from afar — as simply a miracle story demonstrating Jesus' power over the natural world (and particularly the primeval forces of chaos) — is one thing. Looking at it personally — from the standpoint of the terrified disciples, cowering on the floorboards of a wave-tossed fishing boat — is quite another.

Preaching Possibilities

If there's one thing all of us have in common, it's fear. To be afraid is to be human.

Fear isn't necessarily a bad thing. It protects us from many things that would harm us. Fear is a word of warning when danger is near. Yet fear can also be unhealthy. If a person is out for a walk, it may make sense to look furtively around for snakes — if the person happens to be strolling through the Amazon rain forest. Yet, if that same person is plagued with the idea of snakes in a North American living room, then something is terribly wrong.

Snake phobias aside, we're living in a fearful age. Any minister or counselor can readily attest that a great many people today are living lives that are fear-ridden. The fears of today are many: illness such as AIDS or cancer, terrorism, ecological disaster resulting from the hole in the ozone, overpopulation, death, being overwhelmed by debt, intimacy, loneliness, failure, or loss of love.

Today's Gospel Lesson deals rather frankly with this whole matter of fear. On the surface, it seems little more than a miracle story. Jesus is asleep in a boat; a storm comes up, and the disciples get worried; Jesus wakes up and calms the storm. This story elicits feelings of disbelief in many of us — as well it should. It seems to be an act of magic. The rational side of our nature wants to cry out, "It was only a coincidence — the storm was about over anyway!" Sometimes, though, in reading the Bible, it pays to suspend our disbelief, in order to see what the story is saying on a deeper level. This is one of those times.

On one level, this is the story of a gale at sea. That's common enough for anybody who lives by water, but it is also more than that, theologically speaking. For most first-century Jews, that sort of storm would have been the very incarnation of fear. Remember some of the ways the Old Testament talks of the sea — in the creation story, how "waters covered the face of the deep," the waters of chaos. God vanquishes the Egyptians by calling down the waters of the Red Sea upon them. "Deep calls to deep, in the thunder of your cataracts," the psalmist cries out to God (42:7); and then there is the image of the fearsome sea monster Leviathan, who inhabits the ocean depths.

This story offers three easy points of entry for us: the three questions that are asked in it. Two of these questions are asked by the disciples, and one by Jesus. Each of them has a point of contact with our lives.

Question number one: "Do you not care?" That's the question many of us may have asked God, in times of personal struggle. It's the question that even the atheist in trouble hurls into the depths of the cosmos: "Do you not care?" It's the question we wish we could ask our fellow human beings more often, in times of trial — but it's hard even to utter the words. In times of pain — mourning a loved one, putting the pieces together after a divorce, facing the cold terror of unemployment — in such times, when everyone else's life seems to be going well, and ours feels like a shambles, it's hard to ask even a friend, "Do you care? Do you care about *me*?"

To the disciples, it's incomprehensible that Jesus could be sleeping during the storm. So they come out with their haunting question — as haunting as the question of Sam Adams in the Broadway musical *1776*, fearful that he's promoting the American Revolution all by himself: "Is anybody there? Does anybody care? Does anybody see what I see?"

Jesus never answers the disciples' question — not in words, anyway. His answer is to turn to the waves and the wind and say, "Peace! Be still."

Question number two: "Why are you afraid? Have you still no faith?" Of our three questions, this is the one Jesus asks. He does not ask it until after the "dead calm" has descended over the Sea of Galilee. Jesus could have shouted the question through the deafening wind, but he chooses to wait until the storm's fury is over. Jesus could well ask the same question of us — either amidst the gales and tempests of our lives, or after their fury is spent. "Why are you afraid? Have you still no faith?" The question is somehow more compelling after the storm.

All of us have had the experience of feeling paralyzed by a fear, rational or irrational, and then having that fear suddenly calmed. As soon as the storm is over, we feel a bit silly. The goblin wasn't real. "It was only a dream," we say, upon awaking, sweaty and clammy-skinned, from a nightmare. The beast came from within ourselves.

164

Neurotic fears usually have self-interest of some sort at their root. The way to deal with them is to seek out the root cause, naming it for what it is. It is only within ourselves that many of our fears become real, finding flesh to cover their hideous bones — yet although they are born within our very selves, they are still real enough to terrify. "Have we still no faith?"

Question number three: "Who then is this, that even the wind and the waves obey him?" For the Hebrew mind, this is an amazing question. The wind and the sea are the primeval forces of chaos. Jesus commands even these!

Mark's story establishes Jesus as a man of great power. The story has the format and structure of an exorcism — Mark's first-century readers would have recognized immediately that Jesus is exorcising storm-demons. Yet to many of us, the winds and sea within ourselves are as chaotic as any storm on the sea. The pains left over from childhood, the insecurities, the doubts, the outbursts of temper we can hardly control, the compulsion to gossip, to run others down, to distrust even our friends — the sad list goes on and on, the pathetic catalogue of all the hobgoblins within ourselves.

To all these, Jesus Christ has the power to say, "Peace! Be still." And then you and I may wonder, "Who is this, that even the wind and the sea obey him?" Fear has been transformed into awe. The terror of the night has become the righteous fear of God.

Prayer For The Day

I have a sinne of feare, that when I have spunne
My last thred, I shall perish on the shore;
Sweare by thy selfe, that at my death thy sonne
Shall shine as he shines now, and heretofore;
And, having done that, Thou hast done,
I feare no more.

> — John Donne, "A Hymne To God the Father," III, in *Complete Poetry and Selected Prose* (London: Nonesuch, 1946), p. 322

To Illustrate

Psalm 107 vividly recounts the terror of the sea:

Some went down to the sea in ships,
doing business on the mighty waters;
they saw the deeds of the Lord,
his wondrous works in the deep.
For he commanded and raised the stormy wind,
which lifted up the waves of the sea.
They mounted up to heaven, they went down to the depths;
their courage melted away in their calamity;
they reeled and staggered like drunkards,
and were at their wits' end.
Then they cried to the Lord in their trouble,
and he brought them out from their distress;
He made the storm be still,
and the waves of the sea were hushed.
Then they were glad because they had quiet,
and he brought them to their desired haven.

***

Martin Luther King, Jr., used to prepare his people for civil disobedience — for beatings and jail, or whatever needed to be endured — by speaking about faith and fear. Fear, not doubt, is the opposite of faith, King used to tell them: fear is the one power that can neutralize faith — if we let it.

***

As an inscription above the door of an ancient English public-house reads, with all the brevity of a fortune-cookie saying: "Fear knocked on the door. Faith answered. No one was there."

***

I don't gather that God wants us to pretend our fear doesn't exist, to deny it, or eviscerate it. Fear is a reminder that we are creatures — fragile, vulnerable, totally dependent on God. But fear shouldn't dominate or control or define us. Rather, it should submit to faith and love. Otherwise, fear can make us unbelieving, slavish, and inhuman. I have seen that struggle: containing my fear, rejecting its rule, recognizing that it saw only appearances, while faith and love saw substance, saw reality, saw God's bailiwick, so to speak: "Take courage, it is I. Do not be afraid!"

— Philip Berrigan

***

Perhaps no one in our lifetime scaled and conquered the walls of hostility more heroically than Martin Luther King, Jr., and though the hostility of hatred took his life, the power of his love defied that hatred. His dream has given life and justice and strength to a whole generation of Americans — black and white alike.

In an unpublished sermon, King recalls the early days when he was first catapulted into the civil rights crusade. At the tender age of 26, he felt unprepared, scared, powerless. Already the threats were coming in. He was harassed and jailed for going thirty miles an hour in a twenty-five mile zone. And one night around midnight, while his wife and young daughter slept a few feet away, Martin received a phone call.

It was the Klan calling: "N____, we are tired of you and your mess now ... And if you aren't out of this town in three days, we're going to blow your brains out, and blow up your house."

In a sermon, King reflected on that night:

> *I sat at that table thinking about that little girl and about a dedicated, devoted and loyal wife ... and I got to the point that I couldn't take it any longer. I was weak ... And I discovered then that religion had to become real to me, and I had to know God for myself. And I bowed down over that cup of coffee. I never will forget it ... I prayed a prayer, and I prayed out loud that night. I said, "Lord, I'm down here trying to do what's right. I think I'm right. I think the cause that we represent is right. But Lord I must confess that I'm weak now. I'm faltering. I'm losing my courage ... And it seemed at that moment that I could hear an inner voice saying to me, 'Martin, stand up for righteousness. Stand up for justice. Stand up for truth. And lo I will be with you, even*

166

until the end of the world.' " ... I heard the voice of Jesus saying still to fight on. He
promised never to leave me, never to leave me alone. No, never alone. No, never alone.
He promised never to leave me, never to leave me alone.

Sure enough, three nights later a bomb was thrown on the front porch of the King home. Though there was smoke and broken glass, miraculously — providentially — no one was injured. Hostility was to follow King throughout the rest of his life. But he refused to retaliate. He refused to build walls of hatred. Instead, the faith that poured into his heart that dark, lonely night gave him the peace of Christ — a painful peace that sustained him even in the ugliest times.

— Susan R. Andrews, Moderator, 215th General Assembly, Presbyterian Church (U.S.A.),
"Conflict Management 101," A sermon preached at Bradley Hills Church,
Bethesda, Maryland, July 21, 2003. From *Perspectives*, the electronic
magazine of the Office of the General Assembly, PC (USA)

***

One of the legendary football coaches of the early twentieth century was Knute Rockne, coach of the "Fighting Irish" of Notre Dame University. One day, Notre Dame was preparing to play USC, and the coach was aware that his undefeated opponents had a far better team. He happened upon a plan to defeat USC by guile (what he did was legal under the college football regulations of that time, but would not be so today). Rockne sent his assistant coaches out into the city of South Bend and had them bring back 100 of the largest men he could find. He had them suit up in Notre Dame uniforms, and at game time had them run out onto the field ahead of the real team. Although none of these giants ever left the bench during the game, their mere appearance at the beginning was enough. The USC opponents were so rattled that they played a terrible game, and Notre Dame won.

Fear is in our minds.

Proper 8, Pentecost 6, Ordinary Time 13

July 2, 2006

Revised Common	2 Samuel 1:1, 17-27	2 Corinthians 8:7-15	Mark 5:21-43
Roman Catholic	Wisdom 1:13-15; 2:23-24	2 Corinthians 8:7-9, 13-15	Mark 5:21-43
Episcopal	Deuteronomy 15:7-11	2 Corinthians 8:1-9, 13-15	Mark 5:22-24, 35b-43

Theme For The Day   Jesus, who healed people by touch in years gone by, is reaching out to touch us today.

Old Testament Lesson   2 Samuel 1:1, 17-27   *David Mourns Saul And Jonathan*

David has defeated Saul, and has remained in the area while his soldiers mop up the remaining resistance (v. 1). A section the lectionary omits then describes how a messenger comes to David, bringing some of Saul's armor and describing how he himself dispatched the already-dying king. David tears his clothes and weeps, in grief for Saul and Jonathan. The messenger is probably expecting to be rewarded, but instead David calls one of his soldiers in, and at David's command, the soldier kills this man who had killed Saul. As the main part of today's passage begins, David sings a song of lament for Saul and Jonathan, including the oft-quoted line, "How the mighty have fallen!" (v. 19b, 25). Although Saul and Jonathan had their differences in life, at the end, the son died defending his father, and so David sings, "Saul and Jonathan, beloved and lovely! In life and in death they were not divided; they were swifter than eagles, they were stronger than lions" (v. 23). David also confesses his great love for Jonathan, "I am distressed for you, my brother Jonathan; greatly beloved were you to me; your love to me was wonderful, passing the love of women" (v. 26). Few victories in life are without their share of grief.

New Testament Lesson   2 Corinthians 8:7-15   *Paul's Stewardship Advice*

Paul has been commending to the Corinthians, as a positive example, the generosity of the Christians of Macedonia, who have sent large amounts of money to support Paul's ministry. "As you excel in everything" else, Paul tells them, he wants them to excel in generosity (v. 7). Paul is not commanding them to do so, he says, but he wants them to know he will be comparing their giving to that of the Macedonians (v. 8). The true example of generosity, of course, is that of Jesus himself — who, "though he was rich, yet for your sakes he became poor, so that by his poverty you might become rich" (v. 9). It's not the amount of the gift that's important, but the willing heart behind it: "For if the eagerness is there, the gift is acceptable according to what one has — not according to what one does not have" (v. 12). Paul encourages the Corinthians to discover "a fair balance between your present abundance and their need" (vv. 13-14).

The Gospel   Mark 5:21-43   *Jesus Heals Jairus' Daughter And A Woman With A Flow Of Blood*

This lengthy passage contains two healing stories that are intertwined with one another. The first story begins as Jairus, a leader of the local synagogue, comes up to Jesus and begs him to come heal his daughter, who is dreadfully ill (vv. 22-23). Jesus sets off with Jairus, followed by a large crowd of curiosity-seekers. The tumultuous crowd is pressing so closely around him that no one notices a ritually unclean woman, who has suffered for twelve years from a never-ending menstrual flow, come up and touch the hem of his garment. But Jesus notices. "Power has gone forth from him" (v. 30), healing the woman instantly. Jesus stops the entire procession, on its way to Jairus' house, and asks who has touched him. The woman comes forward, "in fear and trembling, [falling] down before him," and confesses what she has done. Far from being angry, Jesus blesses her, saying, "Daughter, your faith has made you well; go in peace, and be healed of your disease" (v. 34). Just then some messengers arrive with the sad news that Jairus' daughter has just died; had Jesus not stopped to speak with the sick woman in the street, he could perhaps have made it there in time. Jesus comforts Jairus, saying, "Do not fear, only believe," then he enters the synagogue leader's house with several of his disciples. He says to the vociferous crowd of mourners there, "Why do you make a commotion and weep? The child is not dead but sleeping," and is met by their derisive laughter (vv. 39-40). Jesus throws the mourners out, takes only his disciples and the girl's parents into her room, and raises her from death, using the gentle Aramaic invitation, *"Talitha cum"* — which means, "Little girl, get up!" (v. 41). The girl does get up, and Jesus asks that she be given something to eat. He charges those present to say nothing of what they have just seen.

Preaching Possibilities

Today's Gospel Lesson tells of a woman who's desperate to reach out and touch Jesus — only here it's not a matter of reaching back through history, but reaching over, in the present, and physically touching him as he stands before her. The woman wants to do this for a reason other than mere adulation: she's sick, and she's certain this rabbi's touch can heal.

But the woman is afraid. The streets are thronged with people, eager to get close to Jesus, yearning to touch him. She has good reason to fear the crowds: for, according to Jewish ritual law, she is unclean.

Mark tells us the woman has been suffering from "hemorrhages" — from what the King James Version calls "an issue of blood" — for twelve years. She's been bleeding, from some intimate part of herself — and because Jewish women are considered unclean for the few days each month when that sort of thing happens, and are required to isolate themselves from the community, this woman has been a virtual exile among her own people. For her to walk up and touch any person who's not also ritually unclean — especially a rabbi, who's required by biblical law to undergo an elaborate purification ritual if that sort of contact takes place — is to risk scorn, or even injury.

Yet, this woman is so desperate to be healed, she's willing to take the risk. "I won't tell him who I am," she says to herself. "I won't tell anybody who I am. I'll throw a cloak over my head, slip through the crowd, and touch him as he goes by. If I can but touch the hem of his robe, maybe it will help." And so the woman does just that — and the instant she touches Jesus, the most remarkable feeling of transformation comes over her. She knows somehow, deep within herself, that she has been healed.

Then the unexpected happens. Jesus stops in his tracks, and looks around. "Who touched my clothes?" he asks. Jesus knows this touch is different from that of others in the crowd. He knows — he just knows — that someone experiencing terrible need has just been helped. Fearfully, the woman steps forward and identifies herself, telling Jesus she's just been healed. Instead of scolding her, he blesses her: "Your faith has made you well; go in peace."

As it was with her, so is it with us. How many of us yearn to reach out and touch Jesus in just such a way? Tentatively, fearfully we stretch out our hand, intending our fingers to graze the hem of his robe and no more. Sometimes we do it as a sort of religious experiment: only half-believing our tentative touch will make any difference at all.

But then, in some way we scarcely understand, it does make a difference. Healing comes to us (if not instantly, then in the fullness of time; and if not in the way we intended, then in the way God intends). Along with the gift of healing comes a response: from the one whom we've touched, who hasn't escaped noticing that power has gone out of him.

So how do we experience that healing touch? We experience Christ's healing, life-giving power in word and sacrament, and through the discipline of prayer. Most notably we experience his touch in the sacrament of baptism: something most all of us received at an early age, probably before we were even aware of it. Yet here inside the font is no empty abstraction, but a real, physical substance: water. That water is, on the face of things, no different from the water that comes gurgling out of the tap, but in a spiritual sense is a means by which God reaches out and touches us.

That touch continues, throughout the life of Christian discipleship, as we encounter Christ in the physical touch of torn bread and poured-out wine. We encounter him as well in the word proclaimed: and whenever, in prayer, our outstretched hand grazes the hem of his garment.

We just may encounter the living Lord, also, whenever — in all innocence and love — we reach out and touch another human being. In the words of Jewish philosopher and theologian Martin Buber, "The world is not comprehensible, but it is embraceable: through the embracing of one of its beings."

Prayer For The Day

We open our hands, O God ... We open our hearts ... We open our lives to you. Reach out and touch us today, as your Son, Jesus, touched those people of old whom he healed of their diseases. Find that place deep within us where we most need your healing. Bring us new life, in your Son's name. Amen.

To Illustrate

In 2002, the newspapers were filled with accounts of what appeared to be a remarkable discovery in biblical archaeology. It was an ancient stone box, called "the James Ossuary." An ossuary is a bone box — a sort of small coffin, used to hold the bones of a person who has died. It was a fairly common thing, in crowded cities of the Roman world, for bodies to be buried in tombs, then disinterred a generation or so later, so another body could be laid in that place. The bones — which had by then been bleached white and no longer needed to be in the ground — were taken away. If the person's family was well-to-do, they stored their ancestor's bones in the specialized stone box called an ossuary.

The ossuary in question turned up in a marketplace in Israel. It seemed to date from the first century A.D.: but even more remarkable, it bore an inscription that said, "James, son of Joseph, brother of Jesus."

How many other James, sons-of-Joseph, brothers-of-Jesus could there be? — it had to be the burial box of James, brother of our Lord — the one who, in the book of Acts, is described as ruling over the early Christian church in Jerusalem.

The impact of this discovery — if genuine — would be nothing short of extraordinary. Apart from the Bible, the only contemporary record of Jesus' existence is one line from the Roman historian Suetonius, who in his *Life of Nero*, speaks of a group of Jews in Rome who stirred up trouble at the instigation of one *Chrestos* — whom many scholars take to be a reference to Christ. Suddenly, there seemed to be hard evidence of the life of the historical Jesus, words scratched not by pen onto flimsy parchment, but carved into hard stone: "James, son of Joseph, brother of Jesus."

Unfortunately, as the newspapers again indicated about a year later, the James Ossuary was ruled a fake. The box itself is ancient enough — probably dating to the time of Jesus — but careful analysis of its inscription proved those words were chiseled into the stone in modern times: probably by some wily antiques merchant, hoping to make a buck.

We've all got a hunger within us for some link, some tangible connection, to greatness. It's that same hunger that leads some to seek baseballs autographed by Babe Ruth, or glossy publicity photos signed by Marilyn Monroe. Pick up such a celebrity artifact, turn it over in your hands, and you feel that somehow, through some sort of autograph magic, you've touched fame.

— Source: Greg Myre, "Israelis Say Burial Box of Jesus' Brother Is Fake,"
New York Times, June 19, 2003

***

When a U.S. president or other famous politician comes to town, there's always someone who holds a baby up to be touched or kissed (that's where the old political expression, "pressing the flesh," comes from). Mothers and fathers, out of some strange motivation they can barely put into words, are seeking some kind of blessing for their child from the touch of this famous person. There's no rational reason to do it — in fact, there's got to be some considerable inconvenience in lugging a baby through the teeming crowd at a political rally — but still they bring their children to be touched.

***

Church leadership consultant, William Easum, says in one of his books, that in the typical worship service people go in and sit down, and for one hour pretend they don't have bodies. They focus their thoughts on the intangible, the spiritual. Part of them believes that the physical aspects of their lives are somehow inferior to that which is spiritual. To reach out and hold the hand, say, of a loved one sitting next to them, or put their arm around that person, seems somehow like it doesn't belong there: that it's a guilty pleasure, an intrusion of the sensual into the realm of the spiritual.

***

There's a famous story of Frederick the Great of Prussia — a powerful ruler of the European Enlightenment, a man of impressive scientific curiosity as well as a leader of armies. Frederick once conducted an unusual scientific experiment into the development of human language. There was a theory of the time that the babbling of infants was, in some unknown way, related to the ancient language of Eden: but that children lost this oldest of all mother-tongues as they grew and learned the language of their parents.

Frederick devised an experiment to test this theory. He had his scientists take some orphaned newborn babies, and isolate them from all physical contact with human beings. The babies would be kept in separate rooms, with no contact with each other. Not a word of language was to be spoken in their presence. Specially trained nurses would see to the babies' physical needs — feeding them, and making sure they stayed warm — but they were forbidden to pick them up and embrace them. Once the children grew old enough to speak, they would be brought into the presence of the other children who were part of the experiment, to see if they could converse with one another.

The experiment was an utter failure. Not one of those poor children lived beyond infancy — let alone to the age when language begins to develop in earnest. The one thing King Frederick learned from his cruel and ill-considered experiment was that the physical touch of another human being is essential to life. If babies are not picked up, and hugged, and caressed, they have but a slim chance of surviving to maturity.

Proper 9, Pentecost 7, Ordinary Time 14
July 9, 2006

Revised Common	2 Samuel 5:1-5, 9-10 *or* Ezekiel 2:1-5	2 Corinthians 12:2-10	Mark 6:1-13
Roman Catholic	Ezekiel 2:2-5	2 Corinthians 12:7-10	Mark 6:1-6
Episcopal	Ezekiel 2:1-7	2 Corinthians 12:2-10	Mark 6:1-6

Theme For The Day Jesus sends his disciples out to travel together, to trust God to work wonders, and to travel light.

Old Testament Lesson 2 Samuel 5:1-5, 9-10 *David's Public Anointing As King Over All Israel*

Samuel anointed the young David as king in a secret ceremony in Bethlehem (see 1 Samuel 15:34—16:13; and comments for the Proper 6, p. 157). Now the time has come to anoint him publicly, and in a way that will involve not only his traditional power base in the southern region of Judah, but the entire nation. The elders of Israel have elected David king by acclamation, declaring that the former shepherd boy will now shepherd the entire nation (vv. 1-2). Now, the elders gather together at Hebron and the thirty-year-old David "makes covenant with them," as they anoint him king (v. 3). Verses 6-8, not a part of this lectionary selection, describe how David captures Jerusalem by stealth. The lectionary selection commences again with verse 9, as David designates Jerusalem — strategically located between Judah and the northern territories of Israel — as his new capital. David "becomes greater and greater, for the Lord, the God of hosts, is with him" (v. 10). The saga of David's long and arduous rise to kingship is now completed.

Alternate Old Testament Lesson Ezekiel 2:1-5 *The Lord Calls Ezekiel To Speak To The Rebellious People*

In classic formula of prophetic revelation, the Lord addresses Ezekiel as "mortal" (literally, "son of man"), commanding him to rise to his feet and listen (v. 1). The Lord tells Ezekiel that he is going to send him to the recalcitrant people of Israel, "a nation of rebels who have rebelled against me" (v. 3). Ezekiel is to say to them, "Thus says the Lord God" (v. 4). At this point, there is no content to the prophet's message — just this prologue, which makes it clear that the prophet will bring not his own word, but the word of the Lord. If nothing else, the Lord says, even if they turn a deaf ear to Ezekiel's message, "they shall know that there has been a prophet among them" (v. 5).

New Testament Lesson 2 Corinthians 12:2-10 *Paul's "Thorn In The Flesh": Power Made Perfect In Weakness*

Apparently, the Corinthians have tended to judge the legitimacy of their spiritual leaders by the ecstatic "visions and revelations" those leaders have received (v. 1). Some of them must have been asking Paul about his credentials in this area. He responds by speaking of "someone he knows" — a friend, supposedly, but he makes it clear in verse 7 he's talking about himself — who "was caught up to the third heaven — whether in the body or out of the body I do not know; God knows" (v. 2). The imagery of "the third heaven" is obscure, but may have some affinities with Jewish mysticism that postulated a three-tiered architecture of heaven, with paradise at the highest level. Paul will boast about such a person, he says (using the third person, here, in a satirical tone), but he will not boast about himself — except about his weaknesses (v. 5). Then, he proceeds to tell his readers about one of his weaknesses — "a thorn was given me in the flesh, a messenger of Satan to torment me, to keep me from being too elated" (v. 7). Despite repeated entreaties to Christ, Paul says, he was not freed from this torment, but he did receive an encouraging word from the Lord: "My grace is sufficient for you, for power is made perfect in weakness" (v. 9). After undergoing this season of spiritual struggle, Paul is now content: "for whenever I am weak, then I am strong" (v. 10). This is a difficult passage, because of Paul's tongue-in-cheek, satirical approach. His message may be summarized as: "You want ecstatic visions of heaven? I could give you ecstatic visions of heaven — I've had them! — but I won't. The only thing I'll boast about is my weaknesses, and how Christ has enabled me to triumph over them."

The Gospel   Mark 6:1-13   *Jesus' Rejection In Nazareth And His Commissioning Of The Disciples*

There are two pericopes in this passage. In the first, Jesus is teaching in his hometown synagogue in Nazareth, but the people there do not receive him kindly. "Is not this the carpenter, the son of Mary and brother of James and Joses and Judas and Simon, and are not his sisters here with us?" they ask. "And," says Mark, "they [take] offense at him" (v. 3). Jesus says in response, "Prophets are not without honor, except in their hometown, and among their own kin, and in their own house." Mark continues — in an understatement that sounds remarkable to modern ears — "He could do no deed of power there, except that he laid his hands on a few sick people and cured them" (v. 4). The second pericope tells of Jesus' commissioning of the disciples. He "[sends] them out two by two, and [gives] them authority over the unclean spirits" (v. 7). The two-by-two nature of the commission emphasizes the importance of community, and also of accountability. He instructs them to travel light, taking little with them and depending on the people they meet for sustenance (vv. 8-10). As for those they visit who will not receive them, Jesus advises: "If any place will not welcome you and they refuse to hear you, as you leave, shake off the dust that is on your feet as a testimony against them" (v. 11). This is, of course, a text whose content is difficult: "shaking off the dust" from one's sandals is a gesture of disrespect in the Middle East, and it is hard to conceive of Jesus writing anyone off so abruptly. Yet, there is also a certain urgency about the disciples' mission, and for every village that does not receive them, there are surely many others that will.

Preaching Possibilities

Jesus calls the twelve and sends them out two-by-two. Before they leave, though, he gives them three gifts, in the form of three pieces of advice. We can consider these pieces of advice to be the Lord's marching orders. They are:

1. that disciples travel together;
2. that disciples trust God to work wonders; and
3. that disciples travel light.

"He called the twelve and began to send them out two-by-two." The call to follow Jesus is always a call to community. That's a hard message to get across to self-sufficient, independent Americans. It's a point of pride, with many of us, that we stand on our own two feet, that we don't need anyone, that we can do for ourselves, thank you.

One of the most durable figures in our national pantheon of heroes is the rugged individualist, the frontiersman — the sheriff who cleans up the crooked little western town, then rides off into the sunset, six-gun still warm from the day's exertions. Does John Wayne need somebody to ride with him on the trail? Not on your life, pilgrim!

Yet Jesus teaches his disciples to go out not as Lone Rangers, as rugged individualists, but in the company of others. They are to lean on one other, to support one another when the going gets tough. The gospel is too big a burden for any one individual to bear.

And so it follows that the task of proclaiming the gospel belongs to all of us. The event of preaching depends just as much on the hearers as on the speaker; and it depends also on what all of us do with this word as we go out into the world — seeking to make the good news real in our lives, sharing with others of the love of Christ as we have come to know it.

Someone has said that the church is like a group of people standing in a circle, with Jesus at the center. Funny thing about a circle — the closer the individual members get to Christ at the center, the closer they get to each other as well.

The second marching order Jesus gives his disciples is that he "gave them authority over the unclean spirits." Now there's an expression that cries out for a translation into the language of today! To the people of Jesus' day, such spirits were the source of everything that was wrong with their world. Sickness, mental confusion, disagreements among people — all could be seen as the work of these demonic spirits, poisoning human life with their meddling mischief.

The disciples, in other words, believe that their faith can make a difference; that it's relevant to human need; that it is a powerful force for good. This marching order of Jesus runs counter to another powerful trend in our society: the tendency to set faith aside as irrelevant. There are powerful forces at work in our land, that would love nothing better than to domesticate Christian faith, to keep it as a loyal but harmless pet, to be trotted out for an occasional invocation at civic occasions. The absolute low point of this way of thinking came in a remark of the late President Dwight D. Eisenhower, who actually said — and I believe I'm quoting him fairly accurately — "It's important that a person have religion, and I don't care what religion it is."

How easily we forget the crucial role that Christianity played in the crises of our nation's history! Read the speeches and writings of the signers of the Declaration of Independence, and you'll discover that most of them were men of deep faith. They saw themselves engaged in a holy struggle to exorcise the unclean spirits of tyranny and oppression from their land. After the contest was over, it is true, they would declare that church and state are to be kept separate — but that was merely to insure that there would never be an established "Church of America," as there is an established "Church of England." Our nation's founders never meant to partition religion off from American life altogether — as some, today, are trying to do.

Jesus' third marching order is "to take nothing for the journey except a staff." What a difficult instruction that must have seemed! We all know how it is when we're packing for a long trip: we lay out all the things we want, then we narrow it down to the things we really need. All along we ask ourselves, "What if it rains?" "What if my flight is canceled, and I have to spend an extra night?" "Do I have enough money for every emergency?"

Before his disciples set out on their journey, Jesus tells them, "take nothing with you: no purse of money, no change of clothes, nothing but a staff." In each town and village, rely on the hospitality of those you meet — and if the people do not receive you, shake the dust off your sandals and go on. Disciples of Jesus Christ are meant to travel light. Everything that could possibly weigh us down or limit our response to human need is to be abandoned by the roadside.

Like the other two marching orders, this one, too, runs counter to powerful tendencies in American life. We are all of us awash in a growing tide of materialism, a thirst for ever-increasing doses of wealth and possessions. Sometimes our possessions seem, truly, to own us.

It's often been observed that there is a crucial decision we, as Christians, need to make about the world: we need to decide that we live not in a world of scarcity, but in a world of abundance. Surrounding us on every side are the fruits of God's good creation — and in that creation, we are never without the things we truly need. There is nothing to be gained by piling on our backs weighty burdens of possessions, useless gadgets brought along "just in case we need them." The lighter we travel through this life, the freer we will be to venture with Jesus into places where his love meets the world's deep need.

Prayer For The Day

Make our ears attentive, Lord, so we may hear echoing through history the thunderous footfalls of a great host: the disciples of your son Jesus, venturing into the world two-by-two, bearing not a single extra burden that would weigh them down. They knew you had given them everything they needed to make their journey, and that you would continue to provide for them along the way. Make our ears attentive, also, to the call Christ extends to each one of us: to join that bold traveling company, following our Lord into all the places where the need seems overwhelming, and where only people of faith dare to go. Amen.

To Illustrate

Following Jesus isn't about arriving somewhere. There is no specific destination, no station whose sign announces, "Found it." Faith serves actual people, but never as a stopping point. Faith uses words like "mansion," "kingdom," "city," and "highway," but as human approximations of divine realities, snapshots of something that is streaming by (already) and yet far ahead (not yet).

Following Jesus isn't about attaining a specific, measurable goal, or grasping a finite, literal truth. Following Jesus is about following. It is about movement. It is about days that haven't happened, people one hasn't met, places one hasn't gone, and forgiveness one hasn't requested — not yet.

Following Jesus starts wherever it starts but then goes on to the edge and around the corner. Clinging to the "hour I first believed" is never enough. Telling yesterday's story and polishing yesterday's truth are never enough.

Faith is a journey. It takes us beyond memory, beyond understanding, beyond comfort, beyond control. Faith is about a road, not a specific place on the road. Along the way, we will see new things, as Jesus promised, hear new words, reconsider old words. New companions will appear, and they will stretch us. New needs will require us to abandon former ways of perceiving reality.

We will feel tongue-tied, confused, rootless, and unsettled, and that is exactly where Jesus wants us to be. For then we can share Abraham's journey to a land he had never seen, and Moses' journey to a land that existed only as promise, and the exiles' return to a home they couldn't find, and Jesus' journey to a hill outside the city and then beyond their sight.

— Tom Ehrich <www.onajourney.org> (subscription), June 24, 2004

***

There's an old story about Jesus' arrival back in heaven following his life on earth. The angels are waiting for him, eager to hear him tell his story. He tells them about everything: his birth, life, death, and resurrection.

One of the angels asks, "Lord, now that you are no longer physically on earth, who will continue to share the good news?"

Christ responds, "I have chosen eleven who were especially close to me, and have given that responsibility to them."

"These eleven of which you speak must be remarkable people. Surely they must be the best and the brightest of God's creations!"

"Well, actually, no," the Lord responds. "These are average people with ordinary abilities. I'd hardly call them 'best and the brightest.' "

"But, Lord, if these are only average people with ordinary ability, how can you be sure that they will get the job done?"

"Well, to be perfectly honest," the Lord replies, "I can't be sure."

"Tell us, Lord, what if they fail to carry out your mission? What is your backup plan?"

"I have no backup plan," Christ answers quietly.

***

Christianity has been made so much into a consolation that people have completely forgotten that it is first and foremost a demand.

— Soren Kierkegaard

***

Christianity, if false, is not important. If Christianity is true, however, it is of infinite importance. What it cannot be is moderately important.

— C. S. Lewis

***

In one of his books, Leonard Sweet tells of an evangelist named Sam "Golden Rule" Jones who held "quittin' meetings" for those who had been converted at his revivals. These meetings were designed to get people to confess their sins (cussing, drinking, gambling, and so on) and then have them publicly pledge to quit their sinning.

At one of these meetings, a woman was asked what she was going to quit. She said she hadn't been doing anything, and she figured she needed to quit doing that.

Proper 10, Pentecost 8, Ordinary Time 15
July 16, 2006

Revised Common	2 Samuel 6:1-5, 12b-19	Ephesians 1:3-14	Mark 6:14-29
Roman Catholic	Amos 7:12-15	Ephesians 1:3-14	Mark 6:7-13
Episcopal	Amos 7:7-15	Ephesians 1:1-14	Mark 6:7-13

Theme For The Day   Amos' example of the plumb line reminds us of the moral code by which God would have us live.

Old Testament Lesson   2 Samuel 6:1-5, 12b-19   *David Brings The Ark To Jerusalem*

Consolidating his power in his new capital of Jerusalem, David orders that the Ark of the Covenant be brought into the city. Quite a scene it must have been: "David and all the house of Israel were dancing before the Lord with all their might, with songs and lyres and harps and tambourines and castanets and cymbals" (v. 5). Verses 6-11, omitted by the lectionary, tell how a man named Uzzah accidentally touches the Ark. God strikes him dead on the spot. After a three-month hiatus following this tragic death, the journey into the city continues — again, with "David [dancing] before the Lord with all his might" (v. 14). David has the Ark set up in a tent especially constructed for this purpose. He conducts sacrifices and distributes food to the people (vv. 17-19). There is an ominous note: as David and the Ark pass under the window of Saul's daughter Michal, she "[despises] him with all her heart" (v. 16). David's establishment of the Ark in Jerusalem and the renewal of regular worship in its presence is a liturgical symbol of the legitimacy of his rule, and a powerful statement of the spiritual values that he intends his reign to demonstrate to all.

Alternate Old Testament Lesson   Amos 7:7-15   *The Plumb Line*

One of the gifts that goes along with prophetic imagination is the ability to communicate in provocative images God's message for the people. In this case, Amos envisions the Lord standing beside a wall under construction, holding a plumb line. "See, I am setting a plumb line in the midst of my people Israel," God says (v. 8). A plumb line, of course, relies upon the unchanging law of gravity to set a standard for constructing a wall that is perpendicular to the ground. If a wall has been built out of plumb, the only responsible thing to do is to tear it down: otherwise, it will eventually fall of its own accord. Amos' ingenious image of the plumb line symbolizes the Lord's unchanging law, to which God's people are expected to conform. The oracle concludes with a prophecy of doom for King Jeroboam (v. 9). Amaziah, priest of Bethel, sends word to Jeroboam about the things Amos has been saying, then advises the prophet to flee for his life (vv. 10-13). Amos' response is to deny that he is a prophet at all. He is just a common man: "I am no prophet, nor a prophet's son; but I am a herdsman, and a dresser of sycamore trees, and the Lord took me from following the flock, and the Lord said to me, 'Go, prophesy to my people Israel' " (vv. 14-15). Even as he denies being a prophet (probably to distance himself from a corrupt, semi-institutionalized prophetic office that had developed by this time), Amos proves by his deeds to be exactly what he denies. God calls whom God will call.

New Testament Lesson   Ephesians 1:3-14   *Heirs To The Promise*

As with many of the other Pauline letters, after the initial greeting the author moves on to a formulaic blessing and ascription of praise to God. Important theological elements include: God's choice of the elect "before the foundation of the world" (v. 4); God's predestination of the elect to be adopted as God's own children (v. 5); redemption through Christ's blood, with the ensuing forgiveness and grace (v. 7); revelation of "the mystery of God's will" (v. 9); and God's "plan for the fullness of time" (v. 10). Following up on the adoption theme of verse 5, Paul indicates that Christians have received a divine inheritance (v. 11) and are "marked with the seal of the promised Holy Spirit ... [as] the pledge of our inheritance toward redemption as God's own people ..." (vv. 13-14). Speaking out against Judaizing factions in the Ephesian church that wanted to exalt Jewish believers over Gentiles, the author makes it clear that all are as God's adopted children together, and all equally entitled to the inheritance.

The Gospel   Mark 6:14-29   *The Death Of John The Baptist Recalled*

King Herod Archelaus hears of the miracles Jesus has been performing, and wonders whether in fact John the Baptist has been raised from the dead (v. 14). Mark then backs up chronologically, to relate as a sort of flashback the details of John's death. Herod had ordered the troublesome John to be arrested and thrown into prison, but did not apparently intend to have him killed. At a banquet, Herod's daughter Herodias dances for the men present, and Herod is so taken by her dancing that he promises to fulfill any wish she may care to make. She asks her mother for advice on what to wish for, and her mother suggests she demand the head of John the Baptist. She does, and Herod has no choice but to fulfill his vow, granting her request. His soldiers present Herodias with John's head on a platter. While this story appears to be a digression from the main narrative, Mark may intend it as a sort of foreshadowing the death of Jesus — who was likewise condemned to death by the rich and powerful, on spurious charges.

Preaching Possibilities

Open up a carpenter's toolbox, and you'll find all manner of tools and gadgets inside: some old, some new. Along with high-tech gizmos like an electric screwdriver, a "stud gun," and maybe even one of those electronic "tape measures" that measures the distance across a room ultrasonically, you'll find some tools that are almost as old as human history.

One of these old standbys is a tool the Egyptians used to build the pyramids. It may be even older: who knows, but maybe the ancient peoples of Britain used it to raise the monoliths of Stonehenge? It's a wondrously simple device: a length of string, with a lead weight tied to one end. The tool is called a "plumb line" — from the Latin *plumbum*, or "lead."

Masons hang a plumb line next to a wall they're building, and the tug of gravity pulls the weight (and the string) straight down. By sighting along the string, workers know whether the wall is straight, or whether it isn't — whether it's perpendicular to the ground, or whether it's leaning over. A wall out of plumb cannot be repaired, but can only be torn down and rebuilt.

Sometimes, in the construction business, there are corners that can be cut. An extra piece of plywood or a coat of paint will cover all manner of sins. But there is one thing no builder can cover up: a wall that's out of plumb. Many people, throughout history, have wished for an exception to the law of gravity, but no one's ever been granted that request. (Just ask Evel Knievel's orthopedic surgeon.)

The Prophet Amos uses the plumb line as a homegrown sermon illustration. Amos is not a speaker of great sophistication: he's a plain-speaking, tell-it-like-it-is sort of person. He got into the prophecy trade because he was convinced his country was going to the dogs, and somebody had to stand up and say something.

When Amos shows up in the neighborhood, the Northern Israel Regional Chamber of Commerce doesn't exactly roll out the welcome mat. First of all, to the people of the northern kingdom, he's a foreigner. Amos hails from the southern kingdom of Judah. Second, Amos isn't much of a diplomat. He doesn't mince words.

Amos is more than upset. He's furious that the poor people of Israel can be sold into virtual slavery for the price of a pair of shoes (2:6; 8:6), while the rich recline on fancy couches and gorge themselves with gourmet delicacies (6:4). More than that, Amos castigates the business community for shady dealings. He's a one-man Federal Trade Commission: insisting that all the stall owners down in the marketplace adopt standard weights and measures, and stop bilking the common folk (8:5).

Amos forecasts the collapse of the out-of-plumb wall that is the kingdom of Israel — and history will prove him right. A few years later, the Assyrian army will sweep through the northern kingdom like a knife through butter. Israel will be utterly annihilated, as an independent state. When that disaster breaks upon the people, some will consider it a sad quirk of politics. Yet most Israelites, paying attention to Amos at last, will see the Assyrian invasion as nothing less than the judgment of God — a harsh, but well-deserved sentence, levied upon a nation grown corrupt and soft, a nation that has long been teetering on a shoddy spiritual foundation.

It is always worthwhile to ask of any nation whether it is constructed on a solid moral foundation. With regard to the United States in our time, there is some cause for concern. A few years back, for example, a team of researchers polled 5,000 Americans. They found the following:

- 93 percent said their judgment about right and wrong was based solely on personal belief
- 74 percent said they would steal from those whom they thought would not miss it
- Almost 50 percent of college students admitted that they cheat
- Upward of 24 percent of all resumés contain materially false information
- 64 percent of people said they would lie when it suits them, if it caused no "real" damage

Another team of researchers interviewed people on the street. They asked them if they were guided, in their daily lives, by the Ten Commandments. A very high percentage of people claimed they were. Then the researchers asked their subjects to name as many of the Ten Commandments as they could. Do you know what was the average number of commandments people could recall? Four.

When construction workers unroll a plumb line, they generally don't touch the line. They let it hang right next to the wall under construction. Looking at it is all they need to do. In the same way, the will of God is something that hangs beside this human life of ours, but which seldom directly touches it. Relying on our own judgment, we cannot always be sure that any given action conforms to the will of God; yet if we take a look at the plumb line — the laws of God in scripture and the example of faithful obedience we see in Jesus' life — we can sense that, yes, in the big picture somehow our lives and the Lord's will for us do run parallel.

Prayer For The Day

Lord, it is a frightening world in which we live. So often, it seems we live in a culture that's morally adrift. Keep us, your people, ever faithful to your will. Remind us of your law. Continue to show us, in Christ, the example of how we ought to live — for his sake. Amen.

To Illustrate

Amos questioned the moral integrity of the political leaders of his own day, but unfortunately, this problem has continued even to our own day. Remember former New York mayor David Dinkins? He found himself in trouble with the IRS. "I haven't committed a crime," Dinkins told reporters. "What I did was fail to comply with the law."

Someone confronted President George H. W. Bush's budget director, Richard Darman, about why the president hadn't kept a campaign promise to preserve wetlands. "The president didn't say that," the budget director shot back. "He read what was given to him in a speech."

The classic political line, though, comes from former Washington, D.C., Mayor Marion Barry: "Outside of the killings, Washington has one of the lowest crime rates in the country."

Now where's that plumb line?

***

There are some who celebrate the heightened "freedom" of having few moral absolutes; but that freedom is rather like the freedom enjoyed by a group of sailors adrift on the open sea, in a small boat, with no compass to guide them. It's a true fact that those sailors can go absolutely anywhere they want; yet do they really want to go *anywhere*? Most them would trade almost anything for a compass.

***

The happiness of the people was the purpose of government, [John Adams] wrote, and therefore the form of government is best which produced the greatest amount of happiness for the largest number. And since all "sober inquirers after truth" agreed that happiness derived from virtue, that form of government with virtue at its foundation was more likely than any other to promote the general happiness.

— David McCullough, *John Adams* (New York: Simon & Schuster, 2001), p. 102

***

I think that what children desperately need is a moral purpose, and a lot of our children here aren't getting that. Instead they're getting parents who are very concerned about getting them into the right colleges, buying the best clothes for them, giving them an opportunity to live in neighborhoods where they'll lead fine and affluent lives and where they can be given the best things, to go on interesting vacations, and all sorts of other things.

— Robert Coles

***

The great masquerade of evil muddles every concept of ethics. Evil appears in the form of light, as good works — even as a historical necessity — or as justice, and utterly confuses one who comes from the traditional world of ethical ideas. For the Christian who lives by the Bible, however, these forms of evil simply confirm its abysmal wickedness. Who is able to withstand this evil? Only he to whom the last measure is not his own reason, his principles, his freedom or even his conscience — but rather his readiness to sacrifice all of these: only he who is called to deeds of obedience and responsibility in faith and single-minded communion with God; only he who will let his life become nothing, as answer to God's request or call.

— Dietrich Bonhoeffer

***

Children today are more likely to cheat, steal, and lie than youths ten years ago, research shows.

A Josephson Institute of Ethics report, which surveyed 12,000 high school students, showed that the number who admitted cheating on exams at least once in the past year had jumped from 61 percent in 1992 to 74 percent in 2002.

Students who admitted to shoplifting within the past twelve months rose from 31 percent to 38 percent. Those who said they lied to their teachers and parents increased substantially.

"The evidence is that a willingness to cheat has become the norm and that parents, teachers, coaches, and even religious educators have not been able to stem the tide," said Michael Josephson, president of the institute, based in Marina del Rey, California. "The scary thing is that so many kids are entering the work force to become corporate executives, politicians, airplane mechanics, and nuclear inspectors with the dispositions and skills of cheaters and thieves," he said.

The surveys underlying "Report Card 2002: The Ethics of American Youth" were administered by 43 high schools throughout the country....

Despite plummeting ethics, this generation appears to possess high self-esteem. Seventy-six percent of the respondents said, "When it comes to doing what is right, I am better than most people I know...."

Despite the increase in cheating, stealing and lying, 95 percent of students agreed, "It's important to me that people trust me," and 79 percent agreed, "It's not worth it to lie or cheat because it hurts your character."

— Judith Person, "Survey of Youths Shows Ethics Slip,"
in the *Washington Times*, October 23, 2002

Proper 11, Pentecost 9, Ordinary Time 16
July 23, 2006

Revised Common	2 Samuel 7:1-14a	Ephesians 2:11-22	Mark 6:30-34, 53-56
Roman Catholic	Jeremiah 23:1-6	Ephesians 2:13-18	Mark 6:30-34
Episcopal	Isaiah 57:14b-21	Ephesians 2:11-22	Mark 6:30-44

Theme For The Day   Christ breaks down the walls of separation between us and our fellow human beings.

Old Testament Lesson   2 Samuel 7:1-14a   *The Lord's Covenant With David*

(This story has already come up this year on the Fourth Sunday Of Advent — see p. 22.) David has established his capital in Jerusalem, and has had the Ark of the Covenant ceremoniously carried into the city and placed in the tabernacle — a special tent-like enclosure similar to the one that has been the Ark's home through all the people's wanderings. Perhaps taking his cue from the grandiose architecture of other near Eastern rulers, David now decides his crowning achievement will be for him to build the Lord a house — to construct a magnificent temple in which the Ark can reside. David shares his plans with the prophet Nathan (appearing here for the first time), who is initially positive. That night, however, Nathan has a vision. The Lord comes to him, delivering an oracle for David: "Are you the one to build me a house to live in? I have not lived in a house since the day I brought up the people of Israel from Egypt to this day, but I have been moving about in a tent and a tabernacle" (vv. 5-6). The Lord reminds David of his humble origins: "I took you from the pasture, from following the sheep to be prince over my people Israel ..." (v. 8). Then the Lord makes covenant with David, promising to make this king great, and all Israel with him (vv. 9b-11a). "Moreover, the Lord declares to you that the Lord will make you a house" — a house not made of timbers, but the dynastic house that will be David's royal progeny (vv. 11b-13). This covenant will become the foundation not only for generations of Davidic rule to come, but also for Israel's later messianic hopes that will follow the crisis of the Babylonian Exile. There is an incipient conflict in 2 Samuel between two styles of royal leadership: the oriental-potentate model of Saul and the rustic-virtue model of the young David. As David moves into maturity, he is adopting more and more the cosmopolitan ways of Saul. The Lord's refusal to allow the construction of a temple calls David back to his simple, rustic origins.

Alternate Old Testament Lesson   Jeremiah 23:1-6   *The Lord Will Raise Up For David A Righteous Branch*

Jeremiah has just finished vehemently uttering prophecies of doom against the kings of Judah. Now he continues that theme, pronouncing, "Woe to the shepherds who destroy and scatter the sheep of my pasture!" (v. 1). But there is a new development. The incompetent shepherds will be punished for scattering the Lord's flock, but the Lord will ultimately have mercy on the long-suffering people: "I myself will gather the remnant of my flock out of all the lands where I have driven them, and I will bring them back to their fold, and they shall be fruitful and multiply" (v. 3). In that new day, the Lord will raise up new leadership for Israel: "The days are surely coming, says the Lord, when I will raise up for David a righteous Branch, and he shall reign as king and deal wisely, and shall execute justice and righteousness in the land" (v. 5). This one shall be called "The Lord is our righteousness" — a deliberate allusion to the corrupt King Zedekiah, whose name literally means "The Lord is my righteousness" (v. 6). Zedekiah's rule is either crumbling at this point, or he has already been overthrown. Jeremiah is saying here that the next ruler the Lord will raise up will truly deserve the name borne by Judah's last, lamentable king. This combination of prophecies of doom and prophecies of comfort is typical of Jeremiah — that great transitional figure who bestrides the fall of the Israelite monarchy and the beginning of the Exile.

New Testament Lesson   Ephesians 2:11-22   *Beyond "Us" And "Them"*

For background on the passage immediately preceding this one, see the Fourth Sunday In Lent (p. 91). This passage addresses head-on the conflict that is at the heart of so many Christian communities in this period: the rift between the "circumcision" and the "uncircumcision" factions: those who believe Christianity to be a refined form of Judaism, and those who see it as a more universal faith, open to Jews and Gentiles alike without a rite of circumcision. Yes, at one time the Gentile believers were "aliens" and were "far off" — but by the blood of Christ, "you who once were far off have been brought near" (v. 13). The author names the division in the church, and declares it ended: "For he is our peace; in his flesh he has made both groups into one and has broken down the dividing wall, that is, the hostility between us" (v. 14). Addressing both factions now, the author asserts that both have equal need to hear the message, "peace to you who were far off and peace to those who were near" (v. 17). Neither group is now "strangers and aliens"; all are brought together to form a single mighty building, with Christ the cornerstone and the prophets and apostles as the foundation (v. 20). This is perhaps an allusion to the Lord's covenant in 2 Samuel 7, to build David a "house" not made of stones (see above). Of this passage, R. P. Martin has written, "No passage of the New Testament could be more relevant to the closing decades of the twentieth century than this magnificent statement of the one hope for our race. The world that we know and inhabit is fallen, divided, suspicious, and full of the possibility and threat of self-destruction. The apostle's teaching holds out the hope and prospect of a reconciled, unified, and amicable society, whose microcosm is seen in the church's worldwide, transnational, and reconciling family." (Martin, R. P. *Ephesians, Colossians, and Philemon*, in the *Interpretation* series [Atlanta: John Knox Press, 1991], p. 32)

The Gospel   Mark 6:30-34, 53-56   *The Feeding Of The 5,000*

(**Note:** Next week's Gospel Lesson is John's version of this same incident.) Jesus' fame is spreading. Some have been calling him a new John the Baptist, and others a reincarnated Elijah (vv. 14-15). Now, Jesus performs his mightiest public miracle to date: cementing his reputation as a prophetic figure to be reckoned with. The feeding of the 5,000 is Jesus' best-attested miracle, the only one occurring in all four gospels (Matthew 14:13-21; Luke 9:10-17; John 6:1-14). Here in Mark's version, Jesus and the disciples are trying to get away for a brief respite from the crowds, but the people find out where they are resting and flock to them. Jesus has "compassion for them, because they [are] like sheep without a shepherd," and begins to teach (v. 34). Thinking logistics, the disciples realize they will soon have a food shortage on their hands. They implore their Master to wrap up his lecture, or else he will have to feed the huge crowd. "*You* feed them," Jesus replies, in either real or mock annoyance (v. 37). The disciples quickly tote up the cost of a grocery-store trip — 200 *denarii* — and object that such a task is impossible. Jesus then suggests that they see how much food they have on hand, but all they can come up with is five loaves and two fish. Jesus organizes the people "in groups of hundreds and of fifties," prays to God, and begins to distribute the meager rations. They prove to be more than enough. Mark's report of Jesus' actions just before the loaves are distributed — he *blessed*, he *broke*, he *gave* — is undoubtedly an allusion to the sacrament of the Lord's Supper. The fact that this occurs in "a lonely place" (*eremos topos*, the desert or wilderness) recalls how, during the Exodus, the Lord provided manna in the wilderness. The detail about the division of the people into fifties and hundreds may hearken back to the way Moses organized the Israelites into traveling companies. Mark wants us to see Jesus as an inspired leader every bit as powerful as Moses.

Preaching Possibilities

Some passages of scripture are replete with quotable phrases, and Ephesians 2:11-22 is one of those. Some examples:

- "you who once were far off have been brought near by the blood of Christ" (v. 13)
- "he is our peace" (v. 14)
- "he ... has broken down the dividing wall, that is, the hostility between us" (v. 14)
- "you are no longer strangers and aliens, but you are citizens with the saints and also members of the household of God" (v. 19)
- "with Christ Jesus himself as the cornerstone" (v. 20)

A passage like Ephesians 2:11-22 offers the preacher an embarrassment of riches. Any one of these richly theological phrases merits a sermon. The temptation will be to lift a single phrase out of context, and use it as the basis for a topical sermon. There is nothing wrong with a good topical sermon, of course, but the historical context of this passage is worth teaching about, for it bears many similarities to the life of the contemporary church, and even of the larger society. A textual approach, dealing with the passage as a whole, has much to commend it.

In almost any human society (and the church is no exception), there is a tendency to have in-groups and out-groups. Sometimes the in-or-out judgment is made on the basis of longevity: there are founding members, longtime members, up-and-coming members, and newcomers (just stick around long enough, and you'll achieve in-group status eventually). In other groups, the in-or-out judgment is made on the basis of some external social criterion: whether one comes from "a good family," for example, or whether one has the "right" racial / ethnic origin or gender. In still other groups, the criterion is frankly financial: pony up the hefty membership fee, and you're in. In certain types of groups, you're in or out on the basis of whether you're courageous — or foolhardy — enough to submit to an initiation or hazing ritual. Finally, there are some groups in which the in-or-out judgment is made on some more subjective basis, such as whether or not the leadership group likes you.

The churches of the New Testament are no exception. A great many of the Pauline letters are devoted to the problem of who's in and who's out. In Ephesus, the question always comes back to circumcision: a criterion that has elements of longevity-in-the-community, racial/ethnic origin, and initiation-ritual.

Here's the situation: as in many Greek cities, Ephesus has a longstanding Jewish community. The Jews are very open to outsiders coming into their community, to study the scriptures and learn about the faith — but the men can never be full members unless they first submit to the painful ritual of circumcision. When Paul shows up in Ephesus, preaching about Jesus Christ, he naturally heads right for the synagogue. He knows that in the synagogue he will find a receptive audience: people who are familiar with the Law of Moses, who speak the same spiritual language as he does. Paul finds some of his most ardent followers not among the synagogue insiders, but rather among those Greek-speaking Jews who sit around the fringes of the synagogue community — with one foot in and one foot out, as it were. As the Christian community becomes more and more distinct from the purely Jewish community, some circumcised Jews naturally come along as well, joining these relative newcomers. But now the ratio of old-timers to newcomers has changed: the newcomers are in the majority. Stubbornly, the old-timers continue to expect that the old rules of inclusion and exclusion will still apply — that their status as insiders will transfer laterally into the new community. A struggle develops between those who want the old, exclusive ways and those who see the invitation to follow Christ as radically inclusive.

Paul is walking a fine line, trying to minister to both groups, but in the end he comes down on the side of full inclusion. Closely following the Pauline tradition, this letter's author begins, here, with an approach that sounds like it's going to please the conservatives: reminding the Gentile Christians that they once were aliens, outsiders. But — and here he introduces a new element, one that will cause the conservatives to start scratching their heads — "you who once were far off have been brought near by the blood of Christ" (v. 13). The author is addressing *both* groups here: Christ "has made both groups into one and has broken down the dividing wall, that is, the hostility between us" (v. 14).

"Okay," say the conservatives, "we can buy that. We believe that we, too, have been saved by Jesus Christ, just as the Gentiles have. But those newcomer men still have to be circumcised. It's the Law of Moses."

But then the author says something truly provocative — almost "in-your-face" as far as the conservatives are concerned. He declares that Christ "has abolished the law with its commandments and ordinances, that he might create in himself one new humanity in place of the two" (v. 15). This is a verse that ought not to be taken out of context, for it could be seen as contradicting Jesus' own teaching: "Do not think that I have come to abolish the law or the prophets; I have come not to abolish but to fulfill" (Matthew 5:17). What the author is saying is that Jesus has come to abolish the now-irrelevant details of the law, its more arcane codicils, so the law's larger, overarching purpose may be fulfilled. Chief among these now-irrelevant details, in his eyes, is the circumcision requirement.

There appears to be an irreconcilable conflict, here, between Jesus' teaching on the continuity of the law in Matthew and the message of Ephesians. Jesus' words, "truly I tell you, until heaven and earth pass away, not one letter, not one stroke of a letter, will pass from the law until all is accomplished" (Matthew 5:18), certainly sound like they contradict Ephesians 2:15. The answer to this seeming conflict is that the author is not talking here about *either-or*; he's talking about *both-and*. This letter offers victory to neither faction in the Ephesian circumcision controversy. Rather, it is saying that the cross of Christ transforms both groups into something entirely new. The law of circumcision still applies, but it is now fulfilled not through the knife, but through the waters of baptism.

In Christ, there is no longer "us" and "them." There is only "us."

Prayer For The Day

Lord Jesus, look kindly upon us when we are too quick to judge. We are all outsiders before you. We praise you that, because of Jesus, you have welcomed us into your house. Help us, always, to share that welcome with others. Amen.

To Illustrate

The ability of the church to ignore the deeper implications of its own scriptures is horribly plain throughout history. Remember it took eighteen centuries for Christians to realise that slavery is against the gospel. Remember that those who supported slavery claimed to do so on biblical grounds.... Remember that Jesus was condemned to death for his own inclusive attitudes, by fundamentalist zealots who believed that they were obeying scripture.

In all these cases those who opposed change could quote the Bible in their defense. With hindsight the church sees that they were wrong; they were killing the spirit with the letter.... In the same way the church will one day look back on the issues that divide us today and find it incredible that it once thought it right and "scriptural" to treat women and other minorities as it does now.

The struggle to make the church inclusive is not based on some secular, woolly "liberal agenda" (the charge endlessly parroted against us) but on a scriptural imperative to do what Jesus did. It is the same struggle to oppose prejudice, bigotry, and oppression and open the kingdom to everyone, especially the most marginalised.

Inclusivity is not a soft option. It is harder to live in a truly diverse and welcoming community than it is to live in a community of the respectably like-minded, just as it is harder to be an intelligent student of scripture than it is to be a fundamentalist.... All of us must be challenged and changed in every department of our life, by the gospel and by one another, whether we are male or female, black or white, gay or straight, rich or poor.
—Anglican Canon Jeffrey John, quoted by Stephen Bates in "Gay Row Dean Attacks Prejudice in Church," in The London *Guardian*, Monday, April 26, 2004

***

Writer Tom Ehrich tells of leading an adult education group in a local church:

Tonight's topic is "inclusion." An easy topic for this church, because it has a heart for inclusion. Anyone is welcome, including folks who aren't welcome at our more self-righteous neighbors except as targets for improvement.

But inclusion isn't that simple, I tell them. Churches tend to have circles of membership. At the center is a "core" group, who attend and usually run everything, and often consume the pastor's time.

Next ring, perhaps three times as large, is what I call "homies," a more diverse group who consider this congregation their "home." Core folks tend to see them as leaders-in-training, but in fact, many homies are content not to join committees.

Beyond that are the "occasionals," more diverse and quite perplexing to the Core folks, because they seem content with so little. Beyond that are "fringe" folks, who come and go and are labeled "unchurched" and "unfaithful."

Populating these circles are "joiners" (jump in), "waiters" (waiting to be invited), "burned" (burned out or burned elsewhere), "loners" (leave me alone), "overloaded" (life is full), and the "changing" (e.g. newly divorced, newly employed).

Churches tend toward a hierarchy of values: core is better than occasional, joining is better than hanging back. They reinforce that hierarchy with labels like "Christmas-and-Easter Christians" and constant appeals for more involvement.

Committee assignments, however, don't equal inclusion. Nor is faith necessarily stronger at the core. Some remarkable relationships with God can be found at the outer circles, if the joiners who populate core groups took the time to listen.
— Tom Ehrich <www.onajourney.org> (subscription), June 18, 2003

For anyone in this troubled, quarrelling center of privilege and power (and as a white, male, middle-class, American, Catholic, professor and priest I cannot pretend to be elsewhere) our deepest need, as philosophy and theology in our period show, is the drive to face otherness and difference. Those others must include all the subjugated others within Western European and North American culture, the others outside that culture, especially the poor and the oppressed now speaking clearly and forcefully, the terrifying otherness lurking in our own psyches and cultures, the other great religions and civilizations, the differences disseminating in all the words and structures of our own Indo-European languages.

    — David Tracy, *On Naming the Present* (Maryknoll, New York: Orbis Books 1994), p. 4

***

A television documentary told of a kindergarten teacher who noticed that the one thing she heard her children saying to each other most often was, "No, you can't play." She decided to make it a rule, in her classroom and also at recess, that children couldn't tell other children they can't play with them.

When the teacher announced her new rule, the children looked back at her in stunned silence. They couldn't believe she could make such a rule. The teacher went further. She visited the classes of each of the other grades, and told them about the kindergarten's new rule. Each of them told her she couldn't make such a rule, it's impossible. But she noticed that the third and fourth graders expressed a certain nostalgia for the simpler days of kindergarten. They admitted that, if the whole school were to adopt such a rule, it would have to start from the very beginning — but it was too late for them, worldly wise third- and fourth-graders that they were.

When the teacher talked to the kindergarteners about the new rule, they all protested — both those who were habitually left out of group play and those who weren't. One girl by the name of Lisa said it wasn't fair: it would make her sad if she had to play with just anyone. Another girl, Christina, said to Lisa, "It's because you don't like me, isn't it?" The class talked about who was sadder: Lisa or Christina, who sat alone while the others played. Everyone agreed that Christina was sadder.

The class agreed to try the experiment. After a few weeks, it felt as though they had never done it any other way. No one was left out, and all the children played when and with whomever they wanted.

In future years, the teacher would occasionally encounter Lisa in the school hallways. Lisa would always ask her how it was going, and seemed happy that the rule was still in place. Many years later the teacher ran into her and her mother in the grocery store and she said she still tried always to follow the rule but that it was hard. Her mother agreed with her that she worked hard at it and it wasn't easy for her.

How early we learn about "us" and "them"!

    — Based on a story shared by Carol Been on Midrash e-mail discussion group,
    April 25, 1999 <www.wpusa.org>

Proper 12, Pentecost 10, Ordinary Time 17
July 30, 2006

Revised Common	2 Samuel 11:1-15	Ephesians 3:14-21	John 6:1-21
Roman Catholic	2 Kings 4:42-44	Ephesians 4:1-6	John 6:1-15
Episcopal	2 Kings 2:1-15	Ephesians 4:1-7, 11-16	Mark 6:45-52

Theme For The Day   If we are so bold as to bring what we have to Jesus, it will prove to be enough.

Old Testament Lesson   2 Samuel 11:1-15   *David Seduces Bathsheba And Murders Uriah*

Israel is at war with the Ammonites. Rather than taking personal leadership of his armies as he has in the past, David chooses to remain in Jerusalem (v. 1). No longer is he the sort of king the Israelites have always craved, a ruler will "go out before us and fight our battles" (1 Samuel 8:20). Walking about the roof of his palace, David looks down and sees a beautiful woman, Bathsheba, bathing on her rooftop. Some commentators have made much of the rooftop location of Bathsheba's ablutions, but in fact the rooftop of a typical Jerusalem house would have been surrounded by a high wall, and would have been relatively private. Were it not for the fact that David's house is so much taller, her actions would have been invisible.

After inquiring into her identity, David sends for Bathsheba, she comes, and they lie together. The author provides the parenthetical detail that, in bathing, "she was purifying herself after her period" (v. 4). This means that not only is Bathsheba acting as a faithful Jewish woman ought to act, but in having sexual intercourse with her, David is violating the religious purity laws. Given the power differential in their relationship, it is hard to justify any fault on the part of Bathsheba in the adulterous affair. The king's action is virtually a rape. When Bathsheba becomes pregnant with David's child, she sends word to him, and he in turn sends for Bathsheba's husband, Uriah, who is deployed in the field as one of the king's military officers. "Go down to your house, and wash your feet," David says to him: a crude soldier's euphemism for instructing him to go home and sleep with his wife (v. 8). This would of course make it plausible for Bathsheba to claim that Uriah is the father of the child.

Uriah, however — out of solidarity with his troops, who do not have a similar opportunity to visit their wives — never visits Bathsheba, sleeping instead in the quarters of the palace guard. Uriah's words, in fact, recall the sort of rustic virtue apparent in the Lord's discussion with David about the superior merits of a tent over a palace: "The ark and Israel and Judah remain in booths; and my lord Joab and the servants of my lord are camping in the open field; shall I then go to my house, to eat and to drink, and to lie with my wife?" (v. 11). Uriah — a foreigner — is, in other words, a man of honor. He lives simply and virtuously, just as David used to do before adopting his cosmopolitan ways. (It no longer occurs to the king to refrain from sleeping with a woman out of solidarity with *his* soldiers in the field.) David tries one more time to convince Uriah to go home — entertaining him at a palace feast until he becomes drunk — but without success.

Concluding that the only way out of the scandal to is for him to marry Bathsheba, David deploys Uriah to the front lines and conspires to have the other Israelite troops fall back, leaving him to certain death (vv. 14-17). Here this week's lectionary passage ends; the story continues next week.

Alternate Testament Lesson   2 Kings 4:42-44   *Elisha Feeds 100 People*

In the previous passage, Elisha has miraculously saved the day for his followers, making a poisoned stew edible (vv. 38-41). He continues to perform mighty works in this story. A man comes up to Elisha, bearing an offering of twenty barley loaves and some unbaked grain. Elisha directs that the food be given to his entourage of 100 people. His servant responds in astonishment, but Elisha simply says, "Give it to the people and let them eat, for thus says the Lord, 'They shall eat and have some left' " (v. 43). It happens just as the prophet predicts. There is more than enough. Through the prophet, the Lord takes care of those people of faith who have risked all to follow the way of holiness.

New Testament Lesson   Ephesians 3:14-21   *Rich Gifts From A Generous God*

In elegant language, the author caps his discussion of "the boundless riches of Christ," given according to "the plan of the mystery hidden for ages" (vv. 7-8), with a magnificent prayer for his readers. He has just been celebrating the "access" believers have to God, through Christ (v. 12). Now, he demonstrates how that access works: by praying to "the Father, from whom every family in heaven and on earth takes its name" (vv. 14b-15). This is a play on words: "father" is *patera* and "family" is *patria* (or, more literally, "fatherhood" or "paternal clan"). *Patria* is the root of the word "patriotism," or love of the fatherland. While the exclusively masculine language may be troubling to some, what is most important here is the close relationship between God and the people. Next comes a request for God's blessings for believers: that they may be strengthened (*krataio*) with power (*dunamis*), as Christ "dwells in their hearts through faith," as they are "being rooted and grounded in love (*agape*)." There is a strong sense, here, of the Holy Spirit's power to address and transform an individual's inner spiritual life. Next, there comes a request for wisdom: that believers "may have the power to comprehend, with all the saints, what is the breadth and length and height and depth, and to know the love of Christ that surpasses knowledge ..." (vv. 18-19). There is a circularity here, that only divine intervention could make possible: knowing something that surpasses knowledge. We cannot say how we could possibly comprehend something so vast as the love of Christ, but by grace, we do. The prayer's closing ascription, which beautifully sums up the prayer's principal theological themes, is often used as a benediction: "Now to him who by the power at work within us is able to accomplish abundantly far more than all we can ask or imagine, to him be glory in the church and in Christ Jesus to all generations, forever and ever" (v. 20). The accent, once again, is on the close, seamless relationship between the living Christ and his church.

The Gospel   John 6:1-21   *Jesus Feeds The 5,000*
And Walks On Water

Inexplicably, the lectionary editors have chosen John's version of the feeding of the 5,000 as this week's text, just one week after choosing Mark's version of the same incident. Much of what can be said about the Markan version applies here (see last week, p. 183), although John does introduce one different element. There is a side story of Philip and Andrew struggling to comply with Jesus' request that they find food for the multitude. One productive preaching strategy is to contrast the roles of the two disciples: while Philip, the cost-counting supply officer, is busy punching his calculator buttons and scratching his head, Andrew, the hopeful scrounger, is out trying to see what food he can scare up. It is Andrew's optimistic response, his boldness in doing something to meet the seemingly fathomless need, that gives Jesus the materials he needs to perform the miracle. Andrew may despair, "But what are they among so many people?" (v. 9), but at least he is holding some bread and fish in his hands as he says those words. The second part of this lectionary selection is the story of Jesus walking on water (vv. 16-21). There are some differences between John's account and the versions of Matthew (14:22-33) and Mark (6:45-52). John's version is fairly sparse, including just the basic details. He does not include Matthew's side story of Peter trying and failing to join Jesus on the waves, nor does he say, as Mark does, that Jesus climbs into the boat with the disciples after the miraculous display is ended. Just at the moment the disciples are wanting to take Jesus into the boat, they suddenly reach land — giving the whole episode an air of mystery.

Preaching Possibilities

Maybe it was a warm, gentle day by the Sea of Galilee. Maybe the soft touch of the sea breeze and the warm glow of the sun are making the disciples feel they haven't a care in the world. The hypnotic splashing of the waves speaks security and comfort to them, as they take a rare moment for relaxation. But reality always has a way of intruding — even on the beach. Reality takes the form of Jesus' question to Philip, "Where are we to buy bread for these people to eat?"

The most difficult questions connected with any large gathering are the ordinary ones — what to eat, what to drink, where to sleep. In the army, they call such questions logistics. Logistics, they say, are key to the success of any military campaign. "An army marches on its stomach," said Napoleon — and he should know. Poor logistics are what did Napoleon's army in on his winter invasion of Russia.

In turning to Philip and asking, "Where can we buy food?" Jesus is asking about logistics. The size of his following has suddenly swelled from twelve to 5,000 — if he's going to keep them very long, he's got to find them something to eat.

John tells us Jesus already knows what he's going to do; he's only testing Philip. It's obvious, though, that Philip takes him at face value. Philip — the realist — takes one look at the crowd and turns back, wide-eyed: "Why, six months' wages wouldn't begin to buy enough!"

Philip must have been the administrator of the little band. He does that calculation in his head. Philip has the sort of mind that takes a problem, and immediately quantifies what it will take to solve it. And what Philip sees is "not a pretty sight," as they say. The fact is, Jesus and his disciples aren't well equipped in the logistical department. Remember that this is the band of men whom Jesus (in another gospel) sends out, with nothing but the clothes on their backs. Jesus and company have barely enough to feed themselves, let alone 5,000.

Fortunately, Philip isn't the only disciple tackling the dilemma. While Jesus and Philip are discussing logistics, Andrew's out working the crowd. After a time, he comes back with a small boy, and the boy's picnic lunch: five barley loaves and two fish — common fare for the poor folk of Galilee.

The quantity of food Andrew comes up with is ridiculous. We can imagine Philip staring at him, open-mouthed. Why did he even bother? Andrew himself senses the futility of it. As he brings the loaves and fishes to Jesus, he says, "But what are these among so many people?"

What are these, indeed? But we all know what happens next. Jesus tells his disciples to start handing the food around, and every time they divide what they have, there's more rather than less. And when they're done, there are twelve baskets left over.

We could well ask ourselves, which sort of disciple are we — a Philip or an Andrew? Do we look at the world as a calculating realist, or as a starry-eyed idealist? Do we observe the problems of life through horn-rimmed bifocals, or rose-colored sunglasses? Do we name the glass of water half-empty or half-full?

It is important to count the cost in life, to make feasibility studies, to plan ahead to avoid disaster. There comes a time, however, when counting the cost becomes an end in itself. Jesus tells a little parable about that elsewhere in the Bible. It's about a group of people who decide to build a tower — only they spend all their time counting the cost, and never get started (Luke 14:28-29).

It's all a question of perspective. Philip and Andrew have two different perspectives. Philip looks out over that hungry crowd and sees a bill for six months' wages. Andrew scans the gathering, and picks out a boy with a picnic lunch. Andrew, in other words, sees possibilities, and as ridiculous as it seems, he has the *chutzpah* to take the little boy by the hand and lead him to Jesus.

Optimism alone is not enough, of course. Andrew's discovery of the boy and his picnic lunch is a valiant gesture, but it's not enough to feed a multitude. It takes the Lord of heaven and earth to do that.

Prayer For The Day

We open our hands, O Lord, and what we see in them seems so pitifully small. The product of our life's labors seems as paltry as five loaves and two fish. Yet we know that you are the God of abundance. Take what we have to offer. Use us, in all our talents and abilities. Make our offering acceptable in your sight — and sufficient for the need at hand. Amen.

To Illustrate

Back in the days of colonial New England, it was the custom for churches to charge families for rental of their pews. These were the old box pews, with little gates on the ends you could open and close. The well-to-do families sat up front, while the common laborers, indentured servants, and slaves — who couldn't afford the rent — sat in the balcony.

Many churchgoers today *feel* like they own the pews they sit in. They come in, week after week, and sit in the same place. After a while they do come to feel kind of like they own the pew. Well, in Colonial days they were one up on us: you could actually rent a pew and have your name on it. Pew rental was like owning a little piece of the church.

The roof of this particular Colonial church began leaking. Some sections of the sanctuary experienced a steady drip in a heavy storm, while others were bone dry. One day, the pastor ascended the pulpit and made an appeal for contributions, so the roof could be repaired. One well-to-do gentleman met the pastor at the door afterward, and declared that he had no intention of contributing to the campaign — because, he said, it wasn't raining on his pew.

The boy on the hillside in Galilee could have taken the same attitude. He could have said, "I've got my lunch. All those hungry people? Not my problem!" But he doesn't. The boy gives all he has to Jesus, and his gift makes all the difference.

***

John Burgess highlights the parallels between the feeding of the 5,000 and Psalm 23: "The feeding of the 5,000 takes place beside the Sea of Galilee ('still waters'). The people are like sheep on a grassy hillside ('green pastures'), and Jesus has compassion on them ('the Lord is my shepherd'). When he feeds them, they are satisfied ('I shall not want'). He will lead them 'in paths of righteousness' and will protect them in times of trouble ('I will fear no evil, for thou art with me')."

— John B. Burgess, "John 6:1-21," in Roger E. Van Harn, ed., *The Lectionary Commentary: Third Readings* (Grand Rapids: Eerdmans, 2001), p. 507

***

A pessimist sees difficulty in every opportunity; an optimist sees opportunity in every difficulty.

— Winston Churchill

***

The greater part of our happiness depends on our dispositions and not on our circumstances.

— Martha Washington

***

If you can't be optimistic, be persistent.

— William Sloane Coffin, speaking about social activism

***

I am not an optimist, because I am not sure that everything ends well. Nor am I a pessimist, because I am not sure everything ends badly. I just carry hope in my heart ... Life without hope is an empty, boring and useless life. I cannot imagine that I could strive for something if I did not carry hope in me. I am thankful to God for this gift. It is as big a gift as life itself.

— Vaclav Havel, Czech playwright and politician,
after surviving years of suffering under Communism

***

When the disciples, charged with feeding the hungry crowd, found a child with five loaves and two fishes, Jesus Took, Blessed, Broke, and Gave the bread. These are the four decisive verbs of our sacramental existence. Jesus conducted a Eucharist, a gratitude. He demonstrated that the world is filled with abundance and freighted with generosity. If bread is broken and shared, there is enough for all. Jesus is engaged in the subversive reordering of public reality.

— Walter Brueggemann, "The Liturgy of Abundance, The Myth of Scarcity," in the *Christian Century*, March 24-31, 1999

***

[It is an] unhappy truth that the world is full of fools who won't believe a good thing when they hear it ... we will sooner accept a God we will be fed to than one we will be fed by.

— Robert Farrar Capon

193

Proper 13, Pentecost 11, Ordinary Time 18
August 6, 2006

Revised Common	2 Samuel 11:26—12:13a	Ephesians 4:1-16	John 6:24-35
Roman Catholic	Exodus 16:2-4, 12-15	Ephesians 4:17, 20-25	John 6:24-35
Episcopal	Exodus 16:2-4, 9-15	Ephesians 4:17-25	John 6:24-35

Theme For The Day   David's repentance demonstrates that there is always a way back to God.

Old Testament Lesson   2 Samuel 11:26—12:13a   *Nathan Accuses David, Who Repents*

Last week's lectionary selection concluded with the account of how David, trying desperately to cover up Bathsheba's pregnancy, deploys her cuckolded husband Uriah to the front lines on a suicide mission. Verses 16-25, omitted from the lectionary, describe how David's commanding general, Joab, sends a messenger back to the king with news of the death of many Israelites in battle. Joab — who is in on David's plot to place Uriah in harm's way, but who also worries how the king will receive news of the heavy casualties — slyly advises his envoy how to manage the king, so as not to become a victim of the kill-the-messenger syndrome. Tell David the bad news first, he suggests, then casually slip in the news that Uriah was one of those killed. The king is initially angry that so many of his soldiers have died, but when the messenger tells him Uriah was one of them, he becomes strangely calm, declaring philosophically that, in war, you win some and you lose some. David sends the messenger back to Joab to tell him to carry on, and better luck next time.

As this week's passage opens, the scene shifts to Bathsheba, who has just learned of her husband's death. We learn nothing of her psychological state, other than that "she made lamentation for him" publicly (v. 26) — exactly what a good wife would be expected to do under those circumstances. Throughout this entire story, in fact, Bathsheba is something of a cipher; she is a two-dimensional figure, more a victim than an actor in her own right. The remainder of this week's selection tells of how the Prophet Nathan exposes David's treachery. He cleverly tells the king a parable of a rich and powerful man who steals the only lamb his poor neighbor owns; when David responds with righteous anger, Nathan indicates "you are the man" (v. 7). David has just said of the rich man in the parable that he "deserves to die" and should make recompense fourfold; now he realizes, to his horror, that this judgment applies to him.

Furthermore, because of Uriah's death, recompense is no longer possible. Speaking for the Lord, Nathan issues this judgment against David: "I will raise up trouble against you from within your own house; and I will take your wives before your eyes, and give them to your neighbor, and he shall lie with your wives in the sight of this very sun" (v. 11). The "neighbor" is, of course, David's son, Absalom, who will rebel against him. David confesses his sin in verse 13a, but the lectionary abruptly ends the story at this point, omitting Nathan's response: "Now the Lord has put away your sin; you shall not die. Nevertheless, because by this deed you have utterly scorned the Lord, the child that is born to you shall die" (vv. 13b-14). When everything about this sordid tale is said and done, the best that can be said of the deeply flawed David is that he is a big enough man to confess his sin, acknowledging his guilt before God and the people.

Alternate Old Testament Lesson   Exodus 16:2-4, 9-15   *Quails And Manna In The Wilderness*

The people of Israel, yearning for the full rations of their Egyptian captivity, are complaining about Moses' and Aaron's leadership. "You have brought us out into this wilderness to kill this whole assembly with hunger," they charge (v. 3b). The Lord advises Moses of a supernatural solution: bread that will rain down from heaven (v. 4). In verses 9-15, Moses and Aaron call the people together and tell them of the Lord's generosity. It happens exactly as they predict, with quails arriving in the evening and manna in the morning.

New Testament Lesson   Ephesians 4:1-16   *Gifts For The Upbuilding Of The Church*

Having prayed for the people, the author now goes on to speak of the unity of the church, the Body of Christ — and of the role of spiritual gifts among the fellowship. He lists the personal characteristics that make for unity: "humility and gentleness ... patience, bearing with one another in love" (v. 2). This verse is a fruitful field for word studies. In verses 4-6, the word "one" occurs no fewer than seven times — a drumbeat of emphasis that leaves no doubt what the apostle is driving at: that the true church of Jesus Christ is characterized by unity. It is possible that these verses are an early baptismal creed. Beginning with verse 7, the emphasis shifts to spiritual gifts, which Christ has "measured" out (*metron*) among the people. Verses 8-10 are a brief detour from the main argument, quoting and very roughly exegeting Psalm 68:18, which in fact is misquoted here (the actual Psalm text says, "You ascended the high mount, leading captives in your train and receiving gifts from people" — not giving them). The point of this excursus is obscure, anyway, and is beside the main point, so it can easily be skipped over. The argument resumes in verse 11 with, "The gifts he gave were that some would be apostles, some prophets, some evangelists, some pastors and teachers, to equip the saints for the work of ministry, for building up the body of Christ...." This is one of the great verses of the New Testament for understanding the life and leadership of the early church.

Similar (but not exactly parallel) lists are found in 1 Corinthians 12:28 and Romans 12:6-8. These are not rigidly defined offices, but rather ecclesiastical functions for which the Spirit raises up gifted people to serve. The very fact that these lists are different from one another suggests a diversity of leadership patterns among the Pauline churches. Even more important than the functions themselves is the theological understanding of what spiritual gifts are for: equipping (*katartismos*) the saints, and building up (*oikodome*) the Body of Christ. The ultimate goal of ecclesiastical leadership is the health of the larger body. All this is provisional, anyway, until the day when we all attain to full "unity of the faith and of the knowledge of the Son of God, to maturity, to the measure of the full stature of Christ" (v. 13). Forsaking the cunning trickery of false teachers (v. 14), we must, "speaking the truth in love ... grow up in every way into him who is the head, into Christ" (v. 15). The passage concludes (v. 16) with a comprehensive, organic understanding of the church as the one, unified Body of Christ.

The Gospel   John 6:24-35   *Bread From Heaven*

Following Jesus' walking on the water, he and the disciples are on the far side of the sea. Some of the multitude who fed on the loaves and fish have taken boats across the sea to look for them, and there they find them. When the crowd (who have seen his disciples get into a boat, but without Jesus) ask him how he got across to the other side, Jesus seems mildly annoyed: "Very truly, I tell you, you are looking for me, not because you saw signs, but because you ate your fill of the loaves. Do not work for the food that perishes, but for the food that endures for eternal life ..." (vv. 26-27a). Perhaps seeking to redeem themselves, they ask what they must do to perform the works of God. Jesus' terse answer: "Believe in him whom [God] has sent" (v. 29). The crowd then asks for a sign, another miracle. They recall the manna in the wilderness (indicating that they have made the connection between that ancient account and what Jesus did for them on the other side of the water). The scripture cited by the crowd is from no single Old Testament verse, but does contain the expression "bread from heaven" from Exodus 16:4. Jesus replies, "... it was not Moses who gave you the bread from heaven, but it is my Father who gives you the true bread from heaven. For the bread of God is that which comes down from heaven and gives life to the world" (vv. 32-33). "Sir, give us this bread always," the crowd responds (v. 34) — although it is still none too clear that they get Jesus' point. They have asked him for miracles, and he has refused, saying obliquely that what they truly need is not another miraculous sign, but himself.

Preaching Possibilities

The White House sex scandals of the 1990s led many news commentators to observe that presidents and their families are now exposed to a higher degree of public scrutiny than at any other time in history. More than one commentator alluded, at the time, to a former "gentleman's agreement" that had once pertained among the White House press corps: journalists at one time agreed that it was in the national interest to shield certain aspects of chief executives' private lives from public scrutiny. This restraint, however, is no more. Considering the very recent nature of this change in our culture, it is remarkable that the author of 2 Samuel, three millennia in the past, shows so little restraint in sharing the details of King David's shocking moral failure. The story of David's adultery and murder is an open wound in Israel's history, one that is never allowed to fully heal.

David is one of scripture's truly colossal figures: a man larger than life, in every respect. When David first comes to the attention of the Israelite nation, he's but a young boy, with a sling in his hand. David places a smooth stone in the leather pocket of that sling, whirls it around his head, and lets it fly. The fearsome giant Goliath crashes to the ground — stone dead (if you'll pardon the pun).

Next, David distinguishes himself in the manly arts of military leadership — soon becoming King Saul's most valued general. At the same time, he excels in an art that is no less manly: composing and singing songs of praise to his God. As King Saul, consumed by pride, slips ever deeper into paranoia and bizarre behavior, David takes up the slack — doing what needs to be done to keep the nation afloat. When Saul finally turns on him, fomenting civil war, God gives David the victory — and before long, this onetime shepherd boy is presiding as king over a nation that has never before been as powerful and free (and never will be again — except, perhaps, during the glorious reign of his son, Solomon).

Yet, as is tragically often the case with great political leaders, this man, too, has the proverbial "feet of clay." David sins — and when this larger-than-life figure sins, he predictably does so in a big way.

There are some who say David falls in love — but, in truth, it's more like falling in lust. David becomes obsessed with the beautiful Bathsheba, the wife of one of his generals, a man named Uriah. While the faithful Uriah's off fighting David's wars, David sends for the man's wife, and — exercising all his kingly authority in a way Bathsheba could not refuse, on pain of death — treats her as though she were his own. When Bathsheba tells David she's expecting his child, the king tries to cover up the scandal, sending Uriah to his death on a suicide mission that has no military significance. David may have committed the perfect crime — but, as Dosteoevsky (in *Crime and Punishment*) and others have borne witness, no crime is perfect as long as the perpetrator carries the burden of guilt.

David's come a long way from his days as a brave and naive young patriot. The years have taken the sparkle of innocent mischief out of the shepherd-boy's eye — and replaced it with the jaded leer of a middle-aged monarch who for years has sought little more than to pleasure his own senses, and build his reputation as a ruler to be reckoned with.

Few in Israel understand how depraved David has become — other than the Prophet Nathan. The Lord sends Nathan on a mission to the palace, to convict the king of his sin. This is no easy undertaking: if Nathan simply walks into David's throne room, points a bony finger at him and cries, "Repent, you sinner!" the king's reaction is not likely to be charitable. Nathan could very well end up sharing the fate of Uriah the Hittite.

Nathan realizes he's got to be circumspect. So Nathan tells the king a story. The prophet presents the story to the king as though it were real, courtroom testimony: a legal case for the king to adjudicate. It's a tale of a poor man, who has a pet lamb, whom he loves very much. Nearby is a rich landowner, with flocks covering many a hillside. When that rich landowner decides to put on a feast — not for anyone important, but only for a passing traveler — the animal he selects for slaughter is not one of his own, but rather the beloved lamb of his poor neighbor.

The king quickly sees the injustice in Nathan's tale. He demands to know where this miserable offender can be found, so he can render justice. It's only at this point that Nathan looks the king in the eye and declares, "You are the man!" It's as though, in that instant, the prophet holds a mirror up to his king. David looks back at him, enraged for the briefest of moments — then he sees his own image in the prophetic mirror.

What happens next demonstrates why David — despite his tragic flaws and his terrible sins — is renowned as the greatest of rulers. David repents. Then he goes out and writes a song. Tradition has it that his song is Psalm 51. It begins with these words:

> *Have mercy on me, O God, according to your steadfast love;*
> *according to your abundant mercy blot out my transgressions.*
> *Wash me thoroughly from my iniquity, and cleanse me from my sin.*
> — Psalm 51:1-2

There's no denial here; no kingly cover-up; no closed-door conclave of the spin doctors to discuss, in anxious whispers, how to handle the media. Instead, David writes a song — a hymn for the public worship of his people, a hymn which makes it clear how dark is his sin and how desperate he is to receive God's forgiveness:

> *Purge me with hyssop, and I shall be clean;*
> *wash me, and I shall be whiter than snow.*
> — Psalm 51:7

What a refreshing change this is from what we see so often in our national life! There's no attempt — as in Bill Clinton's sexual-ethics scandal — to redefine the meaning of the word "is." Nor (to be completely non-partisan) — is there a Ronald Reagan-style attempt to exercise "plausible deniability," as in the Iran-Contra scandal. Once King David takes in the view in the mirror — once he realizes the seriousness of his error, the depth of his sin — he casts all his fortunes on God's grace and mercy, frankly and honestly admitting what he's done.

197

David's honest confession — and his courageous acceptance of the consequences — is the first step on his road to healing. That healing is not automatic, nor is it instantaneous. The grace he receives is not cheap. God doesn't respond by saying, "That's all right, Davey, boys will be boys, don't do it again!" David embarks that day on a long and agonizing road, one that at times will bring its own piercing brand of pain — yet which, as he will discover, is the only road that leads to life.

Prayer For The Day

Generous in love — God, give grace!
Huge in mercy — wipe out my bad record.
Scrub away my guilt,
soak out my sins in your laundry.
I know how bad I've been;
my sins are staring me down....

Enter me, then; conceive a new, true life.
Soak me in your laundry and I'll come out clean,
scrub me and I'll have a snow-white life.
Tune me in to foot-tapping songs,
set these once-broken bones to dancing.
Don't look too close for blemishes,
give me a clean bill of health.
God, make a fresh start in me,
shape a Genesis week from the chaos of my life.

— Psalm 51:1-2, 6-10
— Eugene Peterson, *The Message: The Bible in Contemporary Language*
(Colorado Springs: NavPress, 2003)

To Illustrate

There is a story about a Catholic priest who was hearing confessions. There the priest sat, in his little booth, hearing long lists of sins and dispensing appropriate penances. Nothing the priest heard that day was out of the ordinary — until one particular man walked in, sat down, and closed the door.

The man began to pour out, with great pain in his voice, how it had been many years since he'd gone to confession. For years, this man had — slowly and deliberately, and so cleverly no one had noticed — been stealing building supplies from the lumber yard where he worked.

"How much do you figure you stole, in all those years?" asked the priest.

"Well, let me put it this way," the man replied. "Enough to build my own house, and a house for my son, and one each for my daughters."

"That's a lot of lumber," replied the astonished priest.

"Oh, and did I tell you we also had enough left over to build a cottage by the lake?"

"What you have told me," the priest continued, in his sternest ecclesiastical voice, "is very, very serious. I need to think of a highly demanding penance to give to you. Let me ask you: have you ever done a retreat?"

"No, Father, I have not," said the man. "But if you get me the plans, I can get you the lumber!"

In this world there is repentance, and there is repentance. This particular sinner's repentance was not, apparently, as heartfelt as it could have been.

***

Walter Brueggemann's commentary on the story of David and Bathsheba is written in the staccato style of a detective novel — which, in a certain sense, is what this lurid story is:

David has been resting on his couch (v. 2). He was at leisure and saw what he wanted, a woman "very beautiful." We do not know her name. David asks her name, but he does not measure the cost of his desire. He gets her name; her name is dangerously hyphenated: "Bathsheba — daughter of Eliam, wife of Uriah the Hittite." She has no existence of her own but is identified by the men to whom she belongs. Now David knows who she is — and whose she is. David does not pause, however, because he is the king. The mention of Uriah might have given David pause, but it does not. David acts swiftly, as he has always done. He is not a pensive or brooding man but one who will have his way.

The action is quick. The verbs rush as the passion of David rushed. He sent; he took; he lay (v. 4). The royal deed of self-indulgence does not take very long. There is no adornment to the action. The woman then gets some verbs: she returned, she conceived. The action is so stark. There is nothing but action. There is no conversation. There is no hint of caring, of affection, of love — only lust. David does not call her by name, does not even speak to her. At the end of the encounter she is only "the woman" (v. 5). The verb that finally counts is "conceived." But the telling verb is "he took her." Long ago Samuel had warned that kings are takers (1 Samuel 8:11-19). Gunn (1975) calls it "grasping." Mostly David has not had to take. He had everything gladly given to him by Yahweh, by Jonathan, by Abigail, by his adoring followers.

We have before us in chapter 11 a transformed David, however. Now he is in control. He can have whatever he wants, no restraint, no second thoughts, no reservations, no justification. He takes simply because he can. He is at the culmination of his enormous power.

— Walter Brueggemann, *First and Second Samuel*, in the *Interpretation* series
(Louisville: John Knox Press, 1990), p. 273

***

Aleksandr Solzhenitsyn, the Russian Christian novelist, spent years in a Soviet prison camp. There he witnessed both the cruelties of the guards and the petty selfishness of his fellow prisoners. After that experience, he came to the conclusion that the line dividing human good from human evil is not easy to draw. "If only," he writes, "there were evil people somewhere insidiously committing evil deeds, and it were necessary only to separate them from the rest of us and destroy them. But the line dividing good and evil cuts through the heart of every human being. And who is willing to destroy a piece of his own heart?"

Proper 14, Pentecost 12, Ordinary Time 19
August 13, 2006

Revised Common	2 Samuel 18:5-9, 15, 31-33	Ephesians 4:25—5:2	John 6:35, 41-45
Roman Catholic	1 Kings 19:4-8	Ephesians 4:30—5:2	John 6:41-51
Episcopal	Deuteronomy 8:1-10	Ephesians 4:(25-29) 30—5:2	John 6:27-51

Theme For The Day   We are called to imitate God, with all the joy and abandon of children imitating those they love.

Old Testament Lesson   2 Samuel 18:5-9, 15, 31-33   *David Grieves For Absalom*

At the urging of his generals, David has declined to personally lead his armies against his rebellious son, Absalom. Instead, he has divided his forces into three different groups, under the leadership of three generals. One of them is the wily Joab. The king orders his three commanders, "Deal gently for my sake with the young man Absalom" (v. 5). Absalom's forces are defeated, with 20,000 dead — both in the battle and in the chaotic retreat that follows, in which "the forest claimed more victims that day than the sword" (v. 8). In a freak accident, Absalom is riding his mule under a low-hanging tree limb. His head catches in the branches and he is left hanging in mid-air (Absalom was known for his luxuriant hair — see 14:25-26). In a section the lectionary omits, a messenger brings word of this discovery to Joab. David's general chides the man who brought him the message, asking why he did not kill Absalom himself; the man explains that he was merely heeding David's command to spare Absalom. Joab himself takes three spears, and thrusts them into Absalom's heart as he is hanging there (v. 14). A mob of Joab's armor-bearers finish him off (v. 15, which is included in the lectionary selection). The lectionary now omits a lengthy section in which Joab buries Absalom, and in which a messenger brings news to David of his soldiers' victory. As the lectionary selection resumes with verse 31, a second messenger immediately follows, bringing news of Absalom's death. The lectionary passage concludes with David's impassioned, weeping lament: "O my son Absalom, my son, my son Absalom! Would I had died instead of you, O Absalom, my son, my son!" (v. 33). In instructing his generals earlier, David referred to Absalom impersonally as "the young man" (v. 5); now he is "my son" — a phrase David repeats no fewer than five times, in his anguished grief.

Alternate Old Testament Lesson   1 Kings 19:4-8   *Elijah's Despair In The Wilderness*

Fresh from his victory over the Baal priests atop Mount Carmel (18:20-45), Elijah's fortunes change. The enraged Queen Jezebel, patroness of the Baal priests, is now seeking his life, and the prophet must flee. So rapidly have Elijah's fortunes reversed that he now appears to have completely forgotten the mighty sign the Lord worked through him on the mountaintop. He sinks into depression. A day's journey into the wilderness, he collapses under a broom tree and asks the Lord to take his life (v. 4). Exhaustion overtakes him, and he falls into a deep sleep — until an angel "touches him" and offers him food (v. 5). Elijah eats, then falls asleep again; the thoughtful angel touches him once again, encouraging him to eat more, for he has a long journey ahead (v. 6). Miraculously, this food sustains him over a forty-day journey to Mount Horeb (associated in Exodus 3:1-12 with the call of Moses, and in Exodus 17:6-7 with Moses' producing water from a rock). There is, of course, much more to this story; but the lectionary editors ends their selection here. This passage deals with Elijah's depression, and the rather straightforward, practical insight that a way out of depression may often be found through 1) taking care to nourish one's basic needs, and 2) discovering a purpose, a sense of personal mission.

New Testament Lesson   Ephesians 4:25—5:2   *What The New Life In*
                                                                     Christ Looks Like

Having just urged the people to put aside the ways of their former life (vv. 17-24), the author now provides some details of what the new life in Christ looks like. It involves truth-telling (v. 25); avoidance of excessive anger (vv. 26-27); honest work rather than thievery (v. 28); positive, upbuilding speech (v. 29); and in general, avoiding any behavior that may "grieve the Holy Spirit" (v. 30). Then comes this marvelously comprehensive verse: "Put away from you all bitterness and wrath and anger and wrangling and slander, together with all malice, and be kind to one another, tenderhearted, forgiving one another, as God in Christ has forgiven you" (v. 31).

The next exhortation, to "be imitators of God, as beloved children," appears on the face of it to be impossible — although the latter clause, "as beloved children," perhaps explains what is meant (5:1). Children in their play imitate respected adults not with exact precision, but rather with passionate devotion. We are to "live in love," with our human love at all times finding its home in the larger, all-encompassing, sacrificial love of Christ (v. 2). The rich array of homiletical possibilities in this text include: not coddling and nurturing anger, but acknowledging it and letting it go (vv. 26-27); viewing speech as more than just ethereal words, but as a power for building up other individuals and communities (v. 29); the put away / put on dichotomy in verse 31; and the exhortation to naively but passionately imitate God (5:1).

The Gospel   John 6:35, 41-51   *Jesus Responds To His Opponents,*
                                                                   Who Think Him Blasphemous

Last week's Gospel Lesson concluded with the people's appeal to Jesus to "give us this bread always" (v. 34). Now he proceeds to do just that, saying, "I am the bread of life. Whoever comes to me will never be hungry, and whoever believes in me will never be thirsty" (v. 35).

Skipping some intervening verses about Jesus' purpose in coming to earth, the lectionary jumps to verse 41, which indicates that "the Jews" (in other words, the religious authorities) later took exception to Jesus' identification of himself as "the bread that came down from heaven." It seems blasphemous to them that this man whom they know, a man who has a father and a mother and is living this same human life they are living, can describe himself in such exalted terms. Jesus' response is twofold. First, he appeals to God's authority as the one who sent him and second, he implies that it is God who makes people understand, and that some get it and some don't: "No one can come to me unless drawn by the Father who sent me ..." (v. 44). No one has seen God (except the one who has come from God) — but even so, there are those who have "learned from" God and who are therefore drawn to Jesus (vv. 45-46). In verses 48-51, Jesus reiterates his "bread of life" teaching, making further connections between the bread image and the Lord's Supper.

Preaching Possibilities

Occasionally, there is a piece of advice in scripture that appears to be impossible, and this line from the Letter to the Ephesians is one of them: "be imitators of God, as beloved children."

Following, as this statement does, a long list of challenging ethical instructions, it has the effect of suggesting it's all impossible. Who could ever live up to the demands of Christian life? Speaking the truth, not letting the sun go down our anger, forgiving others — these things are hard enough, but then we're supposed to imitate *God*? We who are created by God, seeking to imitate the Creator? It sounds absurd.

The key that unlocks this problem with Ephesians 5:1 is the second half of the verse: "Be imitators of God, *as beloved children*." We don't have to be around children very long before we realize how much they love to imitate the adult world. That's what play is all about. Over and over, children at play rehearse their perceptions of grown-up life.

What the text tells us is that we can learn something of how to imitate God by observing children at play. There are several things we can say about that. First, children's drive to play — to imitate — is very strong indeed. Psychologists tell us that if children aren't allowed to play — if they're drilled too hard on how to read or count or play a musical instrument before they're ready — they won't grow up well adjusted. Imitation, in other words, is *inevitable*.

Imitation is also a great *joy*. Kids play because it's fun. The games of imagination can keep them busy for hours.

Imitation is also *personal*. The people children imitate most often are the ones they love.

1) *Imitation is inevitable.* Children really have no choice about whether to play or not to play. Imitative play is part of the developmental process. It's part of who children are, of how they're made. It's part of how God has made adults, too. We can't succeed at imitating God by going out and working at it, or by practicing — any more than a person can learn to draw by taking an art course. Who could possibly teach a child how to play? They just do it. They naturally know how, because it flows out of who they are.

Many outside the church often think of Christianity as a system of rules and regulations. They see Christian faith as compliance with a somewhat oppressive book of laws, a list of ethical dos and don'ts. "Good Christians," popular wisdom has it, are those who *do* good. Anyone with real understanding of Christian faith knows this is only a partial picture; yet that is the way many people understand Christianity. It's very much as Martin Luther said: "Those who merely study the commandments of God are not greatly moved. But those who listen to God commanding, how can they fail to be terrified by majesty so great?"

2) *Imitation is joyful.* Children take tremendous delight in their creative play.

Joy is something that bears looking at, because it's often misunderstood. It's misunderstood because we have a natural tendency to emphasize the serious, achievement-oriented aspects of life. As G. K. Chesterton writes, "Solemnity falls out of people naturally; but laughter is a leap. It is easy to be heavy: hard to be light. Satan fell by force of gravity."

One of the best books ever written on the subject of joy is C. S. Lewis' autobiography, *Surprised By Joy.* Lewis, of course, was an Oxford professor who experienced a mid-life conversion to Christianity. He writes how, as a young man, he deeply wanted to experience Christian faith as real. The young C. S. Lewis set out to make himself a Christian. In his prayer life, he concentrated on achieving a certain feeling, a thrill he had felt on some occasions in the past:

To "get it again" became my constant endeavor; while reading every poem, hearing every piece of music, going for every walk, I stood anxious sentinel at my own mind to watch whether the blessed moment was beginning and to endeavor to retain it if it did. Because I was still young and the whole world of beauty was opening before me, my own officious obstructions were often swept aside and, startled into self-forgetfulness, I again tasted Joy. But far more often I frightened it away by my greedy impatience to snare it, and, even when it came, instantly destroyed it by introspection, and at all times vulgarized it by my false assumption about its nature.

— C. S. Lewis, *Surprised By Joy* (New York: Harcourt, 1976), p. 169

Finally, Lewis discovered that he was going about it all wrong. Joy, he learned, is different from pleasure. The difference, as he puts it, is that "Joy is never in our power, but pleasure often is." Pleasure we can make for ourselves. It's as easy as going out to a good restaurant, seeing a movie, seeking the company of friends. Yet joy comes only when we're not seeking it, when we so focus our attention outside ourselves that for a moment we forget who we are, lost in the wonder of what we're experiencing. It's that kind of focus children have as they experience the joy of imitative play. For a moment they cease to be themselves, and become the person they are pretending to be.

3) *Imitation is personal.*

Children don't just imitate anyone. They spend most of their playtime imitating people they love and respect — in many cases, people who also love them. Social workers confirm that children have an amazing capacity to love: even children from the most unhappy, abusive homes still love their parents. Such is the power of personal relationship.

Joy in Christian living flows out of a personal relationship with Jesus Christ. When that relationship matures, it overflows with joy. Mature Christians come to see Christ more as friend than ruler, more as lover than lawgiver. They realize that Christ comes into the world not because he pities it, but because he loves and delights in it — and that he delights especially in the human inhabitants of this world, despite our flaws. As Jesus says in John's Gospel, "No longer do I call you servants ... but I have called you friends" (15:15).

This concept of God as someone who can be known and loved personally was wholly new in the Greco-Roman world. When those Ephesian Christians first heard the words, "Be imitators of God, as beloved children," they would have sounded strange. The gods the Ephesians knew were not personal. How ridiculous it would have seemed to speak of imitating Zeus as a beloved child, or of singing, "What a friend we have in Artemis."

In many ways, those words still sound strange today. The world is not comfortable with a God who knows and loves people personally. And so the world paints God as a stern lawgiver, an oppressive judge — or as an absentminded professor who creates the world only to go off and leave it bubbling in the test tubes. In some ways children have it easier when it comes to faith: for children respond to God simply, without ever having been taught that God is absent or uncaring. They naturally seek to imitate God: and if "imitation is the sincerest form of flattery," there is no greater praise they can give.

203

Prayer For The Day

Sometimes, O God, we see the distance between the way of life Christ wants for us and the ways we actually live as a vast and insurmountable canyon. Sometimes his ethical teachings seem so hard. Help us, we pray, to focus our thoughts not on the canyon's vast dimensions, but rather on the face of the one who is approaching us from the other side, reaching out his hand to help us over. Amen.

To Illustrate

I guarantee you Christ would be the toughest guy who ever played the game. If he were alive today, I would picture a 6-foot 6-inch, 260-pound defensive tackle who would always make the big plays and would be hard to keep out of the backfield for offensive linemen like myself.... The game is ninety percent desire, and his desire was perhaps his greatest attribute.
— A professional football player, describing how he imagines Jesus Christ to be ("Who is imitating whom?" one may ask.)

***

On the subject of truly imitating God — as over against making God into what we would like God to be — Isaiah 44 contains a marvelous satirical section about those who make idols. The prophet describes how idolmakers work: a carpenter first goes out and selects a likely tree, watering it and letting it grow strong in the forest. At the right time he cuts it down, and uses the wood for two very different purposes: "Half of it he burns in the fire; over the burning half he eats flesh, he roasts meat and is satisfied; also he warms himself and says, 'Aha, I am warm, I have seen the fire!' And the rest of it he makes into a god, his idol; he falls down to it and worships it; he prays to it and says, 'Deliver me, for thou art my god!' " (44:16-17).

***

I recently heard the story of a hospice chaplain, who befriended an eighty-year-old woman named Mary who was a hospice patient. He visited her many times, and he was impressed by her faith. One day, he got a call that she had taken a turn for the worse. He was told, if he wanted to see her alive, he'd better go that day. Larry went to visit his friend, and found her in a very deep sleep. The nurse said she really needed to sleep, she'd been in a lot of pain, so Larry didn't wake her up. But just as he turned to go, she opened her eyes wide and stared right at him. She looked intently and then said to him, "Oh, for a minute, I thought you were Jesus."

They laughed about it for a moment. Larry said to her, "Mary, I want you to do something." What's that, she asked. He said, "When you arrive at the gates of heaven and finally do see Jesus, I want you to look at him for a moment and say, 'Oh, I thought you were Pastor Larry!' " Mary smiled and said she would. Two hours later, she died, and she had that opportunity.

I believe we all ought to be mistaken for Jesus, every once in a while.
— Carolyn Winfrey Gillette, in a sermon, "What God Gives"

***

In one of his books, Gordon MacDonald tells about a young Florida man who became devoted to Elvis Presley.

For Dennis Wise, devotion meant spending every bit of money he had to collect Presley memorabilia (books, magazines, pillows, records, and even tree leaves from the Presley mansion in Memphis). Wise never met Presley but he saw him perform several times, and he had once seen him at a distance when he looked through the gates at Graceland (Presley's home). He had stood there for more than twelve hours to get a fleeting glimpse. Wise's devotion is so great that he underwent six hours of plastic surgery to make his face resemble that of the famous singer.

Dennis Wise needs to get a life. Still, when you worship someone, it is natural to want to be as much like that person as possible. When we say that Jesus is the reference point for our lives, it means we want to make our lives as much like his as possible.

— Art Ferry, Jr., from a sermon posted on the Ecunet
electronic bulletin board <www.ecunet.org>

Proper 15, Pentecost 13, Ordinary Time 20
August 20, 2006

Revised Common	1 Kings 2:10-12; 3:3-14	Ephesians 5:15-20	John 6:51-58
Roman Catholic	Proverbs 9:1-6	Ephesians 5:15-20	John 6:51-58
Episcopal	Proverbs 9:1-6	Ephesians 5:15-20	John 6:53-59

Theme For The Day   God calls us to wisely use the time we have been given.

Old Testament Lesson   1 Kings 2:10-12; 3:3-14   *Solomon's Prayer For Wisdom*
     After a long and noteworthy reign, David, the greatest of Israel's kings, finally "sleeps with his ancestors" (2:10). Solomon ascends the throne, "and his kingdom was firmly established" (v. 12). The lectionary jumps ahead to chapter 3, to Solomon's solemn prayer for wisdom as he takes up the kingly responsibilities for which he has prepared for all his life. The Lord appears to Solomon in a dream, inviting him to "Ask what I should give you" (3:5b). Solomon asks for "an understanding mind to govern your people, able to discern between good and evil" (v. 9). This answer "pleases the Lord" (v. 10). Expressing admiration that Solomon did not ask for riches or long life or victory over his enemies, but for wisdom, God promises to give Solomon what he asks: "Indeed I give you a wise and discerning mind; no one like you has been before you and no one like you shall arise after you" (v. 12). Yet, even though Solomon did not request riches and honor, God will give them to him anyway: "no other king shall compare with you" (v. 13).

Alternate Old Testament Lesson   Proverbs 9:1-6   *Come To Wisdom's Feast!*
     In this, one of many poetic passages in Proverbs that personifies wisdom in female form, Wisdom invites passersby into her house for a sumptuous feast. She sends her serving girls out into the streets, calling, "You that are simple, turn in here!" (v. 4). "Come, eat of my bread and drink of the wine I have mixed. Lay aside immaturity, and live, and walk in the way of insight" (v. 5). Divine wisdom, in the way of thinking of Proverbs, *is* a feast. Those who dine at Wisdom's table are not only sustained by what they consume, but are also delighted at the rich fare.

New Testament Lesson   Ephesians 5:15-20   *Wise Living*
     In last week's lectionary selection, we heard advice about how to become "imitators of God, a beloved children" (v. 1). Miscellaneous ethical instructions follow, providing more detail about what this means. Here, in verses 15-16, these instructions continue with an appeal to wise living: to "[make] the most of the time, because the days are evil." The Greek word translated "making the most of the time," *eksagorazomenoi*, is a fascinating compound word of commercial origin, that literally means something similar to "buying wisely in the market-place" (the word *agora*, or "marketplace," is visible within it). Wisdom, in this sense, is not so much a matter of intellectual acumen as resourceful and righteous living. This includes avoiding drunkenness — a common but self-destructive pastime in the pagan world — being "filled with the Spirit" instead (v. 18). The passage concludes with a beautiful statement of how Christians are to worship, singing "psalms and hymns and spiritual songs among yourselves, singing and making melody to the Lord in your hearts, giving thanks to God the Father at all times and for everything in the name of our Lord Jesus Christ" (v. 20).

206

The first verse of this passage overlaps with the last one of the previous week's lectionary selection. Once again we hear Jesus' assertion, "I am the living bread that came down from heaven ..." (v. 51a). Continuing further, we learn that some of Jesus' adversaries have responded with the troubling question, "How can this man give us his flesh to eat?" (v. 52). The question is perhaps not so much one that was raised by Jesus' contemporaries as one that is current in the Johannine church. It affords the opportunity for John to share some of his sacramental theology, with respect to the Lord's Supper. Partaking of the sacramental elements leads to eternal life (vv. 53-55). By partaking of the Lord's body and blood, his followers "abide" (*meno*) or dwell in him. The bread that Jesus gives is qualitatively different from that which the Israelites of old received in the wilderness: "the one who eats this bread will live forever" (v. 58b). Inasmuch as this passage clearly identifies the sacramental meal with the flesh of Jesus, it is possible that it speaks John's answer to the Docetists — those who wanted nothing to do with the reality of Jesus' crucifixion, and possibly abstained from the Lord's table as a result. John is clearly asserting, in response, that nourishment from this spiritual food is essential for survival, in the difficult between-times before the Lord's return.

Preaching Possibilities

The advice from Ephesians 5:15, "Be careful then how you live, not as unwise people but as wise, making the most of the time," is a wisdom teaching. Perhaps in conjunction with the Proverbs Old Testament Lesson, it can provide an excellent opportunity for introducing the biblical ideal of wisdom as not so much a matter of intellectual erudition as a common-sense ideal.

Wisdom. From time immemorial people have sought it — and, for nearly as long, they have been hoodwinked by those who claim to offer it bottled, for convenient consumption. The story is told of one intrepid wisdom-seeker, who climbed to the top of a mountain, and found sitting there the storied wise, old man. "What is the meaning of life?" the traveller asked, as soon as he'd caught his breath.

"Do you mean the breakfast cereal, the board game, or the magazine?" the old man replied. Beware of those claiming to offer wisdom.

That is, unless it's the Bible that makes that claim. In the pages of scripture, we find a very different ideal of wisdom. Far from being something dark and mysterious, a whispered mantra from an eastern mystic, the Bible's idea of wisdom is down-to-earth and practical. It's very similar, in fact, to what we would call "common sense."

Just look at 1 Kings, chapter 3. Solomon, upon receiving the crown of his father, David, prays to the Lord for wisdom. What he desires is not the esoteric secrets of the ages, but merely the clarity of mind to decide judicial cases that are brought before him. The Lord, impressed that Solomon isn't asking for long life or fabulous riches, grants him the discerning mind he craves — and throws in long life and riches to boot.

Or, take a look at the book of Proverbs — that compendium of wisdom reputed to have been compiled by King Solomon himself. You can't get more practical than Proverbs. Here are just a few of the wise sayings of this little book — sayings that have become bywords for our culture:

> *A soft answer turns away wrath,*
> *but a harsh word stirs up anger.*
>   — Proverbs 15:1

Pride goes before destruction,
and a haughty spirit before a fall.
      — Proverbs 16:18

Here's one that perhaps ought to be posted on the wall of every hospital room:

A cheerful heart is a good medicine,
but a downcast spirit dries up the bones.
      — Proverbs 17:22

And what if this one were posted in every corporate boardroom in America?

A good name is to be chosen rather than great riches,
and favor is better than silver or gold.
      — Proverbs 22:1

These are not the inscrutable secrets of the ages; they are homey, everyday, common-sense wisdom. Chapter 9 of Proverbs likens wisdom to the hostess at a banquet: when she invites you in, you will not only be nourished, but delighted at the elegant simplicity of the fare she serves.

"Be careful then how you live," says today's Ephesians passage, "not as unwise people but as wise, making the most of the time...." Then the author goes on to point out what he means by "wise" living: not getting drunk with wine; wives submitting themselves to their husbands; husbands submitting themselves to their wives; children obeying their parents.

Now these may not sound like rare and privileged secrets — but that's not the point. Ephesians doesn't see wisdom as something you have to seek in the rarified air of a guru's mountaintop hideaway, or in an Ivy League lecture hall; no, it has to do with the stuff of everyday life, the faithful living of these days.

When the author writes about "careful" living, he's using a Greek expression that literally means, "be careful how accurately you walk." Wisdom, this letter is saying, has more to do with our ability to place one foot in front of the other, day after day, than it does our acquaintance with Plato, or Einstein, or Freud, or any other great human mind.

It's about living *carefully*. Now in the popular imagination, being careful is much the same as being cautious. A "careful" person, as most people use the word, is one who's hesitant to explore the new and different — who's fearful of the unknown. Yet, "be careful how you live," in this passage, does not mean "be cautious." Rather, it means to "be care-full," filled with caring for others and for the world: "walking the walk" of the Christian, not just "talking the talk."

The final portion of the sermon text advises us to "make the most of the time." "Be careful then how you live," Paul says, "not as unwise people but as wise, making the most of the time, because the days are evil." Literally, the Greek means "redeem the time" — and that's the way some may remember it, from some older translations.

This isn't a first-century treatise on time management — but it is an observation that our lives float in a sea of time. How we choose to act changes the very quality of time itself. Ordinary time may be transformed — by graceful, loving actions — into God's time.

The Greek word for "redeem" is the same word that's used to describe the buying of a person out of slavery. In a certain way of looking at it, we enslave time, by the ways we choose to use it (or misuse it). By living carefully and wisely, we buy time back from its bondage to futility and decay. We make it fruitful; we claim it for God's purposes.

Prayer For The Day

Lord, help us to go forth from this place care-fully: attuned in caring concern to the needs of our neighbors, our community, our world. Help us to go forth wisely: not distracted by the *minutiae* of human knowledge, but seeking with clear head and clear eye your will for our lives. Help us to go forth eager to redeem the time: reclaiming each hour for holy purposes. We ask it in Jesus' name. Amen.

To Illustrate

Once there was a world-famous guru, who claimed thousands of disciples. His followers desired nothing more than to spend a few moments in his presence. The favored few lived close to their teacher and hung upon his every word. Others were less fortunate: they had to gather on the porch of his home. Then there was another group, that spilled out into the road — eager to hear even the secondhand teachings of the great man, repeated by those who had heard him.

The day finally arrived when the great sage lay dying. The three groups waited with eager anticipation for his final words of wisdom. The disciples of the inner circle, those in the teacher's very bedroom, begged him, "Dear teacher, give us your dying words of wisdom."

The guru looked up to the heavens for a moment, then turned to them and answered, "Life ... is like a river."

The disciples on the porch asked, leaning in the windows, "What did he say? What did he say?"

The nearest disciple repeated, "Life ... is like a river."

The followers out on the road heard the commotion, and begged those on the porch, "What did he say? What did he say?"

They repeated, "Life ... is like a river." And the word spread, from one disciple to another.

Everyone nodded gravely at these words of wisdom — until one of the outermost disciples, at the very fringes of the crowd, asked aloud, "Life is like a river? What on earth does he mean by that?"

And so the question passed back through the crowd, from one disciple to another, until it came to the inner circle. The guru's most trusted retainer leaned down and whispered in his ear, "Life is like a river — what does that mean?"

The great sage struggled to lift his head from the pillow, then beckoned as if he had something to say. His number-one man leaned down, inclining his ear to catch the slightest whisper. Then came the reply: "Okay. So maybe life *isn't* like a river!"

***

There's a story from the Jewish tradition, about a famous rabbi and his friends, who had spent an entire morning at manual labor, far from their village. The work was difficult and dirty. At lunchtime his friends brought a pail of water, so their teacher could wash his hands thoroughly, fulfilling the ritual law.

To their surprise, he used only a few drops. How could it be that their wise and pious teacher would avoid the command to wash his hands thoroughly before eating? Cautiously, one of the students asked, "Rabbi, you used so little water. It was not nearly enough to get your hands clean."

Wordlessly, the rabbi pointed to a servant girl walking up the road from the well. Across her shoulders was a yoke, with a heavy jar of water dangling from each end. "How could I do my washing at the expense of this poor girl?" the rabbi asked. "The water I save may prevent one trip to the well for her."

That — and not narrow-minded observance of the law — is truly "care-ful living."

***

A few years ago, a television commercial introduced a new convenience food product: a "breakfast bar." The commercial showed a family doing what families so often do, early in the morning: rushing to get out the door. Dad was all set to leave for work, the kids were slinging schoolbags over their shoulders, Mom was trying to make sense of it all — and they all sort of collided, there in the kitchen. There it was, a second or two of family togetherness before the craziness of the day began in earnest. It would have been nice if they'd had time for breakfast, but there was no time for breakfast. *Must meet minimal nutritional needs ...*

Mom to the rescue! She turned to each of her family in turn, and tossed them a breakfast bar: a little concoction of two layers of cold cereal, with some white substance resembling milk in between. And there — through some kind of television magic — floating in the air over each person's head was a bowl of cold cereal: kind of like the tongues of fire on Pentecost. The message was clear: Your family may not have time for a nice, nutritious bowl of cold cereal, but you can give them all the vitamins and minerals they need by stuffing a breakfast bar in their mouths on the way out the door.

But wait a minute. Isn't *cold cereal* supposed to be a convenience food? Is Madison Avenue now telling us that America now needs a convenience food to substitute for a convenience food? Is that what we mean by redeeming the time?

***

In the tempestuous ocean of time and toil there are islands of stillness where [we] may enter a harbor and reclaim [our] dignity. The sabbath is the island, the port, the place of detachment from the practical and attachment to the spirit. Rushing hither and thither time becomes soiled and degraded; the sabbath is the opportunity to cleanse time.

— Abraham Heschel

Proper 16, Pentecost 14, Ordinary Time 21
August 27, 2006

Revised Common	1 Kings 8:(1, 6, 10-11) 22-30, 41-43 *or* Joshua 24:1-2a, 14-18	Ephesians 6:10-20	John 6:56-69
Roman Catholic	Joshua 24:1-2, 15-18	Ephesians 5:21-32	John 6:60-69
Episcopal	Joshua 24:1-2a, 14-25	Ephesians 5:21-32	John 6:60-69

Theme For The Day   The power God offers to believers is different from the world's idea of power.

Old Testament Lesson   1 Kings 8:(1, 6, 10-11) 22-30, 41-43   *Solomon's Prayer Of Dedication For The Temple*

The lectionary provides some optional verses to help set the context, but the heart of this week's selection is Solomon's prayer of dedication for the temple. It is well to remember the rich symbolism this structure has for the people of Israel. The Lord has prevented Solomon's father David from building such a structure, favoring in those early days the simple, rustic virtue of the tabernacle tent. Now, however, the Lord has relented: during this brief historical interlude when Israel is a political and commercial power in the region, Solomon's temple will be the nation's crowning religious and artistic achievement. Verses 10-11 indicate that, as the Ark is being brought into the new temple, the glory of the Lord fills the entire area, in the form of a dense cloud. In verse 22, Solomon begins his prayer of dedication. Clearly he is, at this moment, the cultic as well as the political leader of the nation. The king begins by recalling God's covenant with the people, and with the royal house of David, in particular. The Lord is a God of covenant (*berith*) and steadfast love (*hesed*). In verse 25, Solomon specifically calls to remembrance the Lord's promise never to let the house of David fail. Will this temple somehow contain the Lord? Of course not: "Even heaven and the highest heaven cannot contain you, much less this house that I have built!" (v. 27). The temple is not so much the place where the Lord dwells, as a listening post, a place where the faithful can come, knowing with certainty that their prayers will be heard (vv. 29-30). God's receptiveness is not limited to the faithful of Israel: even foreigners who come and pray in this house will be heard, to the end that "all the peoples of the earth may know your name and fear you" (vv. 41-43).

Alternate Old Testament Lesson   Joshua 24:1-2a, 14-18   *Joshua Leads The People In Renewing The Covenant*

After the turmoil of the conquest of Canaan is over, when Joshua is "old and well advanced in years" (v. 23:1), he gathers the tribes of Israel together at Shechem, and leads them in a ritual of covenant renewal. Alone among the Israelites, Joshua remembers the full story of the people's unfaithfulness in the wilderness. Now, as he is looking ahead to the time following his own death, he wants to be sure that the people continue to observe the law, "turning aside from it neither to the right nor to the left" (v. 23:6), and not assuming the ways of the Canaanite peoples all around them (v. 23:7). In verse 24:2, Joshua begins a recitation of Israel's history that has some similarities to the famous recitation of the genealogy of Kunta Kinte in Alex Haley's novel, *Roots* — and this one serves much the same purpose. It ends up with verse 13, with the reminder that the Lord has given them the land as a free and undeserved gift. The lectionary selection picks up again with verse 14, which begins the actual covenant-renewal. It is fruitful to focus on the verbs: the people are to *revere* and *serve* the Lord, and *put away* the old gods (reminiscent of Jacob's collection and burial of the idols in Genesis 35:2-4). "Revere" (*yare*) is sometimes translated "fear," but it means something closer to reverence to modern ears. In these times we have largely lost the sense of "fear" as meaning anything other than cringing terror. Joshua places a decision before them, as expressed in these famous words: "choose this day whom you will serve, whether the gods your ancestors served in the region beyond the river or the gods of the Amorites in whose land you are living; but as for me and my household, we will serve the Lord" (v. 15). Verses 16-18 are the people's unanimous and enthusiastic response to Joshua's challenge.

New Testament Lesson   Ephesians 6:10-20   *Put On The Whole Armor Of God*

With one great, concluding metaphor, the didactic section of Ephesians ends. "Be strong in the Lord and in the strength of his power" is the way this pericope begins — a seeming tautology in English, though in fact three different Greek words are at work (v. 10). *Dunamis, kratos,* and *ischus* all appear in this verse, in that order. Physical strength, ruling authority, and the power of personality are a rough approximation of what these words mean. "The whole armor of God" is the controlling metaphor: in the cosmic struggle between good and evil, the followers of Christ are to arm themselves for what they must face. Evil's power is multifaceted: good must contend "against the rulers (*archas*), against the authorities (*exousias*), against the cosmic powers (*kosmokratoras*) of this present darkness, against the spiritual forces of evil (*pneumatika tes ponerias*) in the heavenly places" (v. 12). The weaponry is comparable to what a typical Roman soldier would wear: a "belt of truth," a "breastplate of righteousness," for "shoes [an eagerness] to proclaim the gospel of peace," "the shield of faith," "the helmet of salvation," and "the sword of the Spirit, which is the word of God" (vv. 14-17). Requests for prayers round out this passage — prayers "for all the saints" as well as for the author — who describes himself as "an ambassador in chains" (alluding, no doubt, to Paul's imprisonment).

The Gospel   John 6:56-69   *True Believers*

Overlapping with the last two verses of the previous week's lectionary selection, this passage begins with the thought that, "Those who eat my flesh and drink my blood abide in me, and I in them ... the one who eats this bread will live forever" (vv. 56, 58). Many of the disciples object to this "difficult" teaching — the difficulty consisting in the entire argument, not merely its concluding words (v. 60). The Johannine church evidently struggled mightily over eucharistic theology and over Christology. In verses 61-65, Jesus draws a distinction between true and false belief, and observes that those among the company "who do not believe" will not be saved (there is an oblique reference to Judas here — referred to as "a devil" in v. 70 — but others are evidently included as well). Many of the disciples become disheartened at these harsh words, and subsequently leave (v. 66). Jesus turns to the twelve and asks them if they, too, wish to go away. "Lord, to whom can we go?" asks Peter. "You have the words of eternal life. We have come to believe and know that you are the Holy One of God" (vv. 68-69). Peter — and by extension, the eleven — goes on record here with a confession of absolute faith in Jesus: one that is every bit as pronounced as the one he uttered at Caesarea Philippi.

Preaching Possibilities

Here in Ephesians, chapter 6 we have a remarkable listing of different kinds of power. There are four principal words for power in the New Testament, and a single verse out of this chapter — verse 10 — contains three of them. "Finally," the letter says, "be strong in the Lord and in the strength of his power." It's an awkward and repetitious sentence, and the reason for it is that these three different Greek words are at work, and the translators are hard pressed to convert them into English. The English language just doesn't offer the translators much to work with. Let's take a look at these words, and see what they mean.

First is *dunamis*, often translated "strength." (Here it's in a verbal form, which means "be strong.") The word *dunamis* is of course the basis of our English word, "dynamite"; also, our word "dynamic." A person who possesses *dunamis* — who's truly dynamic — is a strong person: much like Arnold Schwarzenegger back in his iron-pumping days. *Dunamis* is the power to accomplish things.

The second Greek word for power found in this verse is *kratos*, or ruling power. This word is found within our English word, "democracy." *Demos* means "people," so if it's teamed up with *kratos*, or rule, we get "rule by the people." *Kratos* is the sort of power Mr. Schwarzenegger exercises as California's governor. There's no simple, one-word English equivalent to *kratos*, so the NRSV translators take the easy way out and render it "strength" — even though they've just used "strength" to translate *dunamis*, which has a different meaning. The precise meaning of *kratos* in the Greek, having to do with political rule, doesn't come through at all.

The third Greek word for power is *ischus*. This one is a bit harder to define. It's similar in some ways to *kratos* — political rule — but with more of a passive sense. *Ischus* is a quality belonging to a person who governs, that can be seen by others but not directly exercised. If you talked about an "aura of power," you'd be getting close — or charisma, that quality newspaper reporters love to identify in certain politicians. When Ah-nold walks into a room filled with his fans and conversation abruptly stops, he's subtly exercising a kind of personal power — and he's doing it without so much as flexing a bicep. You could call it the Schwarzenegger swagger.

We've said there's a fourth word for power in the Greek language — and though it doesn't occur in this passage, it's worth mentioning anyway. The word is *energeia*, which most will quickly recognize as the root of our word "energy." In the New Testament, though, the word's used a little differently. *Energeia* is strictly reserved, in the Bible, for God's power. When the ancient Greeks speak of energy, they are talking about a mysterious, invisible power that can be traced back, somehow, to the gods themselves.

All this is to say that the little verse, "Be strong in the Lord and in the strength of his power," has a lot more going on inside it than may be apparent at first glance.

It's also a verse that speaks to most all of us, deep inside ourselves. Which one among us does not desire to be stronger? This is true not only with respect to physical strength — the case of the proverbial "98-pound weakling" who gets sand kicked in his face at the beach, and heads off to the gym to pump himself up for the next encounter. Most of us also wish we had more inner strength — the strength to persevere against difficult odds, the strength to tough it out, the strength to not only survive, but prosper.

Inside each one of us there dwells a small child; an insecure, uncertain child. That inner child still believes he or she is fundamentally weak and powerless. What that child wouldn't give for a little strength: physical strength, emotional strength (which we sometimes call "self-confidence"), strength that projects to others a sense of personal authority and importance!

That inner child is looking for a hero. It's that search for a strong, redemptive figure that fuels Hollywood's longstanding fascination with "action movies." The label "action," of course, on the video store shelf really means "violence." It's a euphemism, because the entertainment industry is too squeamish (or more likely, too clever) to use that word.

213

Action heroes are the living icons of a myth our society holds dear. It's a myth that biblical scholar, Walter Wink, and others have called "the myth of redemptive violence." Wink believes that for many, many people, violence is the real religion of our time. Violence — or the threat of violence, in the form of shaking the proverbial "big stick" at our enemies — is the only thing that saves us, in some people's view, from all that's evil in the world. Violence (which by its very nature brings destruction and death) is twisted completely around by this kind of thinking, in a diabolical way, until what is destructive actually comes to be seen as redemptive. It's like the famous comment of that American military officer in Vietnam: "We had to destroy the village in order to save it."

"This Myth of Redemptive Violence," Wink writes, "is the real myth of the modern world. It, and not Judaism or Christianity or Islam, is the dominant religion in our society today." (Walter Wink, *The Powers That Be: Theology For a New Millennium* [New York: Doubleday, 1999], p. 42)

If children (or even adults) nourish their spirits on a steady diet of so-called "action films," they may become brainwashed into believing this destructive myth. They will learn to see the world in stark, black-and-white, good-versus-evil terms. They will learn to locate evil outside themselves and to scapegoat anyone who's strange or different. In time they will come to accept as common knowledge the unthinking assumption that "might makes right" — both on the individual level and on the international stage. They will come to see strength as embodied in the almost mythological figure of a man who slides down a rope out of a helicopter, firing an automatic weapon into a crowd of enemies.

So is this what the Letter to the Ephesians means by being "strong in the Lord," by putting on the whole armor of Christ? Hardly. What the writer's talking about here is no mere human strength, but rather the strength that flows forth from God's love and mercy. The most perfect example of this sort of strength is Jesus Christ. He rejected any thought of an action-hero style escape from the cross, instead submitting to its pain and its shame. We Christians believe it's the death of Jesus on the cross that's ultimately redemptive: not our own deployment of violence. Furthermore, we believe the strength he showed in sacrificially giving himself for the sins of the world is far superior to any merely human strength. As Christ says in 2 Corinthians: "My grace is sufficient for you, for power is made perfect in weakness" (2 Corinthians 12:9).

Prayer For The Day

Great God, we confess that we are often tempted to give in to feelings of doubt, to fears, to creeping insecurity. We present ourselves, now — our whole self; strengths, weaknesses, fears and all — before Jesus Christ. Open our eyes to discover in him power to overcome all our difficulties. Amen.

To Illustrate

In 1966, about a year before he died, J. Robert Oppenheimer — brilliant physicist, co-inventor of the atom bomb — confessed, "I am a complete failure!" Looking back on his life, Oppenheimer saw all his scientific achievements as meaningless. When someone pointed out his numerous discoveries, he replied, "They leave on the tongue only the taste of ashes."

Oppenheimer realized, late in life, that the fire he had brought into the world — like some twentieth-century Prometheus — could leave behind only ashes and destruction. That's the only thing that can come of bombs and missiles; of our crazy, headlong desire to seek wealth and power, and to protect it with military might; of our craving for more and more creature comforts, at the expense of the needy. Indeed, "the taste of ashes" is only thing that can come of any human enterprise that does not have God in it.

***

There's a scene in the film, *Schindler's List*, when Oskar Schindler, the factory owner who spirited so many Jews out of concentration camps, is arguing with the brutish Nazi commandant, trying to get him to release a group of prisoners to labor in Schindler's factory. The commandant is an inhuman monster: for entertainment, he sits at the window of his residence and randomly shoots Jewish prisoners with a high-powered rifle.

Still, Schindler seeks to reason with this barbarian, arguing that his sort of life-and-death authority is not real power. Real power, Schindler argues, is the power not to deal out death indiscriminately, but to hold back — to restrain oneself. Real power is the power to forgive.

Schindler gets his contract laborers, and for a few days the commandant cleans up his act. He gets a sort of perverse satisfaction out of pardoning prisoners. But before long, brutality triumphs over reason, and he's back to his old tricks.

The commandant fails at forgiveness because to truly forgive others, you have to feel something for them — sympathy, compassion, love. He doesn't feel a thing for Jews — or perhaps for anyone (maybe not even for himself). Schindler, however, is the one who, throughout the film, steadily grows in his ability to exercise compassion.

***

Convicted Watergate conspirator, G. Gordon Liddy, once gave a lecture on a college campus in Missouri. Throughout the evening, Liddy — who had just been released from prison — harangued his audience with the idea that only force, brute strength, and an iron will could earn the respect of friends and foes in this "real world which is, in fact, a very tough neighborhood."

During the question-and-answer period, one of the college professors rose to speak. Rather timidly, he objected: "In our country, most people ... after all ... do base their ethics on ... the teachings of Jesus ... and this doesn't sound much like the teachings of Jesus."

Liddy is said to have glared for a moment, before taking in a deep breath, and bellowing: "Yeah — and look what happened to Jesus. They crucified him." To him, the case was closed. The audience responded to his put-down with laughter and thunderous applause.

G. Gordon Liddy was absolutely right. Jesus stood before the terrible, destructive power of Rome in courageous, virtuous silence. And that power rose up and crushed him. To the likes of G. Gordon Liddy — and Pontius Pilate, Caiaphas, and Herod — that should have been the end of the story. But it wasn't the end. There was another power at work in the life — and the death — of Jesus of Nazareth.

That creative, life-giving power began its work in the cool silence of the tomb. That power worked much more rapidly, on that occasion, than it habitually does in our world. A mere three days later, life coursed through Jesus' veins again, and he rose up and walked. Ever since that day, the power of life has continued to contend with the power of death.

Proper 17, Pentecost 15, Ordinary Time 22
September 3, 2006

Revised Common	Song Of Solomon 2:8-13 or Deuteronomy 4:1-2, 6-8	James 1:17-27	Mark 7:1-8, 14-15, 21-23
Roman Catholic	Deuteronomy 4:1-2, 6-8	James 1:17-19, 21-22, 27	Mark 7:1-8, 14-15, 21-23
Episcopal	Deuteronomy 4:1-9	Ephesians 6:10-20	Mark 7:1-8, 14-15, 21-23

Theme For The Day   Listening is at the heart of loving.

Old Testament Lesson   Song Of Solomon 2:8-13   *Praise For The Beloved*

Today provides an opportunity to open a biblical book that is rarely expounded from the pulpit. The Song Of Songs (Song Of Solomon) is a collection of love poetry — although Jewish and Christian commentators over the centuries, uncomfortable with its frank sensuality, have tried to explain the poetry in various other ways. Most notably (and most notoriously) they have sought to describe it as either an allegory of God's love for Israel or of Christ's love for the church. Some have tried to discern a single narrative underlying the poetry, but in fact, the dramatic setting and voices change so often that this is an impossible task. In reality, the Song Of Songs is an anthology of love songs, whose authorship is a mystery. The identification of the book with Solomon is probably the speculation of a later editor. In this passage, the woman celebrates the coming of her lover, with all the strength, agility, and bounding joy "of a young stag" (v. 9). "Arise, my love, my fair one, and come away," he whispers to her, through the lattice (v. 10). The luxuriant springtime growth of the flowers and fig trees encourages the pair to think of love. Intimate communication is at the heart of this passage.

Alternate Old Testament Lesson   Deuteronomy 4:1-2, 6-8   *Moses Urges The Israelites Not To Forget The Law*

The wilderness wanderings are nearly ended, and the people of Israel are on the verge of entering the promised land. Moses wants to be sure that, once Israel crosses over, the people solemnly resolve to "give heed to the statutes and ordinances" he has given to them (v. 1). Israel's steadfast obedience to the law will serve as a witness to the Canaanites, who will then consider them "a wise and discerning people" (v. 6). The Lord of Israel is not only a distant, austere ruler, but responds to the people's needs: "For what other great nation has a god so near to it as the Lord our God is whenever we call...?" (v. 7). To remember the intricately detailed ordinances will require great care: "watch yourselves closely, so as neither to forget the things that your eyes have seen nor to let them slip from your mind all the days of your life; make them known to your children and your children's children" (v. 9).

New Testament Lesson   James 1:17-27   *Be Doers Of The Word*

This passage opens with an excellent stewardship text: "Every generous act of giving, with every perfect gift, is from above, coming down from the Father of lights ..." (v. 17a). James has already identified God as unstintingly generous (v. 5); now he reminds us that all human giving can trace its origin to the primordial giving of God. That God is changeless: and so, presumably, is God's generous nature (v. 17b). We are "a kind of first fruits of his creatures," a living sign in the world of God's generosity (v. 18). With verse 19, James begins a section containing miscellaneous ethical instructions: "let everyone be quick to listen, slow to speak, slow to anger; for your anger does not produce God's righteousness" (vv. 19-20a). Verse 22 can be seen as James' signature idea: "be doers of the word, and not merely hearers who deceive themselves." It is this emphasis on good works, as compared to faith, that led Luther to consider dropping this letter from the canon; he called it, famously, "an epistle of straw." Those who do not enflesh their beliefs in concrete action in the world, James says, are like those who regard themselves in a mirror; as soon as they walk away, the image vanishes (vv. 23-24). Pure speech, care for the needy, holy living: such are the marks of pure faith. "If any think they are religious, and do not bridle their tongues but deceive their hearts, their religion is worthless. Religion that is pure and undefiled before God, the Father, is this: to care for orphans and widows in their distress, and to keep oneself unstained by the world" (vv. 26-27).

The Gospel   Mark 7:1-8, 14-15, 21-23   *Pure Hearts, Not Hands*

Some scribes and Pharisees ask Jesus why his followers do not follow the ritual law, failing to wash their hands in the prescribed way. Jesus responds with hostility, calling them "hypocrites," and quoting Isaiah 29:13: "in vain do they worship me, teaching human precepts as doctrines" (v. 7). In a section omitted by the lectionary, Jesus launches into a debate about "corban" — a regulation, sanctioned by the scribes and Pharisees, that allowed children to satisfy their obligation to provide for their aged parents by making a temple offering instead (vv. 9-13). This, Jesus objects, violates the spirit of the commandment to honor one's father and mother. The lectionary selection resumes with Jesus calling the crowd together and declaring, "there is nothing outside a person that by going in can defile, but the things that come out are what defile" (v. 15). Holy living, in other words, does not consist in washing hands, but rather in what those hands do that is helpful to others. The lectionary then skips the scatological part of Jesus' explanation of this "parable" — an earthy analogy to the workings of the human digestive system (vv. 17-20) — recommencing its selection with his words explaining that "it is from within, from the human heart, that evil intentions come" (v. 21). Jesus thus rejects the entire purification system of Jewish Law. The only purity that matters is moral purity.

Preaching Possibilities

A link between the James and Song Of Solomon lessons is the concept of listening. James urges his readers, "let everyone be quick to listen" (v. 19b). In the Song Of Songs, it is clear that the two lovers are listening rather intently to one another when they are together — and listening eagerly for the arrival of the other when they are apart.

It will be important to say a few words about the Song Of Solomon, and how it has been misinterpreted and marginalized over the years. Most church members have a vague sense that there's something spicy and vaguely embarrassing in that book of the Bible, but few have actually read it — or could even easily find it in their Bibles, sandwiched as it is between the stern philosophy of Ecclesiastes and the soaring prophecies of Isaiah.

Part of the vague sense of embarrassment about the Song Of Solomon has nothing to do with the book itself, and everything to do with our society's ambivalence about human love. Society has a tendency to portray human love in one of only two ways. Love is either completely idealized and spiritual, or it's erotic and physical — and never the twain shall meet. On the one hand are lacy valentine hearts and bouquets of roses; on the other is pornography. One extreme, according to our culture, is good; the other bad. There is no middle ground.

The typical couple, on their wedding day, receive a colossal mixed message. They go from the church (where they've just heard love extolled as a purely spiritual gift), to the reception-hall (where frequently they're treated to an off-color toast by the best man, before going through the degrading ritual of "tossing the garter").

The Song Of Solomon knows no such separation between the physical and the spiritual. "Endless seas and floods, torrents and rivers," the poet writes, "cannot put out love's infinite fires." This author sees no need to construct a wall between the spiritual and the physical; in the Song Of Songs, they are two sides of the same coin.

So what's a preacher to do with the Song Of Solomon, this raciest book in the Bible? One approach is to let scripture interpret scripture: looking first at a New Testament epistle, and its emphasis on listening as a moral virtue.

If there's one thing these two lovers of the Song Of Songs have elevated to a fine art, it's the act of listening to one another. The woman whose voice we hear is listening attentively for her lover: every thought, every action is attuned to his return. When she hears the sound of his eager footstep, and then, moments later, his voice — "Come with me, my love, come away" — her heart thrills within her. James advises everyone to "be quick to listen" — although, for a pair of ardent lovers like this couple, listening is a given. Listening is one thing lovers do especially well, so attuned are they to each other's very heartbeat.

Listening comes easy, when love is new. Yet, as the years go by, and loving relationships — be they marriage or friendship — mature, what then becomes of the listening? It's so easy for married couples, in particular, to become like the one portrayed in a certain magazine cartoon. The husband is reading aloud from his newspaper: "Honey, it says here that one of the reasons for marital problems is that couples don't really listen to each other." Then you look over at where the wife ought to be sitting, and you see an empty chair! Such are the perils of a love that is no longer new.

Listening is, in fact, one of the greatest gifts you or I can give to those we love — or to anyone else, for that matter. There is a universal human need to be listened to — and for those who find themselves suddenly bereft of listeners, life becomes tedious indeed. Such is often the case in hospitals and nursing homes, where patients can go a very long time without having anyone listen to them, about anything other than the occasional question about whether or not the water pitcher is full. The gift of taking the time to truly listen to a person in such circumstances is a precious gift.

James says, "Every generous act of giving, with every perfect gift, is from above...." We listen to others because we have first been listened to. Jesus says, "Ask, and it will be given to you; search, and you will find; knock, and the door will be opened for you." When we pray, God listens. Because God hears us, we can listen to others.

Prayer For The Day

Creator God, we hear in scripture that "in the beginning was the word." You spoke into the silence, and a universe came to be. So eager were you for someone to listen that you created human beings in your own image. We acknowledge, Lord, that we are not always the best at listening to you: but we believe you always listen to us. Help us to be faithful in listening to one another: for such is the way of Christ. Amen.

To Illustrate

One of the legends in the public high school I attended dated back to the days when there was still daily Bible reading in the schools. The daily Bible readings were part of the dreaded "opening exercises." No one paid much attention to that disembodied voice, crackling out of the public address system speaker.

It was school tradition, in those days, to have a different student each week read from the Bible. The chosen student was given freedom to pick any passage at all. It was already Wednesday or Thursday of that fateful week, before the administration noticed what some students had realized instantly on Monday morning: that the student reader that week had chosen the Song Of Solomon, from the venerable King James Version ...

> *How beautiful are thy feet with shoes, O prince's daughter!*
> *The joints of thy thighs are like jewels ...*
> *Thy navel is like a round goblet, which wanteth not liquor;*
> *thy belly is like a heap of wheat set about with lilies.*
> *Thy two breasts are like two young roes that are twins.*
> *Thy neck is like a tower of ivory....*

The effect of those words, I'm told, on a school full of adolescents first thing in the morning, was, shall we say, "memorable." By order of the principal himself, the student reader was instantly sacked — in the middle of the week — despite his fervent protests that all he'd been doing was reading from the Bible! From that day forward — until the Supreme Court banned school Bible reading — students at New Jersey's Toms River High School read from passages that had been chosen in advance by the administration.

Dangerous stuff, those Bible verses!

***

The opposite of talking isn't listening ... [but] waiting.

— Fran Lebowitz

***

When I listen, people speak.

— Seen on a bumper sticker

***

I have often noticed that the more deeply I hear the meanings of [people], the more there is that happens. Almost always, when [people] realize [they have] been deeply heard, [their] eyes moisten. I think in some real sense [they are] weeping for joy. It is as though [they] were saying, "Thank God, somebody heard me. Someone knows what it's like to be me."

— Carl Rogers

***

There's an old legend out of Africa, about a tribe whose custom it was for the men to purchase their wives with livestock. If a woman was especially beautiful, a man might offer her father five goats; if she were plain, only one or two.

There was one young man, who, when the tribe met at the oasis for their annual gathering, set his eye upon one rather ordinary-looking maiden. To the astonishment of all his friends, he went up to her father and bid the princely sum of ten goats. Surprised and delighted with his unexpected good fortune, the father accepted. The two were married straightaway.

A year went by, and as the tribe gathered at the oasis once again, the young men laughed and pointed their fingers at their friend, newly arrived from the hills. "And how is your ten-goat bride?" they asked, snickering behind his back.

Then, at that very moment, into their presence walked the most lovely woman any of them had ever seen. "Don't you recognize the woman I married?" their friend asked.

Truly, they had not recognized her. She had changed. What had changed about her was the knowledge that her husband loved her so much, he had paid ten goats for her. It was this knowledge that had made her beautiful.

In the very same way, the gift of listening — the gift of precious time, offered to another person in love — ascribes worth. It is this sense of self-worth — more than any jewelry, cosmetic, or diet — that makes a person beautiful.

***

An even more poignant story is told by the surgeon and author, Dr. Richard Selzer:

> *I stand by the bed where a young woman lies, her face postoperative, her mouth twisted in palsy, clownish. A tiny twig of the facial nerve, the one to the muscles of her mouth, has been severed. The surgeon had followed with religious fervor the curve of her flesh; I promise you that. Nevertheless, to remove the tumor in her cheek, I had cut the little nerve.*
>
> *Her young husband is in the room. He stands on the opposite side of the bed, and together they seem to dwell in the evening lamplight, isolated from me, private. Who are they, I ask myself, he and this wry mouth I have made, who gaze at and touch each other so generously, greedily?*
>
> *The young woman speaks. "Will my mouth always be like this?" she asks.*
>
> *"Yes," I say, "it will. It is because the nerve was cut."*
>
> *She nods, and is silent. But the young man smiles.*
>
> *"I like it," he says. "It's kind of cute."*
>
> *All at once I know who he is. I understand, and I lower my gaze. One is not bold in an encounter with a god. Unmindful, he bends to kiss her crooked mouth, and I am so close I can see how he twists his own lips to accommodate to hers, to show her that their kiss still works.*

Proper 18, Pentecost 16, Ordinary Time 23
September 10, 2006

Revised Common	Proverbs 22:1-2, 8-9, 22-23 or Isaiah 35:4-7a3	James 2:1-10 (11-13) 14-17	Mark 7:24-37
Roman Catholic	Isaiah 35:4-7a	James 2:1-5	Mark 7:31-37
Episcopal	Isaiah 35:4-7a	James 1:17-27	Mark 7:31-37

Theme For The Day   The good news of Jesus Christ is for all people.

Old Testament Lesson   Proverbs 22:1-2, 8-9, 22-23   *Wise Living*

This section of the book of Proverbs straddles the boundary between two principal divisions of the book. The first two sub-sections of today's lectionary selection, verses 1-2 and 8-9, belong to the collection titled "The Proverbs of Solomon" (10:1). The third, verses 22-23, belongs to the collection titled "The Words of the Wise" (22:17). Not that this matters tremendously to preaching this text, because the proverbial material in both these collections is an assortment of wisdom sayings that are mostly unconnected with each other. The attribution to Solomon attached to the first portion (10:1—22:16) does not necessarily mean Solomon is the author. It means these proverbs were compiled under the patronage of the royal house of David. The varied sayings included in this week's lectionary selection have to do with: the value of a good name (v. 1); rich and poor being equal before God (v. 2); "Whoever sows injustice will reap calamity" (v. 8); the generous who share with the poor being blessed (v. 9); and an injunction against abusing the poor, because the Lord protects them (vv. 22-23). There seems to be an assumption in many of these sayings that the audience is made up primarily of people of means, perhaps young men of the priestly class and / or the royal court — hence, the many admonitions to care for the poor. There is a tone of courtly chivalry echoing through many of these epigrams, that would not have made sense if the destitute were included among its intended audience. Verses 17-21 (omitted from this week's lectionary selection) are a sort of introduction to the second collection, and tell of the editor's purpose in compiling it.

Alternate Old Testament Lesson   Isaiah 35:4-7a   *The Lord Will Redeem*

Scholars have long remarked over the similarities between Isaiah 35 and the work of Second Isaiah (chs. 40-55). Chapter 35 contains both similar imagery and the same sort of hopeful theme, looking to the Lord to redeem the long-suffering Israel. This passage's imagery of the coming of a cosmically powerful God who will save and redeem the people (v. 4), along with miraculous signs such as the healing of physical disabilities (vv. 5-6) and water in the desert (v. 7), all have their counterparts in Second Isaiah. This passage can be the foundation for a sermon on hope, one that encourages believers in trying times to rely on God for redemption and help.

New Testament Lesson   James 2:1-10 (11-13) 14-17   *Faith By Itself, Without Works, Is Dead*

Chapter 2 of James continues the didactic tone of the first chapter, advising Christians to focus on doing good works that give glory to God. There is specific advice here for the ordering of the Christian community's life. Preferential seating for the rich is to be abolished (vv. 1-7), for to do otherwise is to betray the intent of one of Jesus' greatest teachings, to "love your neighbor as yourself" (v. 10a). The Law of God is a unity, and cannot be followed selectively: "whoever keeps the whole law but fails in one point has become accountable for all of it" (v. 10b). The optional verse 13 extols the virtue of mercy, and of avoiding judgment of others: "judgment will be without mercy to anyone who has shown no mercy; mercy triumphs over judgment." Verses 14-17 are the first part of a general philosophical discussion about the inseparability of faith and works. Although many Protestants (including Luther) have responded with horror to verse 17 ("faith by itself, if it has no works, is dead"), if the qualifier "by itself" is not overlooked, it will become clear that James is holding out for a both / and approach, rather than either / or.

The Gospel   Mark 7:24-37   *Jesus And The Syrophoenician Woman*
This is the story of two healings. The first is an exceedingly difficult passage, because of Jesus' remark in verse 27 which makes him sound like a racist. Jesus is out of Israelite territory, near the Phoenician port city of Tyre, and is hoping — for the moment — to remain incognito. A woman of the region discovers he is there, and calls on him in the house where he is staying, asking him to exorcise a demon from her daughter. Jesus' remark certainly sounds like a callous rejection: "Let the children be fed first, for it is not fair to take the children's food and throw it to the dogs" (v. 27). Dogs, in Jesus' society, are not cherished house pets, but are considered a particularly low form of animal life. This plucky woman gives it right back to him: "Sir, even the dogs under the table eat the children's crumbs" (v. 28). Jesus softens at this, declaring to her that the demon has left her daughter — which, as she discovers upon returning home, is exactly the case (vv. 29-30). It is possible that Jesus' remark about not throwing food to the dogs was spoken with a certain degree of irony, perhaps even joking — it's what most everyone would expect him to say, given the feelings of hostility between the two cultures — but the fact that he very quickly heals the girl indicates that this is not, in fact, his personal view. The second healing, verses 31-37, is that of a deaf-mute man. It is a more conventional healing story than the one we have just examined. Notable here is the detailed physical description of Jesus' treatment, including putting his fingers into the man's ears, spitting, and touching his tongue. The man is healed, and the people are delighted, saying, "He has done everything well" (v. 37).

Preaching Possibilities
How ridiculous prejudice is — and yet, sadly, how commonplace! From the earliest days that men and women have walked the earth, we have had this disturbing tendency to build walls, to separate people one from another. Be they barriers of race, nationality, religion, or economic status, all of us can claim a share of guilt for building and maintaining those walls — walls that separate us from brothers and sisters who share this planet. In today's Gospel Lesson, we hear of a woman who has the courage to scale the walls of prejudice.

Jesus and his disciples have crossed over into a foreign country: the Phoenician lands around the city of Tyre (that's present-day Lebanon). Mark doesn't tell us why they've travelled so far out of their way, but it's just possible that Jesus and his friends have gone on a sort of vacation or retreat. Exhausted from the demands of ministry — the crowds that won't leave them alone, the ceaseless harassment of the scribes and the Pharisees — they may just want to get away from it all. (Who could blame them?)

But there is no rest for the weary — not even in Gentile lands. A Syrophoenician woman seeks Jesus out, begging him to heal her daughter. Now that may not seem at all unusual — after all, healing people is Jesus' stock in trade — but remember who this women is. She's not a Jew, but a Gentile. She falls to her knees in front of Jesus, and begs him to help her. The worry etched on her face tells all the story anyone needs to hear: her daughter is sick, and she has nowhere else to turn. This woman will pay any price, will do anything, to see her well again.

Remarkably, Jesus' response to her is lukewarm — even rude. He seems to want nothing to do with the woman. Without even answering her plea, Jesus says to her, "Let the children be fed first, for it is not fair to take the children's food and throw it to the dogs." To our ears that sounds harsh, even cruel — but to understand what's happening here, we have to try to think like a first-century Jew. To a faithful Jew of that day, Jesus' response to the woman is hardly out of the ordinary — it is, in fact, exactly what a rabbi is expected to say. Virtuous women of that society do not approach male strangers and speak to them; and more than that, this woman belongs to an unclean race, the Gentiles. There is no rabbi alive who'd give such a woman the time of day!

In speaking to her at all — in the context of that culture — Jesus is paying her a high honor. He is providing her an opening: allowing her to engage with him in theological debate, as his equal. Jesus is giving her an opportunity to make a theological case for the healing of her daughter. The woman is more than up to Jesus' challenge. In a clever comeback, she responds, "Sir, even the dogs under the table eat the children's crumbs." With that, he tells the woman her daughter is healed: and when she returns home, she embraces a little girl who is herself again.

For whoever is there to witness this encounter, Jesus is teaching an important lesson. Just prior to this passage, Jesus has been explaining to the disciples that the scribes' and Pharisees' idea of ritual uncleanliness is nonsense. It is not what goes into the mouth that makes a person unclean, but what comes out of it. It is not our adherence to the intricacies of the law that God notices, but how we treat other people. According to the minimal requirements of the law, Jesus would have done the right thing by ignoring the woman. Instead, he shows the absurdity of the Pharisees' position by arguing it himself — and allowing the Syrophoenician woman to argue the side of justice and understanding. In engaging her in debate, Jesus honors her for her faith — and at the same time demonstrates to the disciples that all people are equally deserving in the eyes of God.

All of us could stand to hear that same lesson from time to time. It is all too easy for us to grow complacent about the walls of discrimination that are still so prevalent in our society.

Prejudice exacts a heavy toll on those who practice it — just as it does on its victims. How many of us suffer from a sudden twinge of unreasoning fear as we pass a person of another race on a deserted sidewalk? Or how many of us wonder what that person who looks a little different from most others in our neighborhood is doing here, and whether he or she is up to no good? Many are the unconscious judgments we make each day: about fellow human beings, who, like us, are equally made in God's image!

Prayer For The Day
Lord, they pass us in the crowd: the anonymous faces. Some faces resemble our own. Others look different: in color, complexion, bone structure, the pattern of lines that are the remnant of smiles and frowns. Beneath the skin of each face run tiny capillaries, filled with life-giving blood by a beating heart just like our own. Each one was created by you, in your image. Each one is precious to you. Why, O Lord, do we continue to behave as though it were different? Amen.

To Illustrate

There's a famous poem by Robert Frost about the walls we build in life. "Something there is that doesn't love a wall," he writes, looking over at his New England farmer neighbor, who's heaving yet another stone upon the wall that runs between their two properties. The poet asks his neighbor why the wall is necessary:

> *My apple trees will never get across*
> *And eat the cones under his pines, I tell him.*
> *He only says, "Good fences make good neighbors."*

But then the poet is led to wonder,

> *Before I built a wall I'd ask to know*
> *What I was walling in or walling out.*

When you and I build walls between ourselves and others, it is truly an open question whether we are walling the other out, or walling ourselves in!

— "Mending Wall," *The Poetry of Robert Frost*, Edward Connery Lathem, ed.
(New York: Henry Holt and Company, 1979)

***

Sometimes it takes an experience of struggle to shake us out of our prejudices.

That's the way it was for a Dutchman by the name of René Schäfer. Schäfer was a prisoner of war in Japan during World War II. His captors had sentenced him to forced labor in a shipyard in the city of Hiroshima. Through years of harsh captivity, Schäfer had learned to hate his guards with a white-hot passion. He used to pray to God every night that the Americans would attack the city and destroy it, exacting revenge for his years of suffering.

In August 1945, Schäfer's prayer was answered. Hearing an air-raid siren one day, he dove into a ditch. A moment later, he heard the noise, saw the flash — and felt the unearthly heat — of the world's first nuclear weapon used in war. In the darkness and confusion that followed, Schäfer was amazed to find himself helping not only his fellow POWs who had been burned or blinded, but also his guards. Years later, he had this to say:

> *From the moment the bomb went off, you see, there was no hate left. It was a strange experience — how hate can be turned to pity by a single bomb. There was even no difference for me between the Japanese victims and my friends. I felt myself a victim among other victims, not a Dutchman among Japanese. The bomb had killed all hate.*

How sad that it took an atom bomb to blast away the walls of hate, to erase the dividing line between this man and his captors! But that's the way it is with prejudice — the walls between "us" and "them" are not breached very easily.

***

There was an old Native American sheep farmer whose neighbor's dogs were always killing his sheep. It got so bad that he knew he had to do something. As he saw it, he had three options. The first, in true American tradition, was to sue: he could bring a lawsuit and take his neighbor to court. His second option was to build a stronger and higher fence so his neighbor's dogs could not get in. But he discovered a third option. He gave two lambs to his neighbor's children. In due time, the lambs grew into sheep and had other sheep and then the neighbor and his children got to see the sheep not as a impersonal herd, but as something warm and fuzzy, something personal with individual traits and a history and names. They soon penned in their dogs.

Unless you live and eat and sleep with the sheep, almost become one like them, then they will never be unique. They will all look alike. It is the same with us. Unless we get to know others as persons, as individuals, then they are just members of a certain group or class of people. Then they look just like everyone else in the crowd. It is an interesting aspect of prejudice that as soon as someone gets to know another person who belongs to a group against whom they are prejudiced, they do not change their perception of the group. They remove the person they like from the group. If you were to ask them about that little trick of the mind, they would probably say something like: "Oh, they're not like the rest of their kind." Curious, isn't it?

The basis of prejudice and racism, rejection and persecution, is this: reducing people to categories, making them abstractions, not knowing their names, not calling them by name. This depersonalizes them. In order to overcome prejudice, we must see people as individuals with a name and a history.

— Adapted from a sermon by Silverius Galvan, April 23, 1999,
<http://www.deaconsil.com>

***

"It's not so much the things we don't know that get us into trouble. It's the things we know just ain't so."

— Artemus Ward

***

Businessman Chris Kim was inspired to act by listening to the story of a fourteen-year-old African-American boy. The boy stole a pair of pants from the clothing store Chris ran in his mini-mall in a poor south Seattle neighborhood. Chris and another Korean store owner grabbed him, called the police, and were ready to press charges. Then Chris thought about Christ's message of responding with forgiveness, not retribution. He decided to talk with the boy and his parents. "We always say we love our neighbors, but we never do it and risk something that belongs to us. He was a teenager, a young kid. It could have been anyone in a desperate situation, even one of my kids. I thought I should try and understand, not just turn him over to the police."

After Chris and the boy talked, the boy apologized, and said what he really wanted was a job. Chris hesitated briefly, then hired him as a clerk. The boy's mother sent Chris a note saying his compassion had changed her view both of Koreans and her son's life. Moved by the experience, Chris started working with local organizations that educate black youth. "Through my lifetime," Chris admitted, "I didn't have a good feeling about black people. It wasn't from direct experiences, but you hear so much in the media, about all the violence. So I tried to treat this kid as another human being, like myself, my family, my friends. I wanted to be part of solving the problems."

Chris' involvement was supported by an existing foundation of belief, in this case his Christian faith. But it took a direct connection with the boy and his world to induce Chris to put those beliefs into practice. It took a willingness to exercise his moral imagination, to expand his sphere of concern to include someone from a completely different background.

As a result of wrestling with this responsibility to the boy, Chris began questioning himself, especially his business practices. He consulted local neighborhood leaders, brought in new African-American shops to his mini-mall, and sponsored an annual neighborhood festival. He tried to make the mall a place where people of all races and ages would feel welcome. It still felt strange staking his money and time to try to help people who, as he says, "aren't even my own race of Koreans. But I'd wanted to set an example for my children. Once you start to share with others, it gets easier. What I did wasn't anything fancy. But I felt such a priceless taste of love coming back. I got closer to some other human beings who I'd never have gotten to know. Once I've done something like that, I can't go back to what I was before."

— Adapted from Paul Rogat Loeb, *Soul of a Citizen: Living with Conviction in a Cynical Time* (New York: St. Martin's Press, 1999)

Proper 19, Pentecost 17, Ordinary Time 24

September 17, 2006

Revised Common	Proverbs 1:20-33 *or* Isaiah 50:5-9a	James 3:1-12	Mark 8:27-38
Roman Catholic	Isaiah 50:5-9a	James 2:14-18	Mark 8:27-35
Episcopal	Isaiah 50:4-9	James 2:1-5, 8-10, 14-18	Mark 8:27-38 *or* Mark 9:14-29

Theme For The Day   Words have the power to wound, or to heal: we should choose ours carefully.

Old Testament Lesson   Proverbs 1:20-33   *Wisdom Cries Out In the Street To Pay Heed To Her Teaching*

A striking device in the book of Proverbs is the personification of Wisdom as a female figure, introduced for the first time in this passage: *"Wisdom cries out in the street; in the squares she raises her voice ... 'How long, O simple ones, will you love being simple?'"* (20, 22a). Wisdom, here, is taunting those who will not pay heed to her teaching. For those who do not, there are consequences: "I will mock when panic strikes you, when panic strikes you like a storm ... Then they will call upon me, but I will not answer; they will seek me diligently, but will not find me." (1:26b-27a, 28). These stern but loving admonitions are meant to keep young students of the scriptures at their task, in all diligence and faithfulness.

Alternate Old Testament Lesson   Isaiah 50:5-9a   *The Third Servant Song*

This passage has previously occurred in the lectionary on Sunday Of The Passion / Palm Sunday (p. 99).

New Testament Lesson   James 3:1-12   *The Tongue Is A Fire*

James has previously had some things to say about the importance of using human speech in ways that serve God and neighbor, but that effort reaches its climax in this passage. He begins by speaking directly to those who teach the faith: "You know that we who teach will be judged with greater strictness" (v. 1). As a small bridle guides a horse, and a small rudder guides a ship, so "the tongue is a small member, yet it boasts of great exploits" (v. 5). Yet, as a small flame can set a whole forest ablaze, so, too, can the tongue cause terrible damage: for "the tongue is a fire" (v. 6). The tongue is nearly impossible to tame (v. 8). "From the same mouth come blessing and cursing" (v. 10). While James' words may seem at first glance antiquated, in fact, speech is a topic that is constantly in the public imagination. Bitter debates rage in the media about the right to "free speech." E-mail and instant-messaging give us more venues for speech than ever before. We are surrounded by a sea of words: yet so many of them are at best insignificant, and at worst harmful. Truly, this is a timely topic.

The Gospel   Mark 8:27-38   *"Who Do People Say That I Am?"*

This text is one of the turning points of Mark's Gospel. Until now, Jesus has been teaching and performing healings, all the while urging his disciples to remain quiet about what they have heard and seen. Now, in a private moment, he turns directly to his disciples and asks them, "Who do people say that I am?" (v. 27b). Like good campaign workers, the disciples tell him what the most recent polls are saying: "John the Baptist; and others, Elijah; and still others, one of the prophets" (v. 28). But Jesus isn't interested in what the polls say. He wants to know what *they* have say about him, personally. Peter is the first one to speak: "You are the Messiah" (v. 29b). Mark gives no sign of how Jesus receives this news, other than to observe that he commands them to tell no one of this. The second part of this selection has already occurred in the lectionary, on the Second Sunday In Lent (p. 83).

Preaching Possibilities

"Sticks and stones may break my bones," the children chant, "but names can never hurt me."

Oh yes, they can. Mocking names may only be words, but words can wound: sometimes very deeply. It's that sort of criticism James has in mind, as he describes the human tongue as "a fire ... [that] stains the whole body, sets on fire the cycle of nature, and is itself set on fire by hell." You can tame wild animals, he says, but "no one can tame the tongue"; it is "a restless evil, full of deadly poison."

"The tongue is a fire" — Adolf Hitler knew all about that. Just look at that old documentary footage of his Nuremberg rallies: the clipped, staccato speech, the eyes glowing like two black coals, the angry forefinger stabbing the air — then wave upon wave of sheer adulation from the crowd, shouting, *"Sieg heil! Sieg heil!"* It was only words that Hitler spoke; yet those words packed sufficient power to set a continent ablaze, and then a world. Millions perished.

On the other side of the English Channel stood Winston Churchill: hand on hip, watch on fob, bulldog chin extended. They used to say Churchill's tongue could cause more damage to the German cause than a V-1 rocket. In the darkest days of the war, all over England the British people huddled around their radio cabinets, straining to hear what he would say next. James says the tongue is like the rudder of a ship: small in size, but oh-so-important.

Churchill began his service as prime minister by announcing, "I have nothing to offer but blood, toil, tears, and sweat." We can hardly imagine a politician today getting away with that brand of brutal honesty. (How would that sound bite play on the evening news?) But the British people loved it. Churchill told it like it was.

Just a month later, two days before the French surrendered to the Nazis, and the Spitfire pilots stood alone against the mighty Luftwaffe, Churchill came on the radio again. He told the people, "Let us therefore brace ourselves to our duty, and so bear ourselves that if the British Empire and its Commonwealth last for 1,000 years, men will still say, 'This was their finest hour.' "

A blazing fire; a tried-and-true, unfailing rudder — the human tongue may be applied to the cause of evil, or to good! The tongue can deliver a testimonial address; it can also taunt ... and mock ... and needle ... and nag. The tongue can swear allegiance; it can also tell lies ... or cheat ... or vainly boast. The tongue can utter public prayer; or it can befoul the air with profanity. The tongue can offer a wedding vow; or it can whisper sweet, adulterous nothings into a lover's ear.

We've all witnessed the power of the tongue to make a person wilt in embarrassment — to bring that "I-wish-I-could-just-sink-into-the-floor" look to the face. Maybe we've caused that sort of reaction ourselves ... with that little word of cutting criticism, maybe veiled as a compliment: "I'll bet you've been dieting! Why, you're looking sooo good!" or "I'm so glad you didn't go out of your way to clean before we came over!" or "You're going to have big shoes to fill, as the new office manager!"

How much better it is to use our tongues to encourage and build up other people! Mother Teresa of Calcutta once said, "Kind words can be short and easy to speak, but their echoes are truly endless." The author of Proverbs concurs: "Anxiety weighs down the human heart, but a good word cheers it up" (12:25). In another place, Proverbs teaches that "Pleasant words are like a honeycomb, sweetness to the soul and health to the body" (16:24).

When the Holy Spirit falls upon the gathered church at Pentecost, which part of the body does it first affect? The tongue! Not only is the Holy Spirit seen by the apostles as "tongues of fire," that same Spirit empowers them to "speak in other languages, as the Spirit gave them ability."

Pentecost symbolizes, in a certain sense, the redeeming of the tongue. What was it that Peter had done, not long before that day, that still made him feel so desperately ashamed? He had betrayed his Lord. He had used his tongue to say he did not know him. Yet, it is none other than Peter — ecstatically filled with the Holy Spirit — who throws open the doors of the house where they've been huddling, and preaches the gospel. A faithless tongue is redeemed, for holy purposes!

There's a great shortage in our world of kind and gentle words — words that upbuild, words that encourage. Such upbuilding words are so much more than flattery — those cheap compliments handed out wholesale to all comers, merely to grease the wheels of social interaction. No, what we need much more of are words carefully chosen, expressing appreciation of another person's uniqueness. "Make other people like themselves a little better," Norman Vincent Peale used to say, "and they will like you very much."

It's a blindingly simple bit of wisdom — yet so wondrously profound. "From the same mouth come blessing and cursing," says James. Many times each day, we have those two choices offered to us. We may bless, or we may curse. We may tear down, or we may build up. We may speak of kindness and gratitude, or of bitter, selfish striving.

It's all in the tongue — and in the tales the tongue tells.

Prayer For The Day

Great God, you have given us hands to help, backs to bear burdens, feet to rush to where the needs are, ears to listen. You have also given us tongues to speak. May we use them to share words that build others up, rather than tearing them down. Use our tongues, just as you use every other part of us. Amen.

To Illustrate

There's a story about the famous preacher of the last century, Henry Ward Beecher. One Sunday, he ascended the great pulpit of Boston's Plymouth Congregational Church, and there he found a note waiting for him. Beecher glanced at the note, then announced, "I received a letter from one of you this morning. It states quite simply, 'Fool.'"

Beecher paused, then grinned maliciously. "I often receive letters from people who forget to sign their names," he said, "but this is the first time someone has signed their name and forgotten to write the letter."

***

One place where the tongue can cause particular damage is in the church. Two people are hard at work on projects close to their hearts, and they bump up against each other. One person speaks without thinking; the other feels offended. The second person begins avoiding the first, maybe even stops coming to church altogether — because of course you can't express anger in a church setting (that wouldn't be Christian)! Instead, she goes home and starts calling friends, suggesting changes that will keep this sort of thing from ever happening again — for the good of the church, of course.

229

The second person gets wind of the proposed changes, and begins calling his friends. Together they come up with all sorts of reasons why the first group's proposal is not a wise idea. Before long, trenches are dug, barbed wire is strung, and shells are being lobbed so high that no one can tell exactly where they're coming from. Life in the church is suddenly punctuated by mysterious crashes and explosions and puffs of smoke, coming from no-one-knows-where — as people from one side get irritated by things the other side has done (even if they're perfectly innocent).

If the pastor (or anyone else) tries to visit either side, those being visited will steadfastly deny there's any problem — even as they hand the aspiring peacemaker one of their side's uniforms. Rarely is anyone so crass as to ask, "Are you on our side, or theirs?" Instead, they ask pointed questions, to try to find out — or, if they're subtle, they send their friends to do it in their place.

These stealth conflicts can simmer on and on for years — with all parties denying that a conflict exists. People can be found, months or even years later, arguing (with surprising vehemence) over what color to paint a wall, or who should have copies of a certain key. The wall treatment, or the locksmith's fee, is not the issue, of course; it's that real or imagined slight from long ago — those hurtful words that were uttered, but could never be acknowledged, because the unspoken rules declare that all conflict in church is un-Christian!

**

A woman who was known as a harsh critic of other people once told John Wesley, "Mr. Wesley, my talent is to speak my mind."

"Madam," Wesley replied, "God wouldn't care a bit if you would bury that talent."

**

If thou thinkest twice before thou speakest once, thou wilt speak twice the better for it.
— William Penn

**

There's a story about a society woman in London who attended two dinner parties, a week apart. At the first, she was seated next to the prime minister, William Gladstone. At the second, she found herself next to Benjamin Disraeli, leader of the opposition party.

A friend later asked her what she thought of the two men. "When I left the dining room after sitting with Mr. Gladstone," she said, "I thought he was the cleverest man in England. But after sitting next to Mr. Disraeli, I thought I was the cleverest woman in England."

Such is the power of words to build up.

230

Proper 20, Pentecost 18, Ordinary Time 25
September 24, 2006

Revised Common	Proverbs 31:10-31 or Jeremiah 11:18-20	James 3:13—4:3, 7-8a	Mark 9:30-37
Roman Catholic	Wisdom 2:12, 17-20	James 3:16—4:3	Mark 9:30-37
Episcopal	Wisdom 1:16-21 (6-11) 12-22	James 3:16—4:6	Mark 9:30-37

Theme For The Day   Above all else, be kind.

Old Testament Lesson   Proverbs 31:10-31   *A Capable Wife*

"A capable wife who can find? She is far more precious than jewels" (31:10). The author goes on to enumerate the characteristics of this faithful wife. It quickly becomes apparent that this woman is more than a mere extension of her husband. She is a clever and energetic manager, practicing the domestic arts and keeping food on the table of a large and complex household. She supervises the work of various domestic servants (v. 15). She is a small business-owner as well, investing in real estate and planting vineyards (v. 16). She oversees a cottage industry that manufactures clothing (vv. 18, 24). More than being a good businesswoman, she is healthy and virtuous: she is physically strong (v. 17), dignified, confident, and wise (vv. 25-26). Most important of all, she fears the Lord (v. 30). This passage is an acrostic poem, each line beginning with a different letter of the Hebrew alphabet. Its date and authorship are unknown, although some scholars have speculated that, with its strong emphasis on the household as a basic unit of society, it may date from a time when the nation-state of Israel was dominated by foreign overlords. We may read this passage as an example of Israelite "family values" — the family having become the most important institution in a fractured and oppressed society. The "capable wife" is at the heart of this household, and through her good offices many people — children, servants, even her husband (who evidently is a community leader — v. 23) have a decent life. Even beyond the boundaries of her household, the poor benefit from this pious woman's cleverness and hard work (v. 20). She is the embodiment of the practical wisdom that is the central message of Proverbs.

Alternate Old Testament Lesson   Jeremiah 11:18-20   *Jeremiah Laments His Difficult Lot*

Jeremiah is a complicated figure. He is, at various times, both a prophet of doom and a prophet of comfort. Probably the most astute observer of the political scene in Judah, he spends most of his time ostracized by those who hold political power. He speaks truth, suffers for it, then goes back to those who have wounded him, to speak the truth some more. In this passage, a brief poetic interlude, we gain some insight into the prophet's psychological state and inner motivation. "I was like a gentle lamb led to the slaughter," he laments (v. 19). Jeremiah pleads for divine intervention, for God's punishment of those who have schemed against him, and who are working against God's purposes (v. 20). In a little while (although outside the confines of today's lectionary reading), Jeremiah will question God, asking why it is that the wicked always seem to prosper (12:1).

New Testament Lesson   James 3:13—4:3, 7-8a   *Covetousness: Root Of Many Sins*

As with too many other lectionary selections, this one is carefully edited so as to excise the most difficult parts. The resulting product is perhaps easier to preach on, yet less than faithful to the original intent of the author. The passage begins with a condemnation of conflict in the church. The author delves deep into the underlying psychological motives of human conflict, tracing its root cause to covetousness (vv. 1-2). Even murder can be traced back to covetousness. Why be covetous, James wants to know, when all we need do is ask God for what we need, and we will receive (vv. 2-3 — perhaps recalling Jesus' words in Matthew 7:8 and 21:22)? Then comes the passage the lectionary editors have chosen to excise: James responding bitterly, "Adulterers! Do you not know that friendship with the world is enmity with God?" (v. 4). He draws a sharp dividing line between God's realm and the ways of this world, and tells his readers that they cannot have it both ways, displaying allegiance to both. They must choose one or the other. Making this hard choice perhaps a bit easier is the advice he gives in verses 7-8 (now back in our lectionary reading): submit to God, the devil will flee and God will draw near to you. James' worldview is one of unremitting cosmic conflict, in which the forces of good are arrayed against the forces of evil. Any lesser conflicts among those who claim to be on the side of good only detract from the energies and resources that could otherwise be committed to the greater conflict.

The Gospel   Mark 9:30-37   *True Greatness*

This selection is composed of two parts. In the first, Jesus is on the road with his disciples, and confidentially shares with them this teaching: "The Son of Man is to be betrayed into human hands, and they will kill him, and three days after being killed, he will rise again" (v. 31). This is Jesus' second prediction of his passion, in Mark (the first was 8:31-33). His disciples fail to understand, and fail to question him further. In the second part, Jesus notices that several of the disciples have been arguing with each other. When he asks them what the argument is about, they refuse to tell him — although in fact they have been arguing about which one of them is greatest. Jesus must intuitively know what they were arguing about, for he assumes the formal seated position of the rabbi and proceeds to teach them about true greatness: "Whoever wants to be first must be last of all and servant of all" (v. 35). Then, in a parabolic gesture weighty with meaning, he places a small child in their midst and says, "Whoever welcomes one such child in my name welcomes me ..." (v. 37a). Children in that culture have very low status, nearly as low as slaves: so Jesus' word to the disciples is about true greatness being found in humility. This requires some cross-cultural translation for contemporary readers to understand — for in our context, welcoming a child is an ordinary and unexceptional kindness. In Jesus' context, it was very different.

Preaching Possibilities

The Proverbs passage enumerates so many admirable qualities of the "capable wife" that it offers multiple preaching possibilities. One possible direction is to focus on verse 26, "She opens her mouth with wisdom, and the teaching of kindness is on her tongue."

It may be advisable to mention, early on, that the woman lauded in this chapter of Proverbs is an ideal type: her virtues are so numerous, and her facility at multi-tasking so impressive, that she may appear to be a kind of superwoman. (Remember that she does have a staff of servants, so that at least helps to account for her daily accomplishments!) The "teaching of kindness" mentioned in verse 26, however, is a virtue to which anyone can aspire.

Literally, the Hebrew word is *hesed* — a term that's notoriously difficult to translate. Sometimes it's rendered in English as "loyalty," sometimes "mercy," sometimes "love." Here, the Bible translators have chosen the word "kindness": but that choice barely scratches the surface of its meaning. Elsewhere — especially when the subject is God's *hesed* — not just one word will do. The scholars often translate it "steadfast love." The old King James Version likewise uses two words, speaking of God's "loving kindness."

The kindness this admirable woman teaches is like unto the kindness of God. As Bible scholars have grappled with the meaning of God's kindness — with the Hebrew word *hesed* — they have discovered that the word is only used in the case of a covenant relationship: and it's only used of the dominant partner in that covenant relationship. To be kind to someone — to be deeply and truly kind in a way that transcends mere politeness — is not to be subservient, but rather to reach out to someone who is a natural inferior.

The husband in Proverbs 31 — he who sits by the city gate with the boys, while his wife manages the household — admires her not because she's some compulsive workaholic who succeeds (against all odds) in "having it all," but because she's a woman of deep faith. That faith of hers issues in kindness — not toward him, especially, but toward their children, their servant-girls, even toward the beggars in the street to whom she gives alms. This husband who sings her praises is himself a person of faith, and so he sees the inner beauty of her kindness: "Charm is deceitful, and beauty is vain, but a woman who fears the Lord is to be praised" (v. 30).

Few would disagree with the proposition that we could use more kindness in this world. Yet there is a huge difference between the *hesed* of the Bible and what most people think of when they hear the word, "kindness." Kindness, in the popular imagination, is pretty much synonymous with "niceness" — with being pleasant and courteous. The biblical ideal goes much deeper.

God is not especially nice; but God *is* kind. There is a huge difference between those two words. God, it says in the Old Testament, resides in or near the Ark of the Covenant — the box the people of Israel carry with them on their wilderness wanderings, that contains the tablets of the Law. In First Chronicles, a man named Uzzah reaches out and casually touches the outside of the ark; he's struck dead on the spot, as though he were electrocuted (1 Chronicles 13:10). There's nothing especially nice about that. When Moses asks to see God's face, God replies, "No one can see my face and live" (Exodus 33:20). There's nothing especially nice about that, either. When God prepares to pass by the Prophet Elijah, God tells him to keep his distance, so the earthquake, wind, and fire that follow in God's wake won't burn him to a crisp (1 Kings 19:11). There's nothing especially nice about that.

Yet, in each of these incidents, God acts with kindness. God warns the people not to touch the Ark. God tells Moses not to look upon the divine glory about to be revealed. God instructs Elijah where to stand, so he will be safe. Kindness and niceness are not the same. Niceness defines a relationship between two equals; it has to do with politeness and civility and everyday courtesy. Kindness, on the other hand, defines a relationship between a superior and an inferior. The person who's being kind doesn't have to be kind. There's nothing in it for him or her: there's nothing to be gained, no *quid pro quo*, that makes the act of kindness pay off. There is justice, and compassion, and grace — and, most of all, love.

"The teaching of kindness" is on the tongue of the wise woman of Proverbs 31. She is a rich and powerful woman — an accomplished business manager and merchant and farmer who also runs a large and complex household. Yet she also finds time, in dealing with her children and her servants, to reach out in kindness to them. For her, it would seem, kindness is the most important thing of all — for kindness is *hesed*, the steadfast love of God. This kindness she has herself received in abundance, and so she is free to pass it on to others.

233

Prayer For The Day

We are grateful, O God, for the kindness you show us, far beyond our deserving. When we were far off, wandering and lost, you brought us near. You feed us on the bread of life. You nurture us in community. You call us your people. Help us to be kind to others, as well: not as ordinary human courtesy, and not when there is anything in it for us — but out of gratitude, sheer gratitude for what you have done for us. Amen.

To Illustrate

Every time I read this passage, I can't help it: I think about a little ditty from a television commercial of a number of years back — one of those ones we love to hate. A working woman comes home wearing a business suit, kicks off her pumps, pads into the kitchen in stockinged feet, and comes out holding a cast-iron skillet. She prances up to her husband, and in a sultry voice sings these words:

> *I can bring home the bacon,*
> *fry it up in a pan,*
> *and never let you forget you're a man!*
> *'Cause I'm a woman —W-O-M-A-N!*

I've even forgotten what product that commercial was selling. The image of that ridiculous song is burned into my consciousness: ridiculous, because no woman (and no man either, for that matter) can be so thoroughly "all things to all people" as that crooning siren with the skillet in her hand.

Don't think for a moment that the author of Proverbs is talking about that kind of woman!

***

When I was young, I admired clever people. Now that I am old, I admire kind people.
— Rabbi Abraham Joseph Heschel

***

Mohandas Gandhi, the great spiritual leader of India, was once traveling by train. He and a companion were running to catch their train, and just as they pulled themselves up onto the slowly-moving railway car, one of Gandhi's sandals fell off and landed beside the tracks.

Gandhi and his friend stood there for a moment on the train steps, watching his sandal slowly recede into the distance, when Gandhi did a peculiar thing. He reached down and removed his other sandal, throwing it back along the tracks so it landed beside the first.

Gandhi's friend was puzzled by this strange behavior, so he asked him why he had done that — why he'd thrown away the one sandal he had left. "One sandal is no good to me," Gandhi explained. "But if I cast it down beside the other one, perhaps a poor person will come along, discover them both, and be happy that he now has shoes." Kindness was such a large part of Gandhi's nature that — instead of worrying about his loss, as most of us would do — his mind immediately leaped to the happy smile of the poor beggar as he discovered the unexpected bonus of a complete pair of shoes.

***

Teri Thomas, a Presbyterian pastor, tells a personal story about the power of kindness. It's about her grandmother, who, at the age of 95, was slowly slipping away, a victim of Alzheimer's disease.

Each time Teri went to visit her grandmother in the nursing home, she seemed to remember less. Finally, she gave no sign of recognizing Teri at all. Still, Teri found a way to communicate:

As we sat talking about the insignificant stuff you talk about with people you don't really know, I laid my hand on her back. She immediately leaned forward, and as I started rubbing her back she began smiling and purring. When it was time to go, she asked me to come again soon. The next day when I arrived at her door, she looked up and smiled.

"Good morning, Grandma," I said. "Do you remember me today?"

"Of course I do," she replied indignantly. "You are the girl who rubs my back."

— *Thursday Mail*, National Capital Presbytery,
Presbyterian Church (U.S.A.), May 3, 2000

Proper 21, Pentecost 19, Ordinary Time 26

October 1, 2006

Revised Common	**Esther 7:1-6, 9-10; 9:20-22** *or* **Numbers 11:4-6, 10-16, 24-29**	**James 5:13-20**	**Mark 9:38-50**
Roman Catholic	**Numbers 11:25-29**	**James 5:1-6**	**Mark 9:38-43, 45, 47-48**
Episcopal	**Numbers 11:4-6, 10-16, 24-29**	**James 4:7-12 (13—5:6)**	**Mark 9:38-43, 45, 47-48**

Theme For The Day   Christ calls us to lead the wanderer home.

Old Testament Lesson   Esther 7:1-6, 9-10; 9:20-22   *Esther Saves Her People*

Risking her own life, Queen Esther — a Jewish woman — has managed to position herself so that King Ahasuerus of Persia, her husband, offers to fulfill one wish for her. Her wish is that she and her people be saved from a pogrom that the king's wicked minister Haman has been about to begin in the king's name. The king complies with her wish, and Haman is executed, having received no mercy from Esther after pleading with her for his life. The first part of today's passage is the one in which Esther makes her plea to the king. The second section, from chapter 9, deals with the establishment of Purim — the feast celebrated by the Jewish people to this day, to commemorate Esther's courage in saving her people, and God's having placed her in the palace "for such a time as this" (4:14), so she could save her people. Controversy has always swirled around the book of Esther, and particularly its place in both the Jewish and the Christian biblical canon. The name of God is never mentioned in it, and most of the characters, including Esther herself, have significant moral failings. Traditional homiletical approaches emphasize the role of a silent and invisible God, who orchestrates events in such a way that the covenant people of Israel are saved in the nick of time.

Alternate Old Testament Lesson   Numbers 11:4-6,   *God Gracefully Responds To*
                                         10-16, 24-29   *A Grumbling People*

The Israelites, craving meat in the wilderness, are grumbling about the blandness of the manna the Lord has provided: "now our strength is dried up, and there is nothing at all but this manna to look at" (v. 6). The Lord is angry at this, and Moses — rather audaciously — becomes angry at God, complaining that the Lord has saddled him with an ungrateful people who are impossible to lead. Strikingly, this passage contains powerful maternal imagery for God, as Moses complains that he has been, essentially, a wet-nurse to the children borne by Mother God (v. 12). Moses asks that he be relieved of his responsibilities as leader, even if it means his death. The Lord calls a conference of seventy elders of the people, and gives to each of them a share of the spirit that has been upon Moses. The elders then prophesy ecstatically — even two absentee elders, Eldad and Medad, who have not made it to the tent of meeting. When Joshua challenges Moses to stop these two unauthorized elders from prophesying, Moses replies, "Are you jealous for my sake? Would that all the Lord's people were prophets, and that the Lord would put his spirit on them!" (v. 29).

Homiletical possibilities include: 1) how the Lord provides for the people their daily bread, one day at a time, but the ungrateful people distrust the goodness of this provision; 2) how the

Lord graciously accommodates to the needs both of the people and of Moses; 3) the dispersal of spiritual gifts among many people; and 4) the impossibility of confining the Holy Spirit's activity within particular boundaries — as in the episode of Eldad and Medad.

New Testament Lesson   James 5:13-20   *The Power Of Healing Prayer*

In this closing portion of the letter, the author encourages the people to rely upon God in all circumstances. If they are suffering, they should pray. If joyful, they should sing songs of praise. If sick, they should call the elders of the church for prayer and anointing with oil: "the prayer of faith will save the sick" (v. 15). Healing and forgiveness are linked together (v. 16). Elijah is cited as one example of the power of prayer. Verses 19-20 celebrate the contribution of anyone who finds a believer who has wandered from the truth and brings him or her back into the fold: "whoever brings back a sinner from wandering will save the sinner's soul from death and will cover a multitude of sins" (v. 20). This passage speaks to the condition of the church at a time of relative maturity, after the loose ecclesiastical order of previous generations that is seen in the Pauline letters. In these latter days, there is at least one formal church office, the eldership, and a formal rite of prayer and anointing for healing. This is an excellent text for encouraging churches to rediscover the ancient ministry of prayer for healing as a communal act.

The Gospel   Mark 9:38-50   *Competition, Temptation, And Salt*

There are three mostly unrelated pericopes in this passage: one concerning an incident of an unauthorized exorcist casting out demons in Jesus' name (vv. 38-41), another relating Jesus' teachings on the spiritual dangers of temptation (vv. 42-48), and a third containing several sayings that include the concept of salt (vv. 49-50). In the first, the disciples come up to Jesus with some agitation, reporting that a man who is not a visible part of their band is performing healings in Jesus' name. Far from being upset, Jesus instructs that he be left alone: "Whoever is not against us is for us" (v. 40b). The mission of healing and serving others is primary, taking precedence over matters of institutional organization. (Curiously, Matthew 12:30, if considered beside this verse, seems to contradict it: "whoever is not with me is against me." The difference, however, is in the first-person pronouns: plural in the case of the Markan verse and singular in the case of the Matthean one. While the unauthorized exorcist is not against Jesus at all, he can be said to be working independently of the company of the disciples.)

The second pericope has to do with those who would "put a stumbling block before one of these little ones who believe in me" (v. 42); for such a one, the punishment will be harsh. "Little ones" probably refers not to children, but to new believers. Regarding any sort of temptation, Jesus says it is best to resist it by all possible means: even to the point of cutting off one's hand or foot if that is causing one to sin (v. 43-48).

Finally, there is a series of epigrammatic sayings dealing with salt: "For everyone will be salted with fire. Salt is good; but if salt has lost its saltiness, how can you season it? Have salt in yourselves, and be at peace with one another" (vv. 49-50). These salt sayings are rather obscure, and do not seem to directly follow from the narrative that precedes it. The "salted with fire" phrase is particularly mysterious, although it may have something to do with the role of fire and salt in sacrificial rites. Salt, of course, is more than a seasoning; it is a pure substance of great value throughout human history, particularly for the preservation of food. Salt has a job to do, and it does it. A sermon on this passage will probably have to focus on one of its three parts, for it is hard to find a unifying theme that runs through it in its entirety.

Preaching Possibilities

Somewhere out there, on the bumper of one of America's cars, is a sticker with this slogan: "You are a child of God. Please phone home." It gets the point across, doesn't it?

How many children of God do we know who have wandered away from home, never to return? The sociologists tell us our country is full of them, and their numbers are growing all the time. "The unchurched" — as they call them, collectively — is one of the fastest-growing segments of American religious demographics.

Most of the unchurched are not atheists or agnostics — they are those who have a nominal belief in God, but who have drifted away from actively practicing their faith. Some of them feel kindly disposed toward the institutional church. Others of them have had some kind of bad experience that has made them draw a distinction between personal faith and what they would call "institutional religion." Still others are in a kind of waiting mode: they slipped out the back door of the church some time ago, for whatever reason, and are playing a kind of waiting game. They're waiting to see how long it will take for someone to invite them back.

If it's any comfort, this matter of wandering away from the Christian community is nothing new. It's as old as the Bible: as old as the Letter of James, anyway. "My brothers and sisters," he writes, "if anyone among you wanders from the truth and is brought back by another, you should know that whoever brings back a sinner from wandering will save the sinner's soul from death and will cover a multitude of sins" (vv. 19-20).

Jesus tells a few parables about wanderers coming home. He speaks of a lost sheep, who wanders away from the flock. What does the shepherd do, but leave the 99 other sheep grazing on the hillside, and set out after the one that's lost? Then there's the woman with ten silver coins, who loses one of them. Immediately she lights a lamp, takes up her broom, and sweeps out every nook and cranny of the house: hoping against hope that her broom will turn up the lost coin. Finally, there's that famous parable of the prodigal son: the tale of a young fool who demands his inheritance before his father even dies, squanders it, then comes crawling back, hoping for some measure of forgiveness. Dad surprises both his sons — not to mention the world at large — by embracing his faithless son with open arms, showering him with unconditional love (Luke 15).

Maybe some of the people to whom we'll be preaching have been wanderers at some time in your spiritual lives. If so, they know what it's like to wake up and come to the same realization the prodigal son discovered in the pig pen, just before he headed for home. Some of them know the same fear and trepidation he felt, not knowing what to expect at the hand of his father. The reason Jesus told that particular parable — and the reason the Letter of James reads the way it does — is to assure us there's always a way back to God, always a warm welcome for all who have been wanderers at some time in their spiritual lives.

The problem is, those who have been in the church for many years sometimes find it hard to relate to the wanderers out there who may be ready to come home. The old-time evangelist Sam Shoemaker used to refer to certain long-established churches as "aquariums." He would cite Jesus' famous teaching about his disciples needing to be "fishers of men" (and women, too, of course). Then he would point out that many followers of Jesus, in long-established churches, are more like "keepers of the aquarium" than "fishers of people." An aquarium is a closed system. It's a beautiful thing to look at, but aquarium fish just swim around and around in that limited space, enjoying one another's company (or so we presume). Far better, for the sake of the gospel, to be sailing out over the open ocean, encountering newcomers whom God is sending our way.

238

Perhaps the most important thing Christians need to do — in order to be truly hospitable to those who are at that creative juncture in their lives when they may be ready to come back to church — is to listen. Listening, as Henri Nouwen says, is at the heart of hospitality:

> *To listen is very hard, because it asks of us so much interior stability that we no longer need to prove ourselves by speeches, arguments, statements, or declarations. True listeners no longer have an inner need to make their presence known. They are free to receive, to welcome, to accept. Listening is much more than allowing another to talk while waiting for a chance to respond. Listening is paying full attention to others and welcoming them into our very beings. The beauty of listening is that those who are listened to start feeling accepted, start taking their words more seriously and discovering their own true selves. Listening is a form of spiritual hospitality by which you invite strangers to become friends, to get to know their inner selves more fully, and even to dare to be silent with you.*
> — Henri J. M. Nouwen, *Bread for the Journey* (New York: HarperCollins, 1997)

So much of what churches do in the name of evangelism is centered around talking. Certain types of evangelism center around a kind of "witnessing" that has a lot of similarities to a sales pitch. A far more potent form of witness is to spend time not speaking, but listening to what the other person has to say. Only after we've truly listened have we earned the right to reply.

We all crave someone to truly listen to us: to find such a person is a great gift. The "spiritual hospitality" — to use Nouwen's term — that is listening is far more likely than speaking to make an impact on another person, for the sake of Christ. It's one of the best ways to bring the wanderer home.

Prayer For The Day

Give to us, O Lord, a heart for the wanderer. Direct our attention beyond the familiar walls of our church community. Here are people we know and love; but there, beyond the walls, are people you already know and love, whom you are calling us to serve. Give us loving hearts and listening ears, that we might speak the word of affirmation and welcome they need to hear. Amen.

To Illustrate

There's a fable that comes from the Jewish tradition. It's a story about a man who left his own home to seek the great city of light far away. He walked and walked all day, until just before the sun went down. Then he found a likely place to camp for the night. The last thing he did before going to bed was to place his shoes on the ground, facing in the direction he was headed. That way, he figured, he'd set out in the right direction the next morning.

In the middle of the night, though, something happened. A stranger came along and turned the man's shoes around. In the morning he awoke, put on his shoes and set out on his journey again, toward the great city of light — or so he thought. He walked and walked all day, until — just before sunset — he looked up ahead and saw a city that looked rather familiar to him. He entered through the city gate, and found a neighborhood that also looked rather familiar to him. He entered the neighborhood, and came to a house that looked rather familiar to him. He entered into the house ... and he lived happily ever after.

The journey of faith is always the journey homeward.

***

We shall not cease from exploration
And the end of all our exploring
Will be to arrive where we started
And know the place for the first time.

— T. S. Eliot, "Little Gidding," from *Four Quartets*
(London: Faber & Faber, 1942)

***

Sometimes wanderers find their way back to the church on their own — but when they walk through the door, they're not home yet. In such cases, the greeting they receive — or don't receive — is often of crucial importance.

Greeting strangers is not always the easiest thing for Christians to do. Some of us are naturally shy. Some of us are so preoccupied with our own concerns, we may not even notice the person who's sharing the pew. Some of us are afraid of accidentally extending a welcome to someone who's been here all along — and who may not appreciate being mistaken for a newcomer.

Those are the common fears, anyway. Yet the truth is, being greeted is something nearly everyone enjoys. Most first-time visitors to worship are yearning for a welcome. "Is this a friendly church?" they want to know. "Is there a place for me here?" A smile and a handshake go a long way toward helping guests feel at home. As for the fear of welcoming someone who's not a newcomer, but a longtime member — that's easily remedied. Instead of saying, "Welcome to our church" or asking, "Is this your first time here?" just say, "I'm not sure we've had the chance to get acquainted, my name is _____." No one could possibly feel offended at that sensitive approach.

One sort of greeting is to be avoided at all costs. When a familiar, but long-absent face shows up in the pews, some words that may not help at all are, "I haven't seen you for a while," or "It's good to have you back." Most wanderers who have drifted away from the church would rather not have attention drawn to the fact that they've been away.

The single most important word any of us may say, on a Sunday morning, is a word of greeting. Who's to say what sort of wanderings may have led a stranger — or even a returning friend — to worship? Who could possibly know how the Holy Spirit may have been preparing the way before them, making them uniquely receptive to the welcome we extend?

***

Evangelism is spiritual generosity.

— Anonymous

***

We have all been inoculated with Christianity, and are never likely to take it seriously now! You put some of the virus of some dreadful illness into a man's arm, and there is a little itchiness, some scratchiness, a slight discomfort — disagreeable, no doubt, but not the fever of the real disease, the turning and the tossing, and the ebbing strength. And we have all been inoculated with Christianity, more or less. We are on Christ's side, we wish him well, we hope that he

240

will win, and we are even prepared to do something for him, provided, of course, that he is reasonable, and does not make too much of an upset among our cozy comforts and our customary ways. But there is not the passion of zeal, and the burning enthusiasm, and the eagerness of self-sacrifice, of the real faith that changes character and wins the world.

— A. J. Gossip, *From the Edge of the Crowd* (Edinburgh, T & T Clark, 1924); also found online at <http://psalm121.ca/quotes/deqgossipa.html>

Proper 22, Pentecost 20, Ordinary Time 27
October 8, 2006

Revised Common	Job 1:1; 2:1-10	Hebrews 1:1-4; 2:5-12	Mark 10:2-16
	or Genesis 2:18-24		
Roman Catholic	Genesis 2:18-24	Hebrews 2:9-11	Mark 10:2-16
Episcopal	Genesis 2:18-24	Hebrews 2:(1-8) 9-18	Mark 10:2-9

Theme For The Day The hard work of making marriage last is a vital mission for Christians.

Old Testament Lesson Job 1:1; 2:1-10 *Satan And God Contend For Job's Faith*

After quoting the first verse of the book to introduce Job as "blameless and upright," the lectionary jumps to the first part of chapter 2. This is the conclave of "the heavenly beings," in which Satan dares God to let him have his way with his golden-boy, Job, to see if he can shake his faith. The Lord responds, "Very well, he is in your power; only spare his life" (v. 6). The story then tells, in graphic detail, how Satan afflicts Job with "loathsome sores," which he must scrape with a potsherd in order to achieve temporary relief from his physical agony. Job's wife, filled with revulsion (and also with amazement at his unwavering faith, despite the circumstances), says he ought to "curse God and die" (v. 9). Job, still resolute, refuses. The story of Job is hard to translate into the modern idiom. Those who approach it as history must wrestle with the issues of 1) whether God is really supreme in the universe, and 2) if so, why God would so callously abandon a human being to Satan, to suffer every torment imaginable, short of death.

It is better to approach this book as drama, rather than history. Just as Plato composed unhistorical dialogues in which Socrates (a real, historical figure) expounds his philosophy in dramatic settings, so the book of Job is a sort of philosophical dialogue, in which the author wrestles with the problem of human suffering. The figures of God and Satan, in this dialogue, are two-dimensional; they are part of this drama's scenery, as it were, rather than fully developed characters. The only truly three-dimensional character is Job. This text is a classic one for sermons dealing with the problem of human suffering, and how it impacts faith.

Alternate Old Testament Lesson Genesis 2:18-24 *The Creation Of Man And Woman*

"It is not good," says the Lord, "that the man should be alone; I will make him a helper as his partner" (v. 18). God's first response is to create animal life. God brings each creature to the man, "to see what he will call them" (v. 19). Because there can be found no "helper" or "partner" among the species of animals, God creates woman, out of one of the man's ribs. In a tender moment, the man looks upon the woman for the first time and says, "This at last is bone of my bones and flesh of my flesh" (v. 23). Then is expressed the universal principle arising from this ancient tale: "Therefore a man leaves his father and his mother and clings to his wife, and they become one flesh" (v. 24). Here the lectionary passage ends, one verse before the pericope does. Displaying a Victorian discomfort with the human body, the lectionary omits the line about the man and woman being naked but unashamed (preachers who are faithful to the text will add it back in).

Originally addressed to the community of Jewish exiles in Babylon, who were dismayed at signs all around them of the seeming triumph of Babylonian gods, this second of the two biblical creation-stories places the God of Israel firmly in control of creation. It also emphasizes the intimate connection between God and humanity. The human beings are the only creatures, in this narrative, whom God addresses by name. God is the one who speaks the word that calls creation into being, and we are the ones created to respond with words of gratitude and praise, and also to share communicative words with each other. Although this text has been misused in the past to subordinate women to men, in fact there is a strong emphasis on mutuality between the two. Men and women are meant to be helpers and partners. Yes, this mythological account has woman being created out of man; yet if — as we now know beyond a shadow of a doubt from modern genetics — maleness emerges as the result of an addition to the female chromosome, rather than the other way around, then what does that say? The question of which gender emerges from the other is theologically irrelevant.

New Testament Lesson   Hebrews 1:1-4; 2:5-12   *God Has Spoken By A Son*
(**Note:** This passage begins a seven-week run of Second Lesson selections from the Letter to the Hebrews. There is a significant amount of repetition in content, particularly — in the latter weeks of this series — concerning the role of Jesus as the great high priest. As with the First John series back in the spring, it is advisable to look ahead in the lectionary and plan which Sundays will have Second Lesson sermons, so as to avoid repetition.)

This anonymous letter was composed in the late first century, and reflects the concerns of second- and third-generation Christians. It is noted for its elaborate Christology, especially for its concept of Christ as the new and perfected high priest. Hebrews must always be understood in light of the destruction of the Jerusalem temple in 70 A.D.; that watershed event forever changed the way Jews considered themselves as a nation, as well as the way Christians of Jewish background considered their place in the church. Of the form and style of this book, Thomas Long writes, "Even though it has some epistle-like flourishes at the end (see 13:22— 25), the main body of Hebrews bears all the marks of an early Christian sermon, what the author calls a 'word of exhortation' (13:22), a homily of the sort surely preached in many of the first Christian congregations. Early Christian sermons were heavily influenced by the style of preaching done in the synagogue, and in terms of structure and methods of biblical interpretation, Hebrews appears to be an example of a sermon that is rabbinical in design, Christian in content, and heroic in length." (Thomas Long, *Hebrews*, in the *Interpretation* commentary series [Louisville: John Knox Press, 1997], p. 2)

The book begins with this passage, in which — reminiscent of the prologue to the Gospel of John — God speaks a word that resounds through all creation. In former days that word was spoken by the prophets, but in these days it has been spoken "by a Son." The high Christology of Hebrews is laid out right here, at the beginning of the letter, for all to see: Christ is "the one through whom [God] created the worlds," and "is the reflection of God's glory and the exact imprint of God's very being ..." (vv. 2-3). The role of Christ as high priest is also foreshadowed here, with the author's mention of how he "made purification for sins" (v. 4).

The second part of today's selection comes from chapter 2. In words reminiscent of the famous *kenosis* passage of Philippians 2:5-11, the author helps his readers "see Jesus, who for a little while was made lower than the angels, now crowned with glory and honor because of the suffering of death, so that by the grace of God he might taste death for everyone" (v. 9). This passage also introduces another distinctive Hebrews phrase, the description of Jesus as "the pioneer of their salvation" (v. 10; see also 12:2). Jesus is the one who goes before us, blazing the trail of salvation.

A group of Pharisees approaches Jesus and asks, "Is it lawful for a man to divorce his wife?" In doing so, they are posing a well-known theological dilemma that was the subject of frequent debate at that time. Jesus turns the question back on his questioners, asking them to cite Moses' teaching on the subject, which allows divorce in certain circumstances. Jesus responds to their citation, saying the ancient law is only on the books because of human "hardness of heart." He cites the Genesis 2 passage that is our First Lesson today, particularly the line about two becoming one flesh, then adding the line that has become part of our modern marriage ceremony: "Therefore what God has joined together, let no one separate" (v. 9). Later, in a private moment with his disciples, Jesus continues to expound a harder line on the subject of divorce than is present in Jewish law: "Whoever divorces his wife and marries another commits adultery against her; and if she divorces her husband and marries another, she commits adultery" (vv. 11-12). The final portion of this passage describes Jesus' blessing of children, and an exhortation to humility and wonder: "Truly I tell you, whoever does not receive the kingdom of God as a little child will never enter it" (v. 15).

Preaching Possibilities

A commentary on today's Gospel Lesson, written for preachers, pulls no punches: "This week you have two choices: a 'safe bet' sermon and a 'you'll be sorry' sermon — sorry you ever opened your mouth." The "safe bet" sermon is easy: Jesus saying, gently and lovingly, "Let the little children come to me." Then there's the other part of the passage, the first part: "Whoever divorces his wife and marries another commits adultery against her." This part of the text raises uncomfortable questions for all whose lives have been touched by divorce, whether in our own nuclear or extended families (which, with the divorce rate being what it is, is pretty much all of us).

Undoubtedly, it *is* easier to preach on "Let the children come to me." Everyone can go home happy. Yet, there are aspects of that first section of today's passage that every Christian would do well to hear. Not everyone is called to be married, of course: but all of us ought to be concerned with the health of marriage as an institution, which is an essential building block of society.

The question the Pharisees pose to Jesus — "Is it lawful for a man to divorce his wife?" — is something of a rhetorical trap. There were two factions within Jewish theology at that time: one following the conservative Rabbi Shammai, and the other the more liberal Hillel. Both sides consider divorce to be legal; they differ from each other when it comes to the specific circumstances.

Based on his own interpretation of the Law of Moses, Shammai insists that divorces are legal, but that they ought to be extremely rare. Only in the most extenuating circumstances, such as adultery or betrayal of the religion itself, can divorces ever be permitted. Hillel, on the other hand, wants to allow divorce under a wider range of circumstances, all of them depending on the whim of the husband. If a wife ever does anything at all, large or small, to embarrass her husband, she might well live in fear: for her husband could approach her, on that or any other day, and hand her a writ of divorce. Then it would all be over: with no legal recourse, no court of appeal.

The consequences, for the wife, are severe. Quite apart from the emotional pain and trauma, the newly divorced woman is suddenly cast out into the street: homeless and in disgrace. For the husband, there are few such consequences. He gets to keep the house, the property, and the children. She gets nothing. The decision to divorce is his and his alone, as long as he can come up with some explanation of how his wife embarrassed him or damaged his reputation.

It is easy to see how Hillel's permissive approach to divorce could cause all kinds of problems. In opposition to this view is the position of Shammai, who wants to introduce a few modest protections, limiting the reasons for divorce to serious offenses such as adultery. Yet, even with this more liberal school of thought, it's clear that women in that culture are little more than property. Their marriages persist only at the whim of their husbands. It is no accident that the only acceptable reason for divorce is the one thing that threatens their husband's property rights: a wife spending time illicitly with another man.

So when the Pharisees ask Jesus if divorce is ever permissible under the law, they're putting him on the spot. They want Jesus to take sides, with either the followers of Hillel or the followers of Shammai. They hope to see him enter into a raucous debate, and end up bruised and bloodied by the contest.

Jesus gives them no such satisfaction. He takes the side of neither Hillel nor Shammai, ruling instead that divorce is never permitted, under any circumstances. Then he appeals back to a higher authority than the Law of Moses. Referring to the book of Genesis, he says, "For this reason a man shall leave his father and mother and be joined to his wife, and the two shall become one flesh." In doing so, he is taking a position that's extremely radical for his day. He is speaking out in favor of those women, young and old, who live in fear that they are just one divorce decree away from poverty and disgrace. Jesus' complete prohibition of divorce is, functionally speaking, a powerful protective device for the least and lowly of that society.

There is a clash between our two cultures at this point: ancient and modern. Our two cultures are operating under completely different conceptions of marriage. For Jesus' society, marriage is a business arrangement between families. Nearly all marriages back then were arranged by the couple's parents, and there was an exchange of money — the dowry — between the bride's father and the groom's, to seal the bargain. Should there ever be trouble in a marriage — charges of adultery, for example — the bride's entire family would be disgraced, and a call might even go out for a blood feud. Preserving marriages at all costs is absolutely essential for the peace and stability of that ancient society.

Today, by contrast, we assume that marriage is an individual choice, made freely and without compulsion by both bride and groom. It assumes that both parties are free agents, and that they make their vows on a fundamentally equal basis. This is so far removed from the institution of marriage in Jesus' society, that we could almost say they're two separate institutions.

When Jesus quotes the book of Genesis, saying, "God made them male and female," and "the two shall become one flesh," he is not making a universal philosophical statement about the nature of the human marriage bond. Rather, he is speaking a stern, pastoral word to the men of his society. He is telling them to stop using divorce as a means of abandoning one wife, so they can pick up another. Jesus' word about divorce, taken in its historical context, is a word not of judgment but of grace, given: grace for those women who were all-too-often victimized by a harsh and oppressive system that considered them little more than property.

Prayer For The Day

Lord, it is not good us to be alone. You mean us to be in community. In all our communities of commitment — our marriages, our families, our deep friendships — keep us not only faithful, but also hard working: that together we may build relationships that not only strengthen the bonds between us, but also glorify you. Amen.

To Illustrate

How does a lamp burn? Through the continuous input of small drops of oil.

In Matthew, it is said, "If the drops of oil run out, the light of the lamp will cease, and the bridegroom will say, 'I do not know you.'"

What are these drops of oil in our lamps? They are the small things of daily life: faithfulness, small words of kindness, a thought for others; our way of being silent, of looking, of speaking, and of acting. These are the true drops of love.

Be faithful in small things because it is in them that your strength lies.

— Mother Teresa of Calcutta, speaking of the love that makes marriage
(or any other human relationship) last

***

To get divorced because love has died, is like selling your car because it's run out of gas.

— Diane Sollee

***

"In 1400, the average woman died around 27, usually in childbirth," says Dr. John Jacobs, a New York psychiatrist. "The average marriage didn't last twenty years." Contrast that with today, when "we are living so long we can be married three times in a lifetime."

Jacobs, author of *All You Need is Love and Other Lies about Marriage* (New York: Harper-Collins, 2004), is one of a growing number of therapists focusing their practices on helping people make marriages last a lifetime.

Their message is blunt: Marriage is more difficult than many anticipate. But a long-lasting union, held together with hard work, can create a profoundly satisfying relationship. And parents who stay together, even when they know their alliance will never be what they once hoped for, can provide their children with the best possible start in life.

"There has been a lot of rethinking on both the part of therapists and the public," says psychologist Joshua Coleman, who has a practice in Oakland and San Francisco. He is the author of *Imperfect Harmony: How to Stay Married for the Sake of Your Children and Still be Happy* (New York: St. Martin's Press, 2003).

Couples who want satisfying marriages need to dispense with society's romantic "lies" — such as the myth of a perfect soul mate — and face the fact they are apt to experience periods when they are not necessarily happy, Coleman says.

The road to an improved marriage requires improving communication skills, accepting the fact that no partner is perfect and understanding that situations change. A shift in one partner's attitude and actions can cause a positive ripple effect in the other, and sometimes a therapist, who can provide critical outside observations, is needed.

"Imperfect harmony is a given for people who want to stay together," Coleman says. "The vast majority of marriages can be made to be much better than people realize. But navigating by the starlight of happiness and personal affection is a very unreliable source."

— John Boudreau, "Long, Happy Unions are Rare and Require Work,
in 1400 or in 2004, in *Mercury News*, June 27, 2004

***

New love is the brightest, and long love is the greatest; but revived love is the tenderest thing known on earth.

— Thomas Hardy

***

James Jewel Kinnard II and his bride, Bonnie Lou (Chicbonya) Winston, traveled 150 years back in time when they exchanged wedding vows Saturday, September 6, in an authentic Cherokee wedding ceremony.

It was a simple outdoor ceremony that hadn't been performed in the Stockton area since 1849. The couple, both Cherokee Indians, went to great lengths to reconstruct and perform the ceremony. They researched on the Internet and had a lot of help from local medicine man, Al Tihonovich, an Arapaho Indian who officiated at the wedding....

Before heading off to New Orleans for their honeymoon, the new couple had one more ceremony to complete. Tihonovich gave them a large flat rock and told them to carve their names into it. Kinnard then had to throw the rock into the Sac River.

If they ever want to get a divorce they have to retrieve the rock and bring it to the medicine man, who reminded Kinnard that the flood waters get pretty high on that river.

— Justin Ballard, "Cherokee Wedding," in *The Herald Free Press* (Missouri), September, 10, 2003

***

I have no way of knowing whether or not you married the wrong person, but I do know that many people have a lot of wrong ideas about marriage and what it takes to make that marriage happy and successful. I'll be the first to admit that it's possible that you did marry the wrong person. However, if you treat the wrong person like the right person, you could well end up having married the right person after all. On the other hand, if you marry the right person, and treat that person wrong, you certainly will have ended up marrying the wrong person. I also know that it is far more important to be the right kind of person than it is to marry the right person. In short, whether you married the right or wrong person is primarily up to you.

— Zig Ziglar

***

There is nothing more admirable than two people who see eye-to-eye: keeping house as man and wife, confounding their enemies and delighting their friends.

— Homer, Ninth Century B.C.E.

Proper 23, Pentecost 21, Ordinary Time 28
October 15, 2006

Revised Common	Job 23:1-9, 16-17	Hebrews 4:12-16	Mark 10:17-31
	or Amos 5:6-7, 10-15		
Roman Catholic	Wisdom 7:7-11	Hebrews 4:12-13	Mark 10:17-30
Episcopal	Amos 5:6-7, 10-15	Hebrews 3:1-6	Mark 10:17-27 (28-30)

Theme For The Day   Beware of wealth, which is frequently an obstacle on the road to faith.

Old Testament Lesson   Job 23:1-9, 16-17   *Job Yearns To Bring His Case Before God*

Job answers Eliphaz the Temanite, who has insisted that the reason for Job's sufferings must be that he has somehow offended the Almighty by his wickedness. Job replies, "Today my complaint is bitter" (v. 1). He insists that, if he could only find the way to come into the Lord's presence, he would present his case: "He would give heed to me. There an upright person could reason with him, and I should be acquitted forever by my judge" (vv. 6b-7). But Job does not know where the Lord may be found: "If I go forward, he is not there; or backward, I cannot perceive him ..." (v. 8). The result, he says, is that "the Almighty has terrified me; If only I could vanish in darkness, and thick darkness would cover my face!" (vv. 16b-17). One of the most frustrating aspects of a season of suffering is that often there is no tribunal in which to argue our case before God. The Christian answer is that Christ is our mediator, who makes intercession for us.

Alternate Old Testament Lesson   Amos 5:6-7, 10-15   *Amos Cries Out For Economic Justice*

"Seek the Lord and live," says the prophet (v. 6). The way to seek the Lord, he continues, is through righteous living. For those who do not — for those who "trample on the poor and take from them levies of grain" — the day will come when they will no longer enjoy the splendid houses and vineyards they have built with their ill-gotten gain (v. 11). Amos is referring specifically, here, to the way wealthy landowners would often extort exorbitant rents from their tenant farmers, then bribe the judges so the tenant farmers would have no legal recourse. "Seek good and not evil," he continues, "speaking again to the landowners: that the Lord will be gracious and you may live" (vv. 14-15).

New Testament Lesson   Hebrews 4:12-16   *Jesus, Our Great High Priest*

Beginning with the admonition that "the word of God is living and active, sharper than any two-edged sword" (v. 12), the author continues, presenting the image of Jesus as the great high priest. This high priest — unlike others in times past — is "not ... unable to sympathize with our weaknesses." This is seen in the fact that "in every respect [he] has been tested as we are, yet without sin" (v. 15). Consequently, we are able to "approach the throne of grace with boldness, so that we may receive mercy and find grace to help in time of need" (v. 16). The image of Jesus as high priest has been mentioned before, earlier in the letter (2:17; 3:1). The time has now come for the author to explore this metaphor more fully (although today's lectionary passage presents only the first part of that lengthier treatment, which will continue for many weeks of lectionary selections). The accent here is on prayer: because we have a high priest, we have —

through prayer — access to the throne of grace. In the words of Thomas Long, "The preacher wants them to move past fearful prayers, tidy prayers, formal and distant prayers toward a way of praying that storms the gates of heaven with honest and heartfelt cries of human need. He does not want them to pray like bureaucrats seeking a permit but like children who cry out in the night with their fears, trusting that they will be heard and comforted. What the preacher wants to say is gathered up in words of the old hymn, 'Have we trials and temptations? Is there trouble anywhere? We should never be discouraged: Take it to the Lord in prayer!' " (*Hebrews*, in the *Interpretation* commentary series [Louisville: John Knox Press, 1997], p. 63)

The Gospel   Mark 10:17-31   *The Rich Man And Jesus*

A rich man comes up to Jesus, asking, "Good Teacher, what must I do to inherit eternal life?" Jesus testily responds, "Why do you call me good?" then directs him to the Ten Commandments, which the rich man insists he has faithfully observed all his life. "Jesus, looking at him, loved him" — that love is important to remember, as we observe what happens next — "and said, 'You lack one thing; go, sell what you own, and give the money to the poor, and you will have treasure in heaven; then come, follow me' " (v. 21). The man is shocked at this hard teaching, and goes away grieving: "for he had many possessions" (v. 22). This encounter sets up the famous teaching that follows, which has to do with money and possessions: "It is easier for a camel to go through the eye of a needle than for someone who is rich to enter the kingdom of God" (v. 25). The disciples are as baffled and upset by this as the rich man was: "Then who can be saved?" they ask (v. 26). Jesus' only response is the cryptic "For mortals it is impossible, but not for God; for God all things are possible" (v. 27). When Peter protests that he and his comrades have, in fact, done just as Jesus has instructed, leaving everything behind to follow him, Jesus promises that all who have done so will receive "a hundredfold now in this age" ("with persecutions" is added — a note to the Markan church, no doubt, who were beginning to feel oppression), as well as eternal life. Jesus' gospel is a gospel of reversals: "many who are first will be last, and the last will be first" (v. 31). The disbelief with which both the rich man and Jesus' own disciples receive the news about the necessity of leaving everything behind to follow him shows how deeply ingrained is the theological view that God will reward the good in this life. Many of the psalms express this view: "I believe that I shall see the goodness of the Lord in the land of the living" (Psalm 27:13). It is a view that is common enough today, and Jesus' words are equally jarring.

Preaching Possibilities

There are some fundamental assumptions that most of us, in our culture, accept uncritically as true. They include the beliefs:

- that progress is invariably good;
- that more wealth is necessarily better;
- that it is the nature of financial indicators — be they the Gross National Product or the Dow Jones Industrial Average — to grow; and
- that to proclaim anything else is unpatriotic at best, and heretical at worst.

Yet, here we have this difficult teaching of Jesus, delivered to a certain rich man. This high-roller steps right out of his BMW and runs up to the popular preacher: Gucci loafers on his feet, the latest cell phone at his belt, a gold Rolex gleaming on his wrist. "Teacher," he asks, "what must I do to inherit eternal life?"

249

Jesus gives him a Sunday school teacher's answer: "Follow the Ten Commandments."

The man gives him a Sunday school student's answer, in return: "Yeah, yeah, yeah, I know all that stuff already. I go to church; I work hard; I play hard; I keep my nose clean. I set my parents up in that luxury condo in Fort Lauderdale. I've never robbed a liquor store, or run off with another man's wife. But still, I feel empty. Somehow I feel this isn't living. There's got to be more!"

As Eugene Peterson paraphrases Jesus' further response: "Jesus looked him hard in the eye — and loved him! He said, 'There's one thing left: Go sell whatever you own and give it to the poor. All your wealth will then be heavenly wealth. And come follow me.' "

Peterson concludes: "The man's face clouded over. This was the last thing he expected to hear, and he walked off with a heavy heart. He was holding on tight to a lot of things, and not about to let go." (The Message: The Bible in Contemporary Language [Colorado Springs: NavPress, 2003])

This seems, at first glance, like such a harsh story! Who, indeed — as the disciples ask — can ever make it into heaven, if the entryway is tiny as a needle's eye?

Yet Jesus is not condemning the man: far from it! Mark tells us that, when the Lord first cast eyes on him, he "loved him." This is a challenging teaching, to be sure, but one that is framed in gentleness. Jesus really wants the young man to come over and join him — to sell all he has, distribute the proceeds to the poor, and hit the road with him and the twelve.

We need to make it clear, in preaching this passage, that Jesus is not condemning the man. This story has been used too often, over the years, to induce guilt in those who have an abundance of material goods. Remember who initiates the encounter: it is the rich man. It is he who comes running up to Jesus. It is he who is worried about how to attain eternal life. It is he who fears that something in his life is broken, something he doesn't know how to fix.

It's as though the young man is standing in flood waters up to his neck. The river is rising, and he can't swim. There's Jesus, on the bank, and in his hands is a life preserver. Jesus rears back and tosses it to him, with all his strength. But the young man just lets it sit there. "Take it!" Jesus cries; "It's right there!" But the young man just stares at the life preserver, bobbing on the waves in front of his face — and, with a mournful look in his eye, he turns away.

A key to understanding this passage is the list of commandments Jesus gives. Back in the beginning, when the man first addresses him, Jesus answers, "You know the commandments." Then he goes on to list a few. But strangely enough, Jesus doesn't list all the Ten Commandments. He only lists five (well, six, actually, but "you shall not defraud" is really a part of "you shall not bear false witness"). Jesus lists the five commandments having to do with human relationships: murder, adultery, theft, lying, and failing to honor one's parents.

The rich young man has no trouble with these. Nor do many Christians today, whose list of the most important ethical issues begins and ends with human relationships. Sexual ethics is on the list, to be sure — but economic justice? That's nowhere to be found.

Jesus isn't so concerned with these five commandments, numbers four through nine. He knows the young man has kept them, for the most part. It's the others that are a little more problematic. Specifically, number one: "You shall have no other gods before me. You shall not make for yourself an idol...."

There's one thing the rich young man loves — more, even, than God. He loves his material comforts. They are the object of his worship: and when he finds himself in deep spiritual waters, the weight of that golden idol will drag him down for sure.

Prayer For The Day

Great God, you have charged us to have no other gods before you. We want to keep you first in our hearts, but it seems that every time we look around, there is another gleaming idol attracting our attention. The one we cannot seem to look away from is the god of wealth. Give us the courage to let go of whatever weight is holding us back from full devotion to you — golden, or otherwise. Amen.

To Illustrate

Theologian Soren Kierkegaard tells the story of a flock of geese in a barnyard. One of the flock used to speak to them, every seventh day, on the greatness of their ancestors. These ancestors, he told them, were wild geese, strong and mighty. They could take to the heavens whenever they wished, and enjoy the sheer pleasure of soaring among the clouds.

All the other geese would nod their heads solemnly, and tell one another how wonderful was their heritage: but none of them ever did a thing about it. For the corn the farmer fed them was tasty, and the security of the barnyard was unparalleled. Who were they to set off on a fool's errand, into the dangerous skies?

No, it was enough (they told themselves) to hear the tales of their ancestors — and to dream of what it might have been like to fly. In this way, the timid geese sold their birthright of freedom for a small measure of security.

It is always tragic when Christians, called to give with glad and generous hearts, abandon their birthright of stewardship — and chase off (with the rest of the world) seeking the elusive idol of wealth.

***

Jesus calls us from the worship
Of the vain world's golden store,
From each idol that would keep us,
Saying, Christian, love me more.

— From the hymn, "Jesus Calls Us, O'er The Tumult"
by Cecil Francis Alexander, 1852

***

Those who love money will not be satisfied with money.

— The Talmud

***

The truth is that life in America has improved so much in the past century that we have forgotten what it is to struggle. We hear whines that schools are overcrowded today. Actually, the ratio of students to teachers has gone from 30:1 in 1955 to 19:1 now. We hear whining about pay. Yet total compensation, adjusted for inflation, has tripled since 1947, and the cost of necessities has plummeted. Food in 1950 represented about one third of a family's total expenditures; today, it's one seventh.

251

America's Gross Domestic Product is greater than the next five countries combined. Our unemployment rate of 5.7 percent — while higher than it was before the 2001 recession — is still lower than the average U.S. rate in the 1970s, 1980s, and 1990s. Unemployment in France is 9.6 percent. In Germany, 10.4 percent. And we're complaining!

Two-thirds of Americans now own their own homes. We have more cars, more children in college, more cultural institutions. We work shorter hours ... On the whole, we're more prosperous than any other nation in history — and far better off than we were in the past.

— James K. Glassman, "Whine, the Beloved Country!"
in *The American Enterprise*, June 2004, p. 48

***

The concentration of wealth and power in the hands of the few is the death knell of democracy. No republic in the history of humanity has survived this.

— Garrison Keillor, "We're Not in Lake Wobegon Anymore," from
Homegrown Democrat (New York: Viking, 2004)

***

If thou art rich, thou art poor, for like an ass whose back with ingots bows, thou bearest thy heavy riches but a journey, and death unloads thee.

— William Shakespeare

***

G. K. Chesterton once said something to the effect that it may be possible to have a good debate over whether or not Jesus believed in fairies. That could be a rather interesting argument. However, said Chesterton, there is no point to a debate over whether or not Jesus believed that rich people were in big trouble. There is just too much evidence.

— William Willimon, "Jesus vs. Generic God,"
in *Leadership Journal Online*, Winter 2002

Proper 24, Pentecost 22, Ordinary Time 29
October 22, 2006

Revised Common	Job 38:1-7 (34-41)	Hebrews 5:1-10	Mark 10:35-45
	or Isaiah 53:4-12		
Roman Catholic	Isaiah 53:10-11	Hebrews 4:14-16	Mark 10:35-45
Episcopal	Isaiah 53:4-12	Hebrews 4:12-16	Mark 10:35-45

Theme For The Day   Jesus wants us to be winners — but only in the contest of who can be the best servant.

Old Testament Lesson   Job 38:1-7 (34-41)   *Out Of The Whirlwind*

Having kept silence through the long rounds of conversation between Job and his well-meaning but ineffectual friends, the Lord finally answers Job's complaint. God's answer comes "out of the whirlwind" — an unmistakable sign of power. Power, in essence, is the content of the divine answer, which says, in effect, "I am the Almighty, and there is no questioning me." On the way to delivering that answer, the Lord speaks some of the loftiest and most moving poetry in the Hebrew language, recounting in intricate detail the work of creation. "Where were you when I laid the foundation of the earth?" the Lord asks (v. 4) — repeating the same rhetorical question, in somewhat varying form, for dozens of verses. The Lord never does answer Job's appeal — not directly, anyway. The answer is something like that of a president who ducks the special prosecutor's subpoena, claiming "executive privilege." Yet the circuitous journey toward an answer turns out, somehow, to *be* the answer. In a purely legal sense, Job loses the contest: yet, because God is his opponent, the fact that he has heard the divine answer is answer enough. (**Note:** The Preaching Possibilities section of next week's resource deals with a reading from Job that has some applicability to this week's reading.)

Alternate Old Testament Lesson   Isaiah 53:4-12   *The Fourth Servant Song*

For comments on this passage, see the resource for Good Friday (p. 109).

New Testament Lesson   Hebrews 5:1-10   *Jesus Is Superior To Every Other High Priest*

The last five verses of this passage have already occurred in the lectionary, on the Fifth Sunday In Lent (p. 95). Those verses, and the commentary on them, concern the role of Jesus as high priest. Here, the author deals with an implicit question that may be on the minds of his readers, who may be having a hard time reconciling Jesus' role as high priest with the fact that he suffered and died on the cross. The reason any high priest is able "to deal gently with the ignorant and wayward" is because "he himself is subject to weakness" (v. 2). On the Day of Atonement in past generations, the high priest atoned for his own sins, as well as for those of the people. Unlike the high priests of ancient Israel, however, Jesus does not need to atone for his own sins — he has been made "perfect." Nor does he need to return to the holy of holies again and again — the sacrifice he has made on the cross is unrepeatable and "eternal" (v. 9).

The Gospel   Mark 10:35-45   *James And John Ask Jesus For*
                                                                  The Best Seats In Heaven

Following Jesus' teaching about the necessity of giving up all for the sake of the gospel, and his subsequent prediction of his own sacrificial suffering and death, James and John prove they have not yet gotten the message. They approach Jesus and ask him whether he can arrange for them to have the best seats in heaven — at his right hand and at his left. Rather than answering them directly, Jesus responds with a question, asking these two if they are truly ready to drink the cup that he will drink. Jesus is referring, here, to the cup of suffering that, at Gethsemane, he will reluctantly decide to accept (14:36) — though James and John do not yet understand this. "Sure, we'll raise our glass with you, boss," they reply — not knowing what it is they're saying. "Oh, you'll drink it all right," Jesus says, ominously, "but to sit at my right hand or at my left is not mine to grant ..." (v. 39). James and John have asked Jesus for two tickets to the Sky Box, and after leading them on for a bit, Jesus has admitted that he doesn't actually have any tickets. That hardly matters, though, when the other disciples learn what their two comrades have just asked. They're furious. (In truth, they're probably upset that James and John thought of it first!) There ensues such a commotion that Jesus has to quiet them all with a stern teaching about servanthood: "whoever wishes to become great among you must be your servant, and whoever wishes to be first among you must be slave of all ..." (vv. 43b-44a). These circumstances are roughly parallel to those in 9:35, when Jesus has come out with a similar teaching.

Preaching Possibilities

The desire to be a winner runs strong in our culture. We're a competitive people — and getting more competitive, it seems, all the time. Our competitiveness extends even to our children. We pull them out of their neighborhood bike riding and pickup games of softball or soccer, put them in uniform with the names of some business on their backs, and send them off to do battle in organized sports with the children from the next town (not to mention those children's parents, who often get into bitter contests with us of who can yell the loudest).

The desire to be a winner is not unique to our culture. We can see it in the Bible: as in today's Gospel Lesson, when James and John sidle up to Jesus and ask their master a question. "Teacher," they ask, "we want you to do whatever we ask of you."

Jesus must be in a good mood, because he asks them this question in return: "What would you like me to do for you?"

"Oh boy," say James and John to one another, rubbing their hands together in anticipation. "Brother, I think this is our lucky day! (Now quick, before he changes his mind....) Grant us to sit, one at your right hand and one at your left, in your glory." Those Zebedee boys are aiming high. They're asking to be executive vice-president and chief operating officer of heaven, respectively.

But Jesus, who seemed to eager to hear their request a moment before, throws cold water on their ambition. "You don't know what you're asking," he says to them. "Are you able to drink from my cup, or be baptized with my baptism?" It just may be that Jesus understands all too well where he's headed, and what kind of sufferings lie between him and Easter morning. It just may be he knows that the only ones to be granted places at his right hand and his left are the two thieves who will be crucified beside him.

James and John seem to have forgotten the warning their master has just issued. They've clean forgotten his prediction about how he's going to be condemned, turned over for mocking and scourging, and sent to a grisly death. All they can remember is the part about him rising again. Those two have got glory on the brain.

Thomas Long has portrayed this episode, in a memorable passage in one of his books, as though it were an old war movie. Jesus, as he imagines the scene, is the tough, battle-hardened sergeant, about to order his men into combat. They're hunkered down in the trenches, and the bullets are whizzing overhead. The only problem is, the soldiers in his squad happen to be named Moe, Larry, and Curly. Just as their valiant leader cries, "Okay boys, over the top!" and begins to climb out of the trench himself, one of those three stooges pulls on the hem of his uniform jacket. With a goofy grin on his face, he says to his leader, "We have matching ties and blazers, can we sit on either side of you?"

Looking ahead at next week's Gospel Lesson — the passage that comes immediately after this one, in Mark's Gospel — we find Jesus and his disciples leaving the city of Jericho. Sitting right there at the city gate, where the way is narrow and there's no way around him, is a panhandler by the name of Bartimaeus. Bartimaeus is blind, and he makes his living off the coins people drop into his cup. When Jesus passes by, he shouts out, "Jesus, son of David, have mercy on me!" ("Son of David" is a messianic title — it's the first time in the Gospel of Mark anyone's called him that — other than the demons and his own disciples, that is — and Jesus has forbidden them to speak in such terms.) Now, though, the secret seems to be out that Jesus is the Messiah: and this blind beggar seems to have a better understanding of who Jesus really is than his own disciples, James and John.

Jesus asks Bartimaeus exactly the same question he's just asked of the sons of Zebedee: "What would you like me to do for you?" Only instead of demanding, "Make me great, seat me at your right hand!" Bartimaeus simply asks, "Rabbi, let me see again." And without a further word, the beggar's eyes are opened and his sight is restored.

Two encounters with Jesus. Two separate incidents in which Jesus asks exactly the same question: "What would you like me to do for you?" Two completely different outcomes: to one request Jesus says, "No," while to the other he doesn't even have time to say "Yes" before the wish is fulfilled. So what's the difference?

The difference is in the nature of the request. James and John are engaged in some pretty blatant self-promotion; blind Bartimaeus is simply crying out for help. James and John, for reasons of selfish pride, are seeking to be elevated over not only their fellow disciples, but every other human being on the face of this earth. Blind Bartimaeus is merely seeking the gift that is every human birthright: the ability to see.

Jesus doesn't have much patience with self-promoters. His word to us, when we seek to exalt ourselves, is the same word he offers to James and John: "... whoever wishes to become great among you must be your servant, and whoever wishes to be first among you must be slave of all."

This may explain why some of our prayers do not yield the answer we expect. God's not in the business of making winners; God's in the business of making servants. God may intercede in the midst of situations of terrible heartache or difficulty, bringing comfort or healing — in some cases, even restoration — but God's not eager to exalt any one individual over others.

Prayer For The Day

There is within each of us, O God, a small but insistent voice. The voice cries out to be recognized ... glamorized ... glorified. The voice comes from a part of ourselves that we wish were not there — and it has the power to destroy our lives, and the lives of those around us. Give us, we pray, the power to resist that voice. Help us seek after the servant way of Christ. Amen.

To Illustrate

There is, deep down within all of us, an instinct. It's a kind of drum major instinct — a desire to be out front, a desire to lead the parade, a desire to be first.

What was the answer that Jesus gave James and John? It's very interesting. One would have thought that Jesus would have said, "You are out of your place. You are selfish. Why would you raise such a question?"

But that isn't what Jesus did. He did something altogether different. He said in substance, "Oh, I see, you want to be first. You want to be great. You want to be important. You want to be significant. Well, you ought to be. If you're going to be my disciple, you must be." But he reordered priorities. And he said, "Yes, don't give up this instinct. It's a good instinct if you use it right. It's a good instinct if you don't distort it and pervert it. Don't give it up. But I want you to be first in love. I want you to be first in moral excellence. I want you to be first in generosity. That is what I want you to do...."

By giving that definition of greatness, it means that everybody can be great. Because everybody can serve....

— Martin Luther King, Jr., "The Drum Major Instinct," a sermon on Mark 10:35-45, preached on February 4, 1968, at Atlanta's Ebeneezer Baptist Church

***

One of the biggest phenomena in modern religious publishing is the little book called *The Prayer of Jabez*, by Bruce Wilkinson. The book is based on a single verse of 1 Chronicles concerning a minor figure named Jabez. The verse goes like this: "Jabez called on the God of Israel, saying, 'Oh that you would bless me and enlarge my border, and that your hand might be with me, and that you would keep me from hurt and harm! And God granted what he asked' " (4:10).

Wilkinson, who wrote the best-selling book, plucks that verse out of context, and uses it to promise his readers that, if they but utter this prayer with all their hearts, God will bless them with the modern equivalent of an enlarged "border," and God's hand will be with them, granting their every desire. It's almost as though he treats God like some cosmic vending machine: roll your Jabez-prayer into the slot, push the button, and out pops whatever you ordered! (It's no wonder *The Prayer of Jabez* has sold millions of copies in just a few years, and that it's spawned a whole host of spin-off books and related merchandise: it's a very attractive message indeed!)

Would that it were true — that all we need do is utter a prayer according to a certain formula, and God will automatically grant it! But it's not true: Jesus' encounter with James and John is ample evidence of that.

***

I have learned that prayer is not asking for what you think you want but asking to be changed in ways you can't imagine. To be made more grateful, more able to see the good in what you have been given instead of always grieving for what might have been. People who are in the habit of praying — and they include the mystics of the Christian tradition — know that when a prayer is answered, it is never in a way that you expect.... No wonder we have difficulty with prayer, for the best "how-to" I know is from Psalm 46: "be still and know that I am God."

— Kathleen Norris, *Amazing Grace: A Vocabulary of Faith* (New York: Riverhead, 1998), pp. 60-61

***

There's a story from the life of Albert Schweitzer, the great missionary doctor, that illustrates his true character as a servant of Christ. Dr. Schweitzer was working one day, under the hot African sun, building his hospital at Lambaréné — in what was then French Equatorial Africa, but which is now the nation of Gabon. He was struggling to raise a large timber into place, but he couldn't manage it without some help. Looking over, he saw a well-dressed African man standing in the shade of a tree. He asked him to lend a hand.

"Oh, no," the man replied. "I don't do that kind of work. I am an intellectual."

Schweitzer, as it happened, had five doctoral degrees. Before devoting his life to his African mission, he had been renowned both as a New Testament scholar and a concert organist, and had published books in the fields of both biblical studies and music. Wearily, Dr. Schweitzer said to the man, "I used to be an intellectual, but I couldn't live up to it."

***

There is a well-known story about the funeral of Charlemagne, King of the Franks and the first Holy Roman Emperor. As the Emperor's funeral procession arrived at the cathedral of Aix, with all the pomp and circumstance befitting royalty, it was met by the local bishop, who barred the cathedral door.

"Who comes?" the bishop asked, as was the custom.

"Charlemagne, Lord and King of the Holy Roman Empire," proclaimed the Emperor's herald.

"Him I know not," the bishop replied. "Who comes?"

"Charles the Great, a good and honest man of the earth."

"Him I know not," the bishop said again. "Who comes?"

The herald, a bit flustered, could not think of what else to say. But then he responded, "Charles, a lowly sinner, who begs the gift of Christ."

"Him I know," said the bishop. "Enter! Receive Christ's gift of life!"

Proper 25, Pentecost 23, Ordinary Time 30
October 29, 2006 (Reformation Sunday)

Revised Common	Job 42:1-6, 10-17	Hebrews 7:23-28	Mark 10:46-52
	or Jeremiah 31:7-9		
Roman Catholic	Jeremiah 31:7-9	Hebrews 5:1-6	Mark 10:46-52
Episcopal	Isaiah 59:(1-4) 9-19	Hebrews 5:12—6:1, 9-12	Mark 10:46-52

Reformation Sunday

Lutheran	Jeremiah 31:31-34	Romans 3:19-28	John 8:31-36

Theme For The Day   The only real answer to the problem of human suffering is to turn to God in faith.

Old Testament Lesson   Job 42:1-6, 10-17   *Job Repents In Dust And Ashes*

Having heard the Lord's monumental exposition of the wonders of creation, Job is now thoroughly chastened. He has questioned God, and God has heard him. God has not provided the answer he expected, but the fact that God has answered him at all is answer enough (see last week's resource). "I have uttered what I did not understand," Job numbly admits, "things too wonderful for me, which I did not know ... therefore I despise myself, and repent in dust and ashes" (vv. 3, 6). The strong language ("I despise myself") is only what would be expected, in that culture, of a subordinate asking the forgiveness of a superior. "Dust and ashes" are a common symbol of repentance, but also suggest human mortality. The second part of today's selection, verses 10-17, is a prose passage, relating how the Lord subsequently restores all Job's fortunes. Everything that was taken is returned to him, and then some — with the exception, of course, of his family members who have died.

Alternate Old Testament Lesson   Jeremiah 31:7-9   *The Return Of The Exiles*

Jeremiah is finished preaching doom. The time has now come to bring a message of comfort to the dispirited people of God. The time is soon coming, he proclaims, when the exiles will return home: "See, I am going to bring them from the land of the north, and gather them from the farthest parts of the earth, among them the blind and the lame, those with child and those in labor, together; a great company, they shall return here" (v. 8). They will come with tears of joy. The Lord will lead them home, as a father welcomes a long-lost son.

New Testament Lesson   Hebrews 7:23-28   *Jesus The Mediator*

The discussion of Jesus as the great high priest continues. Once again, the author emphasizes that Jesus' high priesthood is permanent, and his sacrifice unrepeatable, since it happened once for all time (vv. 24, 27). Jesus is perpetually ready to intercede for those who approach God through him (v. 25). Unlike the high priests of old, Jesus is not "subject to weakness," but has been made "perfect forever" (v. 28). Today will be Reformation Sunday in many churches. This passage's emphasis on Jesus as the sole mediator between humanity and God is an idea that helped fuel the Reformation, and its dismantling of the system of saintly intercessors that had been so much a part of medieval Roman Catholicism.

Just after Jesus has lectured the disciples on the importance of servanthood, he is walking with them through the city of Jericho. There, a blind man named Bartimaeus, a beggar who sits by the roadside, calls out to him for help. Bartimaeus addresses him by a royal title: "Jesus, son of David, have mercy on me!" This foreshadows the cries of the exultant Jerusalem crowd, who in the very next pericope will welcome Jesus into the city. Jesus calls Bartimaeus over, and asks him exactly the same question he had asked James and John in verse 36, just prior to their appeal for front-row seats in heaven: "What do you want me to do for you?" (v. 51). Bartimaeus appeals for his sight to be restored, and Jesus instantly grants his request, saying, "your faith has made you well." This is in marked contrast to the experience of James and John. Their appeal had nothing of faith about it, only selfishness; Bartimaeus is appealing to Jesus in hopeful expectation, believing with all his heart that Jesus has the power to heal him. The physical blindness of Bartimaeus, the outsider, is ironically contrasted with the spiritual blindness of James and John, the insiders.

Preaching Possibilities

Job is a story about who is in charge of the universe. It assumes the existence of two cosmic powers: God and Satan. In a strange sort of science experiment, God permits Satan to rain down all manner of ills upon the head of the ever-faithful Job — to see if he can be made to recant his faith. The only thing God forbids Satan to do is to take away Job's life.

Job is rich; Satan takes all his money. He is the picture of health; the tempter inflicts upon him a dreadful skin disease. He has a wonderful family; the evil one kills Job's children in a natural disaster, and drives his wife away in despair. Suddenly, Job finds himself stripped of everything he holds dear, except for life itself. And to him, even life itself has become terribly fragile: "A mortal, born of woman, few of days and full of trouble, comes up like a flower and withers, flees like a shadow and does not last" (Job 14:1).

After many pages of philosophical dialogue, in which Job's friends try valiantly to convince him there's nothing left for him to do but "curse God and die," the Lord Almighty finally appears in person. God then calls off the whole dreadful experiment, and restores to Job nearly everything he's lost. Job never has given up on faith totally, but he has certainly wavered; and so, the Lord speaks powerfully to his servants despair, in a voice "out of the whirlwind":

> *Where were you, God asks ...*
> *... when I laid the foundation of the earth?*
> *Tell me, if you have understanding.*
> *Who determined its measurements — surely you know!*
> *Or who stretched the line upon it?*
> *On what were its bases sunk,*
> *or who laid its cornerstone*
> *when the morning stars sang together*
> *and all the heavenly beings shouted for joy?*   — Job 38:4-7

God, here, is the great cosmic architect, the general contractor of the universe. "Who are you," God seems to proclaim, "to challenge my design, or my oversight of all that I have made?" The God who speaks here is the powerful Creator — one who not only assembled the great machine once upon a time and kicked it into motion, but who carefully watches over it even now, correcting its imperfections and fine-tuning its moving parts.

There's a famous story of a preacher who once had a parishioner come into his office, a man he'd counseled through many difficult circumstances. The man had made some progress in dealing with his problems, but always he seemed to fall short of the mark. Always he seemed overwhelmed by life. This day, though, the man was different. He had a smile on his face and a spring to his step. "Pastor," he said, with transparent joy, "I've got something wonderful to tell you: I've just resigned as general manager of the universe, and it's amazing how fast my resignation was accepted!"

That's the sort of realization Job comes to at the end of his long spiritual struggle. When he "repents, in dust and ashes," he is effectively resigning as general manager of the universe. That job is already taken.

When silversmiths create their works of fine art, they engrave, in an inconspicuous place, a tiny letter or symbol known as the "maker's mark." This is what antique dealers look for, as they're asked to appraise the value of an object — say, for example, a silver bowl by Paul Revere. The first step in authenticating the work is to turn it over and search out the maker's mark.

What is it about our lives that displays the maker's mark? Is it the capacity of our brains? Is it our opposable thumb, that anthropologists insist separates us from most other life forms? Is it the ability to reason creatively? Yet as wondrous as our bodies and minds are, it is not in these that we find the maker's mark.

There are some who would seek the maker's mark not in the world within, but in the world without: in the glories of nature. Many's the person who has strolled along a beach at sunset, or climbed a mountain peak, or stood — mouth agape — at the edge of the Grand Canyon, and confessed that this wonder could never have occurred without the intervention of a master artist.

"When I look at the heavens, the work of your fingers," sings the author of Psalm 8, "the moon and the stars that you have established; what are human beings that you are mindful of them, mortals that you care for them?"

Yet the maker's mark is not so unambiguously present in nature that everyone can see it. There are some, after all, who remain unconvinced of God's existence, even after viewing the wonders of nature. There are some who see random forces at work even in the painting of the sunset.

So where do we find the maker's mark? Not in the glories of nature, but somewhere else, in someone who preceded even creation itself. As the gospel writer John proclaims: "In the beginning was the Word, and the Word was with God, and the Word was God. He was in the beginning with God. All things came into being through him, and without him not one thing came into being. What has come into being in him was life, and the life was the light of all people."

It is in Jesus Christ that we see the maker's mark, stamped on creation so that all may know to whom this world belongs. The maker's mark, is not power, or intricacy, or ingenuity ... but love.

Prayer For The Day

When we look at the heavens, O Lord, the work of your fingers, the moon and the stars that you have established ... we are as filled with awe as the psalmist of old. Yet how swiftly we forget that cosmic perspective, as we turn our vision inward and focus only on the pains and problems of life! Keep us ever mindful that you are Lord and maker of all — that you fashioned us and all creatures, and that your plan for the universe is still unfolding as you have intended. Our vision and our faith are not always big enough. When they are not, remind us of your limitless love. Amen.

To Illustrate

Have you ever looked at your hands? I mean, have you ever really studied them as one of the most intricate and beautiful parts of the human body? Nineteen bones arranged to form a cup, an arch, a flat surface or a balled fist, each shape occurring on demand. Fingers able delicately to lift a needle from a table or twist open the stubborn cap of a fruit jar or distinguish between a penny and a dime merely by touch. No engineer designing robot hands has ever come close to such perfection.

— Scott Harrison, a surgeon

***

There is an old Jewish tale about a rabbi's child who used to wander in the woods. At first his father let him wander, but over time he became concerned. The woods were dangerous. All manner of beasts lurked there. The father took the boy aside one day, and said, "You know, I have noticed that each day you walk into the woods. I wonder, why do you go there?"

The boy said to his father, "I go there to find God."

"That is a very good thing," the father replied. "I am glad you're searching for God. But my child, don't you know that God is the same everywhere?"

"Yes," the boy answered, "but I'm not."

***

"I can only write down this simple testimony. Like all men, I love and prefer the sunny uplands of experience when health, happiness, and success abound but I have learned more about God, life, and myself in the darkness of fear and failure than I have ever learned in the sunshine. There are such things as the treasure of darkness. The darkness, thank God, passes, but what one learns in the darkness, one possesses forever."

— Leslie Weatherhead

***

"Okay, question," I say to Morrie, his bony fingers hold his glasses across his chest, which rises and falls with each labored breath.

"What's the question?" he says.

Remember the book of Job?

"From the Bible?"

Right. Job is a good man, but God makes him suffer. To test his faith.

"I remember."

Takes away everything he has, his house, his money, his family ...

"His health."

Makes him sick.

"To test his faith."

Right. To test his faith. So I'm wondering ...

"What are you wondering?"

What do you think about that?

261

Morrie coughs violently, his hands quiver as he drops them to his side.

"I think," he says, smiling, "God overdid it."

— Mitch Albom, *Tuesdays with Morrie* (New York: Doubleday, 1997), pp. 150-151
(*Tuesdays With Morrie* is the account of a series of conversations Albom had
with Morrie Schwarz, a beloved former teacher who is dying
a slow death from ALS [Lou Gehrig's Disease].)

***

Souls are like athletes, that need opponents worthy of them if they are to be tried and extended and pushed to the full use of their powers.

— Thomas Merton

***

Joy is not the absence of trouble, but the presence of God.

— Anonymous

***

Isn't it the greatest possible disaster, when you are wrestling with God, not to be beaten?

— Simone Weil

***

Everything can be taken from a person but one thing: the last of human freedoms — to choose one's attitude in any given set of circumstances ... to choose one's own way.

— Victor Frankl

Proper 26, Pentecost 24, Ordinary Time 31
November 5, 2006

Revised Common	Ruth 1:1-18	Hebrews 9:11-14	Mark 12:28-34
	or Deuteronomy 6:1-9		
Roman Catholic	Deuteronomy 6:2-6	Hebrews 7:23-28	Mark 12:28-34
Episcopal	Deuteronomy 6:1-9	Hebrews 7:23-28	Mark 12:28-34

Theme For The Day   In Jesus Christ, the kingdom of God is near at hand.

Old Testament Lesson   Ruth 1:1-18   *Ruth And Naomi's Covenant*

This passage sets the scene for the story of Ruth and Naomi: two faithful women, unrelated to each other, who in hard times covenant to rely upon each other, despite the traditions of a patriarchal society that would have driven them apart. The relationship between them is mother-in-law and daughter-in-law, a relationship their society would have expected to dissolve at the deaths of their respective husbands. Ruth's words to Naomi, after Naomi encouraged her daughter-in-law to abandon her and return to her own people, have become a classic expression of human devotion: "Do not press me to leave you or to turn back from following you! Where you go, I will go; where you lodge, I will lodge; your people shall be my people, and your God my God" (v. 16).

Alternate Old Testament Lesson   Deuteronomy 6:1-9   *The Shema*

Having delivered to the people the Ten Commandments (5:6-21), Moses now delivers to the people the great commandment of God known as the *Shema*: "Hear, O Israel: The Lord is our God, the Lord alone. You shall love the Lord your God with all your heart, and with all your soul, and with all your might" (v. 4). There are two basic things the people of God are to do: *hear* and *love*. This commandment is given in the context of the ongoing journey toward the promised land. The Lord instructs the people, through Moses, that they must keep this and other commandments "that it may go well with you, and so that you may multiply greatly in a land flowing with milk and honey ..." (v. 3). Obedience is a covenantal responsibility. Keep these words "in your heart," the Lord commands. Recite them to your children. Talk about them with each other. Write them on your foreheads, your hands and on your doorposts, that the law may be an ever-present part of your life (vv. 6-9). Clearly, it is not merely obedient actions that the Lord desires, but a thoroughgoing devotion that indicates an obedient heart.

New Testament Lesson   Hebrews 9:11-14   *The Purifying Blood Of Christ*

The author's exposition of the high priestly office of Jesus continues. Here, we have a detailed account of what the high priest of Israel did during the ritual of atonement. We see the high priest's approach into the holy of holies, the spattered blood of the sacrifice, the sprinkling of the ashes of a heifer. It is a ritual that sounds utterly foreign to modern ears, but to those Christians of Jewish origin for whom this letter is intended, these words would have been fraught with meaning — especially considering the fact that the Jerusalem temple had recently been destroyed by the Romans. The high priestly sacrifice, as the people had come to know it, would never be practiced again. Not to worry: Jesus is the replacement for all that. His blood spilled on Calvary replaces once and for all the blood of the sacrificial animals. His sacrifice has the power to "purify our conscience from dead works to worship the living God" (v. 14).

Not every encounter Jesus has, in the New Testament, with a scribe or a Pharisee is contentious. In this brief account, we hear of a scribe who is appreciative of Jesus' scholarship and faith outlook, and he of his. Jesus has been disputing with the Sadducees based on an arcane question about remarriage and the persistence of marital ties in heaven. A nearby scribe hears the dispute, comes up to Jesus, and asks him to name the greatest commandment. Jesus responds — as would any faithful Jew — with the *Shema* (Deuteronomy 6:4-5), and adds to it the further instruction, "You shall love your neighbor as yourself" (v. 31; Leviticus 19:18). Theologian Emil Brunner once remarked, "The gospel that will not fit on a postcard is not a fit gospel for the kingdom of God." It was common practice in Jesus' day for a student to ask a rabbi to summarize the law in just such a concise format; how the rabbi answered would tell the observers much about his general outlook and theological acumen. The scribe congratulates Jesus on his answer, and Jesus says to him, "You are not far from the kingdom of God." Jesus' answer is evidently a slam dunk: "After that," Mark adds, "no one dared to ask him any question" (v. 34).

Preaching Possibilities

This sermon will be preached just days before Election Day. Although this is not a presidential election year, still there has been ample opportunity, in many of the contests around the country, for voters to hear the candidates contend with one another at an event that's become a great American tradition: the debate.

We all know the drill. The candidates step up to lecterns, and someone starts asking them questions. There is time for rebuttal, and sometimes even for rebuttal to the rebuttal. Watching in the audience (and in the television audience, if the office being sought is important enough) are various commentators and pundits, all of whom are eager to give their instant analysis, and to declare a winner.

As today's Gospel Lesson opens, Jesus has been engaged in some rather contentious debate with the Pharisees and the Sadducees. First, he's had to answer some Pharisees, who asked him if it's lawful to pay taxes to the emperor. Then some Sadducees presented a convoluted theological case study: about a woman who's been married and widowed so many times, she's had seven different husbands. "In the resurrection," the Sadducees want to know, "whose wife will she be?"

These are tough questions, and Jesus handles them pretty well. But then this scribe comes up to him. He's been standing off to one side, quietly observing. He's noticed that Jesus "answered well." And so this man walks up to the Lord and pitches to him his own question: "Which commandment is the first of all?"

Compared to the other questions, this one seems a piece of cake. It's a favorite question of the scribes and teachers of the law, one they've been debating among themselves for years. Jesus has probably had reason to address it many times before. His answer begins with the *Shema* — "Hear, O Israel, the Lord our God, the Lord is one; you shall love the Lord your God with all your heart, and with all your soul, and with all your mind, and with all your strength." Then the Lord adds to this first commandment of Judaism another biblical commandment: "You shall love your neighbor as yourself." Love God; love neighbor. These are the greatest commandments, he says.

Jesus' questioner agrees wholeheartedly. He commends him for answering rightly. And when the Lord hears the scribe's positive endorsement, he commends him in turn, saying, "You are not far from the kingdom of God."

This is an exceedingly odd phrase. We are used to praying, "Thy kingdom come," as we do in the Lord's Prayer, then what does it mean for Jesus to say to a contemporary, "You are not far from the kingdom?" What is the kingdom of God, anyway — this spiritual reality that sometimes draws near, and other times seems far off in the distant future?

The kingdom of God is one of Jesus' favorite topics. It's the subject of his very first sermon. Mark tells how Jesus begins his ministry by proclaiming, "The time is fulfilled, and the kingdom of God has come near." Throughout his ministry, he's endeavoring to explain what he means by the kingdom of God, often using parables. The kingdom, Jesus says, is like a treasure buried in a field.... It's like a pearl of great value, that causes a merchant to sell everything to buy it. It's like a fishing net, cast into the waves, that's hauled back brimming with fish.

It seems, from Jesus' perspective, that the kingdom of God is very close indeed — close enough to touch, almost. It's as though it's a kind of alternative reality — another dimension, if you will — that in special times and places nearly breaks through to our world.

There's a famous comment by the Scottish preacher, George MacLeod, about the Isle of Iona, that holy and historic place off the coast of Scotland. MacLeod said of Iona that it is a "thin place," spiritually speaking. What he means is that whatever barrier may divide the kingdom of God from the kingdom of this world, that barrier does seem, in some very special times and places, to grow porous. The two worlds just about touch — and we know joy.

The same is true with this encounter between Jesus and the inquisitive scribe. When the Lord sees the joy in the man's face, he comments, "You are not far from the kingdom of God." Remember, also, Jesus' words to the thief on the cross, in Luke: "Tonight you will be with me in paradise." In particular times and places, there is this experience of thinness, as the kingdom of God draws near — it may even happen in a circumstance of terrible suffering, as long as faith is there also. The important feature is God's coming to us, unlocking the door that is locked from our side.

The Lord's Table, set before us for this sacramental meal, is one of those "thin" places. It is one of those places where, for a brief and tantalizing moment, earth and heaven seem to come into close proximity with each other. It is so simple, this everyday act of taking nourishment from bread and wine — but in this place, among these people, with Christ spiritually present among us, as our host, it is so meaningful. It is one of the few experiences in life when we are compelled to stop our frenzied activity, to silence in our minds any voice but God's own, and to open ourselves to the signs of God's nearness.

Prayer For The Day

Your kingdom come, O Lord. Your will be done. They are words we say again and again, with scarcely a thought as to their meaning. We wish for your kingdom, Lord, but we hardly know what we'd do with it if it came to us. Attune our spiritual senses to the ways in which your reign of justice and peace is already present among us. Remind us that we are citizens of that realm, and are responsible to its law of love, even as we dwell in a human society where the law of "an eye for an eye" so often seems to be the only standard. Open the eyes of our hearts, so we may see that your reign truly has come near. Amen.

To Illustrate

The kingdom of God is a concept that has always fired the human imagination. The Pharisees of the Bible have their own idea: they imagine the kingdom will result in a nation morally and spiritually renewed by strict adherence to the law.

The Zealots' vision is different. God's kingdom will only come, the Zealots believe, when Messiah appears in Israel, and reestablishes the throne of David. Then he will rule over the people in peace and prosperity. It's a frankly political understanding. It issues in an underground resistance movement, willing to do whatever it takes to drive the Roman overlords from the land.

Then there's the vision of those people who look solely to the future — because, for them, the present is filled with pain. For these oppressed believers, for whom life on this earth holds forth little promise, there is hope to be found in the terrifying prophecies of apocalyptic literature. "Thy kingdom come," for those who are seriously suffering, takes the form of a great cosmic battle between the forces of good and evil, with good emerging triumphant in the end.

We can find elements of all these views in things Jesus says — which is why it's so hard to pin him down to one interpretation over all the others. It does seem, though, that he gives a bit more preference to the kingdom as present in the here and now — just the other side of that thin barrier that separates earth from heaven.

***

If you like, you may refuse to believe you've been drawn into the eternal party. You can't stop the party, though. You may try, if you like, to walk out on it, and look for another bar to drown your sorrows in. But it is the loneliest walk in the universe: there is no other bar, and when you're done with all your walking, you'll find you went nowhere. Jesus does seem to insist that we're capable of being stupid enough to try and stay in hell forever ... Yet even if it's the gospel truth, all of your hell will be at the party, sequestered in the nail print in the left hand of the Bridegroom at the Supper of the Lamb. To say it one last time: even your faith doesn't matter, except to your own enjoyment of what he does for you. You can trust or not trust, but it doesn't change his mind or alter the facts. As far as he's concerned, you're home free forever. That's the deal. It would be a good idea to just shut up and accept it.

— Robert Farrar Capon, The Foolishness of Preaching
(Grand Rapids: Eerdmans, 1998), p. 31

***

What, in fact, could be more "political," a more complete and basal challenge to the kingdoms of this world, to its generals and its lords, both to those who hold power and to those who would seize it, than one who says that his kingdom is not of this world, and yet prays that the kingdom of his Father will come and his will be done on earth? This is an aspiration for the world more revolutionary, a disturbance of the *status quo* more seismic, an allegiance more disloyal, a menace more intimidating, than any program which simply meets force with force and matches loveless injustice with loveless vengeance. Here is a whole new ordering of human life, as intolerable to insurrectionists as to oppressors. It promises that forgiveness, freedom, love, and self-negation, in all their feeble ineffectiveness, will prove more powerful and creative than every system and every countersystem which subdivides the human race into rich and poor, comrades and enemies, insiders and outsiders, allies and adversaries. What could an earthly power, so in love with power as to divinize it in the person of its emperor, do with such dangerous powerlessness but capture and destroy it? It could change everything were it not extinguished, and speedily.

— Alan E. Lewis, *Between Cross and Resurrection: A Theology of Holy Saturday* (Grand Rapids: Eerdmans, 2001), pp. 49-50

***

A mother I know has a different way of asking the same question ["How was your day?"]. As she tucks her children into bed each night ... she asks them a question: "Where did you meet God today?" And they tell her, one by one: a teacher helped me, there was a homeless person in the park, I saw a tree with lots of flowers in it. She tells them where she met God, too. Before the children drop off to sleep, the stuff of this day has become the substance of their prayer.

— Dorothy Bass, *Receiving the Day: Christian Practices For Opening the Gift of Time* (San Francisco: Jossey-Bass: 2001)

***

Jesus was the most dangerous kind of rebel — a rebel who had seen the kingdom and knew it was the only reality. He was the most dangerous kind of rebel because he not merely talked about the kingdom; he lived and manifested its splendor in the beauty of his presence, in the clarity and inner coherence of his teaching, in his fearlessness in the face of opposition. He was the most dangerous kind of rebel because he could not be swerved from his purpose by anything, and he could not be bought by any lure, not even that of being a "master" or a "god"; his integrity was terrible and final.

Jesus was the most dangerous kind of rebel, too, because the vision that guided and inspired him through everything flamed from a direct mystical knowledge of God and would give him the courage to die, if necessary, for what he believed; not even torture, humiliation, and death would destroy his spirit.

— Andrew Harvey, *Son of Man: The Mystical Path to Christ* (New York: Tarcher, 1999)

***

There are places in this world that are neither here nor there, neither up nor down, neither real nor imaginary. These are the in-between places, difficult to find and even more challenging to sustain. Yet they are the most fruitful places of all. For in these limited narrows a kind of life takes place that is out of the ordinary, creative, and once in a while genuinely magical. We tend to divide life between mind and matter and to assume that we must be in one or the other or both. But religion and folklore tell of another place that is often found by accident, where strange events take place, and where we learn things that can't be discovered in any other way.

— Thomas Moore

267

Proper 27, Pentecost 25, Ordinary Time 32
November 12, 2006

Revised Common	Ruth 3:1-5; 4:13-17 or 1 Kings 17:8-16	Hebrews 9:24-28	Mark 12:38-44
Roman Catholic	1 Kings 17:10-16	Hebrews 9:24-28	Mark 12:38-44
Episcopal	1 Kings 17:8-16	Hebrews 9:24-28	Mark 12:38-44

Theme For The Day   Jesus encourages proportionate giving.

Old Testament Lesson   Ruth 3:1-5; 4:13-17   *Ruth Finds A Husband*

Desperate people sometimes do desperate things. Ruth and Naomi, having had little luck in supporting themselves by gleaning (picking the leftover barley remaining in farm fields after the harvest), devise a plan. Ruth, who is still young and marriageable, will go in to Naomi's kinsman, Boaz, while he is sleeping, "uncover his feet" and then "he will tell [her] what to do" (v. 4). The euphemism, "uncover his feet," means that Ruth is to present herself as available to have sex with him. Boaz is not a total stranger to the pair — he is Naomi's kinsman, and the two women have been gleaning in his fields, with his permission — but still this is a desperate and risky maneuver. As for the ethics of it, this is a culture very different from our own; with polygamy and levirate marriage being common practices, there were all kinds of routes for a marriageable widow to become attached to a man, thus becoming a part of his household. While Boaz has no legal responsibility to provide for either Naomi (to whom he is distantly related) or for Ruth (to whom he is not related at all), he is a righteous and benevolent man, and has perhaps been thinking already about establishing such a relationship with Ruth. Naomi has no power or authority to negotiate a marriage for her daughter-in-law, but as a wise woman she is arranging things in such a way that nature may take its course, and romance may blossom. The second part of this lectionary selection tells how Boaz does indeed act honorably, and marries Ruth. They have a child, Obed, who enters into the genealogy as the grandfather of David. For Christians, this means that Ruth, the Moabite widow who had no means of support — and who, without divine favor, would likely have perished — becomes an ancestor of Jesus. The Lord works in mysterious ways.

Alternate Old Testament Lesson   1 Kings 17:8-16   *The Widow Of Zarephath Feeds Elijah, And He Feeds Her*

The Lord directs Elijah to go to Zarephath, in Sidon, and find there a certain widow who will feed him. This is Phoenician country, where the worship of Baal is predominant. Elijah has previously declared that there is going to be a drought in the land (v. 1), and by the time he arrives in Zarephath, the famine is severe. This indicates the failure of Baal, the agricultural god, to provide for the people. The prophet sees a woman gathering firewood. He asks her to bring him some bread, and she says she has only a handful of meal and some oil. She laconically replies that she is going home to bake it into a cake, so that she and her son may "eat it, and die" (v. 12). The woman has evidently been well-off in the past, because she has a house with an upper room (see v. 19). It is the famine that has caused her destitution (although the fact that she is a widow may have made her more vulnerable than most). Elijah tells her to first prepare a little cake of the meal for him, then to do the same for her son and herself. He accompanies this command with a prophetic declaration: "thus says the Lord the God of Israel: The jar of meal will not be emptied and the jug of oil will not fail until the day that the Lord sends rain on the earth" (v. 14). The woman does as she is told, and it happens just as the prophet has predicted: there is enough to feed herself, her household and the prophet for many days. In the pericope that follows (not part of this lectionary selection), Elijah restores her son to life, after he has either died or entered a death-like state.

New Testament Lesson　　　　Hebrews 9:24-28　　　　*The High Priest Who Is To Come*
The comparison between Jesus, the great high priest, and the former high priests of Israel continues. The emphasis, here, is on difference between Jesus' high priestly ministry and that of the others who have held the position. The differences are as follows:

- Jesus does not enter into a sanctuary "made with hands," but into heaven, to intercede with God directly (v. 24).
- Jesus does not need to enter the sanctuary again and again, but has done so "once for all at the end of the age to remove sin by the sacrifice of himself" (vv. 25-26).
- Jesus "will appear a second time, not to deal with sin, but to save those who are eagerly waiting for him" (v. 28).

The author is restating points he has previously made, for rhetorical emphasis. We have seen the first two of these points in 5:1-10 (see Proper 24, p. 253) and in 7:23-28 (see Proper 25, p. 258). The new development is the third point of comparison: that this high priest will return again, "to save those who are eagerly waiting for him." There is no mention of judgment connected with the high priest's return; having already made intercession for the people, he effectively gives them a free pass through the judgment spoken of in verse 27. This is a message of good news akin to that of Romans 8:34 — "Who is to condemn? It is Christ Jesus, who died, yes, who was raised, who is at the right hand of God, who indeed intercedes for us."

The Gospel　　　　Mark 12:38-44　　　　*The Widow's Mite*
Jesus has entered into Jerusalem (11:1-11), cleansed the temple (11:15-19), and engaged in a series of disputes with scribes and Pharisees (11:27—12:37). Now he issues a condemnation of the scribes, who parade their religiosity in ostentatious ways, at the same time as "they devour widows' houses and for the sake of appearance say long prayers" (v. 40). The second part of this selection is the well-known story of the widow's mite — the "mite" being the two tiny copper coins that this impoverished widow quietly places in the temple offering box (the word "mite" comes from the King James Version: "two mites, that make a farthing"). This widow is an example of one of the type of person whose houses the wealthy and powerful have been foreclosing upon. Jesus contrasts the widow's gift with that of the rich people, who visibly "put in large sums" (v. 41). From a proportionate giving standpoint, the widow's gift is vastly larger than that of the wealthy contributors: "Truly I tell you, this poor widow has put in more than all those who are contributing to the treasury. For all of them have contributed out of their abundance; but she out of her poverty has put in everything she had, all she had to live on" (vv. 43-44). The woman has but two coins: she gives them both. By every standard of calculating the amount of offerings — the tithe or any other — this woman would have been entitled to keep one of her two coins (one coin would have been a quintuple tithe). But she gives both anyway. While this passage has come to be known as a classic stewardship text, in its context it

has just as much to do with Jesus' criticism of the scribes and Pharisees as it does with money. The real question, here, is not the amount of the gift, but the generosity of the heart — Jesus' point is that many of the ostentatiously religious of his day are deficient in that department.

Preaching Possibilities

Today is Stewardship Sunday in many churches, and the lectionary provides a classic stewardship text, that of the widow's mite (Mark 12:41-44). It's the classic biblical exposition of proportionate giving.

Some of the old-timers among us may remember the old Jack Benny Show on television — or even, in its earlier incarnation, on radio. One of the longest-running gags had to do with Benny's legendary stinginess. In one famous sketch, a robber comes up to Benny, points a gun at him, and demands, "Your money or your life!" Benny just stands there, staring into space. Again the robber says, "You heard me — your money or your life!" After one of the agonizing slow pauses that are his trademark, Benny replies, "I'm thinking! I'm thinking!"

We smile at that sketch because of the ludicrous idea that a person would actually have to think about the choice between dying or handing over a wallet. We all get attached to money. Money represents psychological well-being, even happiness. It is the fruit of our labors, and is — to some minds — the symbol of our very worth as persons. Even as we laugh at Jack Benny, in the humor there is a twinge of discomfort — because we've all felt that pull money has on us, that makes it difficult to let go.

In a certain sense, "Your money or your life?" is the fundamental question of Christian stewardship — but with one small amendment. Change the "or" to "and" and the full picture emerges: God wants both our money *and* our lives. We can't sequester our financial decision-making in a separate compartment of our lives.

It's a question of *how* we give, not how much. The poor widow in today's reading from Mark is the prime example of the sort of giving our Lord wants us to practice. Jesus is in the temple, watching the noteworthy citizens of Jerusalem place their silver coins in the collection-box. They seem very proud. Then, quietly and without fanfare, a poor widow walks up and drops in two copper coins. It's a trifling sum — but, as Jesus explains to the disciples, it's all she has.

Jesus is teaching the concept of proportionate giving: one of the most basic principles of Christian stewardship. We are to give, he says, not from our abundance — not from what's left over after we've bought everything else we need or want — but from our substance. We are to give, as Nehemiah puts it (10:35-37), the firstfruits of the harvest. For a consumer society like our own, that believes the firstfruits are meant for our own immediate enjoyment rather than for the Lord's work, this represents a complete change of perspective.

Not long ago, there was an advertisement that read: "Now you, too, can own a genuine coin from the time of Jesus: The Widow's Mite. It's a minor miracle that this coin has survived — and now people of faith can study, cherish, and protect it for future generations. It's yet another miracle that they're so affordable." The ad goes on to mention the biblical story of the widow's mite, before delivering its appeal: "While our limited supplies last, you may order the 2,000-year-old Widow's Mite for only $39.95 plus shipping and handling. Remember, this is the genuine coin mentioned in the Holy Bible and it makes a perfect gift for your child, grandchild, or favorite clergyman."

All right, it's a small, antique coin from Jesus' time — probably in poor condition — that may or may not resemble the sort of coin the widow placed in the temple offering box. Like anything else labeled "antique," it's got a certain value to knowledgeable collectors. (That value is probably a good bit less than $39.95, but the coin dealers are counting on the fact that the association they're making with a Bible story may raise its value for some buyers.)

It's not the actual coin the widow held in her hand, of course. How could it be? The widow had two, and the coin dealer has probably got hundreds, if not thousands. To own one of her actual two coins would be to possess a true rarity. Because of its direct association with Jesus, *that* coin would be priceless. Even more valuable still would be something that widow had, that she could not hold in her hand — her generous heart.

Living that way, setting aside God's portion before anything else, and giving it "off the top," is a risk. No doubt about it, but that's Christian stewardship. Stewardship is always a risky business. It was risky for the widow in the temple, and it's risky for us. Yet it's also a joyful business, and a faith-filled business. We Christians can take the risk, knowing that our God will stand by us as we give, confident that our God has promised to provide.

When a ship is launched, it begins from a position on dry land, propped up by wooden beams: "a ship out of water," in every sense of the expression. A ship out of water is a ridiculous thing. It can't go anywhere. It's useless. But then comes the day when someone smashes a champagne bottle across the bow, and somebody else knocks out the supports. With a groaning and a splintering, the newly constructed ship slides down the greased ramp and enters the water with a tremendous splash. The bow sinks down deep, then flies up high, propelled by its natural buoyancy. After a few violent, back-and-forth motions, the craft rights itself.

The ship is afloat. Finally, it's in its element. It's where it belongs. This is the work for which it is made, riding high from wave to wave, upheld by the ocean's supporting hand.

For a Christian, beginning a life of stewardship is like launching a ship. We begin in a sort of shipyard, supported by all the materialistic props society has to offer. It takes courage to forgo the only security we have ever known, and begin the short, stomach-churning slide into the black water. It's risky. It's frightening at times. Yet, unless we undertake that journey, we will never discover the purpose for which God made us. We will trade the hazards of the open sea for a slow death of dry rot in the shipyard.

God doesn't want our money. God wants our lives. The choice God puts before us is not the robber's choice, "Your money or your life!" but a far more profound and far-reaching decision. What God wants is the gift of our very selves. Once we make that commitment, the money, the volunteer time, the talents, and everything else will follow.

Prayer For The Day

Truly, Lord, you have blessed us with a love that knows no bounds. Yet we acknowledge and confess, in all humility, that there are boundaries we put up in life — boundaries that enclose certain parts of ourselves, intended to block the healing light of your love. Chief among those boundaries are the ones that surround our finances. Lord, we give ourselves to you: and may it be, this day and every day, that we open even those dark chambers, sharing out the treasures that sleep in the shadows within. Amen.

To Illustrate

It is said that an old friend of Alexander the Great once came to him asking for money. The friend had fallen upon hard times; he needed some help to get back on his feet. Alexander summoned the royal treasurer, and had him bring a purse filled with many times more than the friend had asked for.

"This is far too much," the king's friend said. "I can't accept it."

"The amount you asked for is sufficient for you to receive," Alexander replied. "It is not sufficient for me to give."

***

We have been called to be fruitful — not successful, not productive, not accomplished. Success comes from strength, stress, and human effort. Fruitfulness comes from vulnerability and the admission of our own weakness.

— Henri J. M. Nouwen, public address at Yale University, March 30, 1995

***

We who are members of the church are the lighthouse of the world. We are responsible for one task above all others — to keep the light of the gospel burning. All else must be secondary.... The church has always put us first before anything else. It took us in as babies, before it knew who we were, what we might be, what we might have. It called us "children of God" and received us into its arms; it walked beside us in good times and in bad times.... It prays for us when we go astray, welcomes us back as a loving mother when we come to ourselves; it is with us in sickness, sorrow, and death. Every other organization we join first ascertains who we are, what we have, what our social standing is; asks if we will "fit in," what we have to offer, etc. How different is the church that turns to us and says, "I don't care who you are, what your background is, what you have. You are a child of God and as such I welcome you without reservation; I offer you all the privileges and blessings; and I shall belong to you and you to me now and forever."

— Martin Luther King, Jr., in an October, 1957 sermon

***

I've learned that you shouldn't go through life with a catcher's mitt on both hands; you need to be able to throw something back.

— Maya Angelou, interviewed by Oprah Winfrey

***

I've seen you stalking the malls, walking the aisles, searching for that extra-special gift. Stashing away a few dollars a month to buy him some lizard-skin boots; staring at 1,000 rings to find her the best diamond; staying up all night Christmas Eve, assembling the new bicycle.

Why do you do it? So the eyes will pop, the jaw will drop. To hear those words of disbelief: "You did this for me?"

And that is why God did it. Next time a sunrise steals your breath or a meadow of flowers leaves you speechless, remain that way. Say nothing, and listen as heaven whispers, "Do you like it? I did it just for you."

— Max Lucado, *The Great House of God* (Nashville: Nelson: 2001)

***

There's an old story about a wise woman who was traveling alone in the mountains. One day as she was crossing a stream, she looked down and saw a precious stone glittering back at her from beneath the clear, running water. She bent down and picked it up. Drying it on her shawl, she examined it carefully, weighed its value and placed it in her bag.

The next day she met another traveler. The man had run out of food a day earlier, and was very hungry. The wise woman offered to share her food with him. When the woman opened her bag to take out some food, the hungry traveler saw the precious stone. Impetuously, he asked the woman to give it to him. Without hesitation, the woman reached into her bag, and gave it to him.

The hungry traveler finished his meal and left, rejoicing in his good fortune. He knew the value of the stone. It was worth enough to keep him in comfort for the rest of his lifetime. A few days later, though, the man searched the old woman out and told her he had to return the stone. "I've been thinking," he said. "I know how valuable this stone is, but I'm giving it back to you in the hope that you will give me something even more precious. Please give me some of whatever you have inside you, that enabled you to give me this stone."

Proper 28, Pentecost 26, Ordinary Time 33
November 19, 2006

Revised Common	1 Samuel 1:4-20 *or* Daniel 12:1-3	Hebrews 10:11-14 (15-18) 19-25	Mark 13:1-8
Roman Catholic	Daniel 12:1-3	Hebrews 10:11-14, 18	Mark 13:24-32
Episcopal	Daniel 12:1-4a (5-13)	Hebrews 10:31-39	Mark 13:14-23

Theme For The Day   When other, seemingly solid foundations of our lives are shaken, the foundation of faith remains strong.

Old Testament Lesson   1 Samuel 1:4-20   *Hannah Is Granted A Son, Samuel*

It's the dearest wish of Hannah, one of Elkanah's two wives, that she be able to have children. Yet, as year succeeds year, only Elkanah's other wife, Penninah, is able to produce offspring — and Penninah regularly torments Hannah with her maternal superiority. Elkanah loves Hannah deeply, but still she feels incomplete. Hannah presents herself at the temple, and offers a solemn vow to the Lord, that if she will only be able to bear a son, she will dedicate him as a nazirite to the Lord — that he will abstain from alcohol, and that "no razor will touch his head" (v. 11). Nazirites, those who practiced ascetic disciplines, were seen as particularly holy before the Lord. Hannah's prayer is so long, and her demeanor so silently intense, that Eli, the high priest, thinks she is drunk. Hannah corrects his misapprehension, and Eli ultimately blesses her, wishing for her a positive answer to her prayer. When Hannah bears a son, she names him Samuel, saying, "I have asked him of the Lord" (v. 20). The chief focus of the book of 1 Samuel is the ascension of David to the kingship, but first the Lord must set the stage with the birth of Samuel — who, as the last of the Judges, is the transitional figure who will make Israel's kingship possible. Samuel is the kingmaker — and it all begins with the humble prayer of a faithful woman, Hannah. Hannah can be seen as a symbol of Israel itself, who cries out to the Lord over many years of waiting, before being surprised by God's graceful response. Hannah's song of joy, 1 Samuel 2:1-10, is an alternate psalm for today. Like Mary's Magnificat (Luke 1:46-55), a song raised under similar circumstances, it is a marvelous poem celebrating God's power of reversal: "He raises up the poor from the dust; he lifts the needy from the ash heap, to make them sit with princes and inherit a seat of honor" (2:8).

Alternate Old Testament Lesson   Daniel 12:1-3   *The Dead Raised*

With Daniel, we enter into the realm of apocalyptic. In the passages that precede this one, the author has been directing his prophetic fury against the corrupt and blasphemous king, Antiochus Epiphanes, who has set up an idolatrous image, "the abomination that makes desolate," in the temple (11:31). Beginning with 11:40, the prophet shifts his attention to the future. The remainder of chapter 11 describes how the king will soon meet an ignominious end in battle, but with chapter 12 — the book's final chapter — Daniel's prophecy takes on a cosmic dimension. He predicts that the archangel Michael shall appear, and those who are faithful "shall be delivered" (v. 1). Then, "Many of those who sleep in the dust of the earth shall awake, some to everlasting life, and some to shame and everlasting contempt. Those who are wise shall shine like the brightness of the sky ..." (vv. 2-3a). In the final chapter of this book, which has probably the latest date of composition of any in the Old Testament, we see the full emergence of a belief in the resurrection of the dead.

New Testament Lesson   Hebrews 10:11-14 (15-18) 19-25   *Approach God With*
                                                               Confidence

The lengthy treatment of Jesus as the great high priest moves toward its climactic conclusion. Christ has made a one-time sacrifice of himself for the sins of humanity: "by a single offering he has perfected for all time those who are sanctified" (v. 14). Christ has opened forever the curtain that once separated God's people from the holy of holies, where the high priest's sacrifices were once made (v. 20). Because of what he has done, we can approach the throne of God in full confidence, knowing that "our hearts [have been] sprinkled clean from an evil conscience and our bodies washed with pure water" (v. 22). While we are waiting for all to be fulfilled, the author encourages us to "provoke one another to love and good deeds, not neglecting to meet together, as is the habit of some, but encouraging one another ..." (vv. 23-24).

The Gospel   Mark 13:1-8   *Not One Stone Will Be Left*
                                                               Upon Another

As Jesus leaves the temple, after presenting his teaching about the widow's mite (see last week's resource), one of his disciples — acting rather like a country rube visiting the city for the first time (which may, in fact, have been the case) — marvels, "what large stones and what large buildings!" The stones of the temple were in fact, almost unbelievably large. Jesus, unimpressed, replies, "Not one stone will be left here upon another; all will be thrown down" (v. 2). A little while later, he is sitting with a few disciples on the Mount of Olives, with the temple in view. These disciples, who have been pondering the meaning of this dark saying, ask Jesus when these things will take place. Jesus urges caution, warning that deceivers "will come in my name and say, 'I am he!' " (v. 6). There will be "wars and rumors of wars" before the end will come, and also natural disasters like earthquakes and famines. These signs, Jesus warns, "are but the beginnings of the birth pangs" (v. 8). Even then, the end is not yet. This passage (along with its parallels in Matthew 24 and Luke 21) is known as the "Little Apocalypse."

These words would have taken on special meaning for the first-century communities for which these gospels were written, who would have recently witnessed the fulfillment of at least some of the predicted events — notably, the destruction of the temple by the Romans in the year 70. The word of Jesus the apostles remembered and recorded, with the needs of the Christians of their own day in mind, is that even when the very stones of the temple have been cast down, the time of the end is not yet. Troubles will abound, but the task of the faithful community is to wait in hope. Later in this chapter, Jesus will warn, "not even the Son knows the day and hour of his coming, but only the Father" (v. 32).

Preaching Possibilities

The date is September 10, 2001. A family of tourists from the midwest steps out of a yellow cab in lower Manhattan. They walk a short distance, until their eyes are pulled upward by the amazing sight before them. It's a massive skyscraper, larger than any they've ever seen: one of the two towers of the World Trade Center. Its twin stands nearby, equally commanding their attention. They are so much bigger than they had imagined, those towers: broad across the base, soaring majestically in height.

Just then the tourist family from the midwest hears a strident voice. "Repent!" cries the voice. "The end is near. One day soon, not one stone of these towers will be left standing upon another!"

"Just some religious fanatic," explains the husband, laughing nervously, before leading his wife and children over to ask for directions to the observation deck.

Had such a scene actually occurred on September 10, 2001, it would hardly have seemed remarkable. Street preachers are part of the life of any major city. Yet who would have taken that man seriously? Who could have known — except, perhaps, for a small group of terrorists, putting the finishing touches on their dreadful conspiracy — that the very next day, the words of that street-corner preacher would prove to be absolutely correct?

Who could have known, either, that Jesus' prediction about the future of the temple is absolutely correct? "Do you see these great buildings?" he asks his disciples — especially the one who'd been walking around like a country bumpkin, gawking at the urban landscape. "Not one stone will be left here upon another; all will be thrown down." To Jesus' listeners, that prediction seems incredible: for what could be more permanent, more stubbornly enduring, than the temple?

The first temple had been constructed by Solomon, richest and most powerful of all Israel's kings. Even in his day, the design of the temple was ancient. Solomon had modeled its floor plan after the tabernacle: the portable, tent-like worship structure the people had carried with them on their wilderness wanderings. Solomon's temple stood proud until the Babylonian invasion, when the soldiers of King Nebuchadrezzar destroyed it. A century later, after the exiles returned from captivity in Babylon, the great reformer Ezra rebuilt it, to Solomon's original specifications. From that day onward, it continued as the center of Israel's worship — though not without times of difficulty. The worst of these times was in 168 B.C., when the Seleucid Greek ruler, Antiochus Epiphanes, briefly tried to eradicate the Jewish faith. He set up a statue of Zeus in the temple, and tried to convince the people to worship there in the Greek fashion. That act of desecration set off the Maccabean revolt, through which the temple was recaptured and cleansed.

Not long after that the Romans took over, and their puppet king, Herod, decided the best way to consolidate his power was to rebuild and refurbish the temple. This he did in grand style, vastly expanding the size of the temple mount and adding great rows of marble columns, after the Roman pattern. The stones Herod used for his new construction were huge — far larger than anything that had been used to date. When Jesus' disciple exclaims, "Look, teacher, what large stones!" he's certainly referring to these huge, rectangular stones of Herod's. The smallest of them weighed two to three tons. Many weighed as much as fifty tons. The largest stone the archaeologists have been able to find is twelve meters long and three meters high; it weighed hundreds of tons. These stones were so immense that no mortar was required; the very weight of the stones themselves held them in place. Who could imagine the destruction of the temple, when stones this massive had been used in its construction?

Well, the Romans would find a way. Four decades after Jesus' death, in the year 70 A.D., these new rulers of Judea had grown thoroughly tired of Jewish resistance. The Emperor Titus ordered that the temple be razed to the ground. For the first time since the return of the exiles from Babylon many centuries earlier, Jewish worship on that spot ceased.

For the Jewish people of that era, this was a catastrophe. It was nothing short of a spiritual holocaust. The elaborate sacrifices, according to the ancient rituals prescribed in the book of Exodus, would take place no longer. No longer was there a holy of holies at the heart of the temple, into which the high priest would venture each year on Yom Kippur, the Day of Atonement, to free the people from their sins. The religious action would shift, more and more, to the synagogues. Synagogues were houses of study, located throughout the Greek and Roman world, where learned rabbis taught the scriptures. There the traditions of the faith were kept alive. While the people might yearn for a rebuilt temple, no Jew would ever see such a building again.

At the time Mark is writing his gospel, the memory of the Roman destruction is a very recent one. The Jews are struggling to make sense of this catastrophe. It's no wonder, then, that Mark would include in his gospel this prophecy of Jesus' about the destruction of the temple. It wasn't literally true that "not one stone would remain upon another," but the Roman devastation was so thorough that further temple worship was impossible. To this day, only the Western wall of Herod's temple complex — the famous "Wailing Wall" — remains.

What are the "stones" on which we depend? What are the building blocks of our lives, which we could hardly bear to see cast down? For some, it's the stone of wealth. For others, the most essential stone is the stone of professional accomplishment. For still others, it's good health, and for others, family stability. Over the course of our lives, all of us construct certain temples, certain structures we judge to be stable or secure. Yet it's surprising how quickly things can change — how rapidly we can descend from certainty into doubt, from consistency into chaos, from comfort into pain.

When temples tumble, let us remind ourselves that no matter how troubled or chaotic life may become, there is one who has known in his life an even fuller measure of pain and heartache. That one is God's own son Jesus Christ, our Lord. That one is close at hand, to comfort and console. He doesn't promise any one of us a life free of trouble. What he does promise, to all who trust in him, are rich resources of faith. That faith allows us not only to persevere through hard times, but to triumph over them: until the day when we achieve final victory in him.

Prayer For The Day

When the temples of our lives tumble, O Lord — when certainties dissolve into confusion, and we wonder where to turn — ground us in the resources of our faith. Help us to know that we are equipped not only to survive, but to prosper: bearing witness to your presence and power in a world where you often seem difficult to behold. Send us signs of your loving presence and bless us with evidence of your grace. Most of all, send us the gift of your Holy Spirit — the advocate, the comforter — that we may be restored to confidence and hope. Amen.

To Illustrate

Here is the story of a man who endured unspeakable suffering in his life, but triumphed in the end. The man was a politician, a member of the New York State Assembly. One day a telegram arrived in his office in Albany. It contained a single three-word sentence: "Come home now!" Not long before, his wife had given birth to a baby girl; he had gone back to work thinking all was well, but it was not.

The young man took the next train back to his home in New York City, and as he walked through the door of his house, his brother greeted him with a strange lament: "There's a curse on this house." Rushing up to the bedroom, he found that his wife, Alice, lay dying, from unforeseen complications of childbirth. He sat and held her, and could be heard pleading: "Let her live, let her live."

Sometime during the night, a family member intruded on their solitude, whispering into his ear, "If you want to see your mother before she dies, come downstairs now." The man left his wife and walked down a flight of stairs into his mother's room, where he held her until she died at 3 a.m.

He returned immediately to his wife's bedside, where he kept vigil until she also died, at two that afternoon. As heavy grief descended on that household, occasionally there could be heard the cry of his infant daughter, who was now without a mother. The man opened his daily diary and slashed a huge "X" across that day's page. There he scribbled: "The light has gone out of my life." The date was February 14, 1884: ironically, it was Valentine's Day.

Two days later, as identical rosewood caskets were brought into New York's Fifth Avenue Presbyterian Church, friends observed that this doubly bereaved man was "in a dazed, stunned state." They wondered if he would ever recover.

He did, though. As difficult and painful as that Valentine's Day was for him, he did recover. Over time, he would find healing. He would marry again. Professionally, he would serve as assistant secretary of the Navy, governor of New York, and president of the United States. His name was Theodore Roosevelt. In his later life, he would triumph not only over personal tragedy, but also over political and professional defeat. (Adapted from a story told by Victor Parachin, "Tending a Wounded Heart," in *Plus* magazine, December, 2002, pp. 25-27.)

Here is what Teddy Roosevelt wrote, after some of these experiences — wise advice, for all who must live for a season through the tumbling of temple stones:

> *It is not the critic who counts, not the one who points out how the strong man tumbled, or where the doer of deeds could have done them better. The credit belongs to the person who is actually in the arena; whose face is marred by dust, sweat and blood; who strives valiantly; who errs and comes short again and again; who knows the great enthusiasms, the great devotions and spends himself in a worthy cause; who at the best knows in the end the triumph of high achievement, and who at the worst, if he fails, at least fails while daring greatly, so that his place shall never be with those cold and timid souls who know neither victory nor defeat.* (From a speech, "Citzenship in a Republic," delivered at the Sorbonne in Paris, April 23, 1910)

***

In Corrie ten Boom's book, *The Hiding Place*, Corrie tells of her first encounter with death. As a girl, she and her mother visited the family of an infant who had died. The idea of losing a loved one overwhelmed Corrie. Sobbing, she told her father that he couldn't die, because she just couldn't handle it. Her father reminded her of their trips to Amsterdam, and how he always gave her ticket to her just before they boarded the train. Her father told her that God does the same for us when a loved one dies: giving us the strength we need, just in time.

***

Without your wounds where would your power be? The very angels themselves cannot persuade the wretched and blundering children on earth as can one human being broken in the wheels of living. In love's service, only the wounded soldiers can serve.

— Thornton Wilder, *The Angel That Troubled the Waters*
(London: Longmans, Green & Co., 1928)

***

Merely accepted, suffering does nothing for our souls except, perhaps, to harden them. Endurance alone is no consecration. True asceticism is not a mere cult of fortitude. We can deny ourselves rigorously for the wrong reason and end up by pleasing ourselves mightily with our self-denial.

278

Suffering is consecrated to God by faith — not by faith in suffering, but by faith in God. Some of us believe in the power and the value of suffering. But such a belief is an illusion. Suffering has no power and no value of its own....

To believe in suffering is pride: but to suffer, believing in God, is humility. For pride may tell us that we are strong enough to suffer, that suffering is good for us because we are good. Humility tells us that suffering is an evil which we must always expect to find in our lives because of the evil that is in ourselves. But faith also knows that the mercy of God is given to those who seek him in suffering, and that by his grace we can overcome evil with good.

— Thomas Merton, "To Know the Cross," from *No Man Is an Island*
(New York: Harcourt, 1978)

Christb The King
(Proper 29, Ordinary Time 34)
November 26, 2006

Revised Common	2 Samuel 23:1-7	**Revelation 1:4b-8**	**John 18:33-37**
	or **Daniel 7:9-10, 13-14**		
Roman Catholic	**Daniel 7:13-14**	**Revelation 1:5-8**	**John 18:33-37**
Episcopal	**Daniel 7:9-14**	**Revelation 1:1-8**	**John 18:33-37**

Theme For The Day   Jesus Christ is King — but not the sort of king the world expects.

Old Testament Lesson   2 Samuel 23:1-7   *The Last Words Of David*

At the end of 2 Samuel are found several appendices. This poem, known as "the last words of David," is the shorter of two poems. The one that immediately precedes it is known as "David's Song of Thanksgiving" (22:1-51). It has undoubtedly been chosen by the lectionary committee for Christ The King Sunday because of the royal theology it expresses concerning Jesus' ancestor, David. If Christians revere Christ as King, then this depiction of David — the prototypical king who receives favor from God — surely has something important to say. Such a king is inspired: "The spirit of the Lord speaks through me, his word is upon my tongue" (v. 2). His rule demonstrates principles of justice, as well as devotion to God: "One who rules over people justly, ruling in the fear of God, is like the light of morning ..." (vv. 3-4a). This kingship is founded upon an "everlasting covenant" (*berith olam* — v. 5). The godless, on the other hand: "... are all like thorns that are thrown away; for they cannot be picked up with the hand; to touch them one uses an iron bar or the shaft of a spear, and they are entirely consumed in fire on the spot" (v. 6).

Alternate Old Testament Lesson   Daniel 7:9-10, 13-14   *Coming On The Clouds*
                                                                                   Of Heaven

Continuing to report on his visionary experience, the author shifts from frightening portrayals of fantastic beasts (representing Israel's enemies), to display a powerful, transcendent figure: an Ancient One (known to readers of the King James Version as "the Ancient of Days"). This is a divine figure on a fiery throne: "... his clothing was white as snow, and the hair of his head like pure wool; his throne was fiery flames, and its wheels were burning fire. A stream of fire issued and flowed out from his presence" (vv. 9-10). There has been considerable discussion of the detail that places wheels on the throne; some have thought this imagery is borrowed from Greek mythology, the image of Helios, the sun god. It is also possible that this imagery comes from the fiery wheels within wheels of Ezekiel's vision (Ezekiel 1:15-21), or from the chariot of fire that appears as Elijah is taken up into heaven (2 Kings 2:11). A vast court of retainers surrounds the throne, as "the books are opened" (presumably, books related the last judgment).

In verses omitted by the lectionary, one of the beasts from the previous vision is put to death in the presence of this royal figure. Then, another royal figure enters the scene: "I saw one like a human being coming with the clouds of heaven. And he came to the Ancient One and was presented before him. To him was given dominion and glory and kingship ..." (vv. 13-14a). This one's kingdom will be forever. The literal translation of "one like a human being" (v. 13) is "one like a son of man." The term "son of man" has a rich and complex history that is too detailed to review here. It has strong links to the visions of Ezekiel (which also likely provide some of the imagery associated with the Ancient of Days). In Ezekiel, the phrase often refers to the prophet himself, but by the time of Daniel, an interpretation seems to have arisen that treats the "son of man" as a separate, eschatological figure. This is the way Jesus himself most often uses the term — although it is not always clear how explicitly Jesus may use the term to refer to himself.

New Testament Lesson   Revelation 1:4b-8   *"He Is Coming With the Clouds;*
                                                        Every Eye Will See Him"

Again, for Christ The King Sunday, a text has been chosen that depicts the triumphant arrival of a divine, kingly figure. The first several verses of this passage are greetings to the seven churches, opening the book in a standard epistolary form. Then, words are shared from what is possibly a contemporary Christian hymn, depicting the triumphant return of Christ: "Look! He is coming with the clouds; every eye will see him, even those who pierced him; and on his account all the tribes of the earth will wail" (v. 7). "I am the Alpha and the Omega," says God (v. 8) — a line that, much later in the book, will be voiced by Jesus himself (21:6 and 22:13).

The Gospel   John 18:33-37   *"My Kingdom Is Not From This World"*

This short segment of Jesus' trial before Pilate is out of season as far as the larger narrative is concerned, but has been chosen for this day because of what Jesus has to say about himself and kingship. Pilate flatly asks him about the title that others have ascribed to him: "Are you the King of the Jews?" Jesus responds with a question, asking Pilate if he came up with this on his own, or if he heard it from others. When Pilate asks him what he has done that has led him to be dragged in for trial, Jesus does not directly answer the procurator's question, but declares, "My kingdom is not from this world. If my kingdom were from this world, my followers would be fighting to keep me from being handed over to the Jews. But as it is, my kingdom is not from here" (v. 36). When Pilate asks him once again if he is a king, Jesus again replies obliquely: "You say that I am a king ..." (v. 37). In general, John portrays Pilate as something of a weakling, rather than an active conspirator — let alone the principal actor — in the condemnation and death of Jesus. There is every reason to think that John portrayed Pilate in a somewhat more favorable fashion, in order not to offend the Roman authorities, who had begun — by the time he was writing — to persecute the Christians. John shifted more of the blame to the high priest and his court, which by the time of his writing had already been annihilated by the Romans anyway.

Preaching Possibilities

Today we end the Christian year, according to tradition, with the day known as Christ The King. This day is a relative newcomer to the liturgical calendar. It's only been around since 1925, when Pope Pius XI introduced it to the Roman Catholic church, as a challenge to the totalitarian governments of the right and the left that were at that time gradually growing strong in Europe. To would-be dictators — like Hitler and Mussolini and Stalin — the message of Christ the King was meant to be that the State does not rule supreme, exercising absolute authority over the hearts and minds of the people. One day, as it says in Philippians, "every knee shall bow and every tongue confess ... that Jesus Christ is Lord...." Only Christ is supreme king over all. Later, as we Protestants went through the process of devising a common lectionary that was ecumenically connected with what other churches were doing, we adopted the Catholic holiday for our own.

When Jesus stood on trial, before Pilate, it was a similar sort of confrontation: the kingdom of God versus the kingdoms of this world. Our text today is from the Gospel of John, and reflects John's outlook that Pilate was not so much responsible for Jesus' death, as a weak ruler who permitted the Jewish authorities to engineer it. In reality, Pilate was an absolute ruler, and did indeed have everything to say about the life and death of Jesus. When he asks Jesus, "Are you the king of the Jews," it is very much an encounter between government at its most raw and authoritarian, and a man who symbolizes a higher authority.

A traveler pulls his car up beside a farmhouse in rural Maine. On the front porch, in a rocking chair, sits an old Mainer: flannel shirt, khakis, baseball cap, L.L. Bean duck shoes on his feet. "How do I get to Boston?" the traveler shouts out.

"Can't get theyah from heeyah," replies the old Mainer.

"Well, what about this road by your house?" the tourist asks. "Where does it go?"

"I've lived heeyah seventy yeeahs," replies the old farmer, "and I've nevah seen this road go anywheyah!" And on it goes, the typical "downeast" dialogue — the native Mainer playing the out-of-towner for a fool.

Jesus' encounter with Pilate contains a similar miscommunication — although one that is not at all comical. The two of them engage in a dialogue about the meaning of the word "king." And, like the tourist and the downeaster from Maine, the two of them seem to mean two completely different things by the word. In much the same way, Jesus and Pilate are talking right past each other.

Who is this Pontius Pilate? Every time we say the Apostles' Creed, we mention his name: the only human name — with the exception of Mary, Jesus' mother — that appears in the Creed. He's a minor character, though, in the great parade of events recorded in the New Testament. Jesus' appearance before him is but one, fleeting chapter in the Passion narrative: a brief, bureaucratic stopover on Jesus' one, horrible day in the Roman justice system — a day that begins with a sleepless night, and ends on a cross.

The early church thought it important to mention Pilate's name in the Creed: not because Pilate himself is such a leading character, but because of what he symbolizes. Pilate is the Roman governor: the sole representative of the Emperor to the province of Judea. Scholars think the Apostles' Creed was written in Rome, by a church under persecution. The early Christians' view — the view from the catacombs (those subterranean burial vaults where Christians lived and worshiped in hiding) — was one that very much took in the emperor. To this little band of persecuted believers, it was important to remember that Jesus, too, had his brush with imperial authority.

It happens that we know a few things about Pontius Pilate, from historians of the day. There's a good deal more written about him, in fact, than there is about Jesus — who's mentioned only once, in passing, in any history book other than the Bible. When Pilate brought Roman Legions to Jerusalem for the first time, he told the soldiers they could bring their regimental standards with them — even though they were topped with busts of the emperor, whom the soldiers revered as a god. To the Jews, of course, this was a horrendous provocation; their second commandment allowed no "graven images."

Pilate was well aware of the insult he was dealing to the people, so he had the standards carried in at night. This ignited a massive protest the next morning, that very nearly ended in a bloodbath; disaster was averted only after Pilate backed down — and this only after Jewish protesters had lain on the ground, and bared their throats to the swords of his soldiers. So Pilate was tough — but also very much a political animal.

He could also be stubborn. There was another incident, in which he had mounted gold shields, with the emperor's name on them, on the walls of his residence in Jerusalem. This, too, led to a near-riot — but Pilate held firm, refusing to take down the shields. Finally, the Jewish leaders wrote to the emperor himself, who personally ordered Pilate to take them down.

Pilate could also be utterly ruthless. There was another time when he had looted the temple treasury, to pay for the construction of an aqueduct. This incited another demonstration: but this time, Pilate had Roman soldiers, dressed as Jews, infiltrate the crowd. At a pre-arranged signal, the soldiers pulled out clubs and beat the protesters, some of them nearly to the point of death.

Pilate served in Jerusalem for ten years, altogether: the second-longest tenure of any Roman governor of that troublesome province. Clearly, the emperor regarded Pilate as a success. By the time Jesus is dragged before him, arms bound, eyes bleary from lack of sleep, Pilate has nothing to worry about. He has clearly established himself as the emperor's right-hand-man in Judea — he has absolute power of life and death over all the emperor's subjects.

"So," the governor begins, looking Jesus in the eye, "are you the king of the Jews?" It's a flippant question, the first gambit in the interrogator's game. Jesus' answer reveals to Pilate something of why the priests and scribes are so upset with him. It is a singularly bold answer. This Jesus has the audacity to answer the emperor's official agent with a question: "Do you ask this on your own, or did others tell you about me?"

"Who's on trial here, anyway?" Pilate wonders to himself, with a touch of amusement. He shoots back: "I am not a Jew, am I? Your own nation and the chief priests have handed you over to me. What have you done?"

"My kingdom," Jesus replies, "is not from this world. If it were, my followers would be fighting your soldiers, even now. My kingdom is not from here."

Like the old Maine farmer and the fresh-faced tourist up from Boston, the two of them talk, they look each other in the eye, they appear to follow the conventions of conversation: but they never really communicate. They never connect, in any meaningful way. "Two ships passing in the night," as the saying goes. "You can't get there from here."

You can't get to where Jesus is, from where Pilate is — or vice-versa. They come from different worlds, those two: and it's more than just a matter of Jew vesus Roman, or church versus state, or rich versus poor. Jesus' reign asking is not fundamentally about human power: it is about divine power, and that power is not yet revealed. The book of Revelation promises that, one day, it will be. But for now, we Christians must live under the rule of civil authorities — most of whom are, we trust, more fair and just than the ruthless Pilate — and await the day when the truly just and benevolent rule of Jesus Christ will be established through all the earth.

Prayer For The Day

Great God, who has given us hearts with which to honor all that is good and blessed and perfect: May our days always be filled with praise for the King of kings and the Lord of lords, the Lamb who sits upon the throne, the one who is Alpha and the Omega of our lives: even Jesus Christ, our Lord. Amen.

To Illustrate

The Thanksgiving holiday we are about to celebrate began with a band of desperately hungry, deeply religious people — they called themselves pilgrims, remember, not just colonists — and their heartfelt gratitude to God, for simple survival. It didn't become an official national holiday until the time of the Civil War: when President Lincoln answered the call for a day of prayer and solemn reflection. Just listen to what Lincoln had to say to the nation, in his Thanksgiving proclamation. It's an extremely revealing statement for any politician to make (although of course Lincoln — with a deep-seated religious faith that not only salted campaign rhetoric, but powerfully informed his actions — was no typical politician):

> *... we have forgotten God. We have forgotten the gracious hand which preserved us in peace, and multiplied and enriched and strengthened us. And we have vainly imagined in the deceitfulness of our hearts that all these blessings were produced by some superior wisdom and virtue of our own. Intoxicated with unbroken success, we have become too self-sufficient to feel the necessity of redeeming and preserving grace — too proud to pray to the God that made us. It has seemed to me fit and proper that God should be solemnly, reverently and gratefully acknowledged, as with one heart and one voice, by the whole American people.*

***

In the Disney animated film, *The Hunchback of Notre Dame*, there is a scene that depicts a raucous Parisian street festival. On that day, everything is topsy-turvy, sings Clopin, the narrator-jester. At that festival, they crown the king of fools, who is actually the ugliest, most hideous person there. Why do they crown the least likely person, sings Clopin? Why, because everything is topsy-turvy! A king becomes a clown and a clown becomes a king. The one they crown that day is Quasimodo, the gentle hunchback who rings the bells at Notre Dame Cathedral.

It is a topsy-turvy act, a reversal — but no more topsy-turvy than for God to enter the world as the son of a humble Galilean artisan and his peasant wife. Throughout his ministry, Jesus demonstrates a remarkable concern for "the least of these" — topsy-turvy thinking again! When he returns on the clouds of heaven, it will be the biggest reversal of all.

***

Leonardo da Vinci knew the centrality of Christ. The vanishing point of his painting of the Last Supper — the point at which all lines converge — is the face of Jesus. All the lines of the painting point to him, with mathematical precision. Art experts have been able to identify many forgeries of this painting, simply by measuring the lines and determining that the figure of Jesus was not precisely in the center.

***

In Jordan some years ago, there was a terrible tragedy in which two Israeli schoolgirls, playing in a park known as the "Island of Peace" in the middle of the Jordan River between their country and Jordan, were shot by a deranged Jordanian soldier. It quickly became apparent that this was an isolated incident caused by mental illness, and an international incident was swiftly averted. And there the story could well have ended.

Except for Jordan's King Hussein. Hearing of the incident, the king left his throne, left his palace, left even his own country, and traveled to the humble homes of the families of the slain Israeli girls. Entering each house, the king fell down on his knees. He bowed before the grieving parents. Then he looked up into their eyes and said, "I beg you, forgive me, forgive me. Your daughter is like my daughter, your loss is my loss. May God help you to bear your pain."

That day, ironically, it was a Muslim king who gave the world just a small glimpse of what a Christlike king is like.

***

There's a story told about George VI, King of England during the Second World War. During the darkest hours of the Battle of Britain, fears mounted that the king and the royal family might not be safe in London. They could be injured, even killed, in a bombing raid. Quietly, and without publicity, the palace staff made secret plans to transport the king and his family to safety in Canada, should the need arise.

Yet despite the urgings of his advisors, George refused to leave his fellow Britons in their darkest hour. Shortly afterward, an incident was reported in a London newspaper, in which the king was inspecting a bombed-out neighborhood. While he was walking through the rubble, an elderly man came up to him and said: "You, here, in the midst of this. You are indeed a good king."

That is what a good king does. A good king lives the life of his people.

U.S. / Canadian Lectionary Comparison

The following index shows the correlation between the Sundays and special days of the church year as they are titled or labeled in the Revised Common Lectionary published by the Consultation On Common Texts and used in the United States (the reference used for this book) and the Sundays and special days of the church year as they are titled or labeled in the Revised Common Lectionary used in Canada.

Revised Common Lectionary	Canadian Revised Common Lectionary
Advent 1	Advent 1
Advent 2	Advent 2
Advent 3	Advent 3
Advent 4	Advent 4
Christmas Eve	Christmas Eve
The Nativity Of Our Lord / Christmas Day	The Nativity Of Our Lord
Christmas 1	Christmas 1
January 1 / Holy Name Of Jesus	January 1 / The Name Of Jesus
Christmas 2	Christmas 2
The Epiphany Of Our Lord	The Epiphany Of Our Lord
The Baptism Of Our Lord / Epiphany 1	The Baptism Of Our Lord / Proper 1
Epiphany 2 / Ordinary Time 2	Epiphany 2 / Proper 2
Epiphany 3 / Ordinary Time 3	Epiphany 3 / Proper 3
Epiphany 4 / Ordinary Time 4	Epiphany 4 / Proper 4
Epiphany 5 / Ordinary Time 5	Epiphany 5 / Proper 5
Epiphany 6 / Ordinary Time 6	Epiphany 6 / Proper 6
Epiphany 7 / Ordinary Time 7	Epiphany 7 / Proper 7
Epiphany 8 / Ordinary Time 8	Epiphany 8 / Proper 8
The Transfiguration Of Our Lord / Last Sunday After The Epiphany	The Transfiguration Of Our Lord / Last Sunday After Epiphany
Ash Wednesday	Ash Wednesday
Lent 1	Lent 1
Lent 2	Lent 2
Lent 3	Lent 3
Lent 4	Lent 4
Lent 5	Lent 5
Sunday Of The Passion / Palm Sunday	Passion / Palm Sunday
Maundy Thursday	Holy / Maundy Thursday
Good Friday	Good Friday
The Resurrection Of Our Lord / Easter Day	The Resurrection Of Our Lord
Easter 2	Easter 2
Easter 3	Easter 3
Easter 4	Easter 4
Easter 5	Easter 5
Easter 6	Easter 6
The Ascension Of Our Lord	The Ascension Of Our Lord
Easter 7	Easter 7
The Day Of Pentecost	The Day Of Pentecost
The Holy Trinity	The Holy Trinity
Proper 4 / Pentecost 2 / O T 9*	Proper 9
Proper 5 / Pent 3 / O T 10	Proper 10
Proper 6 / Pent 4 / O T 11	Proper 11
Proper 7 / Pent 5 / O T 12	Proper 12
Proper 8 / Pent 6 / O T 13	Proper 13
Proper 9 / Pent 7 / O T 14	Proper 14

Proper 10 / Pent 8 / O T 15   Proper 15
Proper 11 / Pent 9 / O T 16   Proper 16
Proper 12 / Pent 10 / O T 17   Proper 17
Proper 13 / Pent 11 / O T 18   Proper 18
Proper 14 / Pent 12 / O T 19   Proper 19
Proper 15 / Pent 13 / O T 20   Proper 20
Proper 16 / Pent 14 / O T 21   Proper 21
Proper 17 / Pent 15 / O T 22   Proper 22
Proper 18 / Pent 16 / O T 23   Proper 23
Proper 19 / Pent 17 / O T 24   Proper 24
Proper 20 / Pent 18 / O T 25   Proper 25
Proper 21 / Pent 19 / O T 26   Proper 26
Proper 22 / Pent 20 / O T 27   Proper 27
Proper 23 / Pent 21 / O T 28   Proper 28
Proper 24 / Pent 22 / O T 29   Proper 29
Proper 25 / Pent 23 / O T 30   Proper 30
Proper 26 / Pent 24 / O T 31   Proper 31
Proper 27 / Pent 25 / O T 32   Proper 32
Proper 28 / Pent 26 / O T 33   Proper 33
Christ The King (Proper 29 / O T 34)   Proper 34 / Christ The King /
                                              Reign Of Christ

Reformation Day (October 31)   Reformation Day (October 31)
All Saints (November 1 or   All Saints' Day (November 1)
   1st Sunday in November)
Thanksgiving Day   Thanksgiving Day
   (4th Thursday of November)   (2nd Monday of October)

*O T = Ordinary Time